MW01620581

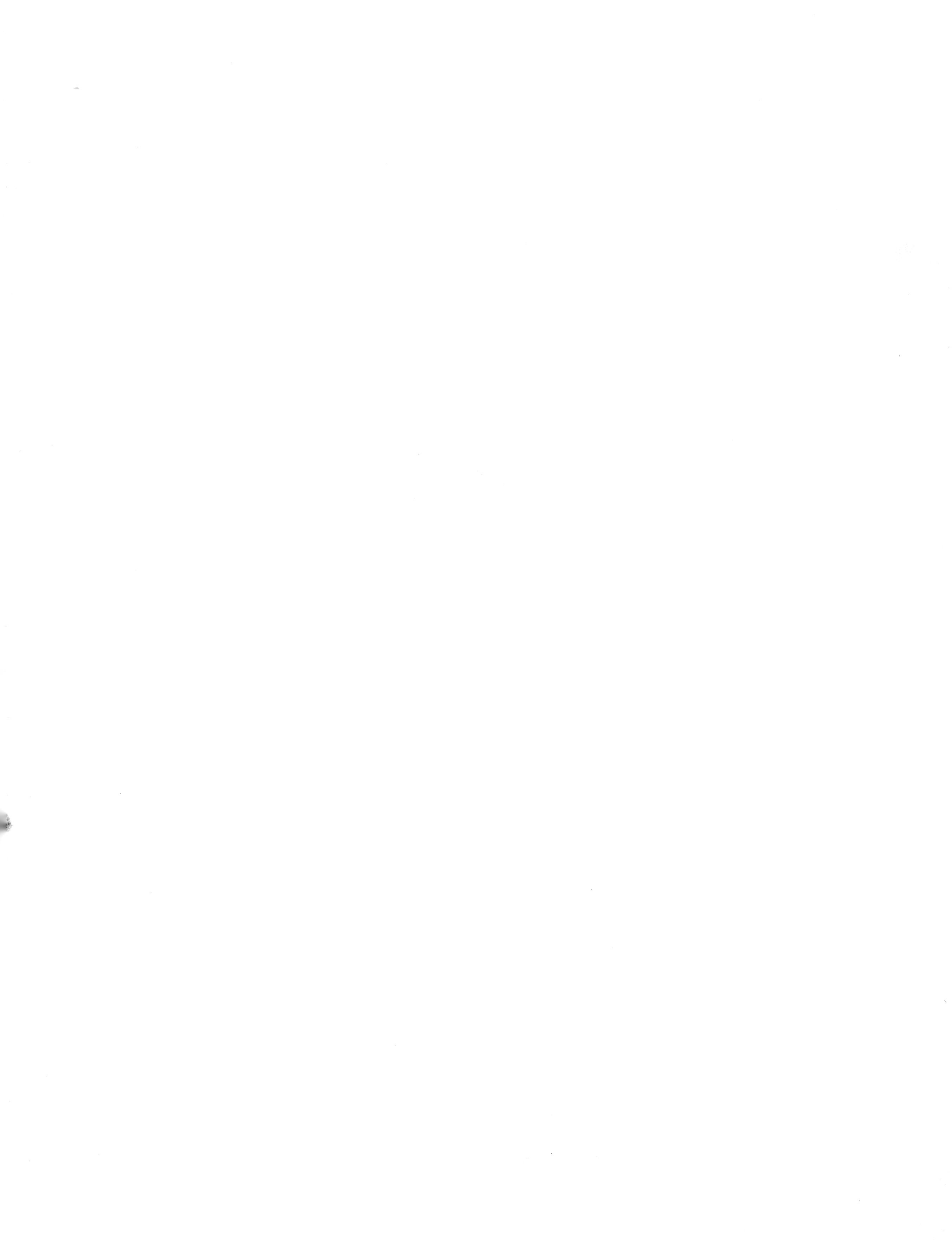

# *Ground/work*

Edited by Molly Epstein and Abigail Ross Goodman

With texts by Courtney J. Martin, Jenelle Porter, Pavel S. Pyś, Lumi Tan, Yesomi Umolu, and Robert Wiesenberger

Clark Art Institute, Williamstown, Massachusetts
Distributed by Yale University Press, New Haven and London

The Clark Art Institute sits on the ancestral homelands of the Mohican people. We acknowledge the tremendous hardship of their forcible removal from these homelands by colonial settlers. A federally recognized Nation, they now reside in Wisconsin and are known as the Stockbridge-Munsee Community. We pay honor to their ancestors (past and present) and to future generations by committing to build a more inclusive and equitable space for all.

| | |
|---|---|
| JCJ | Jennie C. Jones<br>*These (Mournful) Shores* |
| AS | Analia Saban<br>*Teaching a Cow How to Draw* |
| HY | Haegue Yang<br>*Migratory DMZ Birds on Asymmetric Lens –*<br>*Tee-Cher Tee-Cher Vessel (Great Tit)*<br>*Hou-Ke-Kyo Vessel (Japanese Bush Warbler)*<br>*Duiitt Duiitt Vessel (Gray-Backed Thrush)* |
| EL | Eva LeWitt<br>*Resin Tower A (Orange)*<br>*Resin Tower B (Yellow)*<br>*Resin Tower C (Blue)* |
| NB | Nairy Baghramian<br>*Knee and Elbow* |
| KA | Kelly Akashi<br>*A Device to See the World Twice* |

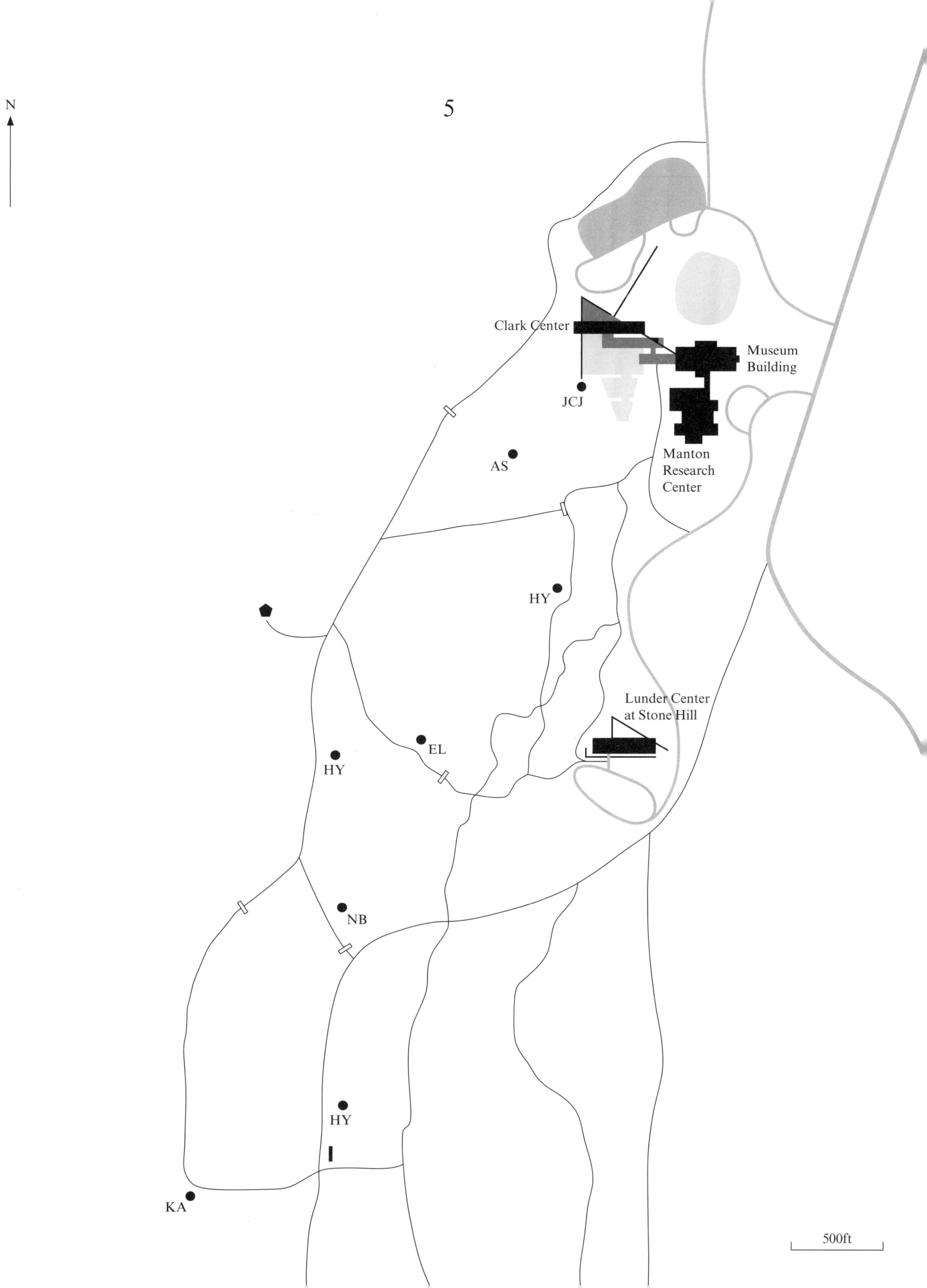

N

5

Clark Center

Museum Building

JCJ

AS

Manton Research Center

HY

Lunder Center at Stone Hill

EL

HY

NB

HY

KA

500ft

# Contents

## Foreword

Following its completion in 2014, the Tadao Ando–designed Clark Center turned the view of the Clark Art Institute away from the street and toward Stone Hill. As a result of this reorientation, the Clark's grounds—140 acres open to the public day and night—increasingly became a site of exploration for visitors. The expanded use of the museum's campus was the catalyst for the exhibition that would eventually be named *Ground/work*. This rethinking of the grounds has enlivened the landscape and furthered the Clark's engagement with contemporary art.

Since the 1970s, the Clark has exhibited the work of and collaborated with living artists. In 1977, for example, Robert Morris's sculpture *Untitled (Williams Mirrors)* appeared in the courtyard of the Manton Research Center during the artist's residency at nearby Williams College. In the 1970s and 1980s, the Clark often collaborated with Williams and other local colleges on contemporary projects. In 1980, the institute staged a major exhibition of Helen Frankenthaler's prints (reprised by two more shows, of her woodcuts and paintings, in 2017). With the addition of Tadao Ando's Lunder Center at Stone Hill, in 2008, the Clark expanded its contemporary offerings, mounting exhibitions by artists including Juan Muñoz, El Anatsui, David Smith, Jennifer Steinkamp, and, most recently, Lin May Saeed. And, in 2015, the site-specific commission and installation of Thomas Schütte's *Crystal* on Stone Hill marked a new chapter for the Clark, of extending art and programming into the landscape.

In partnership with Molly Epstein and Abigail Ross Goodman, *Ground/work*'s two guest curators, we began to connect with artists and invite them to visit. All six artists—Kelly Akashi, Nairy Baghramian, Jennie C. Jones, Eva LeWitt, Analia Saban, and Haegue Yang—came to the Clark to spend time with the collections, study the architecture, and explore the surroundings. Through long walks with staff from many different parts of the institute, the artists became familiar with the grounds. It was important that each artist drove the selection of the site for her work, which in turn became an integral part of the creation and installation of the sculptures throughout the campus. This autonomy is part of what makes this exhibition distinctive—each artist led the process for determining the conception and location of her work, creating six forceful, specific, and personal installations that interpret nature, the history of art, and our interaction with both in surprising and provocative ways. These new perspectives are ones we hope will stay with visitors long after their time at the Clark.

Although the Clark has been planning *Ground/work* for many years now, we feel fortunate to be able to share this exhibition in 2020–21. In the face of isolation and distance, consequences of the safety measures implemented to protect our communities from the COVID-19 pandemic, many people turned to the Clark's grounds as a place to safely spend time outside and connect with a broader community. Opening this exhibition during the global pandemic presented challenging circumstances for the artists, exhibition curators, Clark staff, and fellow collaborators, but creating opportunities for people to connect with art, nature, and one another—safely and at no cost—was a commitment we were proud to keep. We are happy to be able to provide that space for all visitors, and in a way that is still true to our mission as an arts institution. Despite the difficulties of the past year, we have seen an increase in the number of visitors to our campus and the surrounding trails; going forward, our grounds will no longer be seen only as a backdrop to the galleries, but also as a true part of the experience of the Clark and who we are.

As director, I add my hearty thanks to the long list of people who worked tirelessly to realize this project, as outlined in Molly and Abi's acknowledgments. Additionally, I would like to extend my great appreciation to the donors whose contributions helped bring *Ground/work* to fruition; the full list of their names appears on pp. 232–33 in this catalogue. Finally, however, I must extend special thanks to Molly and Abi themselves—whose expertise, vision, and dedication ensured the great success of this project.

Olivier Meslay
Hardymon Director

# Acknowledgments

*Ground/work* was initially conceived in 2016, installed in 2020, and remains on view in 2021, as we prepare to publish this book. A project of this duration, ambition, and scale does not come to fruition without the efforts and generosity of many people; therefore, we are eager to acknowledge and thank the following individuals, all of whom were instrumental to the exhibition and the catalogue that documents its making.

To the six artists who accepted our invitation to visit the Clark Art Institute and to generate new site-responsive commissions that form the *Ground/work* exhibition: we will forever be indebted to you for broadening our perspectives on art and nature, on material and process, on innovation and collaboration.

To Olivier Meslay, the Hardymon Director of the Clark Art Institute, who approached us in the spring of 2017 to share his interest in mounting a major outdoor exhibition on the Clark's grounds and kindly entrusted us with this important task: we cannot thank you enough for your vision, your generosity, your faith in us, and your enthusiasm and unending support for the artists and their work.

As guest curators, and therefore temporary participants in the activities of this esteemed institution, we had the distinct privilege and pleasure for the past several years of working and being affiliated with an extraordinary group of individuals at the Clark, each of whom treated this project with great care and commitment.

First, to Kathleen Morris, Marx Director of Collections and Exhibitions, who shepherded this project from beginning to end with unparalleled skill, managing a rather unwieldy exhibition with extensive moving parts through a global pandemic with ease and grace: we are grateful for your partnership and leadership. To Larry Smallwood, deputy director, who connected the dots from fabrication to installation and made myriad complicated concerns look easy: thank you for being our strategic partner in making the show a reality and for always putting the artists' ambitions first. To Teresa O'Toole, assistant exhibitions and collections manager, whose exemplary attention to detail and expert coordination made the show possible: we are grateful for your steady hand and all of your work on the project from conception to conclusion.

To our distinguished colleagues in the curatorial department at the Clark, we are honored to have had the opportunity to work alongside you for *Ground/work*. Thank you for your support of and enthusiasm for the project and for welcoming us into your ranks with warmth and generosity. Lipp Chief Curator Esther Bell was a constant source of wise counsel, gracious encouragement, and illuminating expertise. In addition to writing for this publication and giving countless tours of the show in both sun and snow, associate curator of contemporary projects Robert Wiesenberger worked alongside us to ensure that this endeavor would amplify the institute's contemporary programming. To Anna Siedzik, our intrepid registrar for *Ground/work*, and her colleagues in the Clark's Registration Department, led by Mattie Kelley, with Angela Liporace and Patty Tainter: thank you for all of your care and work in ensuring the works on view were properly looked after from shipping to installation and beyond. The Clark's grounds manager Matthew Noyes, whose love for the land paired with his depth of knowledge and sheer joy in sharing it, was an ongoing source of inspiration. To his team, Nathan Alibozek, Justin Sullivan, and Kyle Thayer: thank you for making everything work in concert with the Clark's 140-acre campus. Enormous thanks are due to Jed Cleary and his entire team at Func Art Design—Eric Laning, Dylan Soares-Kern, Tom Nicol, Henri Broyard, Amy O'Shea, and Lauri Kobar—who managed the complex installation of each of the projects on the Clark's grounds over the course of several months in 2020. We owe a debt of gratitude to Jonathan Briggs and Dominique Chenail-Briggs of Carpenter Hill Construction, who made the impossible possible—and did so while maintaining the integrity of the Clark's landscape and protecting its ecosystem. Thanks are also due to Clark preparators Tom Merrill in particular, and Paul Dion and Nathan Ahern, for their care in installing and maintaining the works. To others whose work contributed to the success of the exhibition, including Jeremy Broadwell and his team, Brad Dilger, Jay Dube, Helene Gillette-Woodard, Vince Guntlow, Rich Hailey, Charlie LeBatt, Michael Mucci and his team, Mike Pereira, Sarah Pike, Josh Safdie, Mike St. Pierre, Nicole Sullivan, and Greg van Houten, we extend our thanks.

To Vicki Saltzman, who championed the exhibition from the outset and worked tirelessly to spread the word far and wide, and to everyone on the Communications and Design team, including Josh Maher, Amy Coon, and David Edge: thank you. Many thanks to the teams at FITZ & Co. and Becca PR for promoting the exhibition and bringing members of the press to visit the show. Laurie Glover oversaw the audio guide that accompanies the exhibition and allowed us to share the artists' voices with a broad public, whether they were able to visit Williamstown or not. Nora Considine and Rebecca Cross stewarded the *Ground/work* microsite and managed the exhibition's presence on social media, which brought the exhibition to online audiences around the world. Ronna Tulgan Ostheimer and her team in the Education Department made the show come alive for visitors both young and old. Finally, our graduate interns from the Williams College MA program in art history, Julie Reiter and Eliza Harrison, were invaluable participants in the early work on the show.

To the six writers who accepted our invitation to lend their voices to this volume: thank you for your work and scholarship. Anne Roecklein and Kevin Bicknell in the Publications Department at the Clark were extraordinary collaborators and project managers for this volume. Thomas Clark, who photographed the exhibition throughout the seasons in all kinds of weather and conditions, helped us capture the shifting truths and realities that surrounded these objects during their time on site. Laura Coombs designed the book with sensitivity and vision, and Kristin Swan served as our trusted copyeditor. David Murphy skillfully managed image permissions.

Our gratitude to the artists extends with great sincerity and appreciation to those who work with them in the studio and beyond. To Valerie Veator of Kelly Akashi Studio, Michel Ziegler of Atelier Baghramian, Darcy Ripley of Analia Saban Studio, and Liene Harms and Jeesu Lee of Studio Yang in Berlin and Seoul: we appreciate all your efforts and collaboration on this project over these past few years.

The fabricators and production partners for each of the projects went to great lengths to complete the works during a particularly challenging global moment, and we will forever be in debt to them: John Doloszycki and his team at Benchmark Arts, Los Angeles, and George Roth and Chris Piazza at Pour House–Art Casting, Los Angeles, who collaborated with Kelly Akashi on *A Device to See the World Twice*; Paolo Carli and Manuela Della Ducata of Henraux S.p.A, Lucca, Italy, who worked with Nairy Baghramian on *Knee and Elbow*; Andrew Pharmer and Vincent DiDonato at Workshop Art Fabrication, Kingston, New York, and Bill Brovold, who collaborated with Jennie C. Jones on *These (Mournful) Shores*; Karen Atta and Naomi Van Der Lande of ATTA Inc., New York, who worked with Eva LeWitt on her *Resin Towers*; Todd Storti of New England Fence, Inc., Pittsfield, Massachusetts, who collaborated with Analia Saban on *Teaching a Cow How to Draw*; and Kostas Papalexiou and Maddie Udayakumar of Neoset Designs, Brooklyn, along with Michael Brotherton, Dillon Johnson, and Andrew Emmet of SITU Fabrication, Brooklyn, David Spergel at Microsol Resources, and Dave Cortes and Heather Pirnak, all of whom worked with Haegue Yang on *Migratory DMZ Birds on Asymmetric Lens*.

We also extend our thanks to the gallerists who support and represent the participating artists, all of whom we are lucky to count as friends and collaborators: Esperanza Rosales of VI, VII, Oslo; Alexander Gray and John Kunemund of Alexander Gray Associates, New York City and Germantown, New York; Francois Ghebaly and Gan Uyeda of François Ghebaly Gallery, Los Angeles; Bree Zucker, Lissa McClure, Jose Kuri, and Monica Manzutto of kurimanzutto Mexico City / New York; Marian Goodman and Jessie Washburne-Harris of Marian Goodman Gallery, New York, London, and Paris; Olivia McManus, Julia Fishbach, and Emanuel Aguilar of PATRON Gallery, Chicago; and Tanya Bonakdar, Ethan Sklar, and Joel Draper of Tanya Bonakdar Gallery, New York and Los Angeles.

To the donors whose generosity made the show possible, Karen and Robert Scott, Denise Littlefield Sobel, and Paul Neely: our heartfelt thanks for your major support of the exhibition. Additional funding was generously provided by the Terra Foundation for American Art; the National Endowment for the Humanities: Exploring the human endeavor; Maureen Fennessy Bousa and Edward P. Bousa; Amy and Charlie Scharf; Elizabeth Lee; MASS MoCA; Chrystina and James Parks; Howard M. Shapiro and Shirley Brandman; Joan and Jim Hunter; James and Barbara Moltz; a gift in honor of Marilyn and Ron Walter, and many additional generous patrons. Thanks to the Clark's Advancement Team, including Tom Woodward, Emily Daunis, Jackie Moran, Tucker Bair, and Maureen Hart Hennessey, for their devotion to sharing this project with the Clark's members and supporters.

Thanks to Maria Taft, Jane Booth, Michelle Lamuniere, Bethany Morris, Danielle Cook, and James Kenny for their enthusiasm and support as we worked to bring this project to fruition.

To our families—Gordon, Jonah, Rebecca, Hannah, Esmé, and Mark—who have been an incredible source of support and cheering on throughout this endeavor and all it has entailed: thank you for reveling in our joy in the process of making the show a reality (and for your understanding each time we temporarily needed to relocate to Williamstown!).

Finally, once again, to Kelly Akashi, Nairy Baghramian, Jennie C. Jones, Eva LeWitt, Analia Saban, and Haegue Yang: it has been an unbelievable privilege to be in your orbit and to be in close dialogue with you over the past several years. Thank you for welcoming us into your practices with generosity, for giving so richly of yourselves, and for bringing us into your respective worlds—all are places we would like to remain in for years to come.

Molly Epstein and Abigail Ross Goodman

# Landscape as Found Object
## Molly Epstein

*Art itself might be partially defined as an expression of that moment of tension when human intervention in, or collaboration with, nature is recognized.*
—Lucy Lippard

"Landscape humanizes land," declares historian Mitchell Schwarzer. "It extends mind, body, and technology into nature. It constructs social and temporal awareness out of wood, water and wilderness. . . . But in all cases—in the flesh, represented on canvas, influenced by canvas—landscapes deepen a person's line of perception in a present moment."[1] When I landed on Schwarzer's observations, which frame an elucidating examination of the post-industrial landscape shaped by car travel, cinema, and the rise of the digital age, I found he might as well have been describing the Clark Art Institute—its collection and the distinctive natural setting within which it is cozily ensconced. Throughout the development of *Ground/work* over the past four years, I have been struck by the realization that a real place, an imagined place, and a depicted place coexist at the Clark, where humanizing forces have created a revelatory encounter with art and nature that happens both inside and out.

Renowned for its permanent collection and research institute, the Clark is a cultivated idyll teeming with treasures and ideas, from the venerable works hanging in its galleries (see Jacob van Ruisdael's c. 1660 *Landscape with Bridge, Cattle, and Figures* [fig. 1] whose composition echoes features found in the Clark's own scenery), to the extensive woodlands and open meadows linked to the museum buildings below through a series of integrated paths and footbridges. Despite the elaborately conceived landscapes held both within the Clark's architecture and beyond it, the campus—generously open to all, day and night, free of charge—conveys a sense of the natural world unmitigated, unfettered, unbound. Reflecting on her first site visit to the Clark on a cold and blustery winter day in 2019, artist Jennie C. Jones described a sense of discovery in "going out on such an adventure into that terrain" (fig. 2).[2]

How, then, to invite contemporary sculptural practice and inquiry into this landscape, both *of* the institution and accessible 24/7 as an unrestricted public space? How could sculptural responses

1

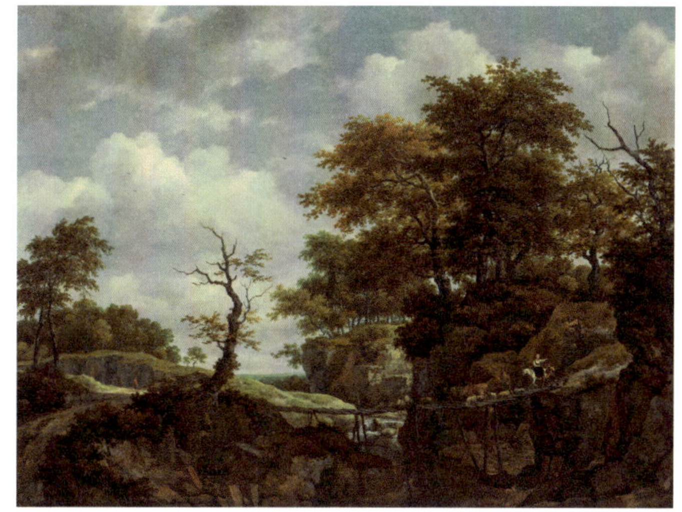

2

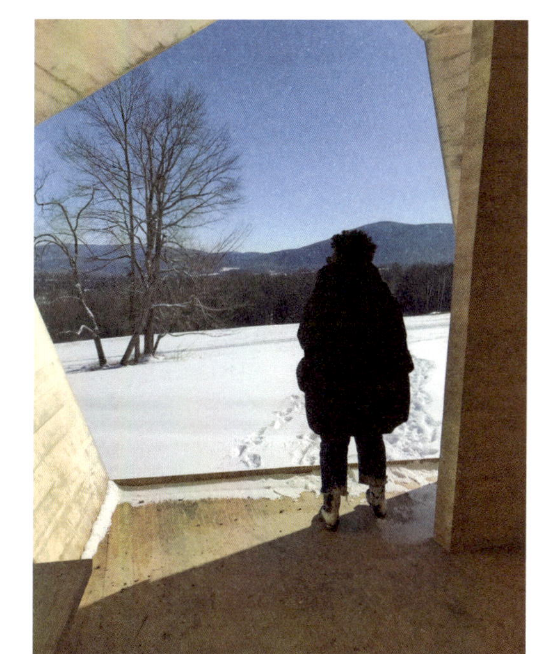

Fig. 1 Jacob van Ruisdael, *Landscape with Bridge, Cattle, and Figures*, c. 1660. Oil on canvas, 37 5/8 x 51 1/16 in. (5.6 x 129.7 cm). Collection of the Clark Art Institute. Acquired by Sterling and Francine Clark, 1922, 1955.29

Fig. 2 Jennie C. Jones standing inside Thomas Schütte's *Crystal* during a visit to the Clark in January 2019

embedded within the landscape heighten perception, slow time, engage material innovation, and encourage close looking and listening? The landscape's openness and four distinct seasons offered a layered and shifting environment to which *Ground/work*'s participating artists could respond, pushing against the convention of the inflexible, static monolith with an ensemble of encounters that unfurls throughout the Clark's grounds.

Interested in creating an opportunity for novel considerations of space, material, scale, and the renegotiation of traditional conditions of display out of doors, Abigail Ross Goodman and I invited six contemporary artists to visit the Clark and conceive of new works of art to be installed in the landscape. While not all had previously worked outside the white cube, their research-driven practices investigate how materials and context convey meaning, here prompted by the Clark's collection, architecture, flora and fauna, topography, and weather, which served as an open invitation to each. The resulting works of art incorporate aspects of the landscape and the artists' own materials and methods in equal measure. The site in each case is privileged, each project integrated within the found environment for the year it would spend on view.

The intertwining of sculpture and nature is a long and winding tale, a chronicle of prehistoric monuments, of garden decoration, of private and public pleasure parks merging environment and culture for (first) the few (fig. 3) and (then) the many. Then earth became architecture, time and scale material. Since the parameters and traditional definitions of sculpture in the twentieth and twenty-first centuries have morphed and dissolved, site has come to rely on the relationship between object and place with artworks asserting themselves as estranged from their environments as in those found in manicured or domestic outdoor space, contingent as in 1960s and '70s Land Art, or critical as in the discursive practices of recent decades.[3] For *Ground/work*—whose title came first, long before any of the commissions were fully envisioned or completed—we wanted to signal that there was labor to be done by the site. Not as plinth or pedestal, but as a mechanism for collage. Place and context would participate actively, with the works intimately

3

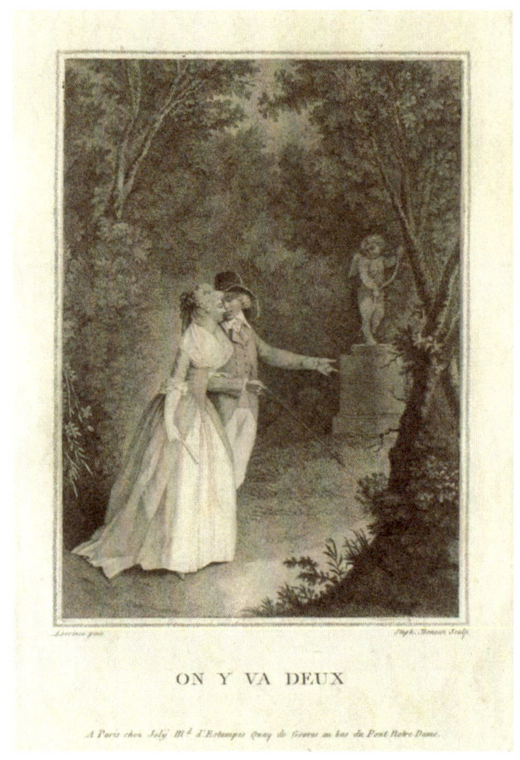


Fig. 3 Stefano Benossi, *On Y Va Deux*, c. 1788. Stipple engraving on laid paper, 13 3/8 x 9 ½ in. (33.9 x 24.2 cm). Clark Art Institute, Williamstown, MA. Acquired by Sterling and Francine Clark before 1955, 1955.2239

connected to the Clark's physical and ephemeral qualities, its associations through its collection, its landscape, and its built environment.

The artists' works are at once dependent upon and outside landscape: local birds can perch atop and drink from Haegue Yang's *Migratory DMZ Birds on Asymmetric Lens*; a monumental ash tree lies prostrate as a magnificent ruin, framed by Kelly Akashi's *A Device to See the World Twice*; the view from the top of Stone Hill doubles as the third element in Nairy Baghramian's *Knee and Elbow*; shifting weather conditions set in motion the harp strings of Jennie C. Jones's *These (Mournful) Shores*; slanting afternoon light refracts through Eva LeWitt's *Resin Towers*, casting colorful shadows; and seasonal bovine residents are treated to a drawing lesson in Analia Saban's *Teaching A Cow How to Draw*. The six artists in *Ground/work* have welcomed the existing landscape into the production process as both unofficial medium and acknowledged collaborator.

In *A Device to See the World Twice* Kelly Akashi reflects on the explicit relationship between site and outcome: "This work to me could only be created in an environment like the Clark. . . . Honestly, my mind can't separate development of this project from my visit to the landscape."[4] Akashi first visited the Clark in February of 2019 in the midst of a dramatic winter storm. After trekking through the grounds, she identified a natural niche in the woods that captured her attention, primarily due to the presence of an ash tree, standing tall and proud in a clearing abutting the trail. Her device directs visitors to engage with the occurrences and exchanges, both macro and micro, that she observed happening in the constant environmental chaos of the Clark's landscape. Akashi was also interested in what she calls the "evidence of moments" that take place in relationship to the sculpture, whether or not a human visitor is present.[5] The artist returned to the East Coast in March of 2020 to finalize siting for the work (fig. 4) and two and a half months later, the ash tree fell, the result of decades of rot taking hold. The once-vertical tree form was now earthbound, a spectacular monument to decay. Despite this dramatic and unanticipated change in conditions, Akashi kept the location. The tree's unexpected descent seemed apt, evidence of exactly what the artist was interested in directing our attention to as viewers. Akashi revels in chance manifest as change that is undeniable and irrefutable—a natural world of entropy, energy, and the unknown made plain in unanticipated ways. The experience of the sculpture is an ever-changing one: the fixed nature of the cast-bronze branches reminds us that the surrounding tree forms are in flux, while the lens reveals what transpires in the present, never to repeat. For Akashi, sculpture, like nature, is not static.

Similarly, when Nairy Baghramian visited the Clark for the second time in September 2019 (fig. 5), she characterized the relationship between nature and sculpture in *Ground/work* as "like a polite handshake; it's not forever, it feels like there is no misuse of each other, when we talk of the politics of it . . . more how we can live with and without each other."[6] This meaningful connection, a regard between the objects on view and their natural surroundings, emphasizes the collapse of the hierarchies and boundaries that one has come to expect where art and nature are concerned. For this exhibition, Baghramian noted, "the nature is not a playground for sculpture"; rather, in the artist's contribution, *Knee and Elbow*, the view from the top of Stone Hill where her work is sited becomes an integrated aspect of the sculpture as well as the prompt for its making.[7] Time spent out in the Clark's landscape reinforced for Baghramian that walking in nature can provide mental rest; her visits in preparation for the exhibition demonstrated how the very act of gazing down at the museum buildings and the town below created an opportunity for physical respite and repose. To arouse this feeling of rest, Baghramian created a sculptural evocation of what anatomical release could look like. The artist's practice has, from the beginning, concerned itself with the release of a discrete object from its traditional support or base structure. Here, Baghramian creates an integrated sculptural gesture where the object, its physical site, and the view become a single experience, unbounded by the edges where marble and stainless steel meet earth and sky.

Following her first visit to the Clark in September 2018, Haegue Yang remarked that the landscape surrounding the museum was at once utterly foreign and yet familiar. The New England setting reminded her of the lush and ecologically diverse world of the

4

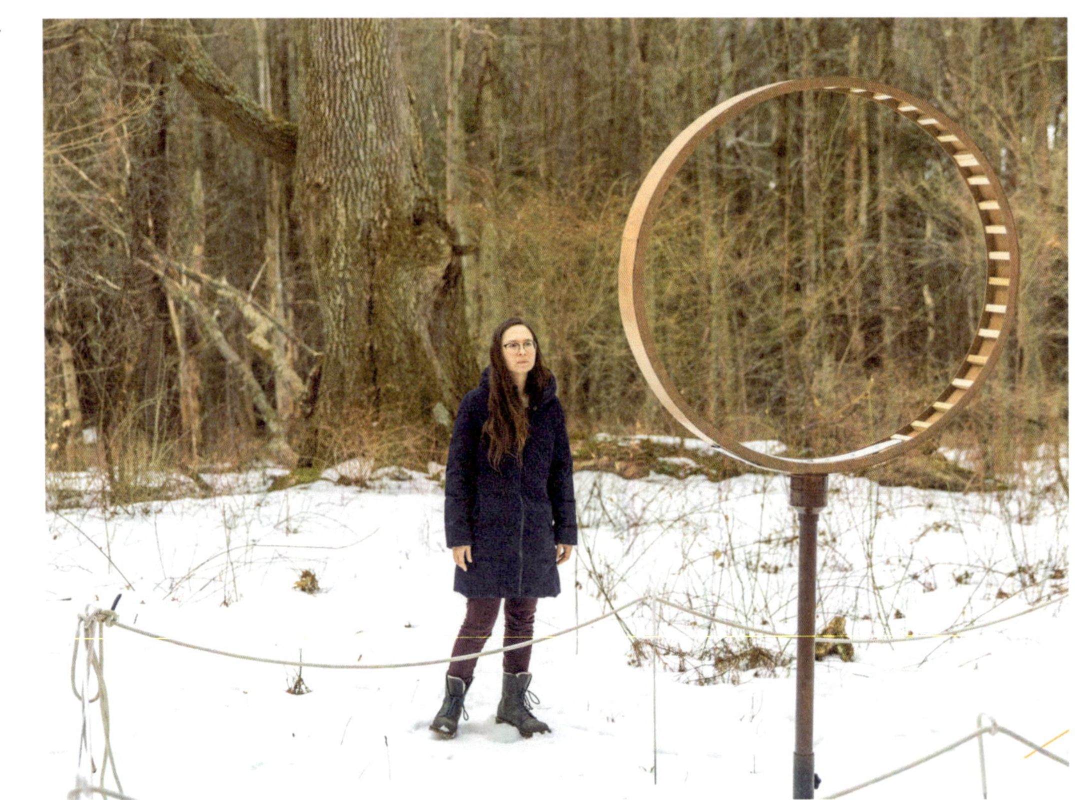

5

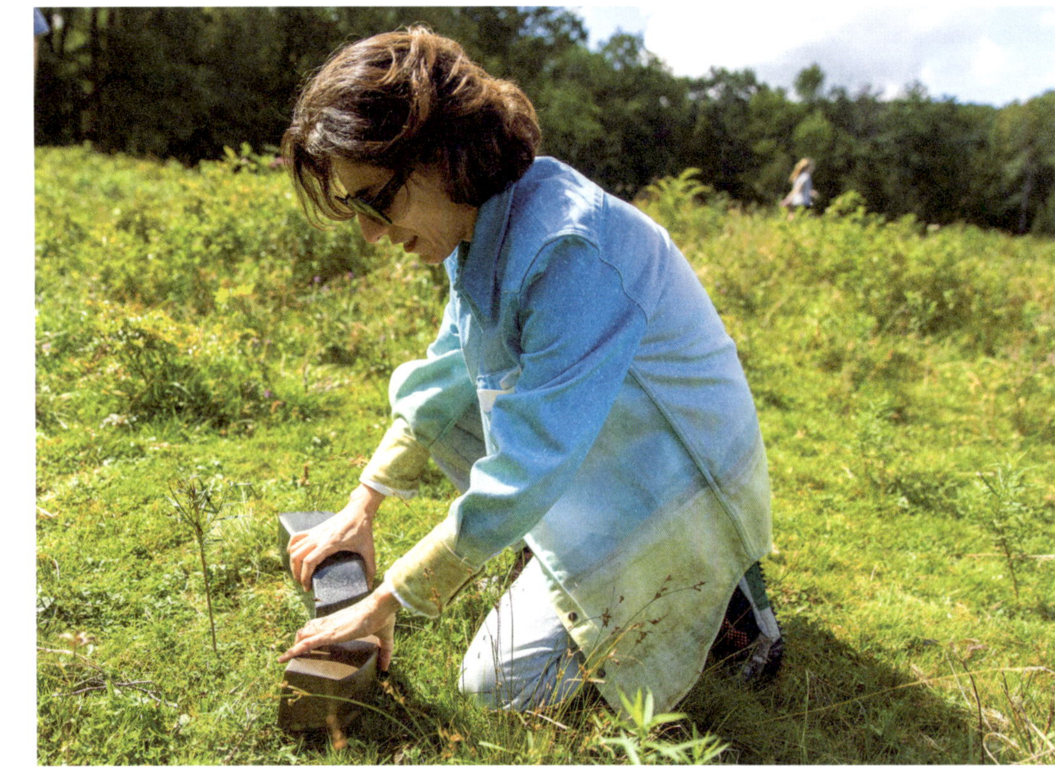

Fig. 4 Kelly Akashi on site at the Clark to finalize site placement with a maquette of *A Device to See the World Twice* in March 2020

Fig. 5 Nairy Baghramian with an early maquette for *Knee and Elbow* on site at the Clark in September 2019

6

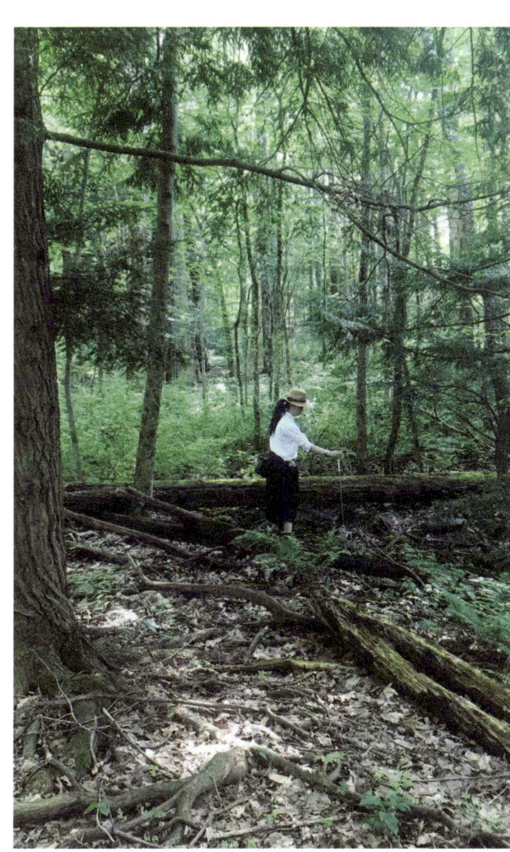

Fig. 6 Haegue Yang exploring the landscape during a visit to the Clark in July 2019

Demilitarized Zone, which separates North and South Korea, encouraging the artist to draw a through line between the DMZ and the Clark's landscape (fig. 6), thereby collapsing time and space to conceptually bridge two disparate environments that registered to Yang as somehow parallel. Given the presence and potency of the natural world in both settings, from the outset, the artist envisioned a work in which birds from the DMZ would have an imagined chance meeting with the local species in Williamstown, Massachusetts. Yang's three sculptures, scattered in disparate locations across the Clark's campus, were always intended to have the potential to be useful to species endemic to Stone Hill. Atop robotically milled stone pedestals, 3D-printed biocompatible resin birdbaths collect rainwater and snow, providing drinking water or a site for bathing.

Yang's series of works stage a metaphorical encounter between birds at the Clark and those from the DMZ, whose song was unexpectedly broadcast around the globe in real time during the historic inter-Korean summit in April 2018. In recent projects, Yang has incorporated a recording of the moment during the summit when the two leaders stepped away from the press and spoke privately on a bridge. This open-source audio file captures birdsong and the sound of camera shutters during what was a nearly unprecedented political event. The tape itself can be considered a readymade, an unmediated primary source, which Yang has woven into recent sculptural installations. This is the first time, however, that the artist pushes the recording into three dimensions, giving three of the bird species heard on the tape a physical, sculptural form birthed from their sonic selves. Yang's related use of found objects in her practice is evident in her extensive body of work *Series of Vulnerable Arrangements* (for example, fig. 7), begun in 2006, which employs light fixtures, venetian blinds, and other daily household objects in new positions and communication patterns. Reorienting assumptions about identity, borders, and constructed realities that divide similar beings, Yang embraces the Clark's landscape as medium, creating a reunification of species that could never truly interface in real time and space.

Georges Hugnet wrote of Duchamp's readymades in *Cahiers d'Art* in 1932, "The 'simple' thing is consecrated."[8] Hugnet's statement and broader discussion of Duchamp's practice within the context of Dada conveys the radical (and scandalous) presentation of simple objects in the sacred spaces of fine art and effectively articulates the way a found object can be elevated through its reframing. The sculptures on view in *Ground/work*, in turn, consecrate the landscape and the specific sites chosen by their makers. The works engage fully with their surroundings, but never recede into the landscape; as a result, these works of art and their environments both come into sharper relief. Our attention is directed toward how the forces of chance, time, distance, light, and seasonality can change our perspective and our experience of physical space.

Eva LeWitt found in the Clark's landscape an opportunity for various natural components—light and shadow, the expanse of sky and the colors of the shifting seasons—to become active elements in the perception and totality of her *Resin Towers*. Drawn immediately to a site of transition between the cloistered woodland trails and the meadow, LeWitt positioned her works like punctuation points, calling down the hill to the architecture of the Clark's buildings below (fig. 8). The transparency of the resin reflects and refracts the changing light each day, projecting colorful shadows onto the ground in an ever-shifting performance. The spheres within each tower mirror a shape commonly found in nature, echoing the diagrammatic truths of the natural world in material suspended in resin. Throughout the seasons—which LeWitt considers to be the fourth sculpture in her work—the luminous resin acts as a channel through which all of the natural matter surrounding the sculptures is absorbed, processed, and telegraphed back through the shifting conditions of site.

In developing her first artwork to be installed out of doors for *Ground/work*, Jennie C. Jones found herself "thinking about what is affected by its environment that would emanate a sound" and landed on the form of an Aeolian harp "as a haunting thing."[9] The Clark's landscape—its wind and weather patterns in particular—releases the sonic potential of *These (Mournful) Shores*: on windy days, the harp emits a low, atonal reverberation as gusts mobilize the strings in a doleful, improvised composition, calling out to the landscape in an organic duet with the nearby water feature. This is the first work in three dimensions by Jones that has the latent possibility to generate sound. Previous sculptural works by the artist refashioned sonic found objects—from headphones to cassette tapes to instrument cables—but were always muted: alluding to the audio activity of their former lives, but never audible in their new orientation. The artist, who uses techniques of both physical and conceptual assemblage in her practice, has often spoken about how she considers existing and operating on the periphery as a radical act.[10] Here, Jones situates herself and her work at the edge of the building, the threshold of landscape. The harp, a minimalist color study, repeats the precise dimensions of the adjacent granite wall, appearing as a nearly seamless extension of the architecture. Separated by only four inches, together they nod to the linear armature of a musical score. In this small gap Jones urges a new reading not just of the iconic Winslow Homer seascapes within the galleries that inspired this sculpture, but of all of the works in the Clark's collection and in the canon as a whole. Just as Duchamp's readymades invited the viewer to reassess works of art that came both before and after them, *These (Mournful) Shores* asks us to look again at images, objects, and histories that we think we already know, creating space for the subsequent deconstruction of dominant narratives.

While Jones responded to the Clark's architecture, in *Teaching A Cow How to Draw* Analia Saban focused on an unlikely extant structure on the institute's campus. The artist remarked after visiting the Clark for the first time in May of 2018 that the presence of cows in the landscape caught her attention. Seizing the opportunity to integrate this wholly unexpected aspect of the site into her work, she adopted the existing pasture fence (fig. 9), which served as a dividing line between the institute's lower campus buildings and the landscape of Stone Hill, as a found object, redesigning the running fence line as a primer in strategies of image making—for a bovine audience. Saban creates opportunities for both whimsy and a kind of formal reappraisal, reframing the view of Stone Hill in both directions, thereby asking us to look anew at familiar forms and reflexive assumptions.

7

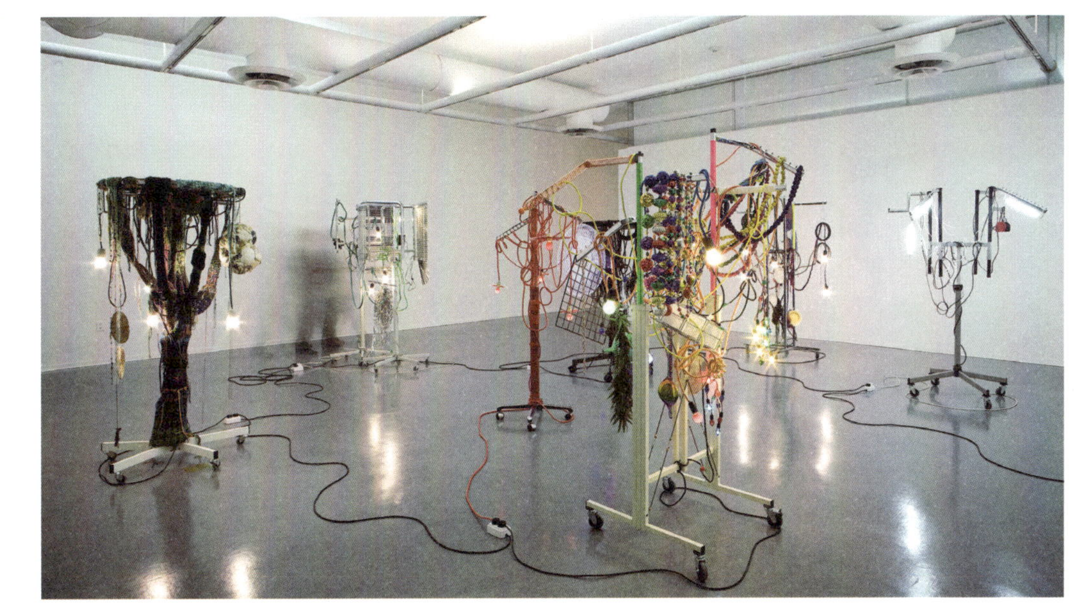

8

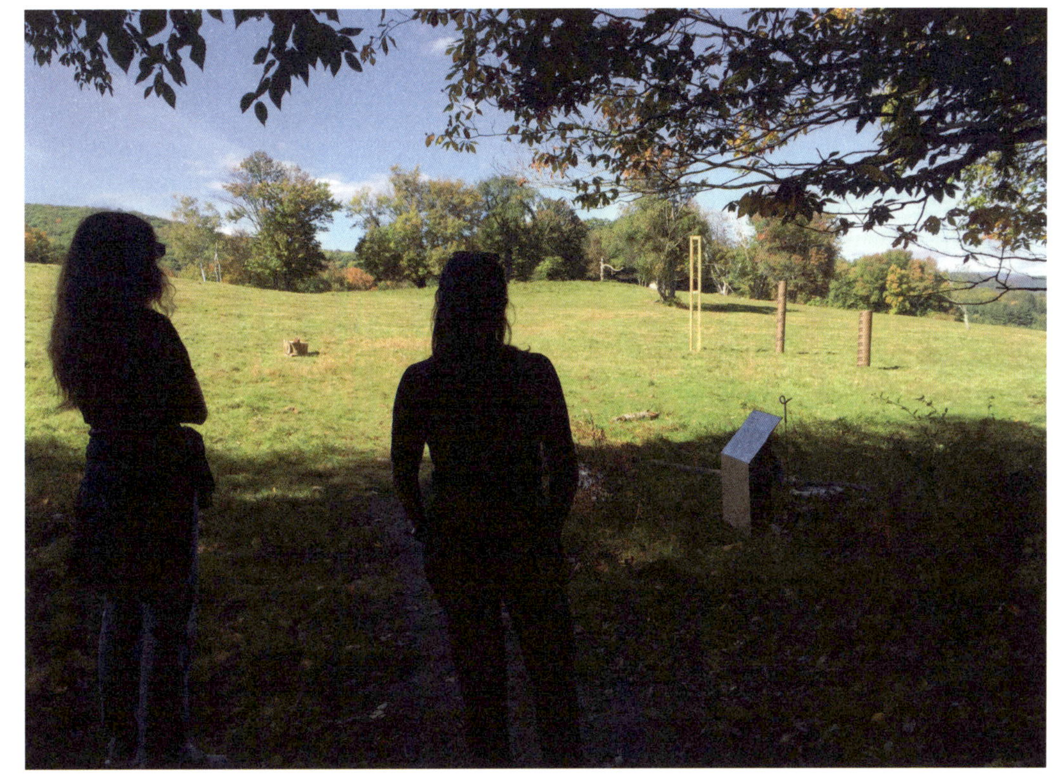

Fig. 7 Haegue Yang, *Series of Vulnerable Arrangements—Concerns toward Personal Limits*, 2009. Seven light sculptures. Private collection, Seoul. Installation view of *Assume Nothing: New Social Practice*, Art Gallery of Greater Victoria, Canada, 2009

Fig. 8 Eva LeWitt and *Ground/work* co-curator Abigail Ross Goodman finalizing placement with maquettes for *Resin Towers* in September 2019

As Schwarzer writes, "Landscape is both a thing seen and a way of seeing."[11] Saban's work is instructive: whether you encounter the surprising complexity of the fence's composition as you begin your walk through the exhibition, or it greets you at the end of your wandering as you make your way back to the museum buildings below, it inevitably shifts your perspective around image making, objectness, space, and audience. As with all of the works on view in *Ground/work*, *Teaching a Cow How to Draw* transforms the visitor's relationship to the landscape from a thing to be seen and experienced to an altered way of looking where everything is three-dimensional and multisensory.

In 1955, when the Sterling and Francine Clark Art Institute opened in Williamstown, Massachusetts, the original museum building included galleries with large windows specifically designed to allow visitors to experience views of the outdoors while enjoying the objects on view inside. Drawing on its founders' values, the Clark's focus on the landscape beyond its buildings as a place of repose, activation, and deepened perception has only increased over time. *Ground/work*, the Clark's first exhibition of outdoor sculpture, therefore, feels like a natural progression for the institute and its identity. In 1979's "Sculpture in the Expanded Field," Rosalind Krauss wrote: "[Sculpture] sits in a particular place and speaks in a symbolic tongue about the meaning or use of that place."[12] By continuing to extend its focus up the hill and mounting an ambitious exhibition out of doors, the Clark has demonstrated the importance of its specific landscape to its work as an institution and the significance of its site to its public. And by inviting six artists to make new works that will likely have lives elsewhere beyond the Clark, the institute has simultaneously declared a renewed commitment to living artists and the art of the now: these works of sculpture do not belong to this particular place and will go on to demand close looking as they disperse to new sites in the future. Installed on a rolling basis in 2020, they remain on view through the four seasons until the exhibition concludes in October 2021, when they will leave the landscape that has permeated and informed them, but on which they are not contingent. Ultimately, there will be no physical trace that they were here, even though each has thoroughly transformed its site by reshaping perception and experience.

Haegue Yang has often referred to communication or interaction as "condensation," a tangible reaction or visible event that results from the meeting of two disparate forces: people, materials, forms.[13] The artist has also drawn attention to the "temporary rendezvous" of artworks in an exhibition where the "separation had been pre-planned," alluding to the temporal nature of a gathering of objects that characterizes all exhibition-making endeavors.[14] Although these works of art will each have a future life beyond the Clark's campus, they will inevitably leave a residue of memory and meaning behind, just as the Clark's landscape as found object and material will ineffably migrate with them. To borrow Yang's language, when the temporary rendezvous of *Ground/work* concludes and the pre-planned separation takes place, the condensation created through the making of these works and the year they have spent on view will remain suspended: a rubbing up of objects and landscape, leaving both forever changed.

*Molly Epstein is a curator and art historian based in New York.*

Epigraph: Lucy Lippard, *Overlay: Contemporary Art and the Art of Prehistory* (New York: New Press, 1983), 4.

1 Mitchell Schwarzer, "The Moving Landscape," in *Monuments and Memory, Made and Unmade*, ed. Robert S. Nelson and Margaret Olin (Chicago: University of Chicago Press, 2002), 83.

2 Jennie C. Jones, unedited Acoustiguide interview conducted by Molly Epstein and Abigail Ross Goodman, April 21, 2020, 1:00.

3 For an accounting of a broad range of histories, theories, and designations regarding art in public space, see the extensive glossary section included in Brigitte Franzen, Kasper König, and Carina Plath, eds., *Sculpture Projects Muenster 07* (Cologne: Walter König, 2007), 323–475. See also Miwon Kwon's text on the evolution of site-specific artistic practices *One Place After Another: Site-Specific Art and Locational Identity* (Cambridge, MA: MIT Press, 2002).

4 Kelly Akashi, unedited Acoustiguide interview conducted by Molly Epstein and Abigail Ross Goodman, April 27, 2020, 29:37.

5 Kelly Akashi, site visit and conversation at the Clark Art Institute, video recording, March 2, 2020, 31:00.

6 Nairy Baghramian, site visit and conversation at the Clark Art Institute, video recording, September 4, 2019, 4:28.

7 Baghramian, video recording, 28:55.

8 Georges Hugnet, "L'Esprit Dada dans la peinture" (part 1), *Cahiers d'Art*, no. 1 (1932): 64–65.

9 Jones, Acoustiguide interview, 8:18.

10 See Jennie C. Jones, artist talk at the Art Institute of Chicago, February 17, 2017, accessed November 4, 2020, http://www.youtube.com/watch?v=ROum0hPFsaY.

11 Schwarzer, "Moving Landscape," 87.

12 Rosalind Krauss, "Sculpture in the Expanded Field," *October* 8 (Spring 1979): 33.

13 See "A Conversation: Haegue Yang and Eungie Joo," in *Haegue Yang: Condensation*, exh. cat. (Seoul: Arts Council Korea; Berlin: Wiens Verlag, 2009), 19. See also "The Mystic Landscapes of Haegue Yang: Haegue Yang in Conversation with Stuart Comer," *MoMA Magazine*, October 25, 2019.

14 Haegue Yang, quoted in "Arrived: A Conversation between Haegue Yang and Yilmaz Dziewior," in *Arrivals*, ed. Yilmaz Dziewior (Bregenz: Kunsthalle Bregenz, 2011), 70.

9

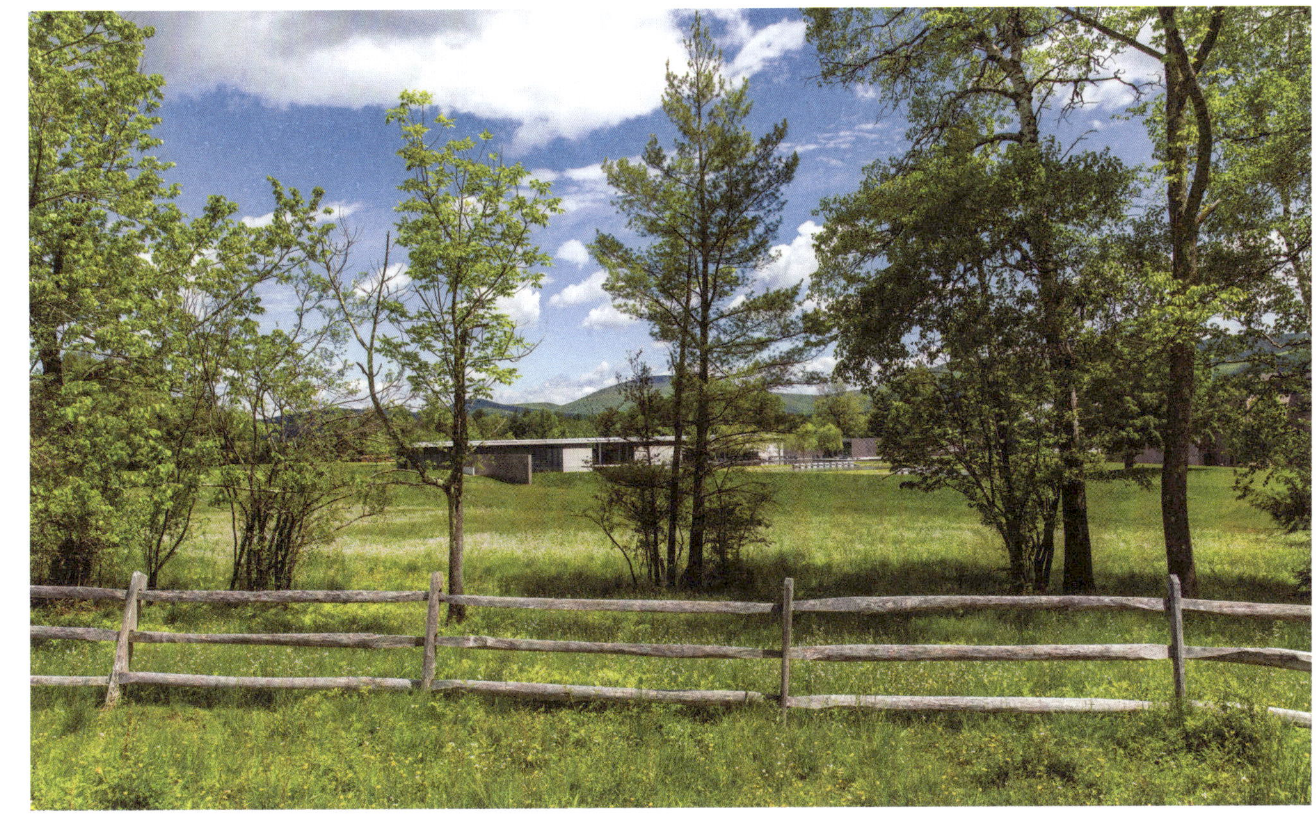

Fig. 9 The original split-rail fence at the Clark in June 2019

# Site and Somatic Scale: Six Possibilities on Stone Hill
## Abigail Ross Goodman

Contending with scale is an unavoidable challenge of any outdoor intervention. The six *Ground/work* artists commissioned to create site-responsive sculptures for the Clark Art Institute's 140 acres and varied terrain, ranging from grassy field to open pasture, wooded trails to hemlock groves, had to grapple not only with which spaces to occupy, but also how much space to take up. Within their unique approaches to the setting, Kelly Akashi, Nairy Baghramian, Jennie C. Jones, Eva LeWitt, Analia Saban, and Haegue Yang each prioritized nuanced, embodied encounters with their works. Rather than attempt to dominate the landscape, the artists absorbed the qualities of the institute's campus and collection, making proposals that acknowledged the site and the environment. Despite the distinctions between projects, they all claimed space in a manner that, even in the most expansive gestures, privileges a body-centered relationship to scale and viewers' awareness of their experience of perception.

In his 2004 article "No More Scale: The Experience of Size in Contemporary Sculpture," James Meyers lays out the evolution of, and relationship between, the terms scale and size.[1] Somatic scale places value on the phenomenological experience—the relationship between object, body and, later, context—while an interest in size emphasizes sheer volume, at times irrespective of context. While producing works of substantial dimensions and heft, the *Ground/work* artists managed to avoid the crutch of going bigger for bigger's sake. They channeled their ambition into innovations within their practices, engaging new materials and new methods of production and fabrication, and championed the ideals of somatic scale—especially for how it focuses the act of looking and cultivates attentiveness to place and self.

Analia Saban's *Teaching a Cow to Draw* marks space through an expression of scale that is experienced as much as it is seen. At 620 linear feet, her installation is the largest in the exhibition, and yet, in many ways, it is the most subtle intervention. Reimagining the Clark's existing split-rail fence as a study in perspective aimed equally at the institute's human and nonhuman audiences, Saban leveraged the entire, extensive border between the adjacent pasture and the museum grounds. The artist reflected on the viewing experience as being "expanded" in part by "the fact that you have to really walk for a few minutes, or probably for quite a while to get the whole picture of the piece" (fig. 10).[2] That is, she approaches monumentality with an idea beyond physical scale: that of duration. She claims not just the space her work occupies in the landscape, but also the time it takes to absorb her intervention fully; she is gently requiring something we are more used to offering to experiences of new media: our presence. Nevertheless, in spite of the running dimensions of the artwork and the interval needed to take it in, Saban's didactic fence presents as something born of the place, a drawing in space purposefully reverent of the landscape and of the functional object that it replaced. With a poetic sensibility and a witty sense of humor, Saban balances elegance with the handmade and the humble, the formal with the perceptual, the monumental with the approachable.

Jennie C. Jones's *These (Mournful) Shores* highlights another mode of perception: the sonic. Her site-responsive sculpture, the first of her works to be made for the outdoors and also to be fabricated outside of the studio, meticulously echoes the precise height and depth of a wall that extends from the Clark Center alongside a reflecting pool, both constructed during the institute's 2014 expansion. The sculpture's hue—a mix of rust, purple, and gray—echoing the adjacent ruddy granite wall designed by Tadao Ando, also harkens back to colors found in two Winslow Homer paintings in the galleries.[3] A continuation of Jones's interest in reframing histories of art and music to include Black voices, *These (Mournful) Shores* invites us to look anew at familiar images and to consider other possible readings of their content. As a Black artist, Jones shares her subjectivity to express how Homer's North Atlantic seascapes might be considered portraits of the Middle Passage. Scaled to the Clark's architecture, the towering, sixteen-foot-tall modernist interpretation of an Aeolian harp, played by the wind, creates an immersive landscape/soundscape experience (fig. 11). This aural component reinforces Jones's savvy and deft weaving of multiple narratives and visual vocabularies into objects and encounters that transcend categorization. By any definition formidable, in both size and subject matter, *These (Mournful) Shores* seamlessly fits within its

10

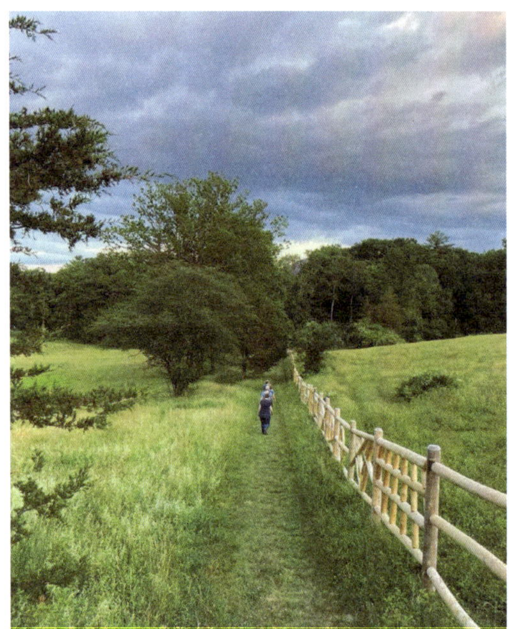

Fig. 10 Visitors walk alongside Analia Saban's *Teaching a Cow How to Draw* in June 2020. Courtesy of Destination Williamstown, Instagram.com/destinationwiliamstown

site and context. To go back to Meyer's distinctions between size and scale, though the work is large, it is in direct and purposeful relationship with the campus, the collection, and the viewer. Jones described her enthusiasm for the opportunity to "manifest ideas larger than my hands" at the Clark.[4] Reflecting on scale, form, and color, she explained, she intentionally tried to draw out the strength of the place: "I was also mindful of the changing seasons and the environment around the sculpture when thinking about a color that would be neutral, so that the landscape could sing just as much as the instrument."[5] This responsiveness to the site invites the viewer to be "present," she added.[6]

In another contribution that centers the act of looking, Nairy Baghramian reveals a shared desire to create moments of pause and presence. When visiting the Clark for the first time, Baghramian remarked on the siting of Thomas Schütte's *Crystal*, a long-term loan that was installed on Stone Hill in 2015. Baghramian found it to be "an indication of . . . an open but still intimate space from which you can get a specific vantage point in order to test your own perceptions."[7] Inspired by this quality, she settled her marble and polished stainless steel *Knee and Elbow* (2020) on a perch atop the upper Stone Hill pasture with a nod to the museum at the foot of the fields, as well as the theater of the hill and the Green Mountains beyond. Weighing approximately 2,500 pounds combined, the sculpture's two components are not unlike their bovine companions beyond Saban's fence—capable of asserting their bulk while appearing surprisingly disarming and gentle. From a distance, at least in the summer and fall, the massive work commands the landscape with its pink and white punctuation of the terrain (fig. 12). Yet as one approaches, suddenly the thing once giant improbably becomes something much more tender and accessible. In his *Phenomenology of Perception*, the French philosopher Maurice Merleau-Ponty asserts the primacy of experience, the way that the comprehension of an object shifts as one's body moves around it, even when the object of concern and its setting are static.[8] One can feel this sensation when circumnavigating *Knee and Elbow*. Drawing on her interest in contemporary choreography and dance, Baghramian has made an artwork that seems to fold and unfold before the viewer. *Knee and Elbow*

11

12

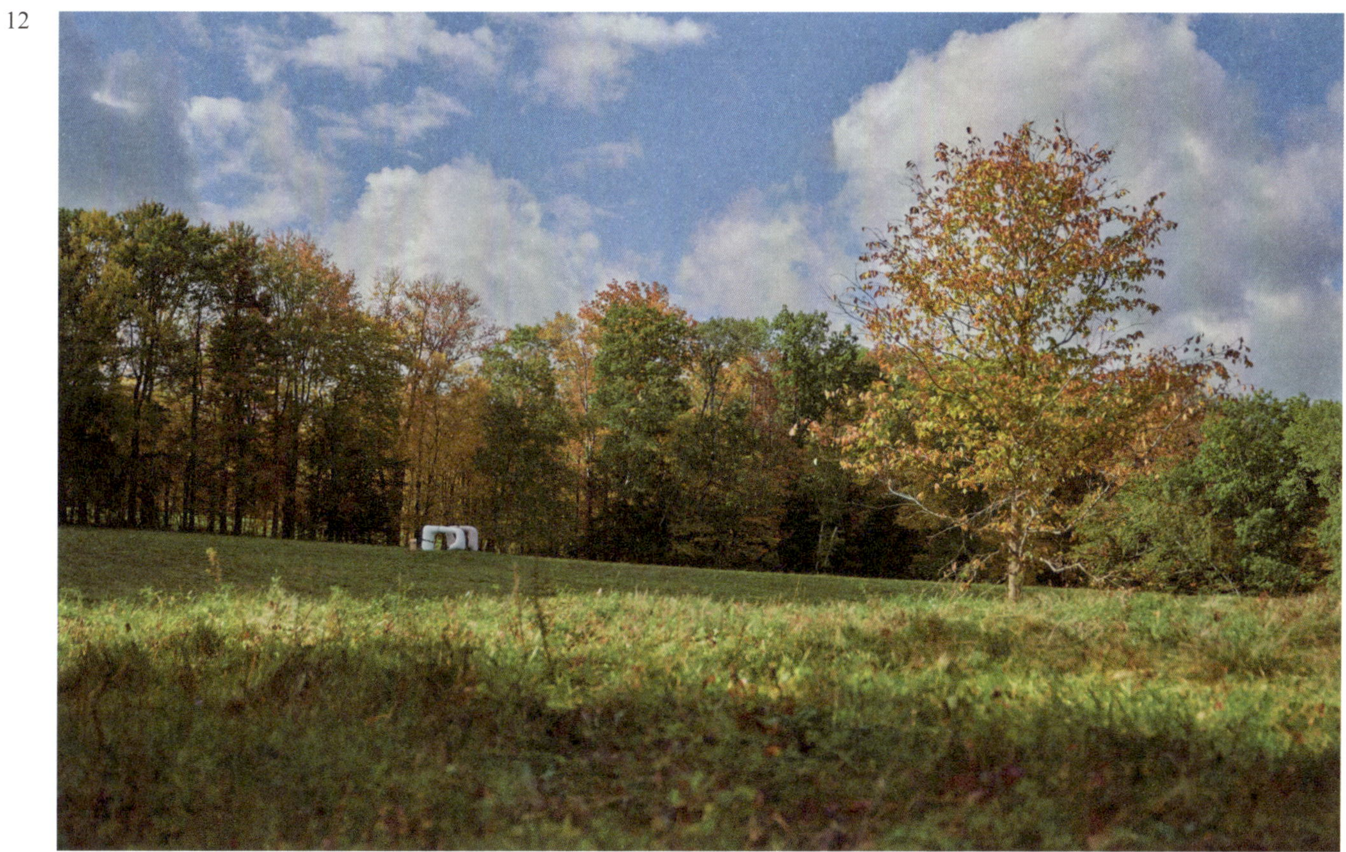

Fig. 11 Jennie C. Jones, *These (Mournful) Shores*, 2020
Fig. 12 Nairy Baghramian, *Knee and Elbow*, 2020

epitomizes Baghramian's nuanced and intuitive sense of form and amplifies her engagement with the performance of her works—their ability to stand in for the body while also eliciting motion and emotion from other bodies.

In *A Device to See the World Twice*, sited a brief walk across the upper pasture and through a forest path from *Knee and Elbow*, Kelly Akashi approaches ideas of perception and scale from a distinct vantage point. She focuses our view toward the mysterious deep of the woods, offering a fixed lens through which to behold all that is transpiring in the theater of the natural world. The "device" is an *aide-memoire*, tuning the viewer into this specific place, which then operates as a portal to a space beyond what the body-sized lens captures. With her background in photography, the artist has long been interested in how to fix objects or bodies in time despite the inevitable entropy of all living things. Throughout her practice, Akashi has often utilized cast objects as an index and origin point in her works, presenting them life size or even enlarging them (fig. 13); here, the base of the lens is fashioned out of cast-bronze branches, while the lens takes the form of a magnifying glass scaled to a human armspan. The dimensions of the object engage directly with the body—most adults find themselves facing the center of the lens—and this relationship between the object and the viewer firmly roots the work in somatic scale. Yet form aside, the artist approaches scale through how she wrestles with time: human and geologic. Initially planning to focus her lens on a two-hundred-year-old ash tree standing at the far reaches of the Clark's grounds (fig. 14), she recommitted to the site after the majestic tree fell during a particularly violent spring storm. In the resulting work, Akashi inverts ideas of monumentality, creating a device for the observation of grandeur rather than building something expressly grand itself. The artist's project for *Ground/work* engages the mechanics of sight as an entry point for conceptual questions about perception and the lived understanding of place, including its volume and dimension. The humanistic geographer Yi-Fu Tuan writes, "Place is a special kind of object. It is an object in which one can dwell."[9] Akashi underscores this sentiment and provides a means by which one can inhabit such space.

13

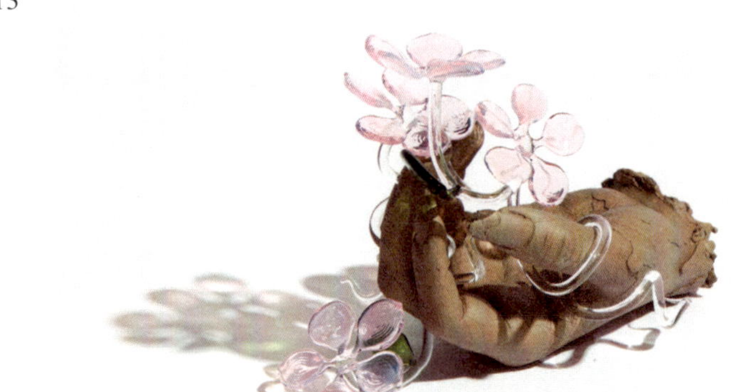

Fig. 13 Kelly Akashi, *Cultivator (Hanami)*, 2021. Flame-worked borosilicate glass, bronze, overall: 9 x 10 x 4 in. (23 x 25.5 x 10.2 cm); bronze: 4 x 6 x 4 in. (10.2 x 15.2 x 10.2 cm). Courtesy of the artist and Tanya Bonakdar Gallery, New York

14

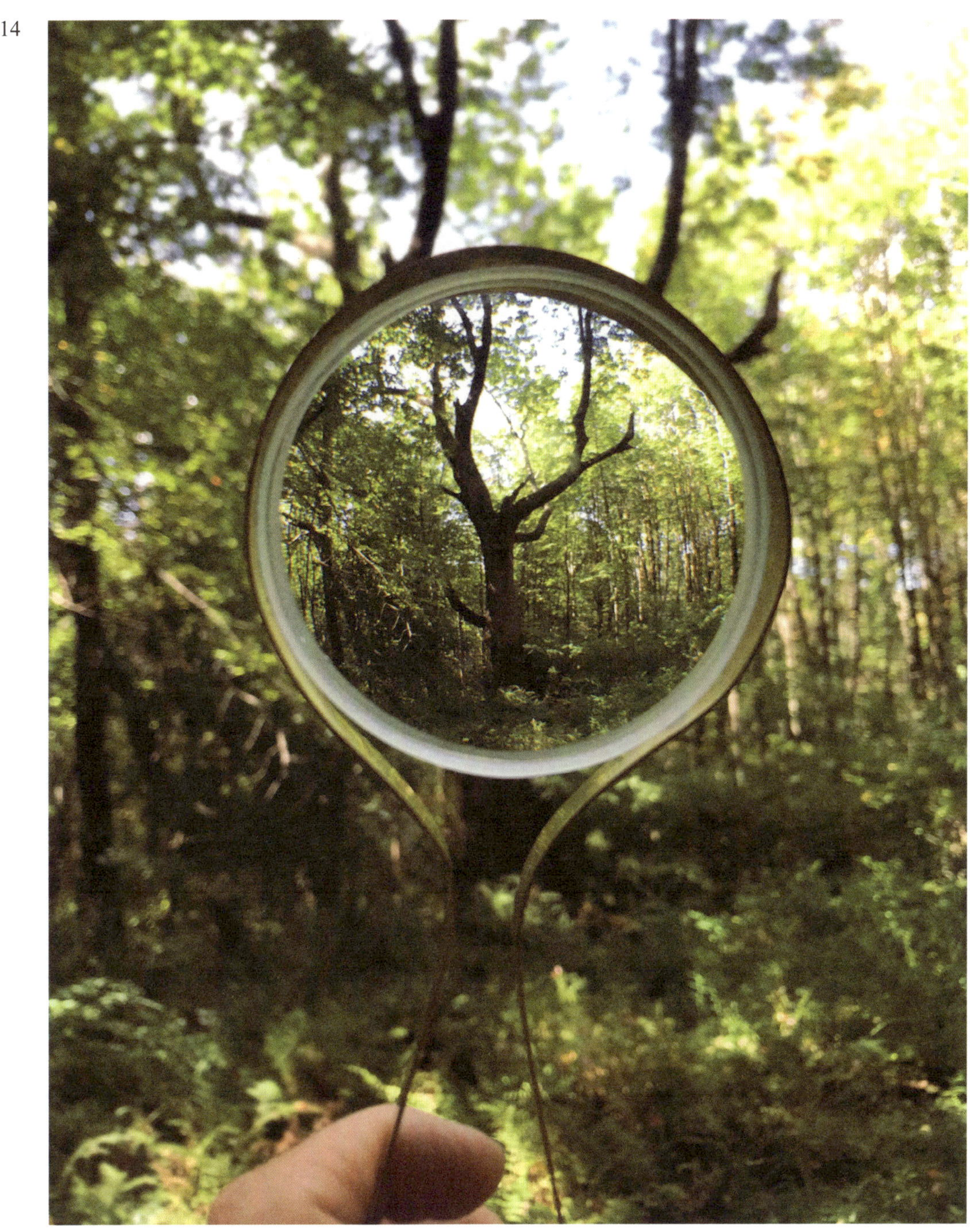

Fig. 14 Preliminary maquette for Kelly Akashi's *A Device to See the World Twice* on site at the Clark, 2019

With *A Device to See the World Twice*, she offers both a physical object and the possibility to experience place as object.

At eleven feet tall and ten inches square, Eva LeWitt's resin forms are legible from a distance. The artist explicitly sited her three equivalent columns, *Resin Tower A (Orange), Resin Tower B (Yellow), and Resin Tower C (Blue)* (fig. 15), to operate as beacons, objects that lure visitors into the landscape. Perceptually seductive, their translucent forms catch and fragment light; as the sun's position shifts, these slender yet towering forms cast shadows and perform as sundials. In spite of their height, and likely thanks to their narrow circumferences, the works occupy a scale that viewers can still understand as relating to their own proportions; Lewitt's forms are twice as tall, and half or a third as wide as many human bodies. As much as these objects assert themselves in the terrain, in her choice of color for each tower, the artist references the durational experience of the exhibition, anticipating the changes in the environment over the many months and seasons of the columns' installation. Each of LeWitt's hues advances or retreats depending on the time of year; she was interested in the recessive qualities of particular colors in certain periods. In this way, she nods to the passage of time and suggests how our sensory experience shifts in variable conditions. Unlike the other projects in *Ground/work*, LeWitt's does not point outside itself to tell a story or reveal anything beyond formal and perceptual concerns. Instead, the *Resin Towers* employ materiality, seriality, and the basic forms of the circle and the sphere, the square and the column. The artist describes the interior of the towers as animations of shapes, or rather, as documents of how these essential shapes might be made in a moment. By way of example, imagine the blue forms in *Tower C* illustrating a circle contracting and expanding within the clear resin column. LeWitt's limited actions, materials, and forms heighten the perception of everything else—one's own size in relationship to the towers, the color of the landscape, the quality of the light. Time slows, and one arrives at a state of (self-) conscious observation. Starting with her early wall-bound works in latex, plastic, and foam, LeWitt demonstrated finesse at making viewers aware of their perception of weight and form. The expansion of these ideas into serial, rhythmic installations, like her 2019 project *Untitled Mesh (A through J)* at the Aldrich Contemporary Art Museum set the stage for her departure from the prop of architecture, into the round (fig. 16). As with such precedents, LeWitt's trio of *Resin Towers* employs repetition as a means for shaping space and asserting the sculpture's presence in the landscape. This progression of emphatically linear forms, which are enriched by the proximity of their sister towers, expresses quite clearly the artist's interest in how related parts make a whole.

If LeWitt utilizes proximate seriality—viewers encounter her resin towers side by side in *Ground/work*—Haegue Yang harnesses scattered seriality to engage the scale of the Clark's landscape and also of memory: hers of the inter-Korean summit of 2018, and viewers' as they discover her sculptures at three sites across Stone Hill. Yang describes "time and geographical distance" as vital in her life,[10] and the new tripartite sculpture she created for *Ground/work* has already sparked a series that will continue halfway around the world. An expression of her recurring explorations of dispersion and congregation, opacity and transparency, *Migratory DMZ Birds on Asymmetric Lens* comprises three works: *Tee-Cher Tee-Cher Vessel (Great Tit)*, *Hou-Ke-Kyo Vessel (Japanese Bush Warbler)*, and *Duiitt Duiitt Vessel (Gray-Backed Thrush)* (all 2020). Even as the component parts of these sculptures are consistent—each incorporating a 59-inch-high, robotically milled base in the sacred lens-like form of a *vesica piscis* (fig. 17)[11] with the inscribed longitude and latitude of the Clark and the DMZ, topped with a translucent 3D-printed bird centered on the ridge of the form—each is distinguished by individual traits: different colors of soapstone, as well as language pertaining to the site etched into the milling grooves, the material, the bird. Though somewhat whimsical in effect, no detail is haphazard, no nuance by chance. In the essay "The Architecture of Opacity," curator Philippe Vergne describes how Yang consistently "formalizes a true phenomenology of perception in which all senses are called to task."[12] This is borne out again at the Clark. Unlike some of her works, these sculptures are not kinetic and do not emit sound, but the they do have a subtle synesthetic

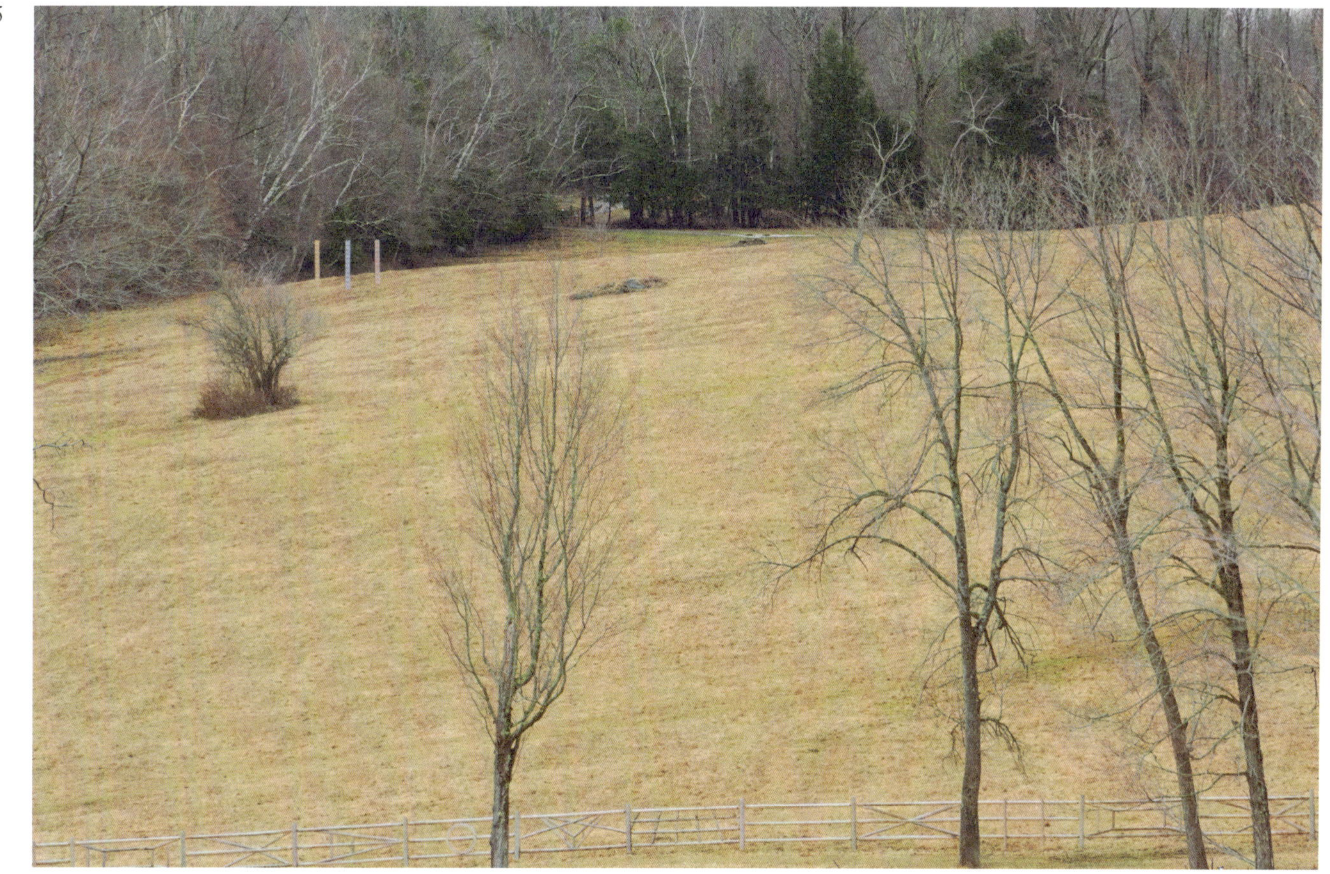

Fig. 15 Eva LeWitt, *Resin Tower A (Orange), Resin Tower B (Yellow), and Resin Tower C (Blue)*, 2020

16

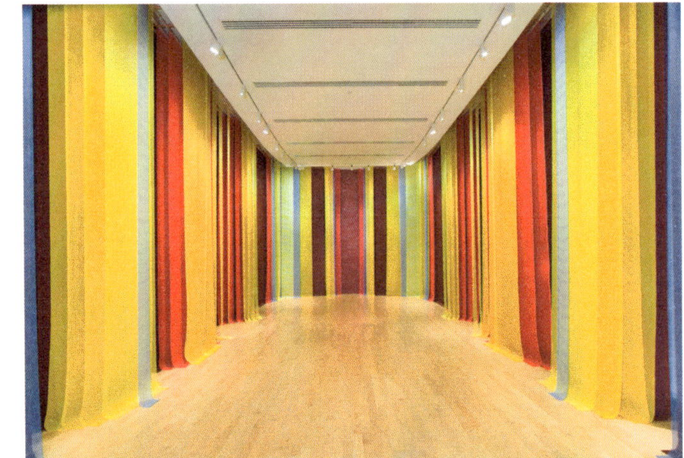

Fig. 16 Eva LeWitt, *Untitled Mesh (A through J)* (installation view, detail), 2019. Aldrich Contemporary Art Museum, Ridgefield, CT. Courtesy of the artist and VI, VII, Oslo

quality—one can imagine the translucent birds bringing their song to Stone Hill—and the forms morph as their lens-like shapes shift to flat discs depending on the viewer's vantage point. The grooved surfaces of the bases seem to crave touch, and the etched texts offer evocative, sensate descriptions like *arid air* or *dry dust*. The tension between the intimacy of the encounter with these objects and the vast possibilities that they attempt to describe is core to the work. Though Yang's sculptures themselves reflect a very human scale, the massive bases positioning the tiny resin birds at eye level, the artist insists on a certain freedom for territorial expansion and the opportunity to create possibilities for discovery through wandering. This is a technique she has long employed when conceiving her exhibitions, both indoors and in the landscape. Yang explained in an interview that "the accidental encounter is probably [the] most vital experience one could get while one is wandering," in part because it develops and subverts expectations.[13] In distributing her works across the landscape, Yang merges the physical scale of her objects with the topographical scale of the distance traveled to find them, creating opportunities for meetings of chance and discovery. The glimpses of these works as they catch one's eye while meandering along the wooded trails or cresting the pasture touch something tender and poetic, speaking to the artist's witty and playful yet often-melancholy practice.

In conceptualizing their respective projects, Akashi, Baghramian, Jones, LeWitt, Saban, and Yang examined the limitless possibilities for expressions of size and scale offered by the Clark and the landscape of Stone Hill. Fundamentally, *Ground/work* sought to highlight progressive and varied approaches to sculptural practice, and it is intriguing that the artists independently gravitated toward site-sensitive and somatically scaled forms. When work began on the exhibition in 2017, the pandemic of 2020 was unimagined. Yet when *Ground/work* opened that year, it offered a counterpoint to the isolation and fear of the moment and provided an opportunity for visitors to find spaciousness again. In ways the artists could not have anticipated, the return to public spaces, even bucolic ones, brought a heightened sense of one's body due to pandemic protocols of maintaining "social distance" from others. The novelty, too, of encountering

17

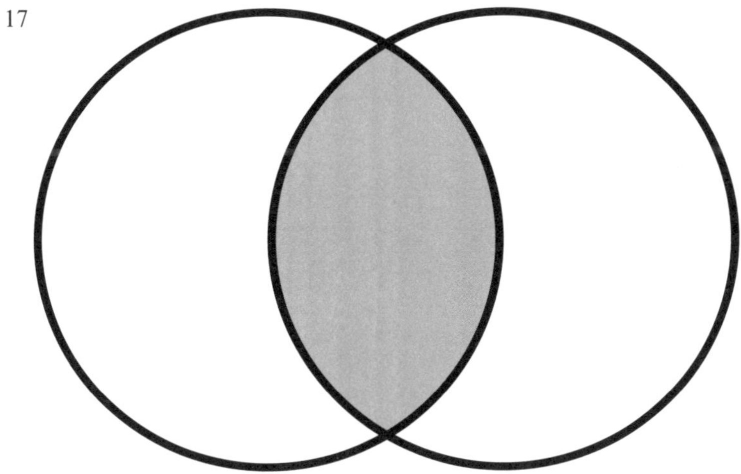

somatically scaled artworks in a time when most human interaction was mediated by technology also strangely amplified the works' intent. Nearly half a century before lockdowns constrained our physical worlds, Yi-Fu Tuan wrote, "Spaciousness is closely associated with the sense of being free." He continued, "Freedom implies space; it means having the power and enough room in which to act."[14] With the full expanse of the Clark's grounds at their disposal, the *Ground/work* artists prioritized the relationships between their works, their sites, and their viewers, not feeling the need to make size as an expression of their power. Instead, these artists understood the concept of spaciousness—physical, conceptual, material—that *Ground/work* offered, and they celebrated the opportunity to innovate free of limitations.

*Abigail Ross Goodman is a curator based in Cambridge, Massachusetts.*

1 James Meyers, "No More Scale: The Experience of Size in Contemporary Sculpture," *Artforum* 42, no. 10 (Summer 2004), http://www.artforum.com/print/200406/no-more-scale-the-experience-of-size-in-contemporary-sculpture-6960.
2 Analia Saban, unedited Acoustiguide interview conducted by Molly Epstein and Abigail Ross Goodman, recorded March 11, 2020, 43:11.
3 Winslow Homer, *Eastern Point* and *West Point Prout's Neck* (both 1900, see figs. 23 and 24).
4 Jennie C. Jones, unedited Acoustiguide interview conducted by Molly Epstein and Abigail Ross Goodman, recorded April 21, 2020, 13:01.
5 Jones, Acoustiguide interview, 40:53.
6 Jones, Acoustiguide interview, 40:53.
7 Nairy Baghramian, unedited Acoustiguide interview conducted by Molly Epstein and Abigail Ross Goodman, recorded July 8, 2020, 5:36.
8 Maurice Merleau-Ponty, *Phenomenology of Perception*, trans. Colin Smith and Forrest Williams (New York: Routledge, [1945], 2012), 5.
9 Yi-Fu Tuan, *Space and Place: The Perspective of Experience* (Minneapolis: University of Minnesota Press, 1977), 12.
10 Haegue Yang, unedited Acoustiguide interview conducted by Molly Epstein and Abigail Ross Goodman, recorded June 23, 2020, 9:08.
11 A vesica piscis, which translates to "bladder of a fish," is the lens-like shape formed by two overlapping discs of the same radius. It is a considered a component of sacred geometry.
12 Philippe Vergne, "The Architecture of Opacity," in *Hague Yang: In the Cone of Uncertainty*, Silvia Karman Cubiñá, Leilani Lynch, and Philippe Vergne (Berlin: Hatje Cantz Verlag, 2019), 57.
13 Yang, Acoustiguide interview, 58:14.
14 Tuan, *Space and Place*, 52.

Fig. 17 Diagram illustrating a *vesica piscis*

Powder-coated aluminum, wood, harp strings
197 1/16 x 72 x 18 in. (500.5 x 182.9 x 45.7 cm)

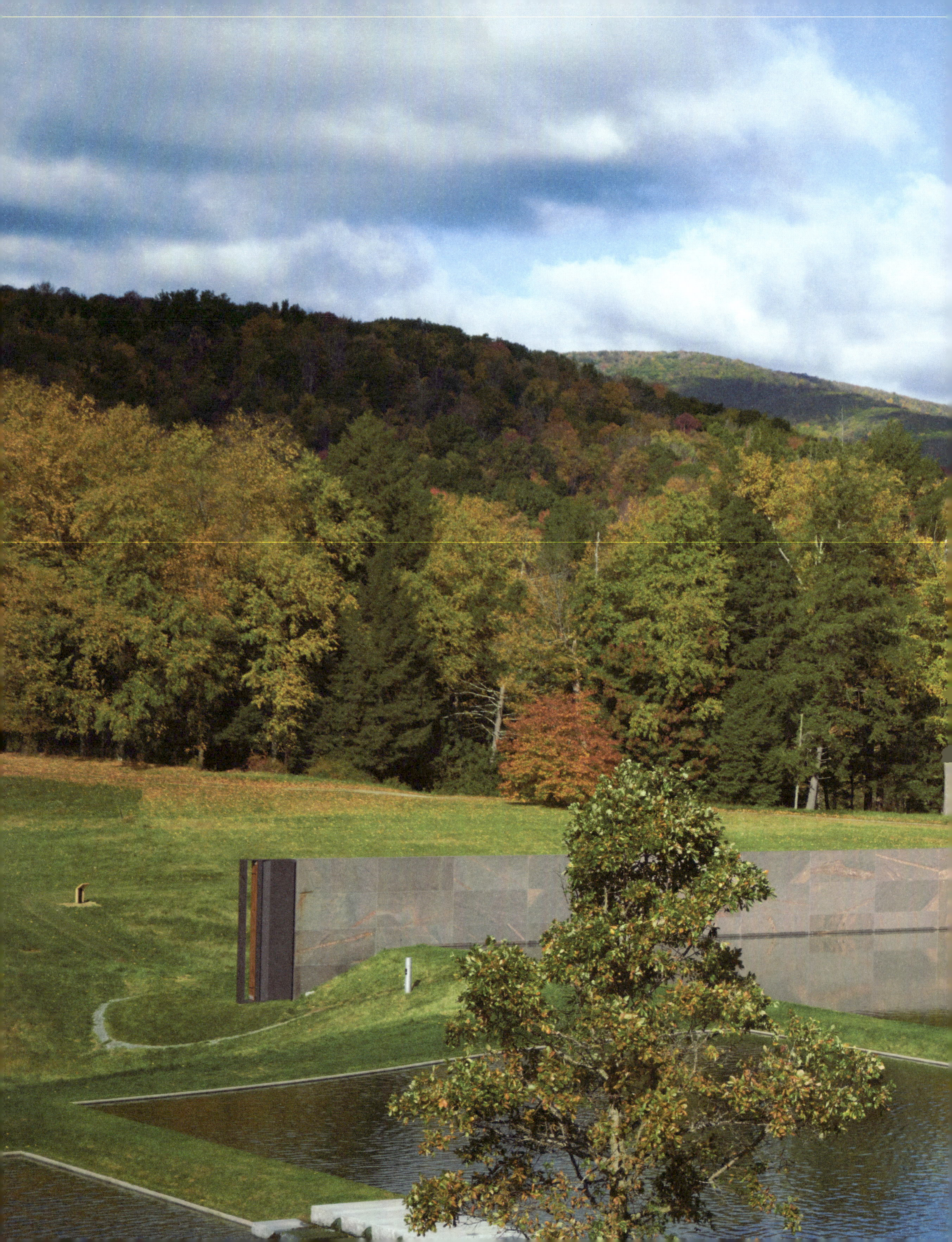

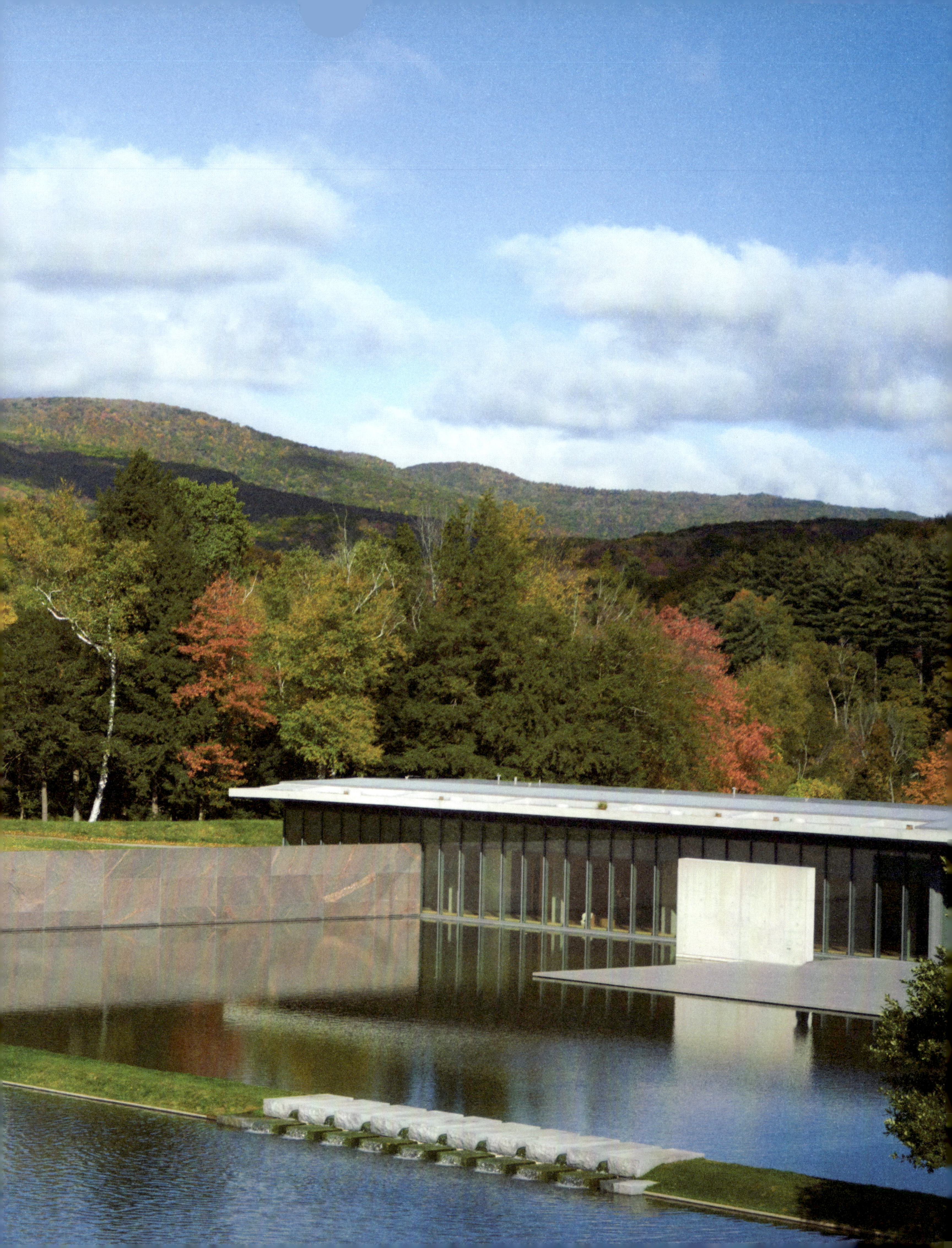

# Rupture and the Sound of Silence: Jennie C. Jones's *These (Mournful) Shores*

Yesomi Umolu

Being in the company of Jennie C. Jones's work requires attentive looking and listening, a multisensory engagement she continues with *These (Mournful) Shores* at the Clark Art Institute. Throughout her practice, the artist revels in parsing the annals of history to reveal the confluence of Minimalist art and other modernist practices with experimental music traditions and their attendant sociopolitical agendas, particularly those connected with African American culture. Jones's paintings and sculptures closely adhere to the strict formalism of Minimalism—deploying limited color palettes and primary forms, utilizing industrial materials, and working in an iterative manner—while at the same time introducing unexpected gestures that aim to disrupt and subvert these conventions. For example, in the artist's ongoing signature series of *Acoustic Paintings*, piercing lines and accents of vibrant reds, blues, and yellows interrupt flat fields of monochromatic color (fig. 18). Drawing on processes of repetition and variation found in Minimalism and modes of experimental music, these paintings consistently incorporate literal breaks in their structure: they feature raised blocks and surfaces, separate into two components, or shift perspective by curiously traveling across corners.

Jones's spatial experimentation goes even further: constructed from industrial sound panels that absorb and minimize echoes and reverberations, the *Acoustic Paintings* create a baffled sonic environment within which they are viewed. This leads to an interplay between silence and noise in the gallery space that mirrors the tension between flatness and perspective found across the paintings' surfaces and forms. By calibrating sound and moving beyond the conventional materiality of painting in this way, Jones interrogates the medium's auditory and spatial potential alongside its surface qualities. This exploration of hybrid forms simultaneously "fine tunes" a viewer's visual, aural, and physical acuities in a manner that demands attentive engagement. Jones previously extended this approach to the scale of architecture with site-specific projects at the modernist buildings of the Hirshhorn Museum and Sculpture Garden and the Philip Johnson–designed Glass House and Sculpture Gallery,[1] as she does now in concert with the Clark's 2014 addition designed by the noted Japanese architect Tadao Ando. While this latest work activates the museum's exterior and is Jones's first sculpture with the potential to generate sound, on both earlier occasions she manipulated audio recordings and ambient soundscapes to bring the experience of sonic dissonance and harmony into museum spaces as a counterpoint to their overriding minimalist lexicon.

At the Hirshhorn Museum in 2013, Jones created a listening area by introducing an offset, curved wall that mirrored the circular form of the museum's architecture, upon which she installed a selection of the *Acoustic Paintings* (fig. 19). Within this architectural and object-driven context, Jones filled the galleries with edited sound fragments from African American avant-garde musicians. In 2018, at Johnson's influential modern house in New Canaan, Connecticut, Jones further honed her site-responsive approach by creating the durational sound piece *RPM (revolutions per minute)* composed of a range of solfeggio frequencies.[2] Enlivening the aural experience of the building and swelling through its spaces, this work could also be heard as an undertone in the Sculpture Gallery, where Jones presented *Year of Construction: 1970*. This latter sound work comprised recomposed musical fragments by prominent Black sonic practicioners and composers, including Alice Coltrane, Alvin Singleton, Milford Graves, and Yusef Lateef.

Through the artist's lens, both modernism and experimental music share an ethos of deconstruction and improvisation, generating new sonic and aesthetic languages via the intersecting paths of minimalism and abstraction. By harnessing latent and recorded sound to enliven the auditory and bodily experience of both the Hirshhorn and the Glass House sites—spaces that are often associated with simplified geometries, monochrome colors, and muted acoustics—Jones opened up the possibilities of experiencing architecture through extemporaneous interventions beyond the architect's intention.

Marking the first time that Jones has left the white cube of a gallery or museum space and relinquished the production of her work to outside fabricators, her sixteen-foot-tall sculpture *These (Mournful) Shores* takes stock of nature, architecture, and history. Ando's recent reimagining of the Clark's campus nestles single-story buildings and a three-tiered reflecting

18

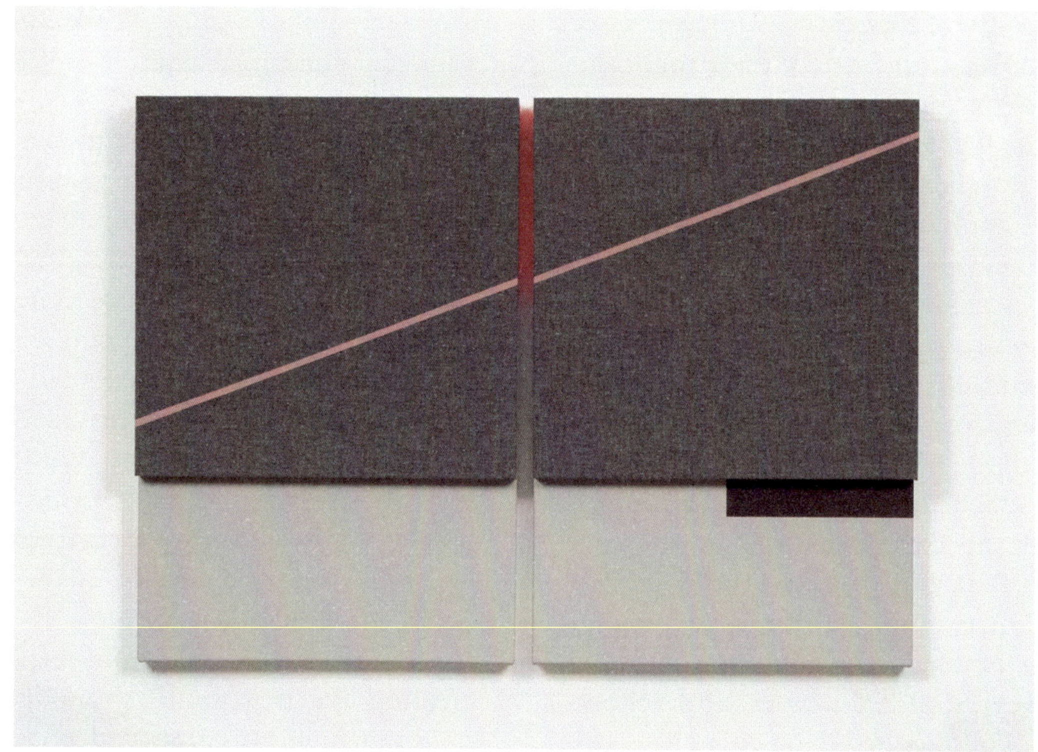

19

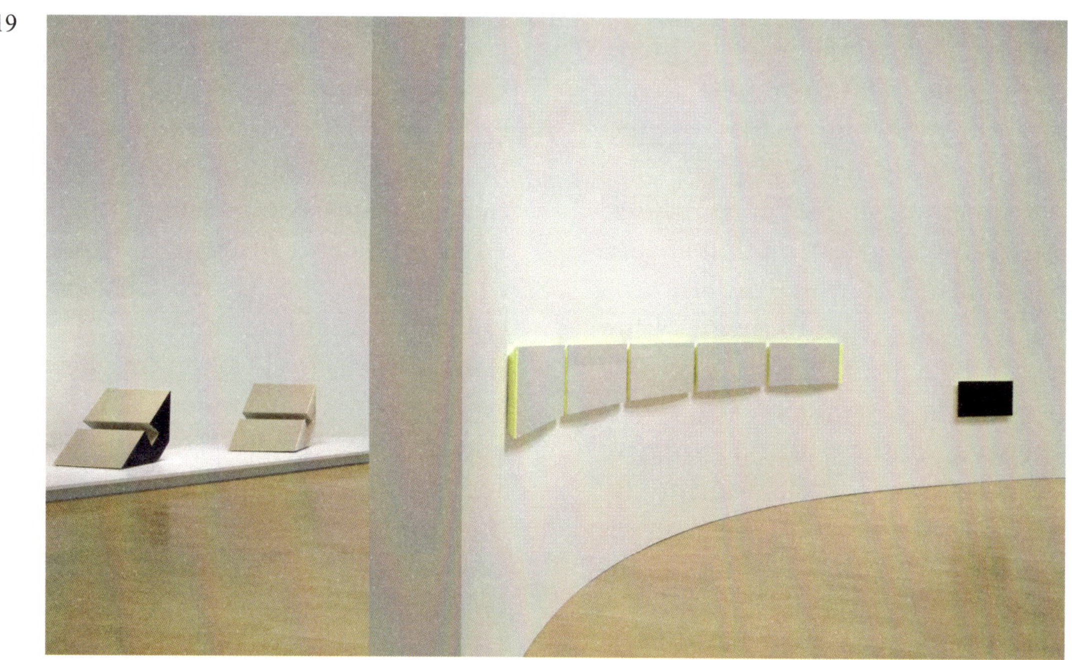

Fig. 18 Jennie C. Jones, *Fractured Crescendo, Rest*, 2019. Acoustic panel, acrylic on canvas, two parts, overall: 49 1/2 x 36 x 3 in. (123.7 x 91.4 x 7.6 cm). Courtesy of the artist; PATRON Gallery, Chicago; and Alexander Gray Associates, New York and Germantown, NY

Fig. 19 Installation view of *Directions: Jennie C. Jones: Higher Resonance*. Hirshhorn Museum and Sculpture Garden, Washington, DC, 2013

pool in a surrounding landscape of lush meadows, woods, and wetlands.[3] Constructed in simple geometric forms of concrete, stone, and glass, Ando's minimalist architecture lends an air of austerity to a place known for the deep contemplation of art. The architect's design provides ample opportunity for interplay between inside and outside, drawing attention away from the close looking and study of artworks carried out on the interior and toward the natural expanse of the Clark's grounds.

Adjacent to Ando's reflecting pool, a long granite wall extends from the museum building into the landscape. Protruding from the wall and matching its height and thickness to appear as a subtle and nearly seamless extension of the wall, Jones's monumental sculpture is inspired by a late nineteenth-century design for an aeolian harp.[4] An instrument that can take on an architectural scale, the aeolian harp relies solely on the variable character and force of the wind to produce its harmonic frequencies. It may come as no surprise that Jones was interested in fashioning a harp at the Clark, given the significance the instrument holds within the musical histories that the artist regularly culls. Alice Coltrane, whose work Jones references throughout her practice, was an accomplished harpist (fig. 20). Her husband, John Coltrane, had commissioned a harp to be made for her, but he died before she received it.[5] In the mythology of experimental music, Contrane's harp could thus be seen to represent the passing on of musical legacy as well as the embodiment of personal grief.

Jones's sculptural works often reference contemporary and historical sound technologies to create prototypical listening devices and environments. For example, in the 2014–15 work *Duchamp's Inner Ear* (fig. 21), Jones manipulates the horn-shaped speaker of a 1923 Victrola record player to create an object that pays homage both to Marcel Duchamp's conceptual readymades and to John Cage's famous silent score *4'33*. Although soundless, *Duchamp's Inner Ear* intimates the reproduction of sound in the viewer's mind through its composition of forms that act as signifiers for sound. Jones's experimentation with sound-as-sculpture and sculpture-as-instrument builds on the work of other noted avant-garde practitioners such as Tony Conrad, Terry Adkins (fig. 22), and key figures from the Fluxus movement who invented new acoustic devices by retooling readymade objects and parts of well-known instruments. Like Duchamp and Cage, these pioneering thinkers posed key questions about our conception and perception of sound, the form and function of everyday objects, and the strictures of performance.

Jones's sound constructs and paintings are rarely intended to be "played" by the human hand per se, neither are they intentionally activated through performance as was so often the case with the cited precedents. *These (Mournful) Shores* operates in a similar arena by manipulating the design, scale, and coloration of a musical instrument that is instantly recognizable. Of course, this sculpture-cum-instrument also has the potential to produce sound within an ecosystem rich with nature's melodies and reverberations, from birdsong to the rustling of tree leaves, from the ripple of water to the quiet hiss of a breeze.

There is a strong element of indeterminacy in Jones's sound works, which is no doubt inspired by the improvisational processes and chance procedures deployed by avant-garde artists and musicians that led to a radical break from artistic conventions. Her listening devices are effectively passive objects as they calibrate sound—through reducing and extracting noise from the surrounding environment—rather than produce it, relying on invisible forces for their activation. Jones is clearly fascinated with exploring what exists at the periphery of our knowledge and perceptions, attending to other sensory receptors beyond the visual and embracing the overlooked spatial possibilities of painting. Jones works through these ideas at the monumental scale of architecture with *These (Mournful) Shores*. Here, the artist recognizes that architecture can affect the sound of a given space through its sheer mass, shape, and materiality. Placing her sculpture as an addendum to Ando's construction, she introduces a new variable to the building that has the potential to shift not only the acoustic and physical experience of the Clark, but also the perception of the works of art it houses.

Looking back toward the museum, the sightline from *These (Mournful) Shores* directs the eye to the location where two paintings by Winslow Homer in the Clark's permanent collection typically reside.

20

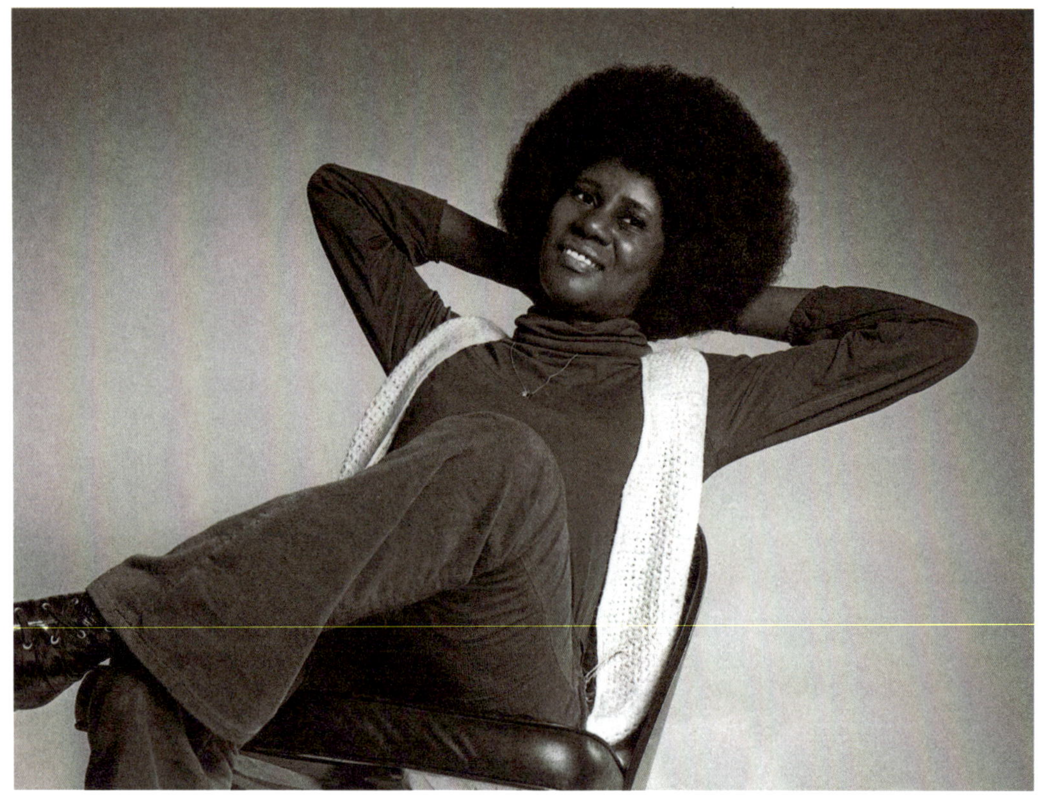

21

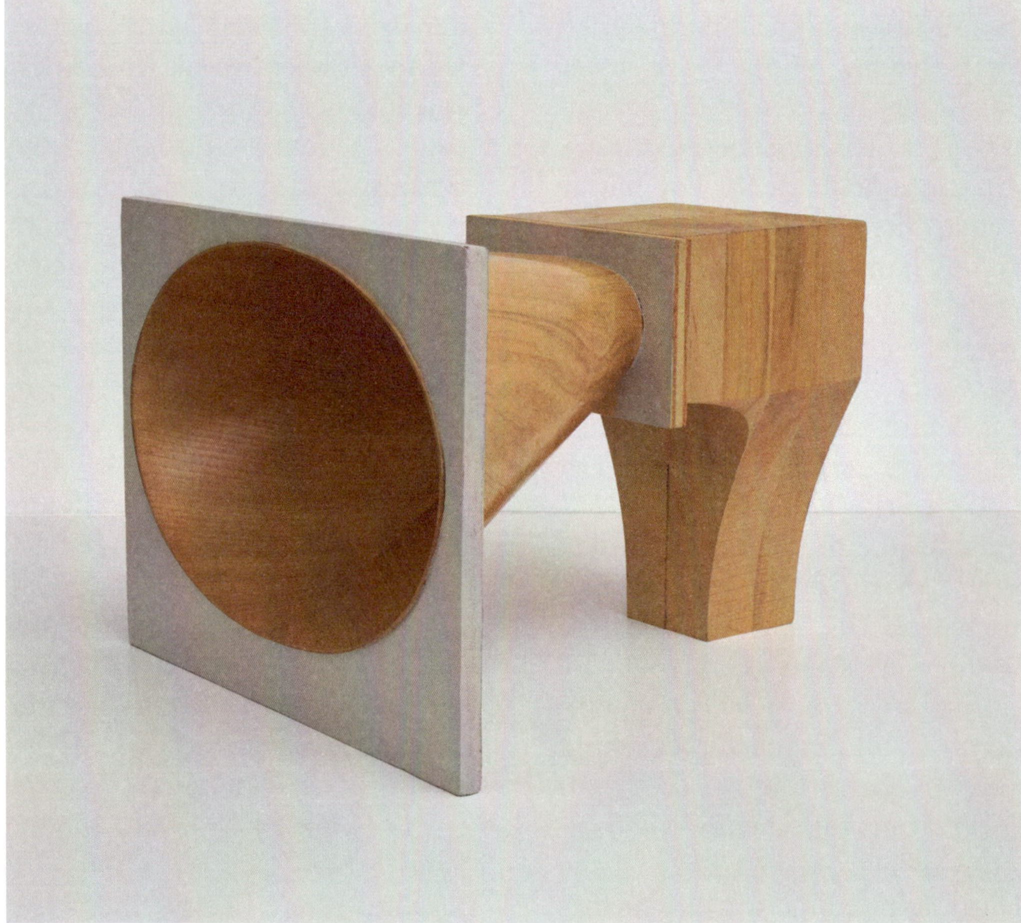

22

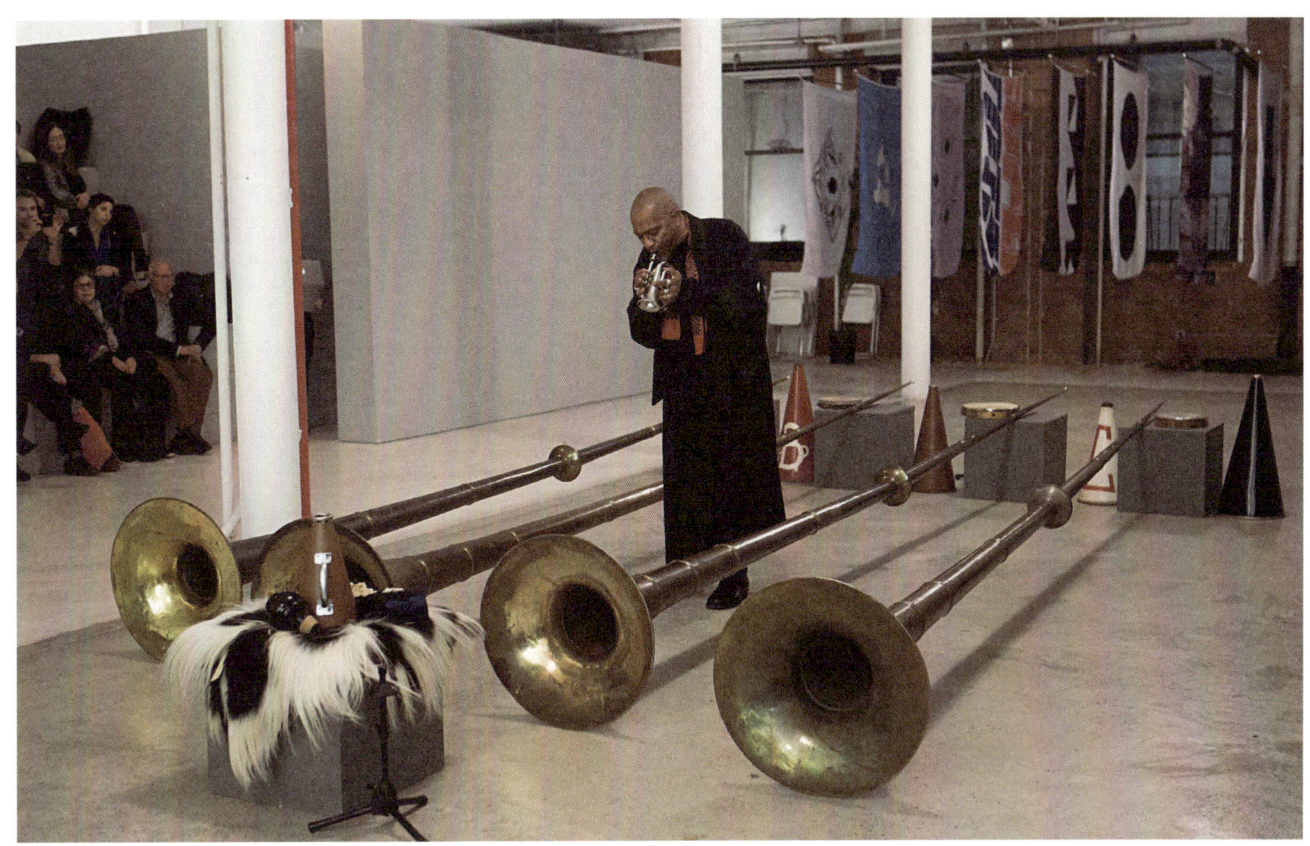

Fig. 20 Photograph of Alice Coltrane by Chuck Stewart. Chuck Stewart Jazz Photographs, Archives Center, National Museum of American History, Smithsonian Institution. © Chuck Stewart Photography, LLC/Fireball Entertainment Group

Fig. 21 Jennie C. Jones, *Duchamp's Inner Ear*, 2014–15. Altered 1923 Victrola Part, 13 x 17 x 16 in. (33 x 43.2 x 40.6 cm). Contemporary Arts Museum, Houston. Courtesy of the artist; PATRON Gallery, Chicago; and Alexander Gray Associates, New York and Germantown, NY

Fig. 22 Blanche Bruce and the Lone Wolf Recital Corps perform Terry Adkins's *The Last Trumpet* as part of the Performa Biennial 2013, at Salon 94. © The Estate of Terry Adkins / Artists Rights Society (ARS), New York

Created in the ten years before the artist's death, the richly textured canvasses of *Eastern Point* and *West Point Prout's Neck* (both 1900, figs. 23 and 24) depict the surf breaking fiercely upon rocks off the coast of Maine. The turbulence of these scenes, which according to Jones illustrates Homer's skill at freeze-framing the buoyancy of the open seas, contrasts with the apparent placidness of Ando's water feature.[6]

As an artist working in the minimalist tradition, Jones might be expected to reject the strong pictorial sensibilities, the abundance of ornament and symbolism found in the Clark's permanent collection of American and European works from the fourteenth to the early twentieth century. Yet Jones has drawn inspiration from Homer's epic realism. The gray brown and rich cherry hues of *These (Mournful) Shores*' aluminum and wood construction derive directly from Homer's melancholic color palette, as well as from objects in the Clark's collection of decorative arts and furniture. Moreover, Jones's evocative title imbues her sculpture with narrative associations, prompting reflection on nature's power and the impermanence of human life, themes that Homer explored throughout his lifetime.

Throughout her work, in its convergence of multiple histories and cultural touchstones, Jones has always attempted to integrate African American perspectives and creative production into our broader understanding of the Western canon. Jones acknowledges that in Homer's seascapes she saw beyond mere representations of nature's majesty to recognize the Atlantic Ocean as a site of loss and mourning.[7] The significance of the aeolian harp should not be understated here. Its ethereal and atonal harmonies evoke the alluring voices and lyres of sirens that, according to classical mythology, caused shipwrecks and lured sailors to their deaths. This imagery is particularly pertinent in the context of the transatlantic slave trade, the harp's otherworldly songs lamenting the lives lost at sea during the Middle Passage, when European ships carried millions of enslaved Africans across the Atlantic to the "New World." For Jones, the "mournful shores" of the Americas Homer depicted are inextricably linked to European settler colonialism and its pursuit of conquest through violence. By implicating this history in her sculpture and evoking the story of bereavement associated with Alice Coltrane's harp, Jones moves beyond the reverence for nature that is apparent in Ando's building and Homer's paintings to conceptualize the natural world as threshold between freedom and subjugation, life and death, the real and the mythical.

The themes of *These (Mournful) Shores* take on a more optimistic cast in another Black artist's monumental sculpture, Augusta Savage's *Lift Every Voice and Sing (The Harp)* (1939, fig. 25), inspired by the musical instrument's traditional triangular form. Originally presented at the 1939 New York World's Fair, Savage's sculpture took the form of a harp composed of a group of Black singers of graduating heights, the tallest larger than life size, whose striated robes resembled harp strings. Savage made the work in homage to what has come to be known as the Black national anthem, composed by the poet James Weldon Johnson (1871–1938). Reflecting the spirit of liberation and the promise of progress in the pre–Civil Rights era, *The Harp* was a significant public monument for the African American community—albeit only temporarily. The work was destroyed at the close of the World's Fair in the absence of sufficient funds to cast it in bronze.[8] As a sculpture that doubly implies sound through its form and the aghast mouths of its singers, *The Harp* is also conceptually aligned with *These (Mournful) Shores*.

It is rare among Minimalist practitioners to allow space for metaphor and meaning to emerge from their work beyond the movement's formal language. Jones has remarked that, for her, there are unique "social and political ramifications to rejecting 'subject' and embracing 'object'—as an African American woman, much more is at stake. Minimalism becomes a radical gesture empowering a refusal to sell my narrative or bodies."[9] Yet her choice to gesture toward narrative in *These (Mournful) Shores* highlights her distinctive contribution to the minimalist tradition and indeed suggests a renewed interest in reclaiming subjectivity in her work. Her aeolian harp evokes the work of radical practitioners across time who have broken from the canons of art history and music—Coltrane, Duchamp, Cage, Atkins, and others. In this way, Jones

23

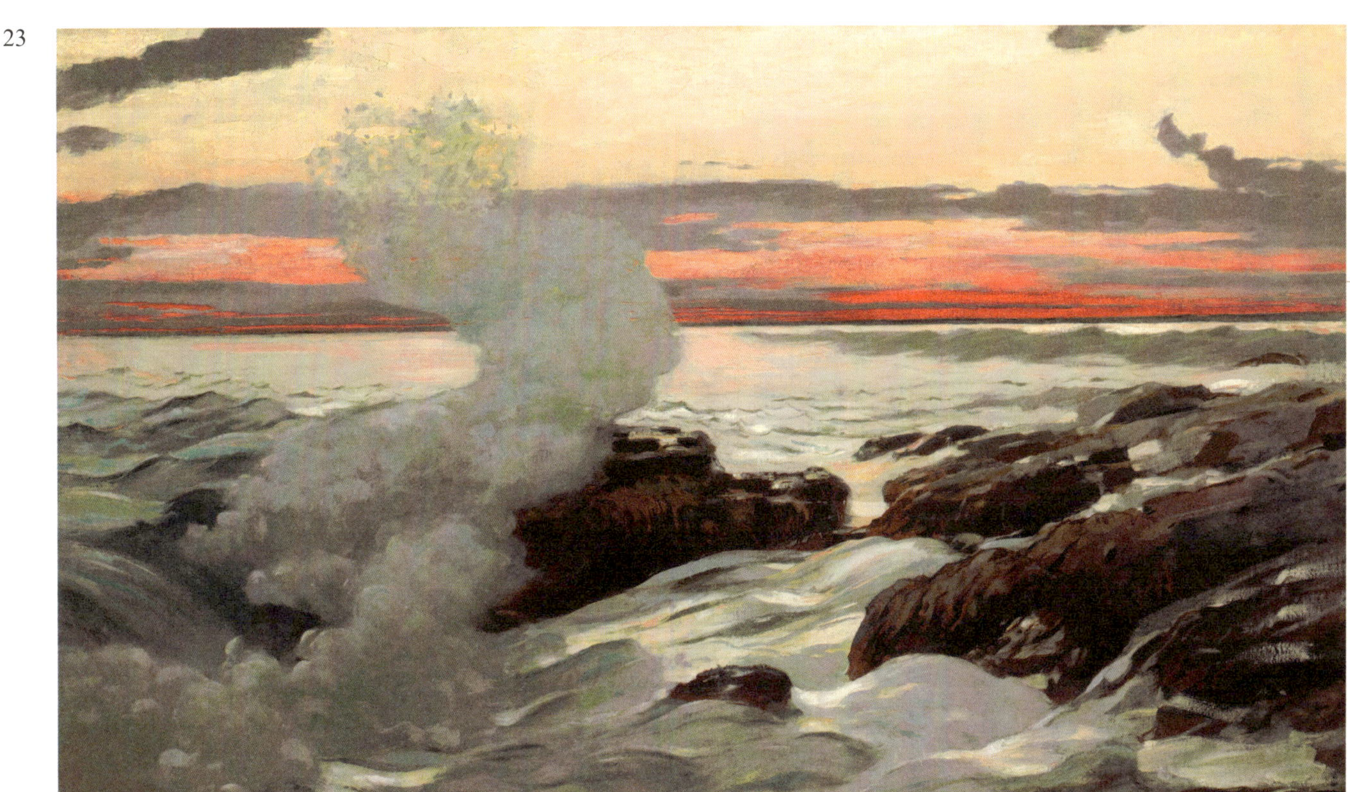

24

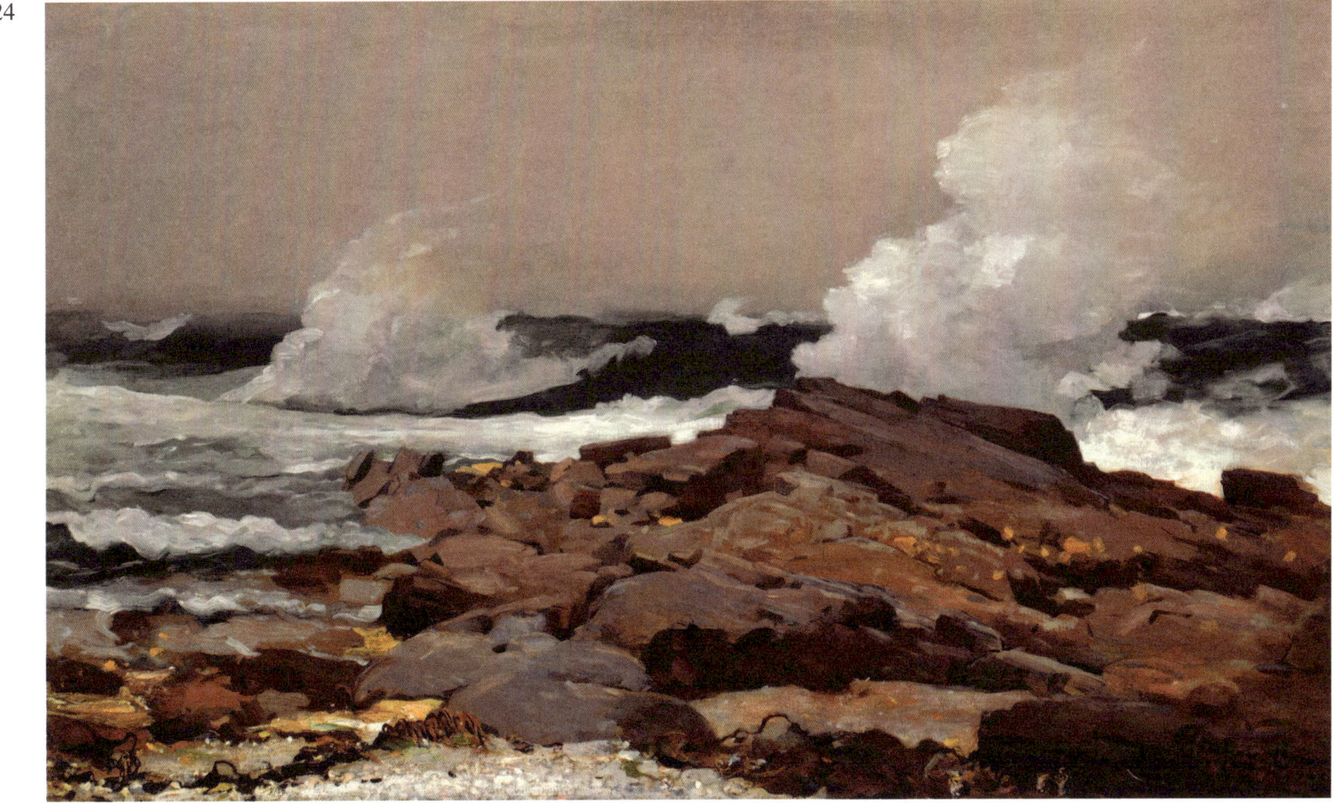

Fig. 23 Winslow Homer, *Eastern Point*, 1900. Oil on canvas, 30 1/4 x 48 1/2 in. (76.8 x 123.2 cm). Clark Art Institute, 1955.6

Fig. 24 Winslow Homer, *West Point Prout's Neck*, 1900. Oil on canvas, 30 1/16 x 48 1/8 in. (76.4 x 122.2 cm). Clark Art Institute, 1955.7

makes a bold statement about how different urgencies can surface and recede across individual practices and art histories.

While Jones embraces the potential of narrative in *These (Mournful) Shores*, it remains one undercurrent among many in the work. Much in the same way that her paintings imply the potential of listening, so does *These (Mournful) Shores* imply other stories. Layering historical references, the possibility of sound, and an expansion of the museum's physical form, Jones's sculpture acts as a potentially disruptive feature in the landscape and beyond: it considers harrowing ruptures in the course of human history and points to breaches in the art historical canon.

*Yesomi Umolu is director of curatorial affairs and public practice at the Serpentine Galleries.*

1 *Directions: Jennie C. Jones: Higher Resonance* (May 16–October 27, 2013), http://hirshhorn.si.edu/exhibitions/directions-jennie-c-jones-higher-resonance/; and *Jennie C. Jones: RMP (Revolutions per Minute)* (September 1–November 30, 2018), http://theglasshouse.org/whats-on/jennie-c-jones-rpmrevolutions-per-minute/.

2 The six-tone music scale that comprises the solfreggio frequencies dates back to the religious music of medieval Europe.

3 The reflecting pools were conceived by Tadao Ando and developed by Reed Hilderbrand Landscape Architecture.

4 Jones's sculpture references a design created by the famous French violin maker Nicolas Eugène Simoutre (1834–1908).

5 Jude Rogers, "'It's Like You're on Top of the Alps': Alice Coltrane's Spiritual Jazz Rediscovered | London Jazz Festival," *The Guardian*, November 17, 2017, http://www.theguardian.com/music/2017/nov/17/alice-coltrane-london-jazz-festival.

6 Jennie C. Jones, "*These (Mournful) Shores*," SoundCloud audio, Clark Art Institute, 4:18, http://www.clarkart.edu/microsites/ground-work/about-the-projects/jennie-c-jones. Edited from an interview conducted by Molly Epstein and Abigail Ross Goodman, recorded April 21, 2020.

7 Jones, "*These (Mournful) Shores*," SoundCloud audio.

8 See "American Art Today, *The Harp*, by Augusta Savage," 1939 New York World's Fair website, http://www.1939nyworldsfair.com/worlds_fair/wf_tour/zone-2/the-harp.htm.

9 "Structure without a Center: Jennie C. Jones Interviewed by Jared Quinton," *Bomb Magazine*, July 29, 2020, http://bombmagazine.org/articles/structure-without-a-center-jennie-c-jones-interviewed/.

25

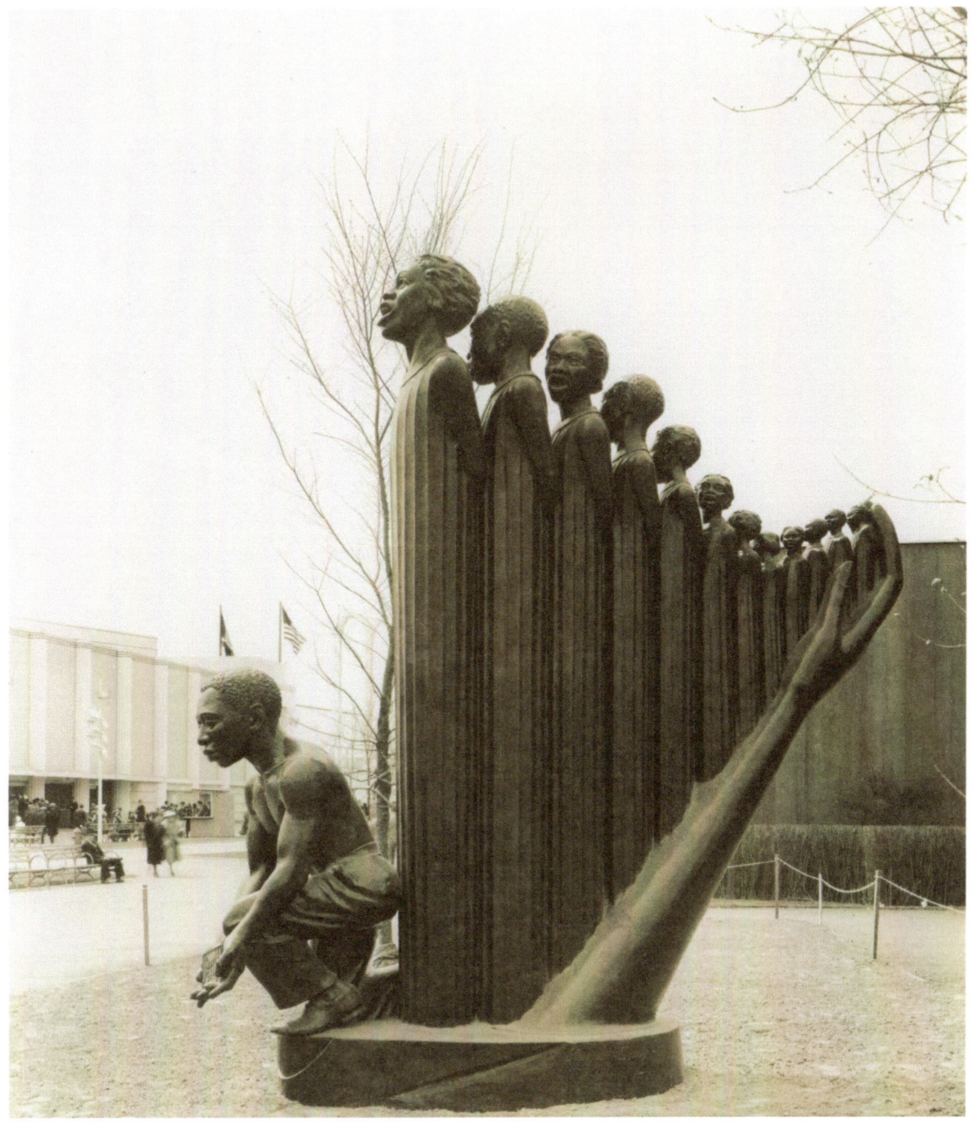

Fig. 25 Augusta Savage, *Lift Every Voice and Sing (The Harp)*, 1939. New York World's Fair, Inc. Records, Manuscripts, and Archives division, New York Public Library

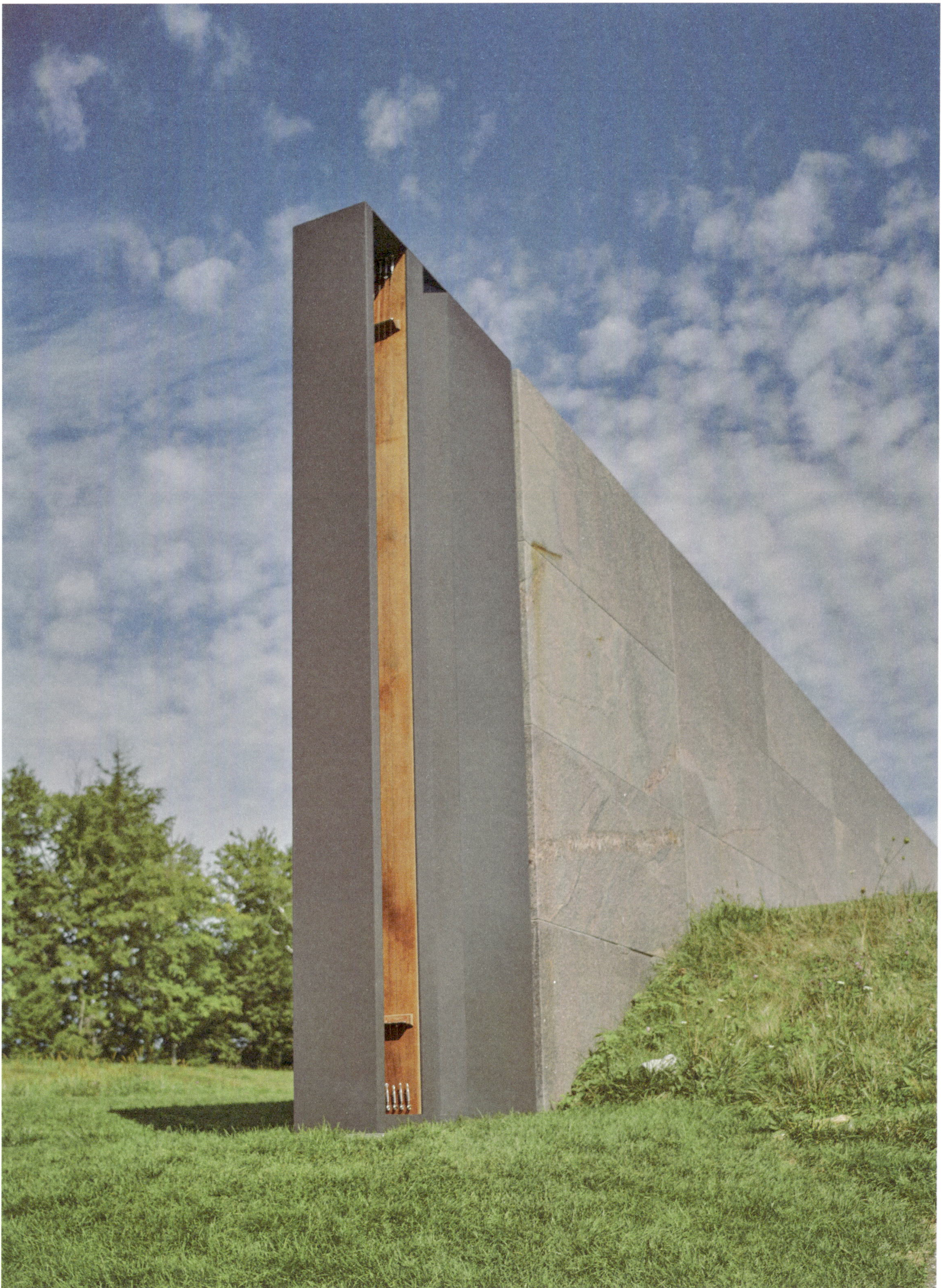

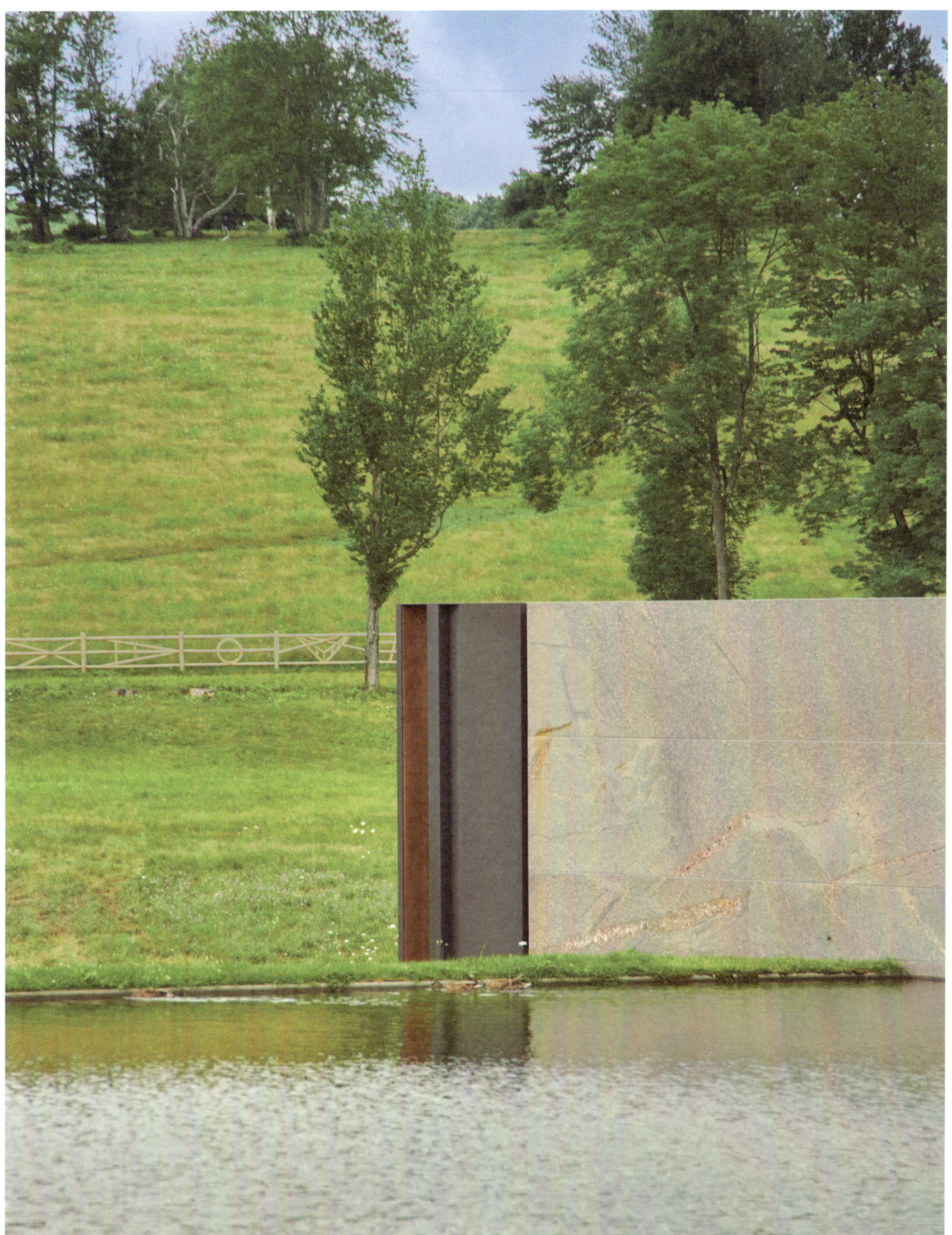

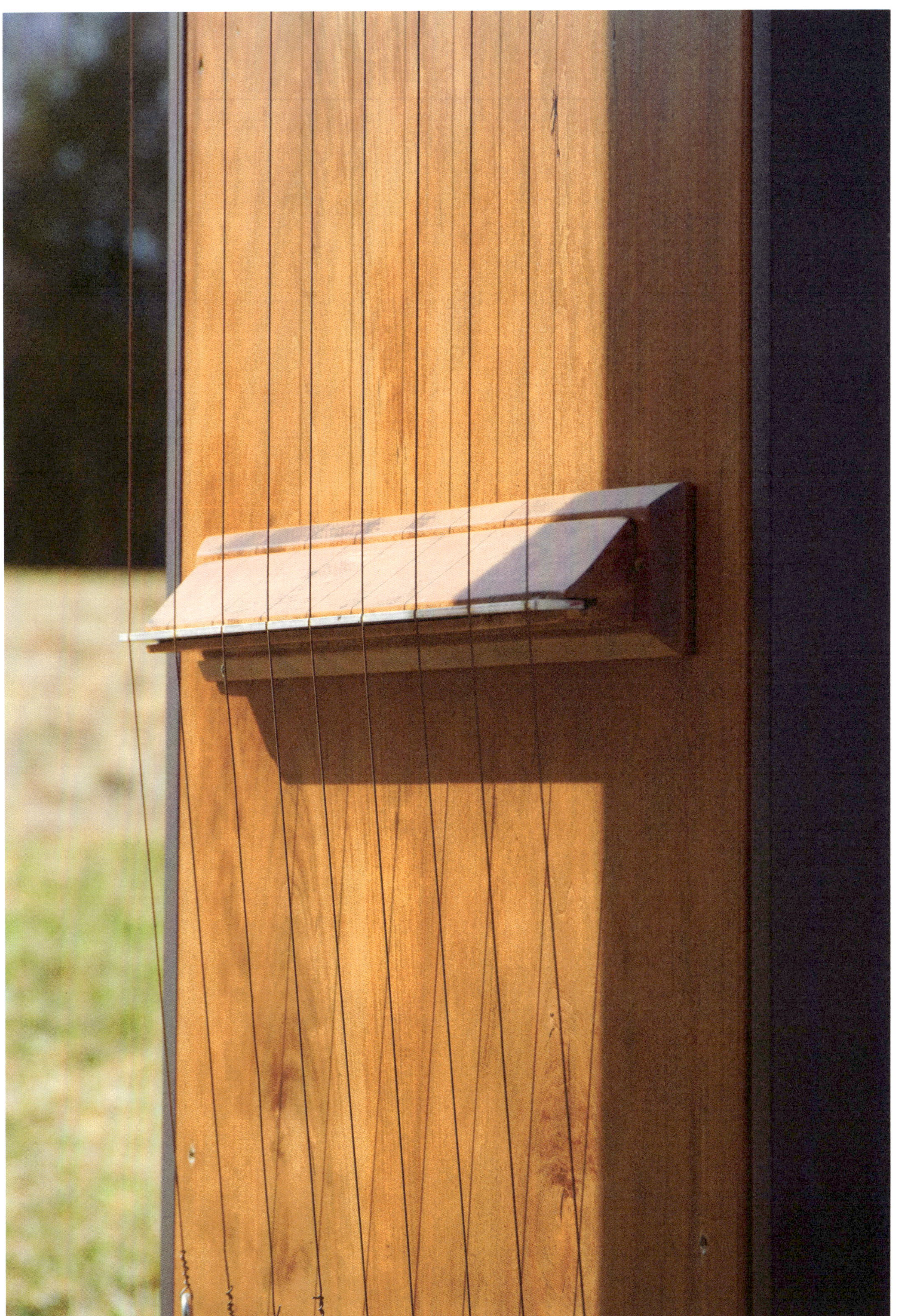

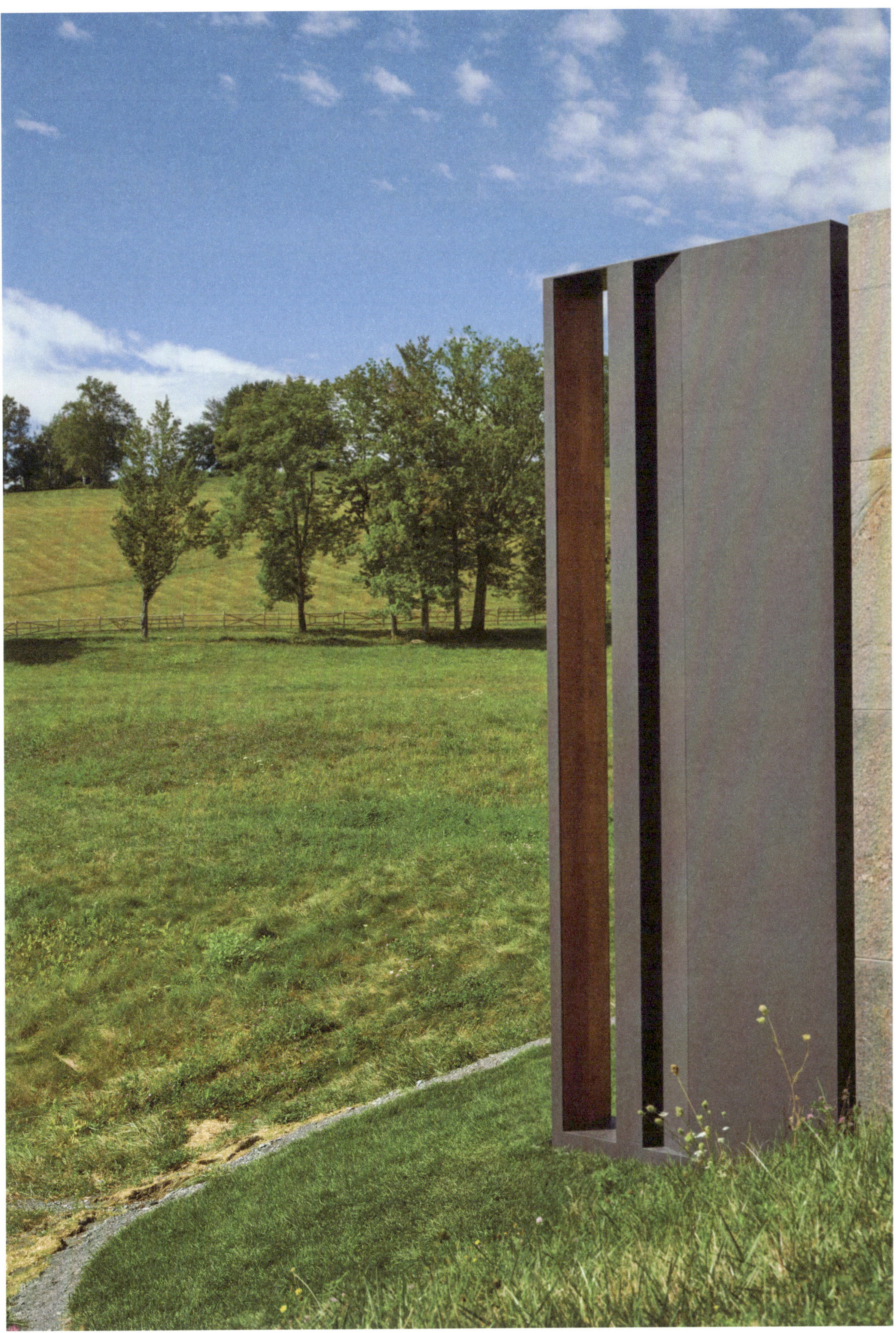

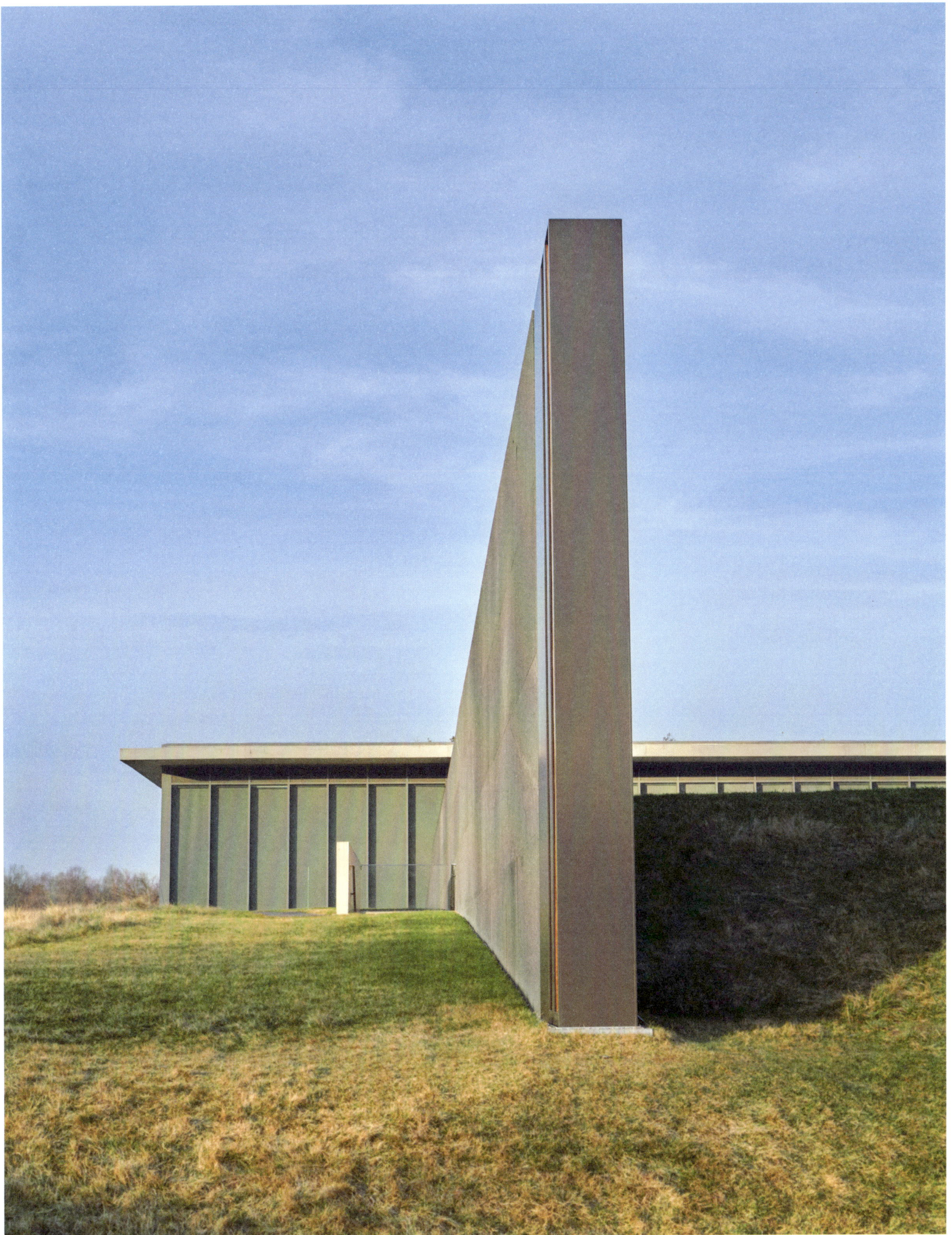

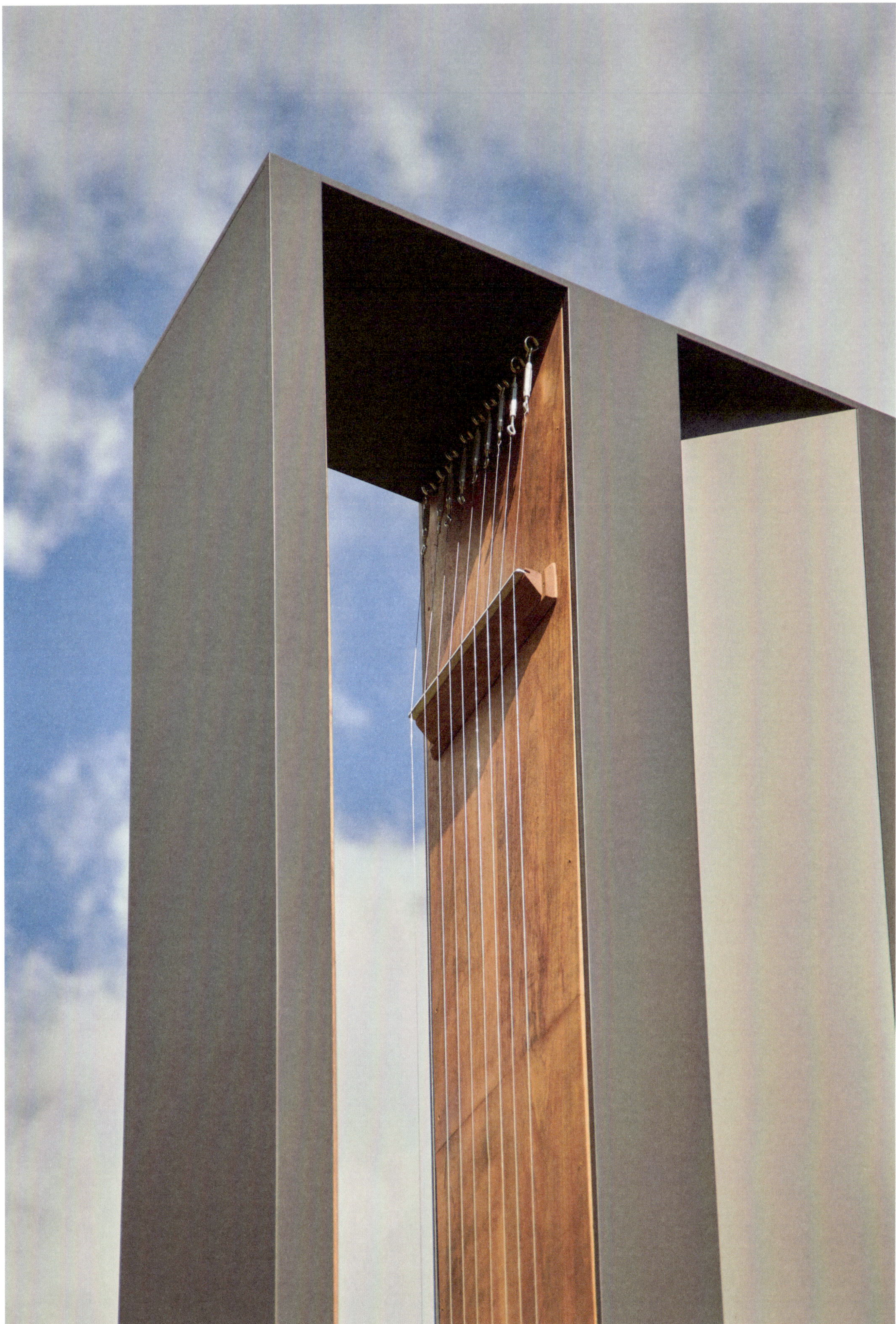

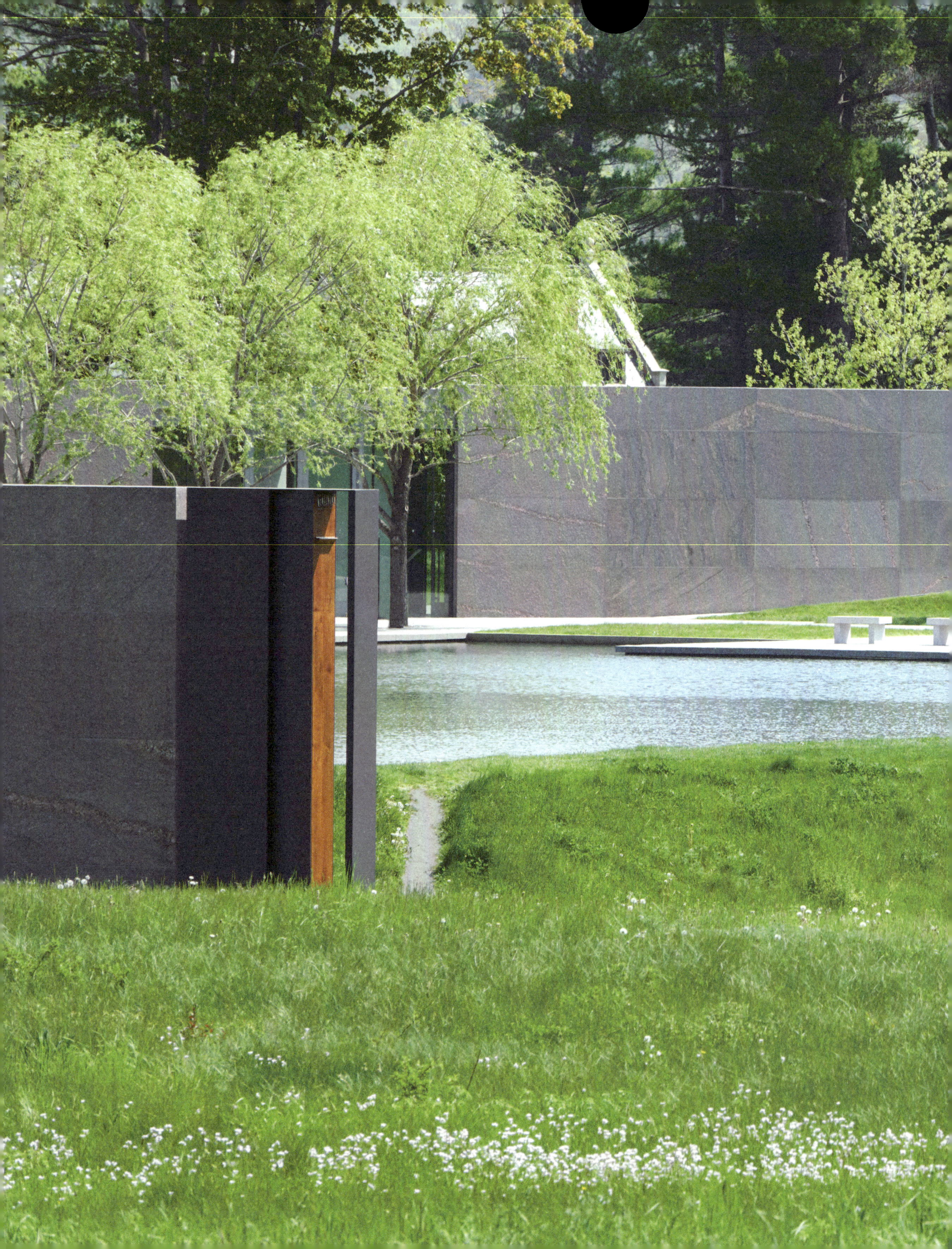

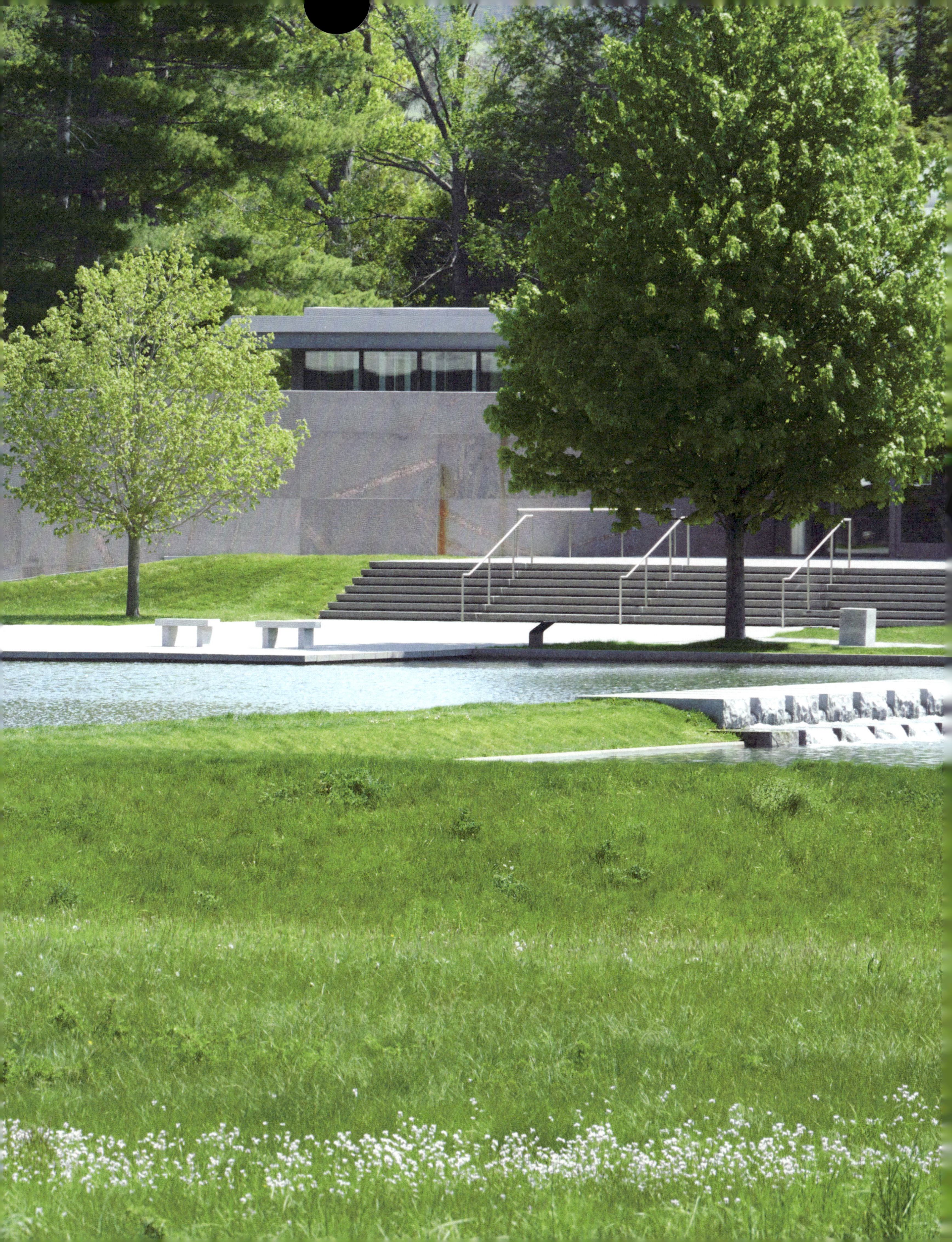

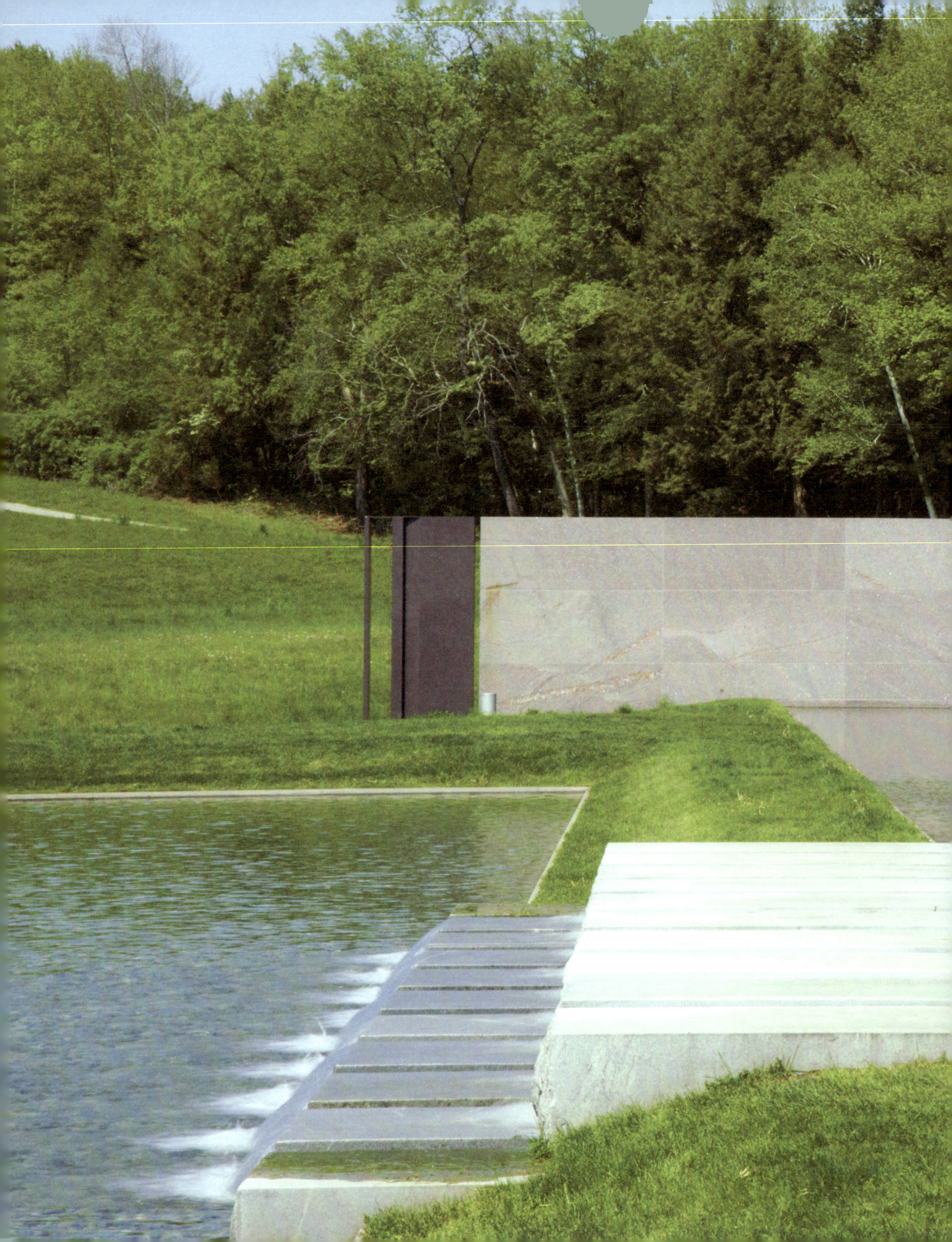

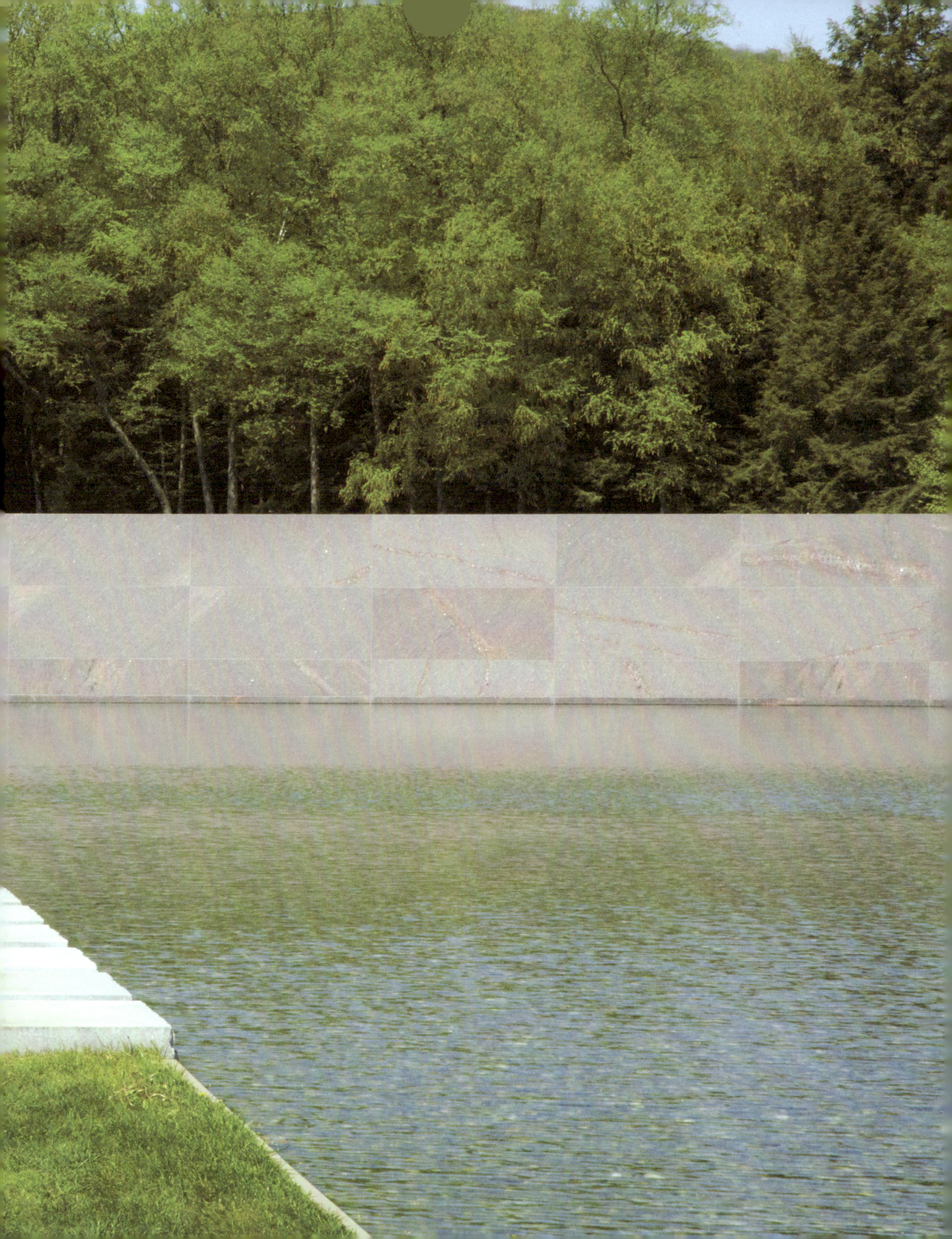

Cedar wood
620 ft. (189 m)

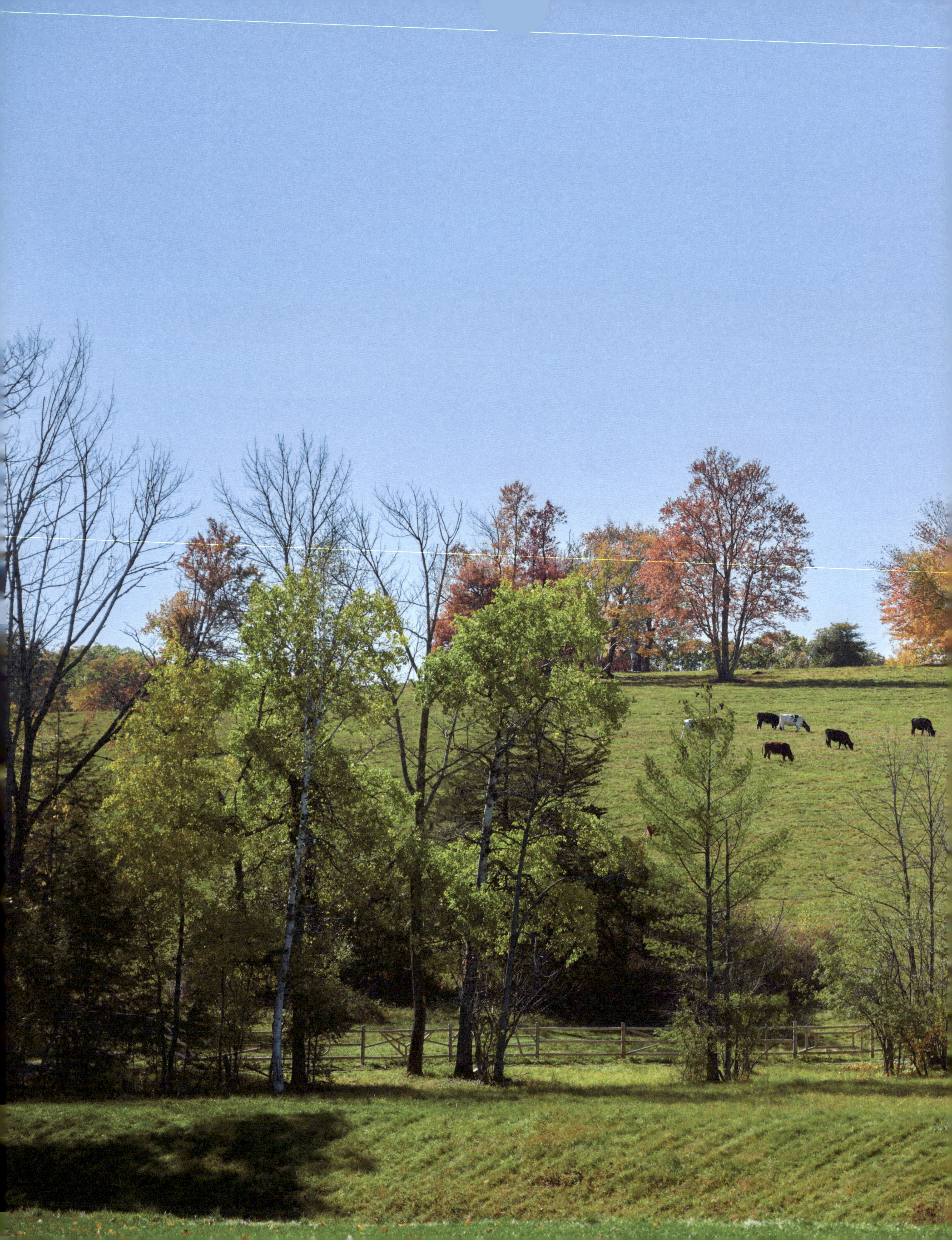

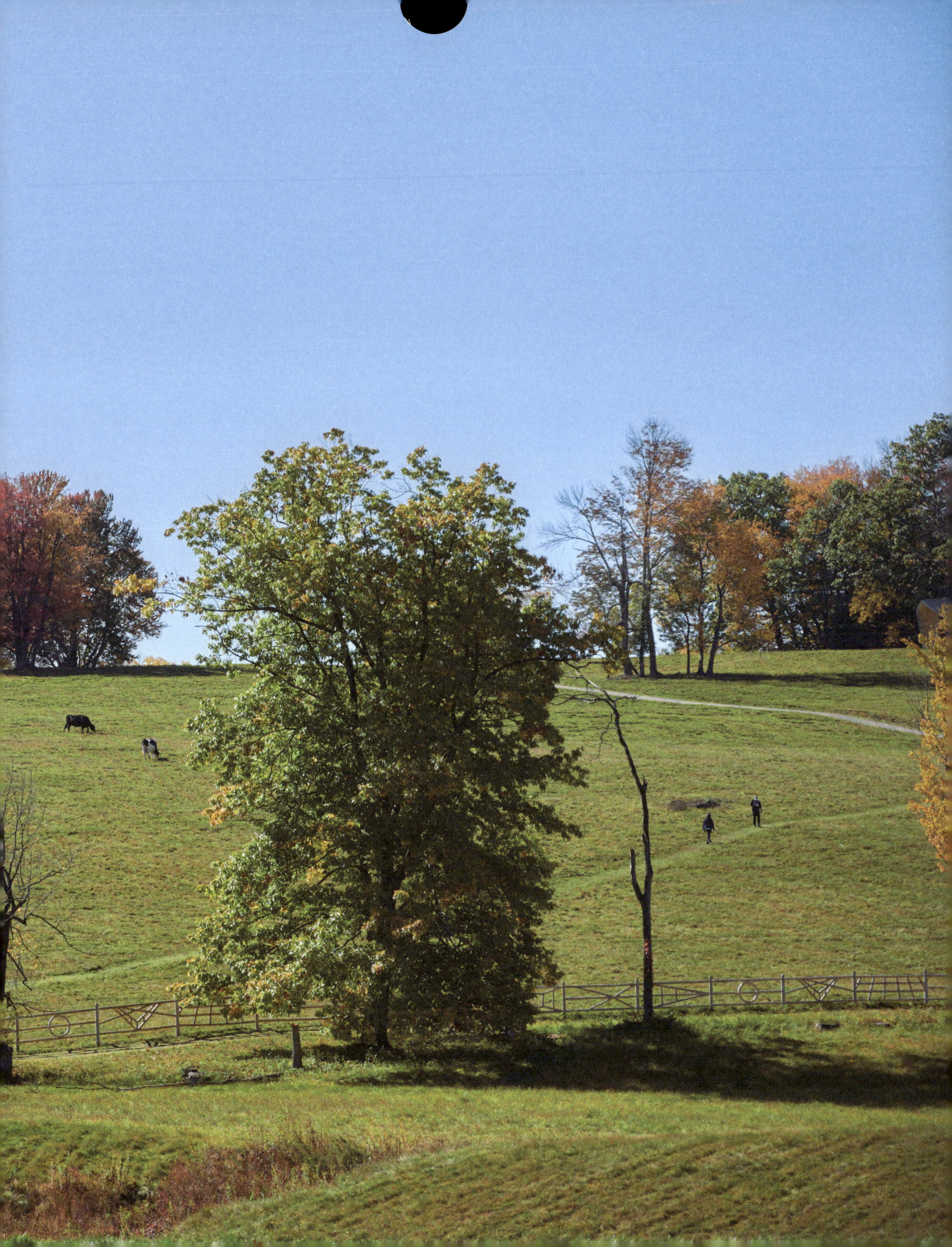

# Remarks on Rural Scenery, or Analia Saban Teaches a Cow How to Draw
Jenelle Porter

*The field that you are standing before appears to have the same proportions as your own life.*
—John Berger

*Teaching a Cow How to Draw* is an artwork in the form of a 620-foot-long cedar fence that borders a sloping pasture behind the Clark Art Institute. Commissioned for the temporary outdoor exhibition *Ground/work*, Analia Saban's remarkable sculpture replaced an existing pasture fence corralling up to two dozen seasonally resident Holstein, Belted Galloway, and Jersey cows. Of this fence-cum-sculpture or sculpture-cum-fence, Saban remarked, "I was thinking that the cows are used to seeing this fence on a regular basis, and maybe if we can make a more complex fence, they could somehow be intellectually entertained."[1] The sneaky, art-y twist is that the sculpture/fence (as I'll call it) diagrams, in its constructed segments, theories of composition and perspective.

The overall structure of *Teaching a Cow How to Draw* is based on a typical split-rail fence: three uniformly spaced, horizontal rails supported by vertical posts. This utilitarian design reminded the artist of the rule of thirds, an artist's technique for producing harmoniously balanced compositions.[2] Saban expanded the idea to include eight sections of fence that diagram the following rendering strategies: the rule of thirds (the rectilinear grid), a room in perspective, a vanishing point, one-point perspective of a grid (two versions), a circle, two-point perspective, and a centered vanishing point. Adopting the compare-and-contrast methodology at the core of art historical pedagogy, she also included one section of traditional split rail. These motifs repeat in sequence seven times to compose a 620-foot span of "intellectual entertainment": a drawing lesson. For cows.

## Fences

Saban's sculpture/fence can be considered within the history of Land Art and environmental art gestures and, in its use of materials and serial logic, in relation to works by likeminded North American artists who emerged during the 1970s. For example, both Mary Miss's 1970 *Room Fence* and Jackie Winsor's *Fence Piece* (1970, fig. 26) adapted Minimalist tenets to utilitarian, vernacular structures. Miss's 1979 *Veiled Landscape* (fig. 27), set on a hillside in Lake Placid, New York, offered "a three-dimensional landscape view" staged and disrupted through a sequence of rectilinear structures, writes architect Christian Zapatka. The work "not only frames the landscape in the distance, but imprisons portions of it within the frames of its grid, abstracting the textures of sky and foliage. The view . . . is thus made part of the project, while the immediate obstacles . . . call attention to the nature of the materials and to the materials of nature."[3] Another of Miss's 1979 works, *Staged Gates*, introduced architectonic apertures along a wooded slope as a means of framing, enacting a transformation of real nature into mediated views that points to the history of painting. In contrast to Saban's enclosure for the Clark, Christo and Jeanne-Claude's astonishing *Running Fence* (1972–76), a twenty-four-mile-long white fabric "fence" that spanned two counties in Northern California, was designed so that animals (and humans) could move safely through it during its two-week installation. All of these artworks point to the ubiquity of fences, the most prevalent, and predictable, of human-imposed landscape interventions (leaving aside roads, houses, pollution, etc.). Take a road trip to the middle of Anywhere USA and you'll find fences, lots of them, keeping something or someone in, keeping something or someone out. Yet, as artists from Miss to Saban remind us, fences are drawings on the land as much as they are physical barriers.

Like Miss, Nancy Holt trafficked in perception with her Land Art works. In characterizing Holt's practice, art historian Pamela M. Lee adapts the work of German social theorist Niklas Luhmann to look "beyond the usual binaries" ascribed to 1970s Land Art ("art world/desert, culture/nature, inside/outside, etc.").[4] Lee writes that according to Luhmann, "distinctions between perception and communication are paramount yet nonetheless converge upon that strange thing called the work of art."[5] Key to this formulation is the role of the observer, and Luhmann makes a distinction between what he terms "first-order" and "second-order" observers. The latter, according to Lee, "is essentially engaged in the 'observation of observations'. . . the act of differentiation—and

26

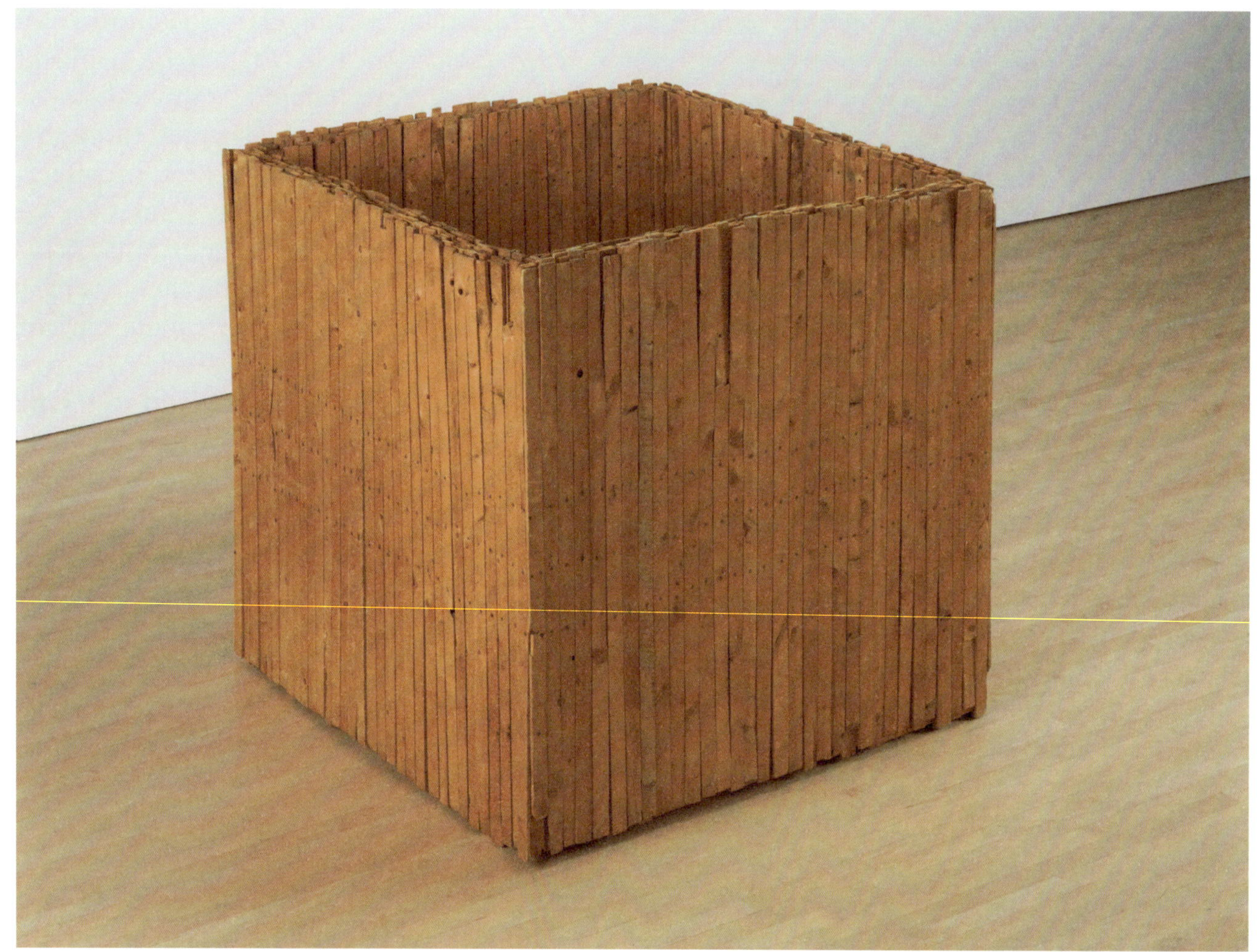

Fig. 26 Jackie Winsor, *Fence Piece*, 1970. Wood and nails, 49 1/2 x 49 x 49 in. (126 x 124 x 124 cm). Rose Art Museum, Mortimer and Sara Hays Acquisition Fund

27

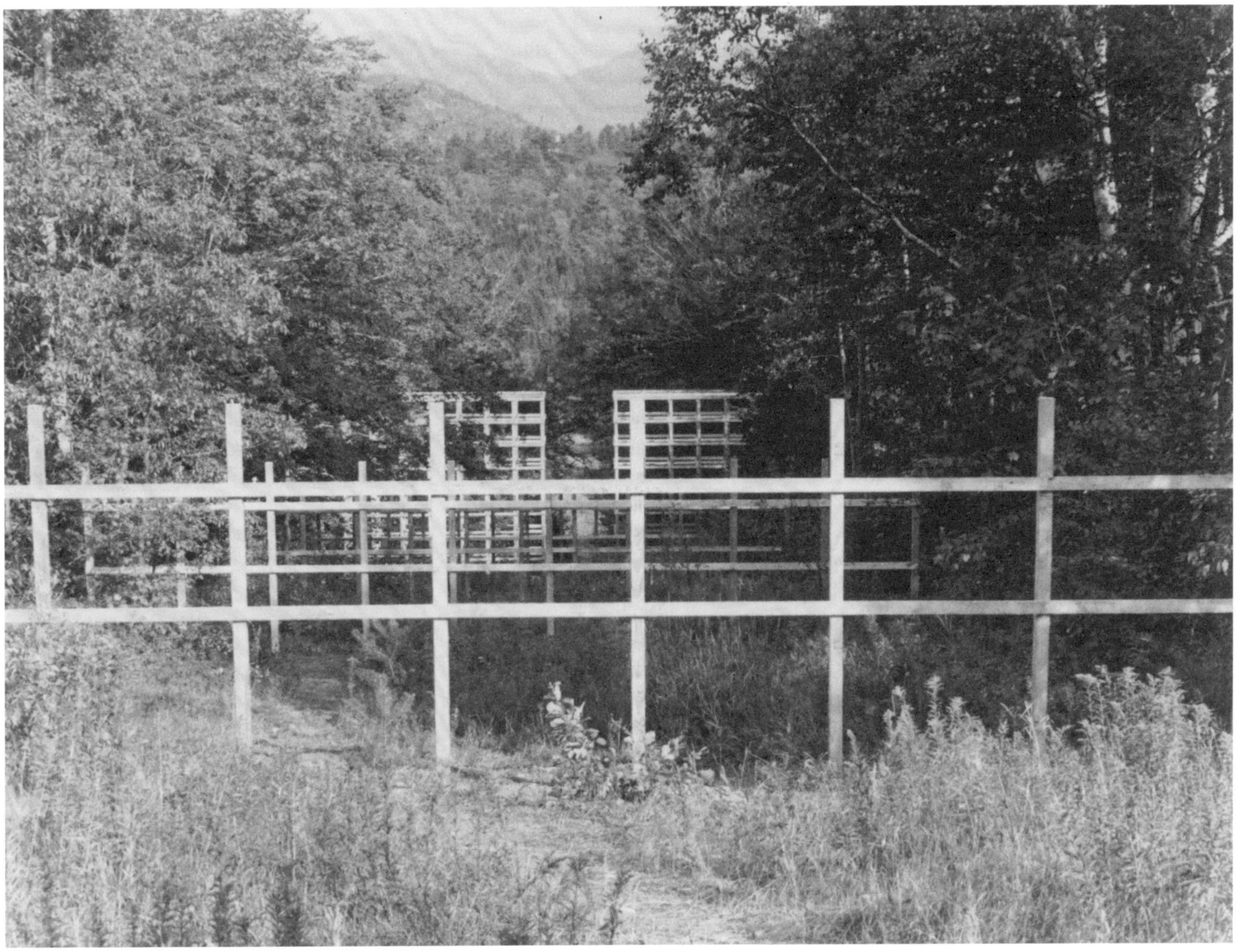

Fig. 27 Mary Miss, *Veiled Landscape*, 1979. Wood, steel, wire mesh, 400 in. (1,016 cm). Commissioned as part of the XII Winter Olympics, Lake Placid, New York, 1980. Courtesy of the artist

28

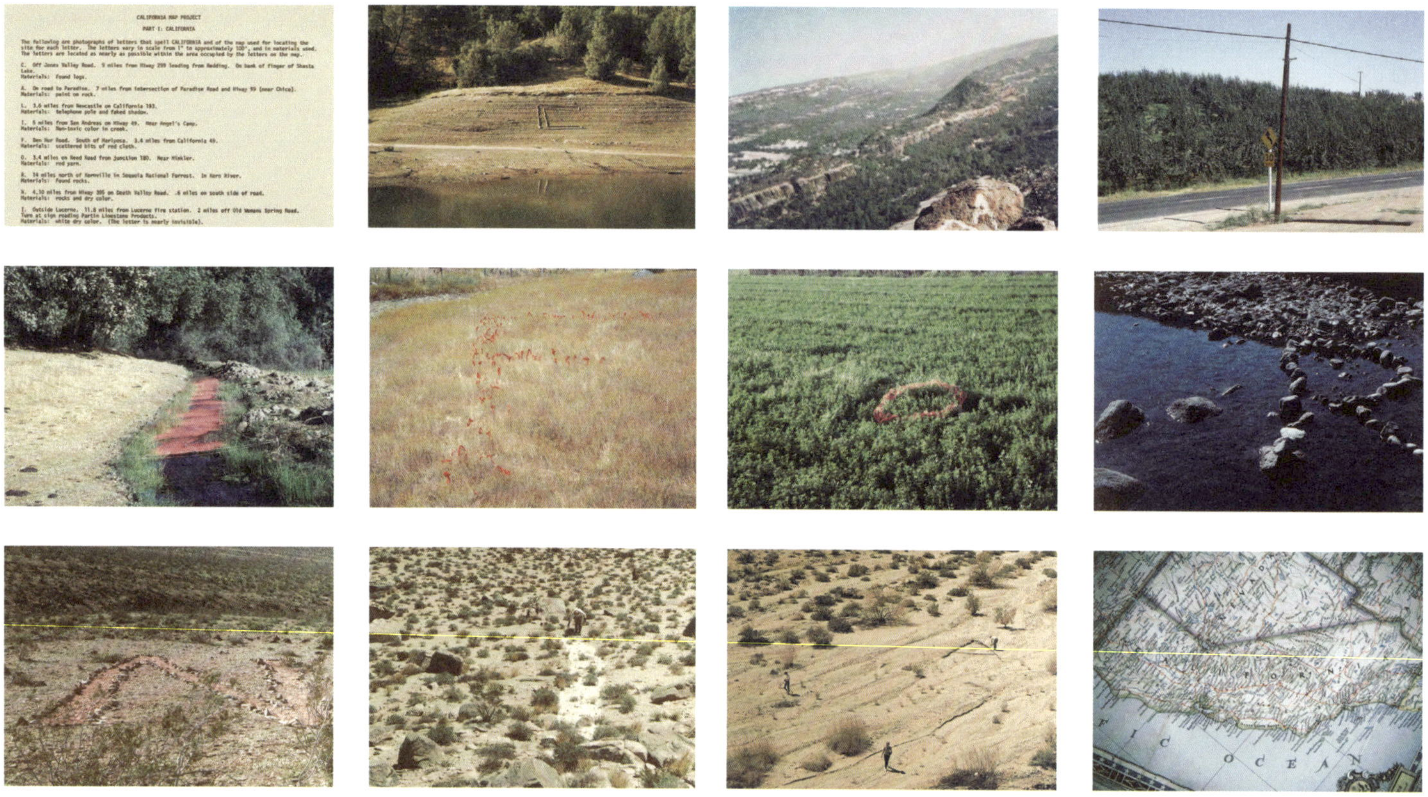

Fig. 28 John Baldessari and George Nicolaidis, *California Map Project Part 1: California*, 1969/2000. Twelve archival inkjet prints. Courtesy of the Estate of John Baldessari and Marian Goodman Gallery, New York, London, and Paris

the border—required to mark works of art from other things."[6] If one considers the literal border formed by a fence—that is, Saban's sculptural intervention—this theory grows ever more charged, ever more enlarged by the concept of an observer tasked with formulating distinctions. Therefore, what does Saban's sculpture ask us to observe? The cow viewing the sculpture? People observing the cow viewing the sculpture? The pasture and the cows seen through the fence-as-lens, or the fence-as-frame? Does the sculpture/fence function as a kind of transitional object bridging the divide between art (the museum) and nature (the pasture)? What distinguishes this work of art from the other things of this world?

## Folly

Saban's witty title is an homage to a 1972 video work by her teacher and mentor, artist John Baldessari. In *Teaching a Plant the Alphabet*, Baldessari presents English alphabet flash cards to a potted banana plant while repeating the letter sound—for example, C-C-C-C-C, and so on—for over eighteen minutes. The deadpan futility nonetheless tantalizes with the possibility of cross-species comprehension. Perhaps one can teach a plant the alphabet if one tries hard enough. While Baldessari's video assimilated then-emergent theories of semiotics and structuralism, it was also something of a riposte, and perhaps homage, to Joseph Beuys's 1965 performance work *How to Explain Pictures to a Dead Hare*. For three hours, the artist whispered to the eponymous corpse, which he cradled in his arms, about the objects in an art gallery. One supposed that the shamanistic Beuys might just succeed in breathing art into the furry being, just as Baldessari might just conjure plant literacy. Moreover, both Baldessari's and Beuys's works explore the contingencies of communication, including the authority of the speaker, the reception (or potential lack thereof) of the subject/object, the context and era in which the works were created, the propagation of meaning, and the slippery roles of humor, satire, and parody. Saban's site-responsive sculpture assumes similar contingencies.

Injecting language where it perhaps didn't belong, as a means of query and critique, was an aspect of Baldessari and George Nicolaidis's *The California Map Project, Part 1: California* (1969, fig. 28). Traveling the state from top to bottom, the artists "found" or marked the letters C-A-L-I-F-O-R-N-I-A (for example, a utility pole and its cast shadow pressed into service as an "L"; a river rock "R"; a spray-painted "O") at the precise corresponding location where they appeared on a printed state map, documenting their landscape incursions in eleven color photographs (ten letters and one map). Baldessari described the work as "an attempt to make the real world match a map, to impose a language on nature and vice-versa."[7]

The witty earnestness of these earlier works plays through, especially, Saban's invocation of interspecies communication via instructional "edutainment" and landscape incursion. The word folly comes to mind, not only its origins in the French *fou* or *folie*, for madness, but as a term for elaborate architectural structures with no practical purpose. A folly is envisioned as a conversation piece, typically located in gardens and parks, and intended to enliven a view and focus the eye. It is a decoration, an ornament for a site, just as Saban's sculpture is, in its way. It is a folly in the form of a decorated fence, to coin a phrase (with a nod to Venturi, Scott Brown, and Izenour's decorated shed[8]). These connotations of decoration and ornament complicate Saban's artwork. Are we to consider it as sculpture or folly, art or design? By adapting a vernacular style particular to wooded regions such as northwestern Massachusetts, where the raw materials are in ready supply (we'll set aside the region's equally ubiquitous stone walls and the legendary poems about them[9]), *Teaching a Cow How to Draw* masquerades as an ordinary fence. The folly is its extra-ness, both its instructional intentions and the "madness" of the attempt. In addition to addressing the often-confining categories of art and design, Saban's work questions the very status of the viewer: is it art if the intended audience is cattle?

## Landscapes Are Paintings

Saban describes *Teaching a Cow How to Draw* as an attempt to "keep things together, hold the image, or hold the horizon line."[10] But while it may attempt to fix the horizon, this is, as you might imagine, an exercise in futility. The horizon cannot be fixed. The fence will change; if left to nature, it will degrade and collapse. Its appearance is contingent upon seasons, cows, and humans, as well as our subjective formulations of inclusions and exclusions. The fence holds the landscape by way, paradoxically, of division. It is a border, the frame for a picture or view.

Consider the words that connect a landscape with a painting: field, edge, border, surface, incident, space, horizon, ground. Visual theorist John Berger wrote, "The ideal field would apparently have certain qualities in common with (a) a painting—defined edges, an accessible distance, and so on; and (b) a theatre-in-the-round stage—an attendant openness with a maximum possibility for exits and entrances."[11]

The first use of the English word landscape emerged in the sixteenth century from a Dutch painter's term for a depiction of natural scenery. From painters it was adopted by poets, then finally entered regular usage to describe, for example, scenery, topography, and panoramic vistas. In other countries, landscape painting traditions—and the words to describe them—are much older. Paintings of nature and its flora and fauna have appeared in every culture, in every form, since the beginning of human history.

A painter of landscapes is called a landscapist.

## Slippage

*Teaching a Cow How to Draw* is Saban's second landscape-sited artwork. In 2018, at the invitation of Art Safiental, she made *Circuit Board for Rock Painting* (fig. 29), a twenty-six-foot-high limewash painting of a computer circuit board executed on a rock face in the Safien Valley, Switzerland. Both of these outdoor works align with a studio practice that focuses on painting—specifically, the interrogation of its fundamental materiality. Saban combines processes from photography, printmaking, weaving, sculpture, and painting—often in one work. She forces materials to do what they aren't designed to do: for example, absurdly excessive quantities of paint poured into linen that sags, bulges, and seeps; or paint used like plaster to cast prosaic objects such as sheets, towels, and trash bags. Other works, conversely, subvert additive painterly strategies, such as a series that subtracts paint from a surface with a laser cutter. All that remains of the linen ground in *Erosion (Cube) #2* (2011, fig. 30) is a floating cube tethered to the stretcher by perspectival guidelines.

Saban's approach to making art expresses her attention to the dissolution of borders between nature and technology. As she's begun to utilize technology—such as CNC (computer numerically controlled) machines—in the studio, Saban has turned it inside-out by portraying its circuit boards and microchips as a way to link technology with art—and, more broadly, with making. Present-day computing technology originated in the punch-card programmed jacquard loom, an industrial-era mechanization of what was (and is) a simple and ancient human technology: the interlocking of threads to make a textile.[12] And weaving is another process Saban introduces into her painting by using a loom to interlace a linen warp with a weft of long strips of dried acrylic paint. If one considers both the literal and metaphorical potential of weaving as the interlacing of linear pliable elements, then Saban's hybrid object can seem extraordinarily generative, an object that is consequential as both exemplar and provocateur: a prod for radical material experimentation and a strategy for eliding the borders between art and craft, analog and digital.

But painting is not the only discipline where Saban demolishes media and their attendant categories. The fact that *Teaching a Cow How to Draw* is a barrier reminds me, formally, of her *Draped Marble* sculptures (fig. 31), in which the artist draped sawhorses with folded slabs of rigid stone. The marble "drape" enfolds an exquisitely crafted walnut sawhorse (more nature, more artificiality!) inspired, according to the artist, by crowd-control barriers used by law enforcement. I appreciate the hubris of bending stone, of looking at the carved drapery of a marble statue and thinking, What if one literally draped stone? To do so requires not carving but demolition—sledgehammering marble. Affixed to fiberglass mesh that holds in place the shattered fragments, the slab is "folded" at its middle point over a creased steel armature. The shards both enhance and disperse the marble's veining, resulting in a kind of mannerism: nature made artificial, instability and tension foregrounded.

29

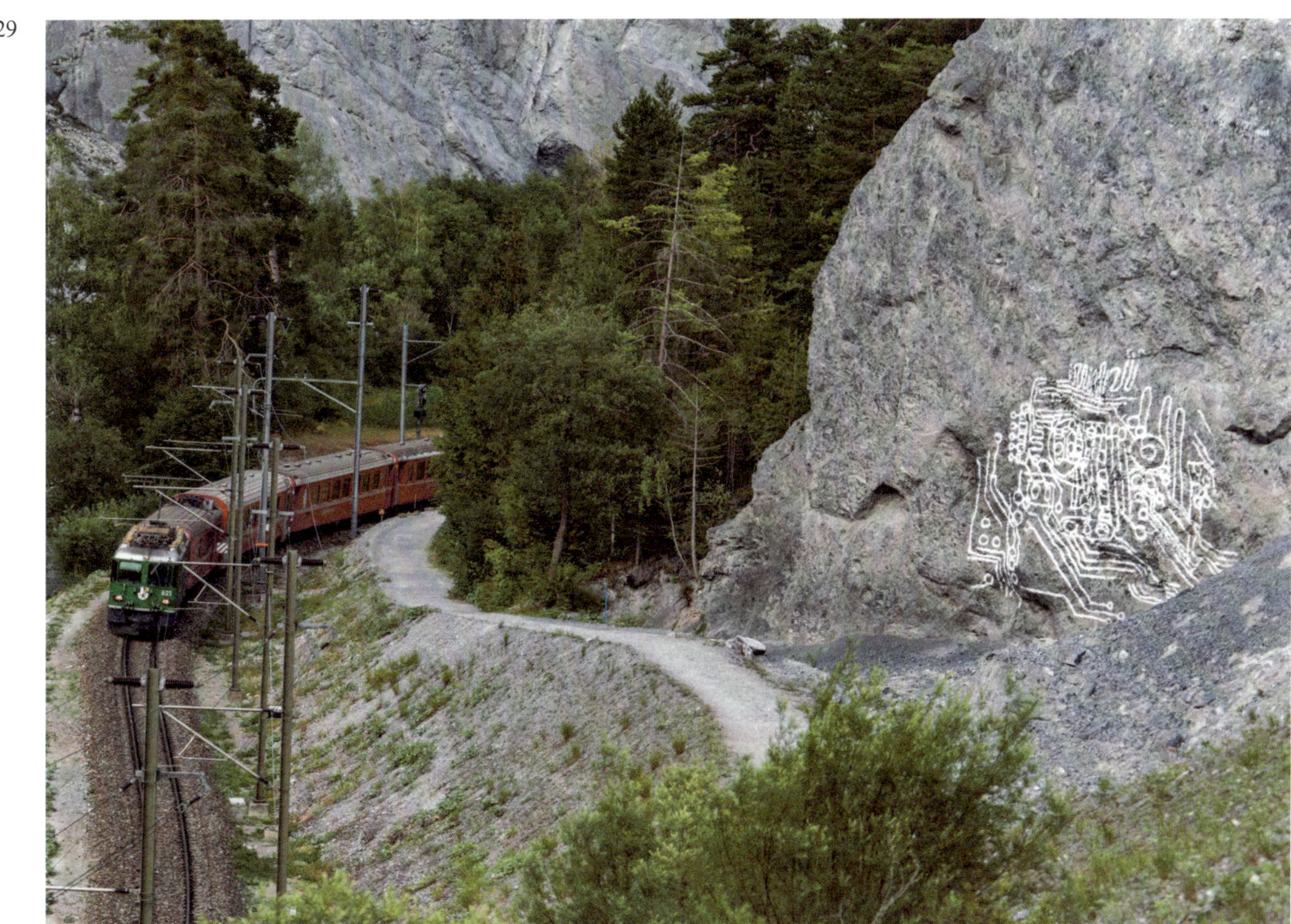

30

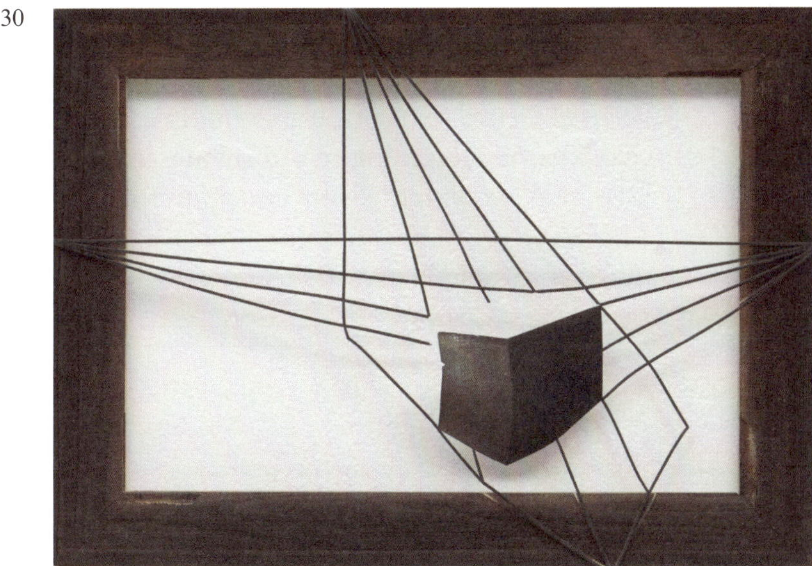

Fig. 29 Analia Saban, *Circuit Board for Rock Painting*, Art Safiental Biennale, 2018. Limewash paint on rock, 26 1/4 x 32 3/4 ft. (8 x 10 m). Image courtesy of ILEA Institute for Land and Environmental Art

Fig. 30 Analia Saban, *Erosion (Cube) #2*, 2011. Laser-sculpted acrylic paint on canvas, 12 x 16 x 2 in. (30.5 x 40.6 x 30.5 cm). Image courtesy of the artist, Tonya Bonakdar Gallery, Sprüth Magers, and Galerie Praz-Delavallade

The juxtaposition of these two projects underscores the fluidity with which Saban navigates often-contradictory materials and concepts.

## Cows

According to industry data, cows outnumber humans in Argentina, Australia, Brazil, New Zealand, and Uruguay. In the United States, the human population of nine states is eclipsed by that of cows; South Dakota's human-to-cow population ratio is approximately 850,000 to 3.6 million.[13] As of January 2019, the global cattle population was 989 million. I find this data staggering, the "more cows than people" absurdity of it all. Though I've no idea how to parse—literally, metaphorically, or morally—these numbers, they strike me as relevant to Saban's intentions (not to mention her childhood in Argentina). So persuaded was I by the artist's consideration of the resident cows, I inquired about her philosophy on food. I found myself presuming that only a vegetarian could conceive of an "intellectually entertaining" pasture fence. She does not abjure meat eating, but that does not preclude empathy with nature and animals. Feeling oneself into different perspectives is among the tender aspects of the artist's project.

As I considered Saban's artwork, one of my first questions was, Why are there cows on the museum grounds? The Clark's grounds manager, Matt Noyes, explained that cows have grazed on Stone Hill, as the land behind the institute is named, since the late nineteenth century. Today, the Haley family grazes its cows and cuts hay in the meadow from spring to late fall, as they have since the Clark opened in the 1950s. The cows develop pathway systems that allow them to come and go as they like from the meadow to their nearby barn.

When I think about cows and art (cows in art; art cows?), my sentimental favorite is Mark Tansey's painting *The Innocent Eye Test* (1981, fig. 32) in the collection of the Metropolitan Museum of Art (New York state human-to-cow ratio: approximately 19.6 million to 1.45 million). The picture portrays a group of dark-suited white men unveiling one of the most celebrated works in European art history for a bovine audience of one. The life-sized painting is Paulus Potter's *The Young Bull* (1647), a pastoral scene rendered in a kind of grand scale and loving detail (flies, frogs, birds, sunshine) that, in seventeenth-century Europe, was not typically afforded farm stock. The naturalistic verisimilitude Potter sought is, in Tansey's translation, subjected to the ultimate test: will the cow recognize its own species? Will it be soothed (two more cows amid all these humans, thank goodness), alarmed, bored, or perhaps manifest its judgment corporeally (one man holds a mop at the ready). Will Claude Monet's 1891 *Grainstack (Snow Effect)*, hanging to the right, draw the cow's hungry gaze? While Tansey's work operates in the realm of the critique of representation, it nonetheless poses enduring questions: What do we see, and how do we see it? Is there such a thing, pace John Ruskin, as an innocent eye?

Saban's sculpture, by contrast, acknowledges that cows are sentient beings and therefore potentially capable of learning from their surroundings. They see the sculpture/fence, just not the same way that humans do. And I mean this literally. Cattle experience 300 degrees of vision compared to the human eye's 180 degrees. The human blind spot is much larger. Given its panoramic vision, a cow apprehends a view of the horizon that the human eye can never attain. But, compared to humans, cattle have slow visual processing, poor depth perception, and limited vertical vision. Given these animal facts, what will the cows learn from Saban's drawing instruction? The idea that we might even consider this question (of which the probable answer is "very little to nothing") illustrates the effectiveness, and sly wit, of *Teaching a Cow How to Draw*.

## Perspective

I've appropriated the title of this essay, "Remarks on Rural Scenery," as a way to frame *Teaching a Cow How to Draw*.[14] I've deliberately seeded this text with open-ended questions as a way to echo the remarkable generosity of Saban's artwork. Much of its conceptual and formal elegance, I suspect, lies in how it makes space while dividing it. As well, it invites us to slow and to look closely, in the artist's words, "at the fence and the beauty of the material, how the joints

31

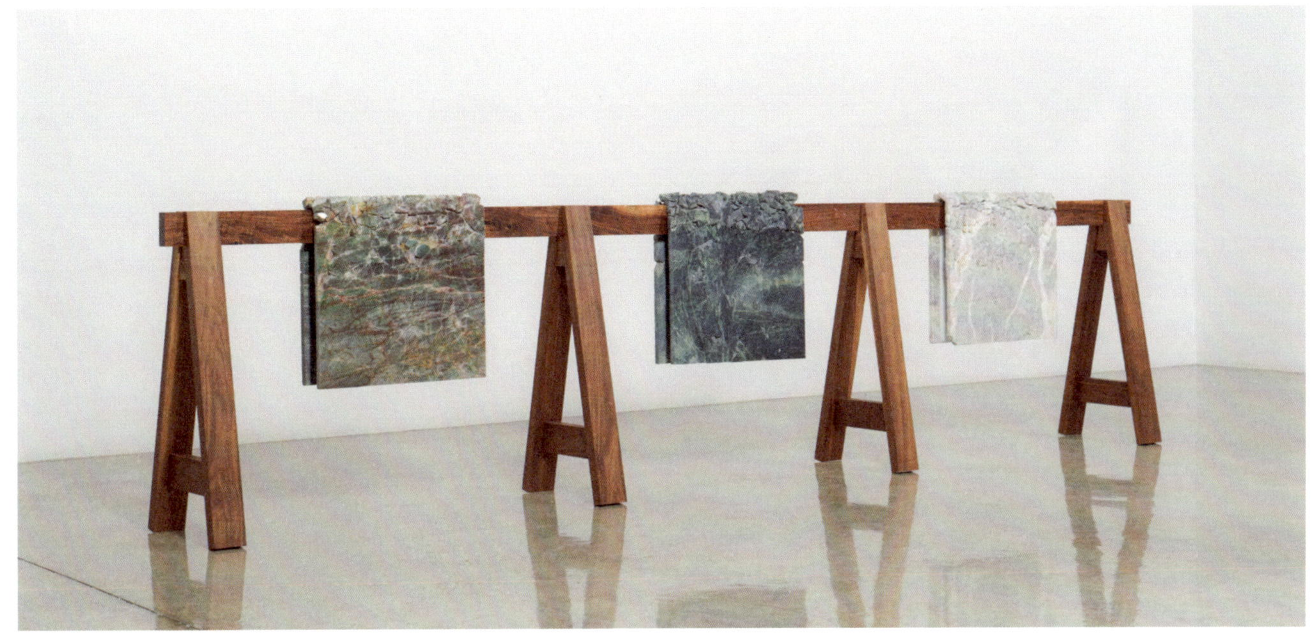

Fig. 31 Analia Saban, *Draped Marble (Emerald, Jade, Fior di Pesco Classico)*, 2015. Marble mounted on steel on wooden sawhorse, sawhorse: 33 11/16 x 144 x 15 3/4 in. (85.6 x 365.8 x 40 cm); emerald marble slab: 20 1/2 x 20 1/8 x 4 1/4 in. (52.1 x 51.1 x 10.8 cm); jade marble slab: 20 5/8 x 20 1/16 x 4 3/8 in. (52.4 x 51 x 11.1 cm); Fior di Pesco marble slab: 20 3/4 x 20 1/8 x 4 1/8 in. (52.7 x 51.1 x 10.5 cm). Image courtesy of the artist, Tanya Bonakdar Gallery, Sprüth Magers, and Galerie Praz-Delavallade

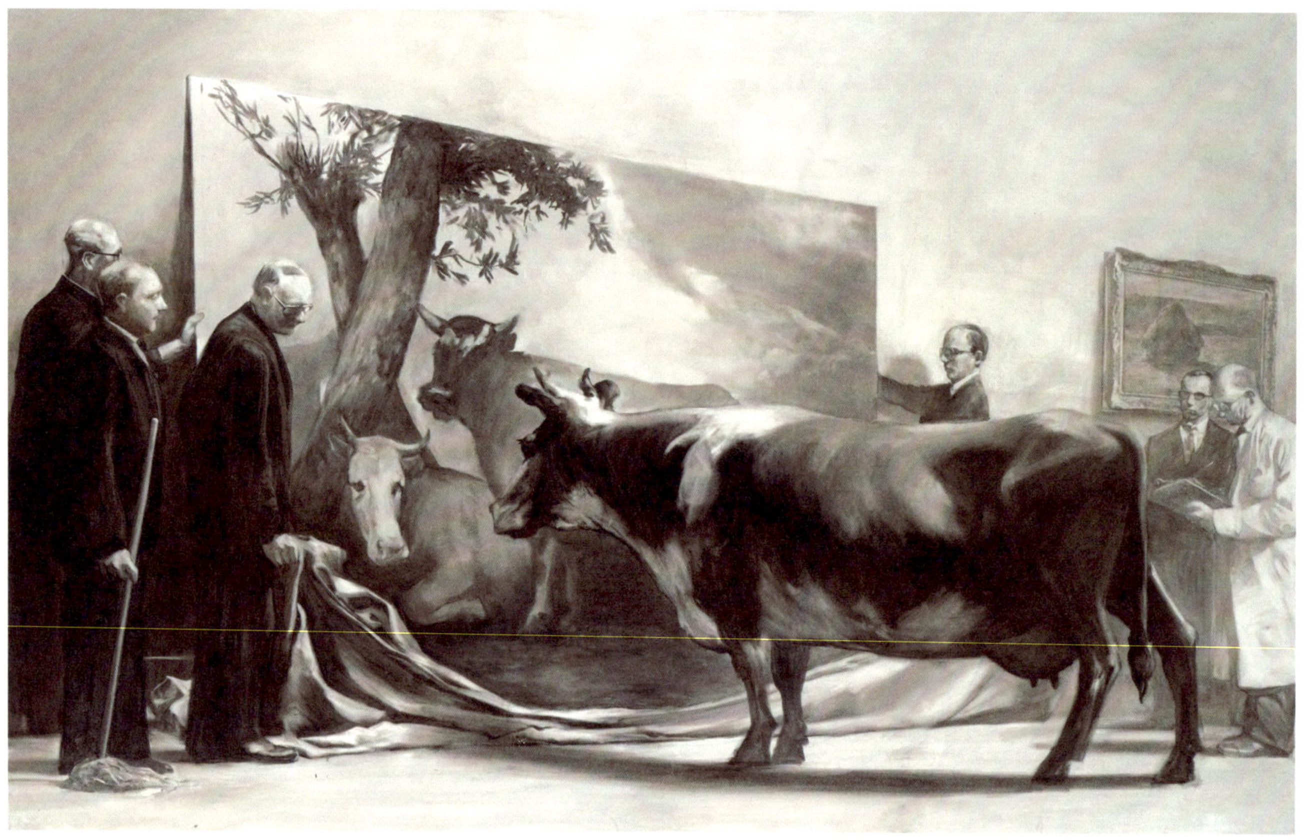

Fig. 32 Mark Tansey, *The Innocent Eye Test*, 1981. Oil on canvas, 78 in. x 10 ft. (198.1 x 304.8 cm). Metropolitan Museum of Art, Gift of Jan Cowles and Charles Cowles, in honor of William S. Lieberman, 1988. Courtesy of the artist and Gagosian Gallery. © Mark Tansey

are made, how it's pieced together. The fence plays a very important role in the land. I wanted to see if that fence could engage in the dialogue of drawing, and whether the complexity would invite the viewer to look again."[15]

One last remark, in the form of a question, with one possible—and very open-ended—conclusion: Do we gain perspective by studying perspective? When art is most relevant, it transforms vision and knowledge; it informs how we look. In the midst of writing this essay, I traveled to the Eastern Sierra and, there, along the interstate, I glimpsed a split-rail cattle enclosure draped with animal hides. Though it was a somewhat macabre arrangement (the living penned by the skins of their deceased kin), I couldn't help but envision it as a bizarre combination of Saban's *Draped Marbles* sculptures with *Teaching a Cow How to Draw*. Moreover, in the writing of this essay, I have learned a lot about cattle, which points to the convoluted ways we develop knowledge—constantly, and in consideration of fluid categories and contingencies—about what art can do, what it can be, for whom and/or what it is intended, and how the boundaries that contain such theories are perennially eroded and reassembled. In this, *Teaching a Cow How to Draw* offers as much instruction to humans as it does to cows.

*Jenelle Porter is an independent curator and writer.*

Epigraph: John Berger, *About Looking* (New York: Pantheon Books, 1980), 198.

1 Analia Saban, "Teaching a Cow How to Draw," SoundCloud audio, Clark Art Institute, 4:28, http://www.clarkart.edu/microsites/ground-work/about-the-projects/analia-saban. Edited from an interview conducted by Molly Epstein and Abigail Ross Goodman, recorded March 11, 2020.

2 Tracing the rule to its origins, this essay's title derives from John Thomas Smith's 1797 *Remarks on Rural Scenery*, in which he coined the phrase "the rule of thirds." Smith's book expanded on and quantified Sir Joshua Reynolds's earlier guidance to painters on balancing dark and light in their work. See also John Thomas Smith, *Remarks on Rural Scenery: With Twenty Etchings of Cottages, from Nature: And Some Observations and Precepts Relative to the Picturesque*, 1797.

3 Christian Zapatka, *Mary Miss, Making Place* (New York: Whitney Library of Design, 1997), 59.

4 Pamela M. Lee, "Art as a Social System: Nancy Holt and the Second-Order Observer," in *Nancy Holt: Sightlines*, ed. Alena J. Williams (Berkeley: University of California Press, 2011), 42.

5 Lee, "Art as a Social System," 42.

6 Lee, "Art as a Social System," 42.

7 John Baldessari, quoted in Patrick Pardo and Robert Dean, eds., *John Baldessari Catalogue Raisonné: Volume One, 1956–1974* (New Haven, CT: Yale University Press, 2012), 376.

8 In *Learning from Las Vegas* (1972), Robert Venturi, Denise Scott Brown, and Steven Izenour deploy the comparative method to differentiate the "duck"—a "building-becoming-sculpture," that is, the symbolic novelty structures of midcentury roadside America—from the "decorated shed," in which ornament is applied to ordinary box structures.

9 See, for example, Robert Frost's "Mending Wall," with its cows and fences.

10 Analia Saban, phone conversation with the author, September 16, 2020.

11 Berger, *About Looking*, 194–95.

12 It was computer scientist and graphic artist Janice Lourie who, in the late 1960s, pioneered (and holds IBM's first software patent for) computer-aided design for textile manufacturing.

13 According to beef2live.com, accessed September 29, 2020.

14 See note 2.

15 Saban, "Teaching a Cow How to Draw" (edited slightly for clarity).

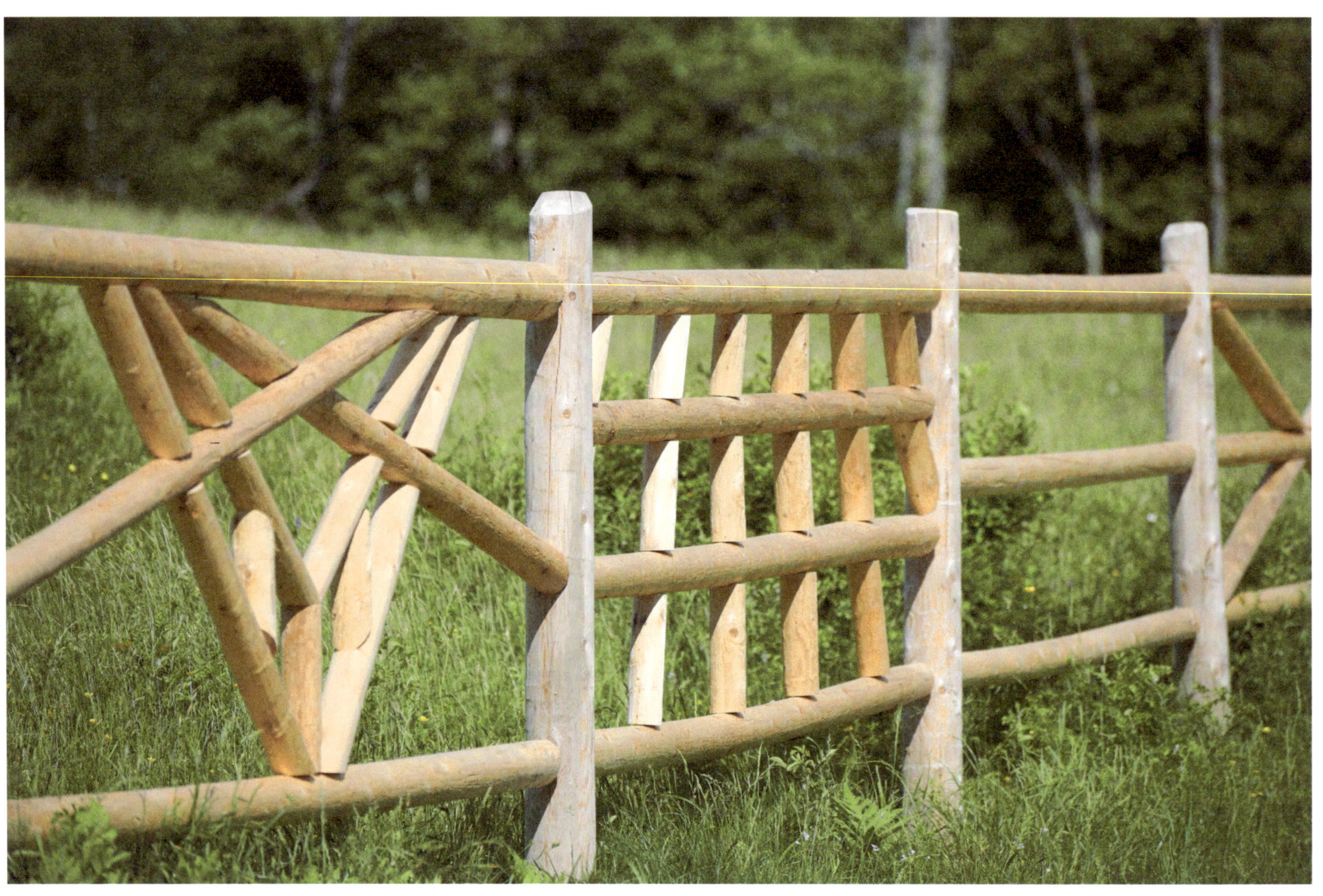

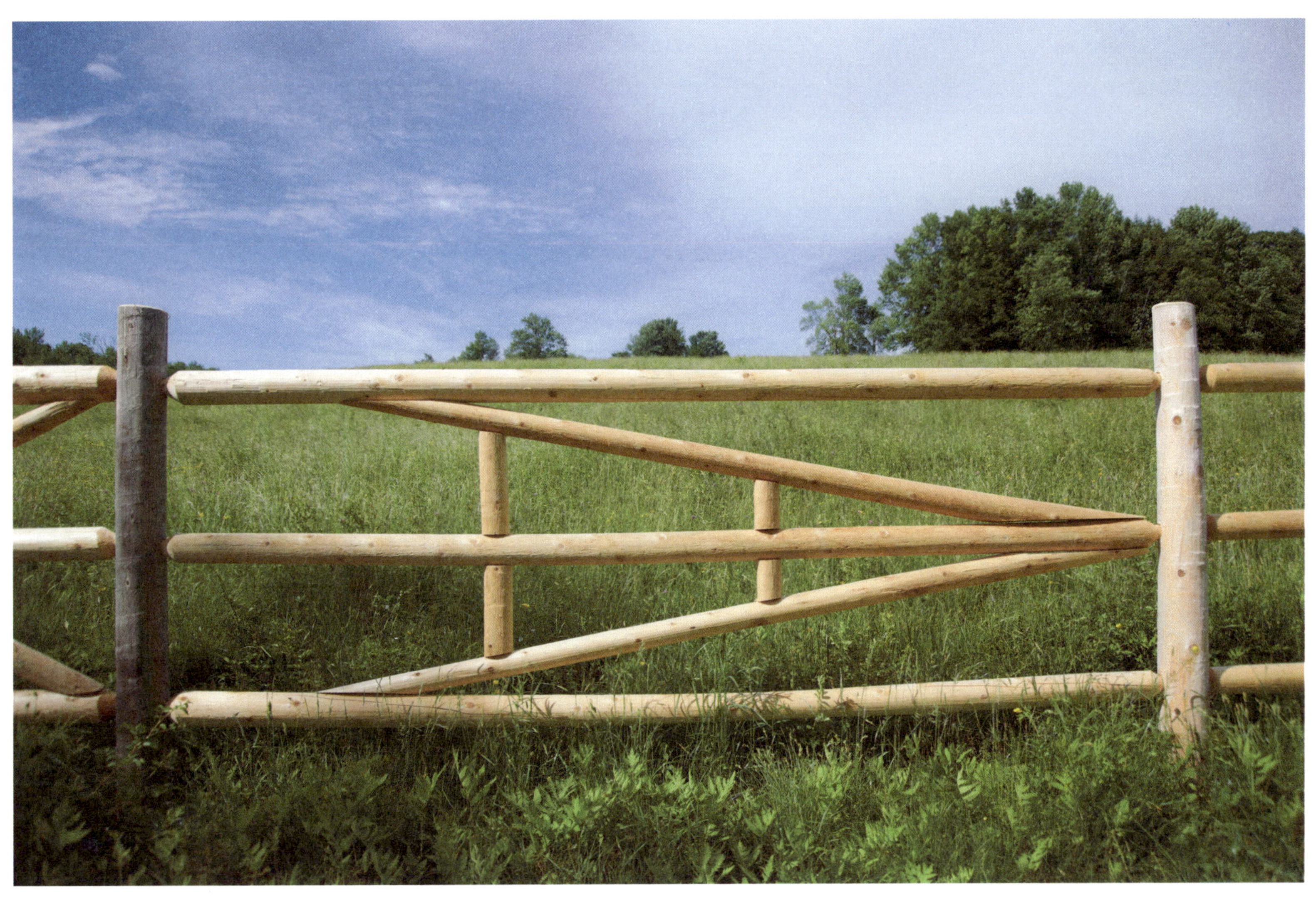

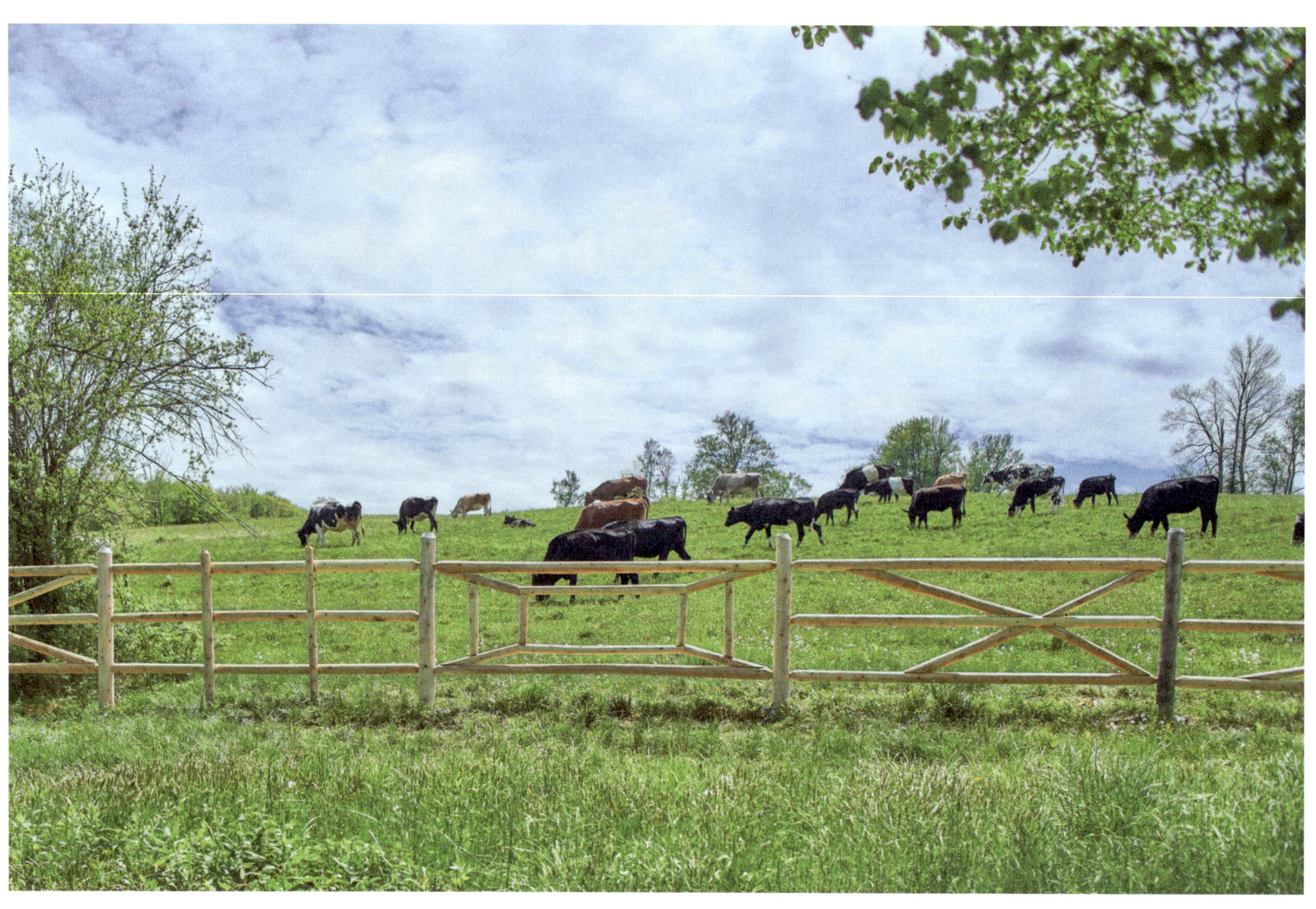

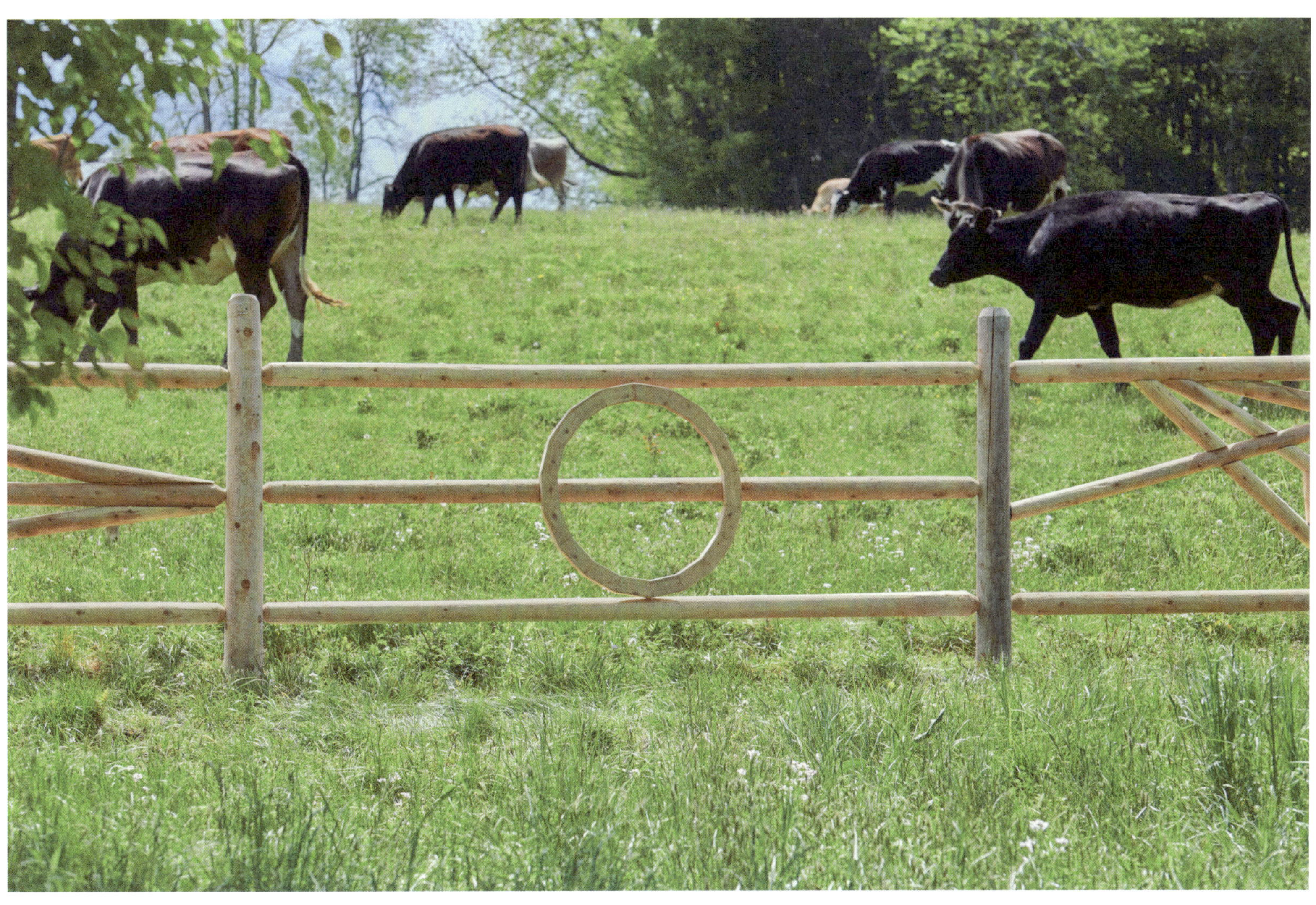

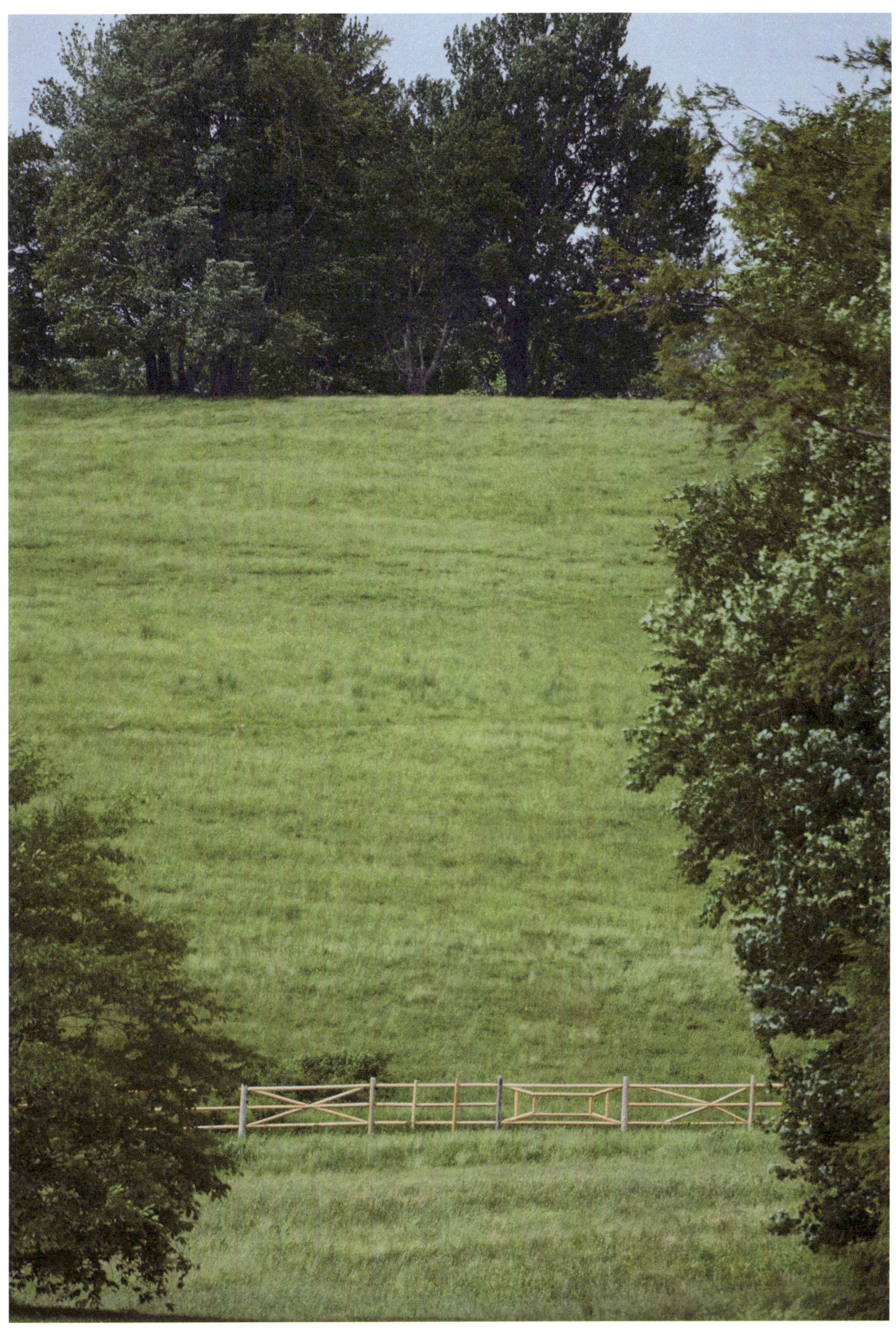

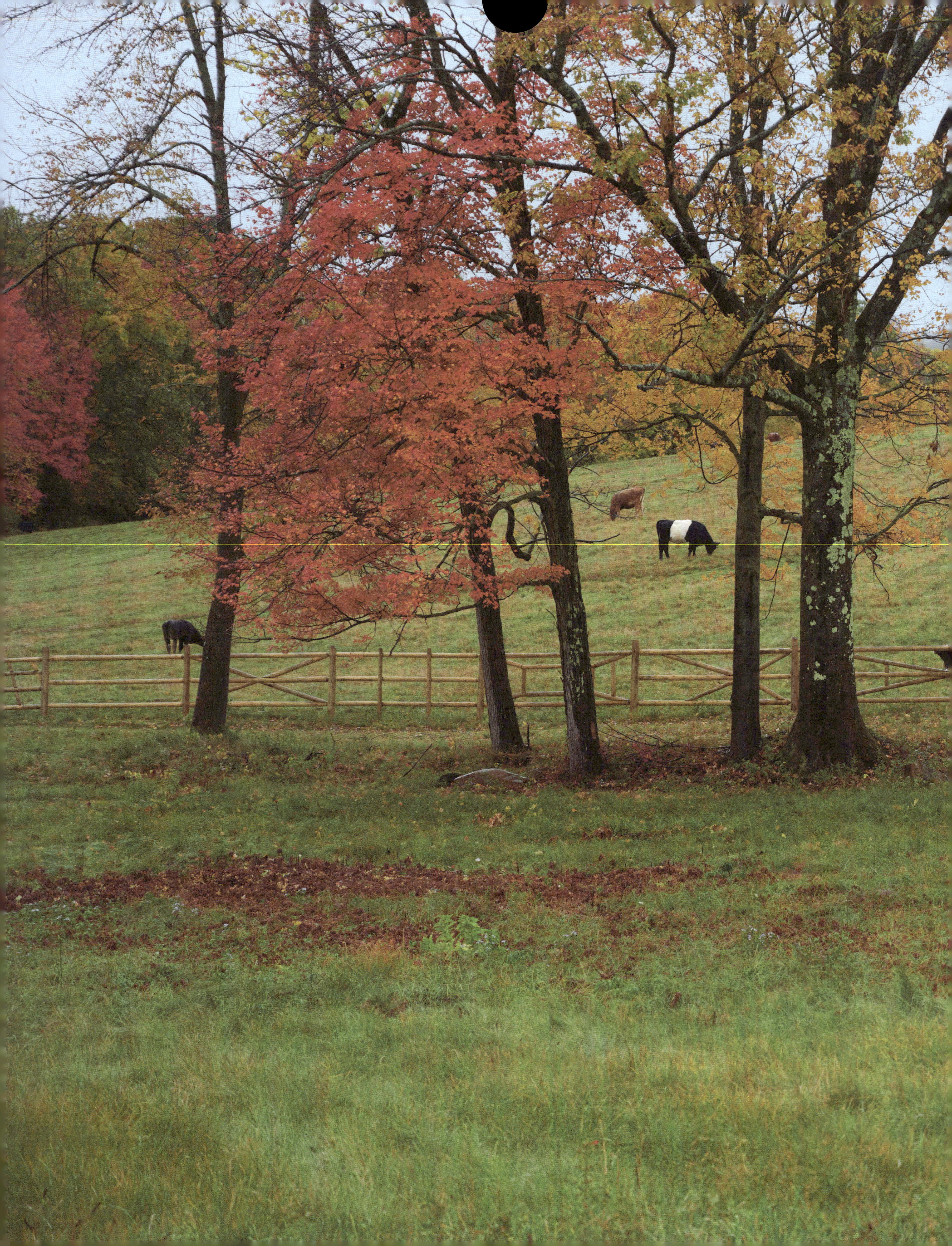

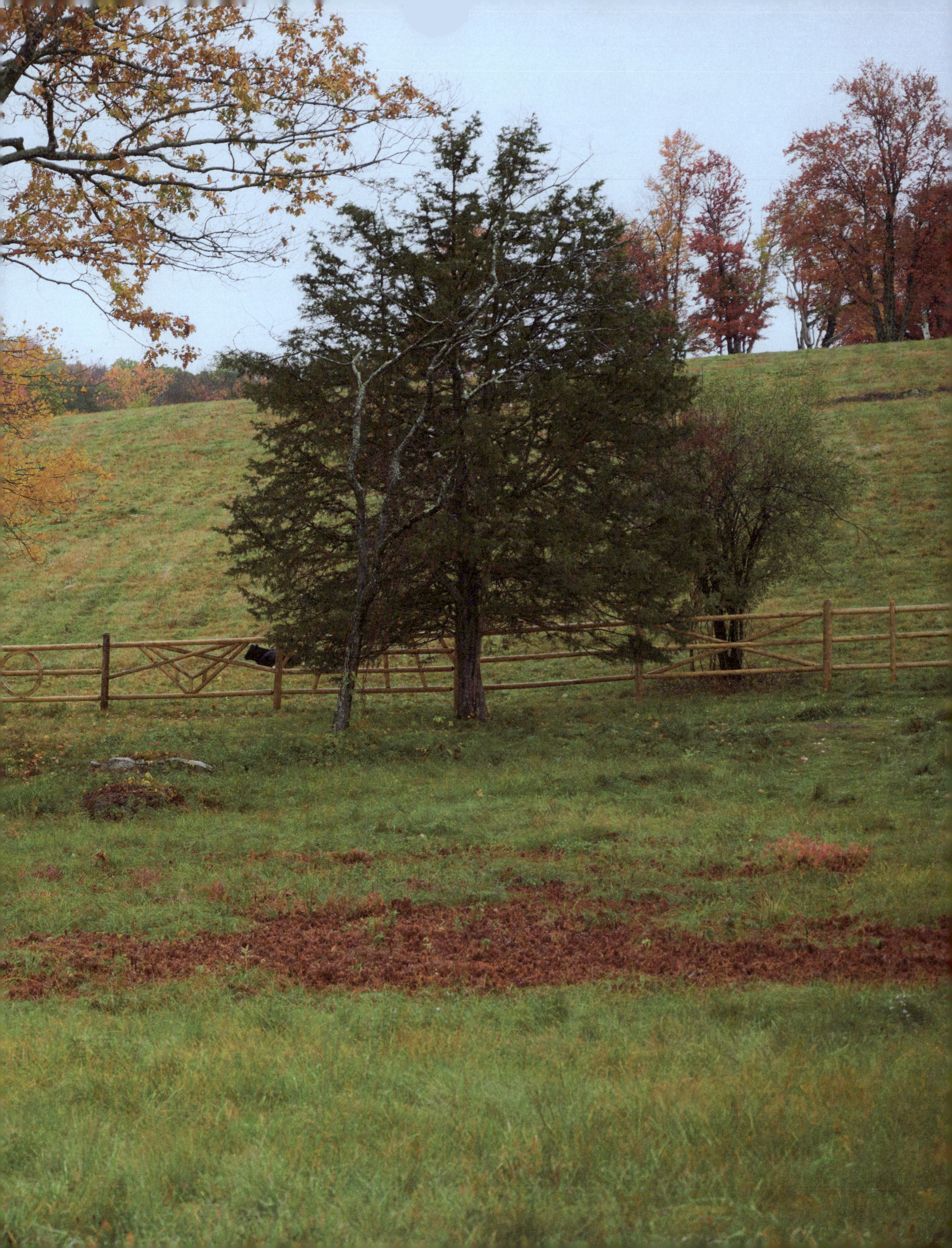

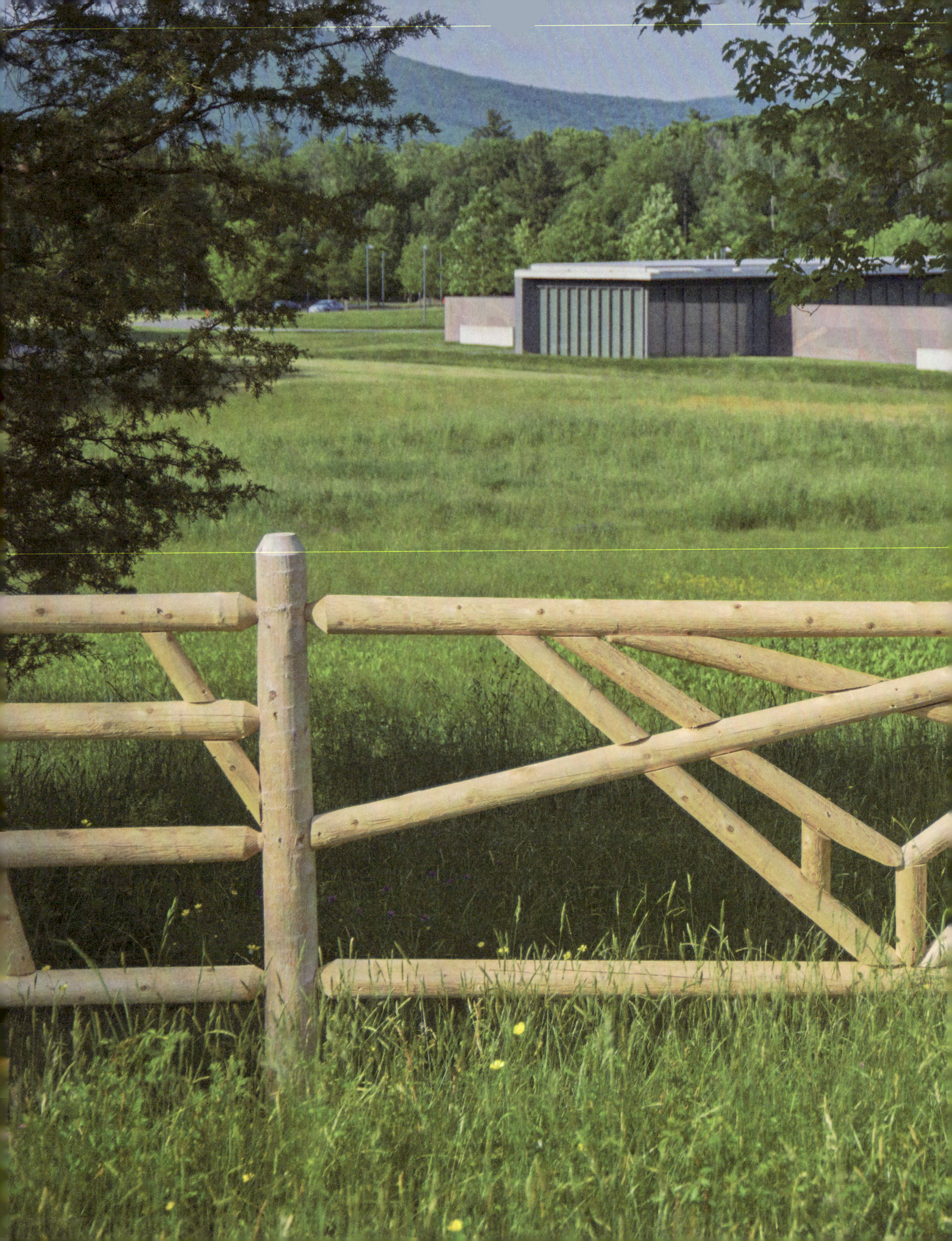

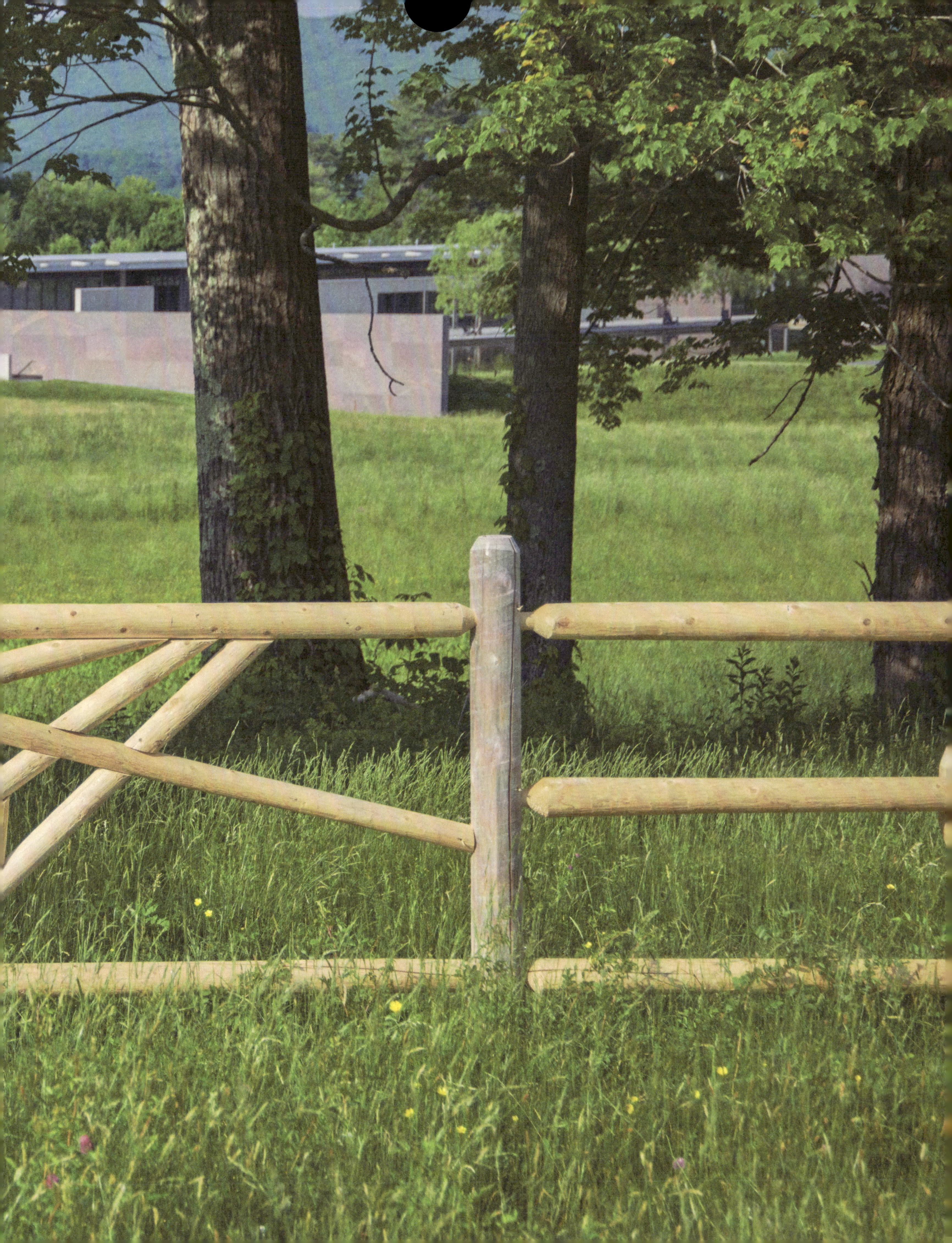

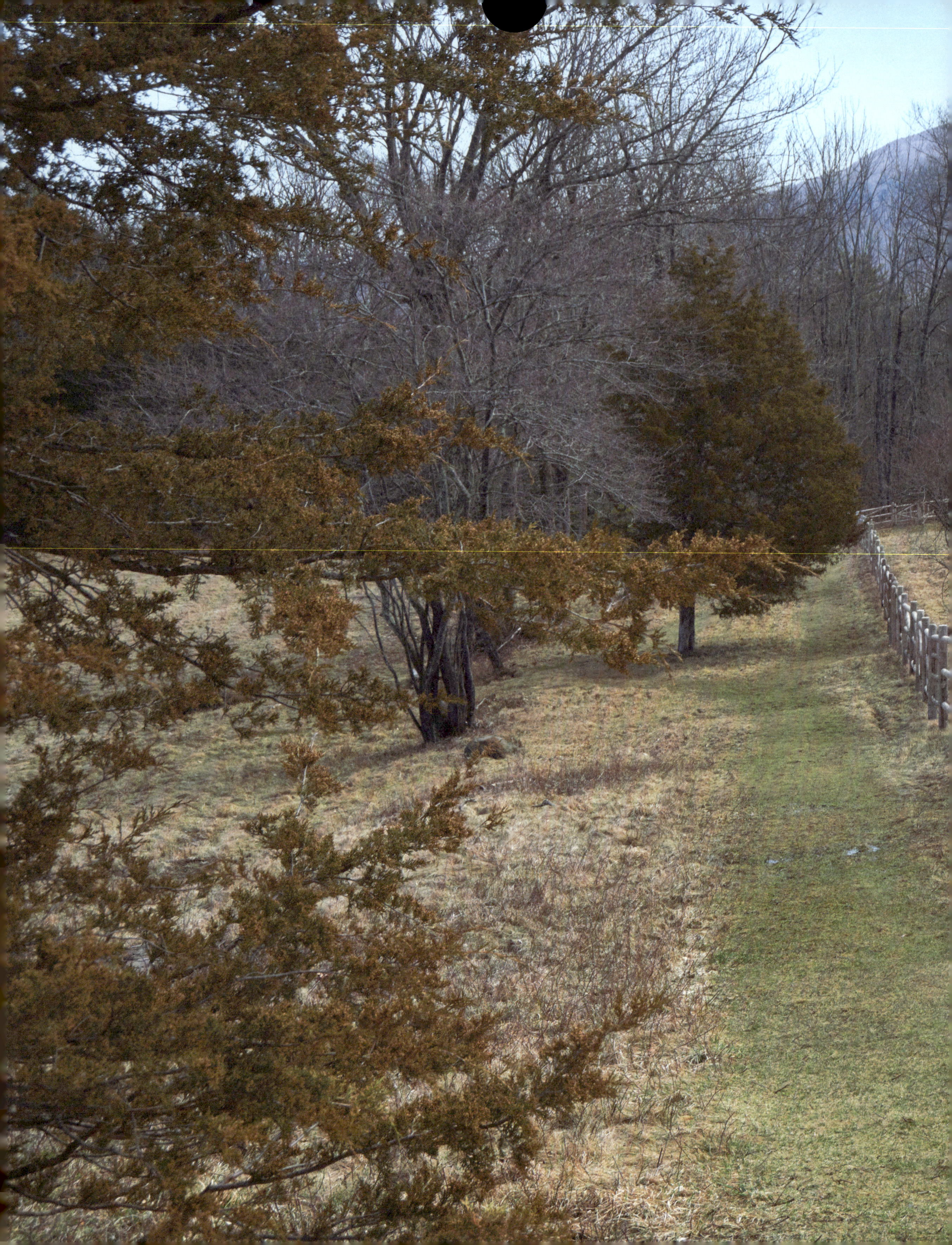

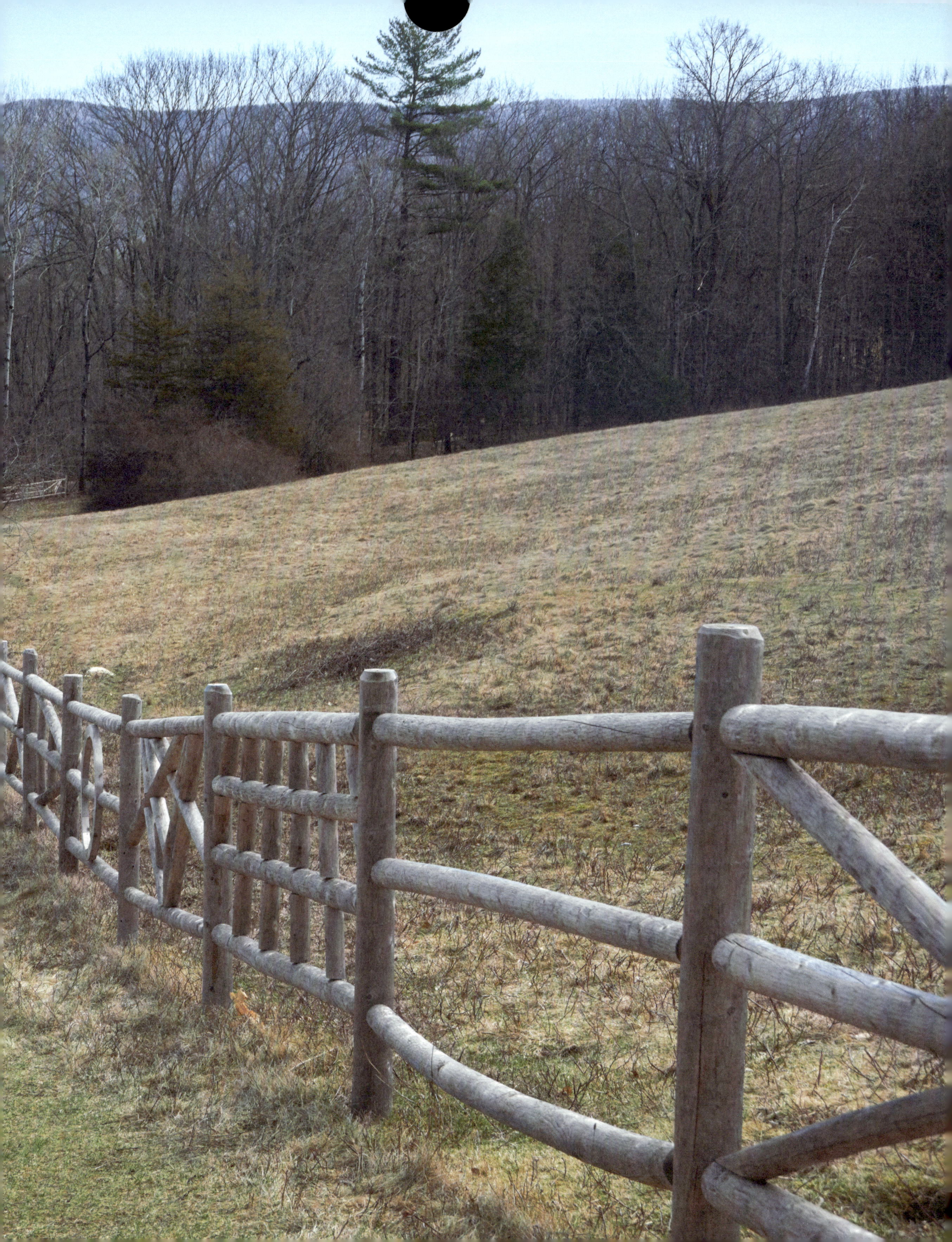

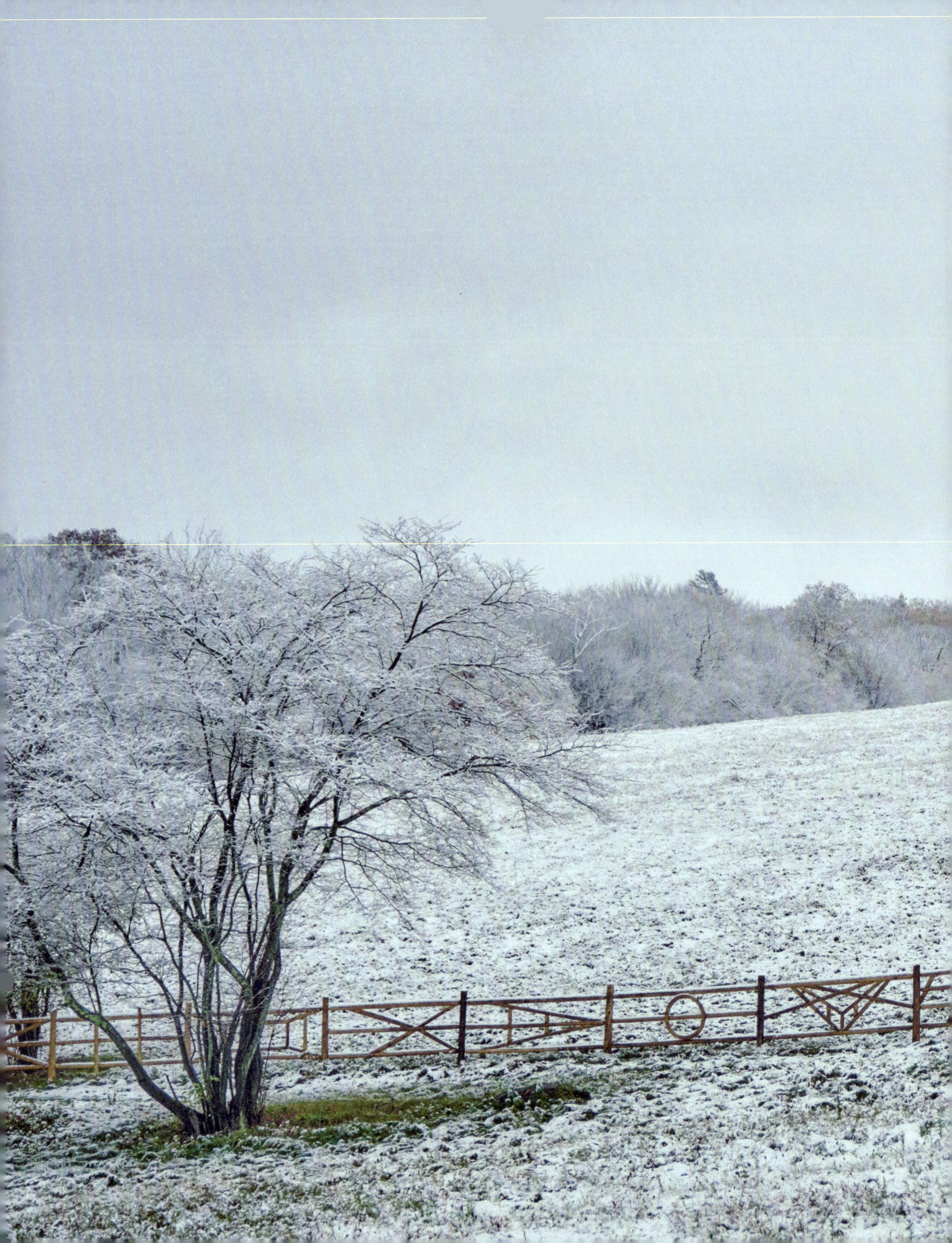

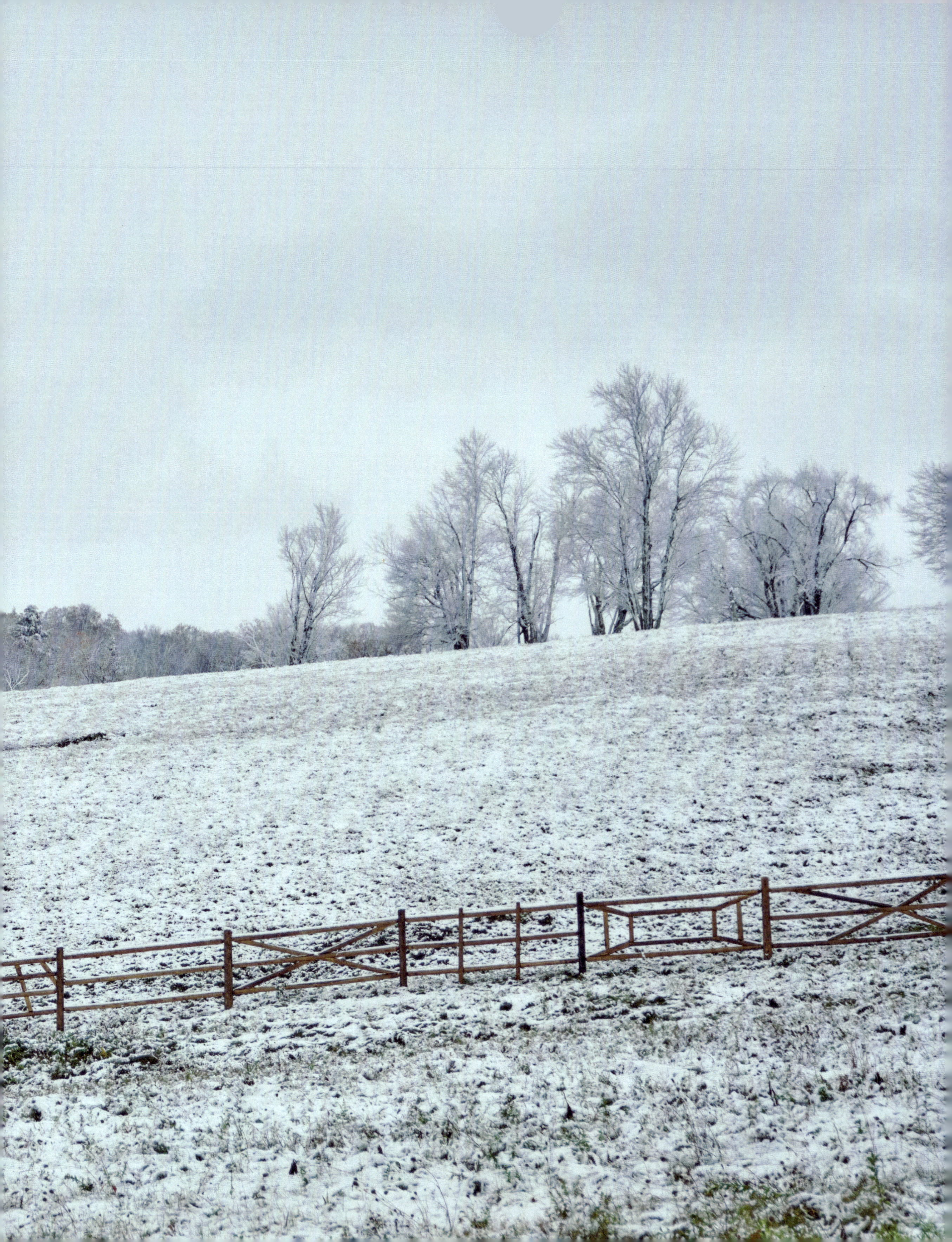

Soapstone, 3D-printed resin
62 x 58 1/4 x 28 3/4 in. (157.5 x 148 x 73 cm)
62 x 58 1/2 x 33 1/2 in. (157.5 x 148.6 x 85.1 cm)
62 x 58 x 35 in. (157.5 x 147.3 x 88.9 cm)

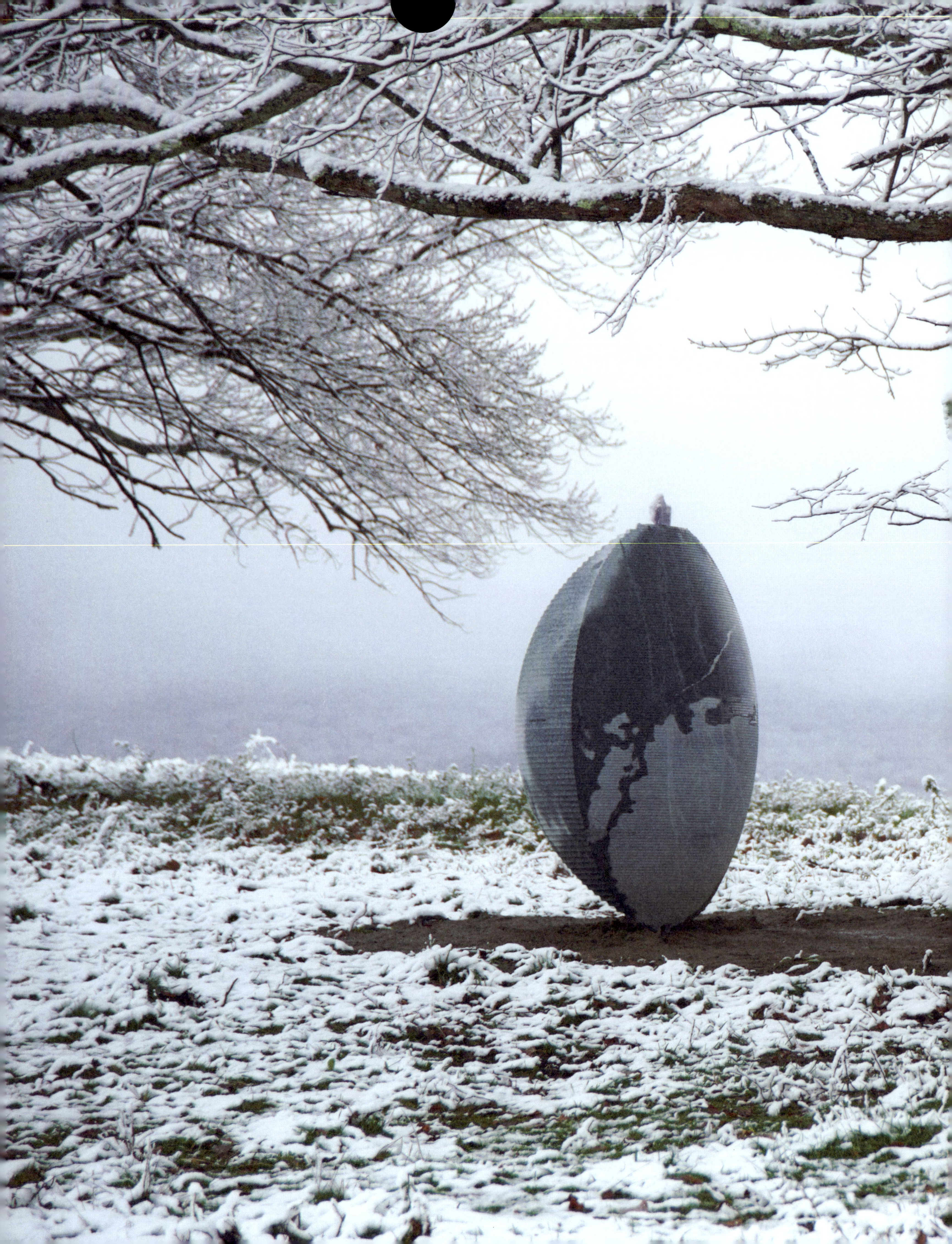

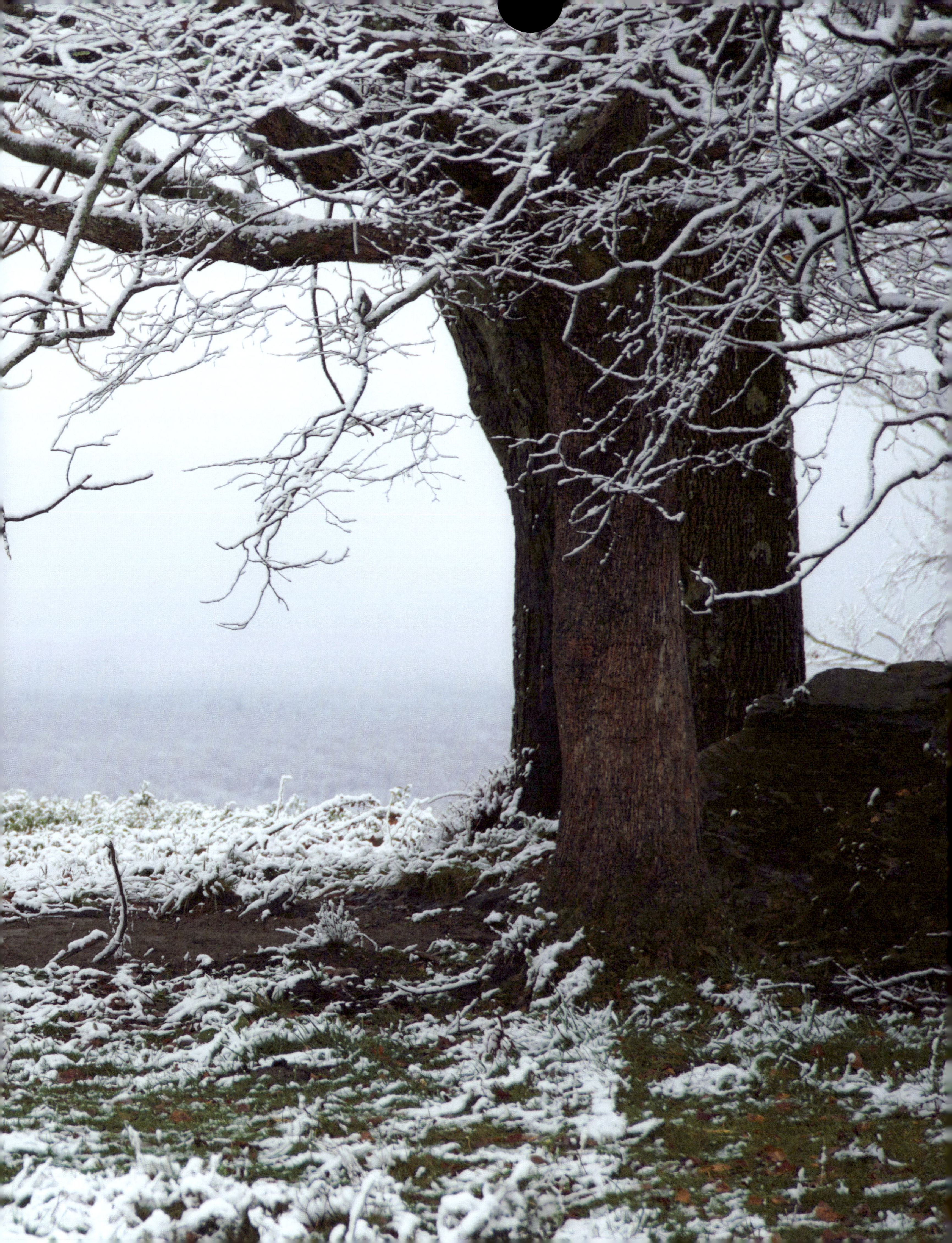

# A Proposal for an Encounter: On Haegue Yang's *Migratory DMZ Birds on Asymmetric Lens*

Pavel S. Pyś

On April 27, 2018, South Korean President Moon Jae-in and Kim Jong-un, Supreme Leader of North Korea, met in a historic summit that marked the first time a North Korean leader had stepped into the South since the end of the Korean War in 1953. Potent with symbolic gestures, the meeting culminated in the signing of the Panmunjom Declaration for Peace, Prosperity, and Reunification of the Korean Peninsula, which seeks to bring an end to the Korean conflict. At one point during the summit, the two heads of state held a private conversation on a footbridge within the Joint Security Area, the single meeting point between the two Koreas within the 155-mile-long Demilitarized Zone (DMZ). While in view of reporters, their conversation remained out of earshot (fig. 33). As the cameras clicked away and footage was livestreamed, only birdsong was audible. Unable to overhear the exchange between the two, audiences around the world who had tuned in to the broadcast found themselves listening instead to chirping, trilling, and whistling. This temporary reversal of hierarchies—the privileging of nature over culture—inspired Haegue Yang's three *Migratory DMZ Birds on Asymmetric Lens* sculptures (2020), created for the grounds of the Clark Art Institute. Perched at eye level atop each of three massive soapstone disks is a life-size bird form, 3D-printed in transparent resin, that also doubles as a birdbath. Each sculpture is titled for the bird species it depicts and its call: *Tee-Cher Tee-Cher Vessel (Great Tit)*, *Hou-Ke-Kyo Vessel (Japanese Bush Warbler)*, and *Duiitt Duiitt Vessel (Gray-Backed Thrush)*. All three birds are native to the DMZ; none is found in the local North American avian population. As temporary visitors to the Massachusetts outdoors, Yang's works draw attention not only to ecological relationships, but also to the assumptions we hold surrounding the primacy of our species over others.

For all the gravitas of the momentous meeting she references, Yang has propelled nature from circumstantial backdrop to the main event. The historic summit takes on new dimensions as the artist urges us to consider the symbolic meaning of birdsong. Humans have looked to nature since time immemorial, seeking clues to our own destiny in meteorological and astrological events. The animal kingdom is equally rich with associations that trickle into cultural texts and everyday sayings (a canary in a coalmine, like a duck to water). Within the context of the 2018 inter-Korean summit, one key avian metaphor is brought into sharp relief: freedom. Able to traverse swathes of land and sea (and by extension—cross borders and boundaries), birds are seen as the embodiment of liberty: flying "free as a bird." They feature prominently in heraldic imagery, usually in the form of eagles (found on the late nineteenth-century Korean imperial emblem and, of course, in the iconography of the United States), but also of owls, roosters, and hawks. A brief anecdote illustrates just how loaded such symbolism can be: during World War II, the Nazis mandated the removal of any sovereign imagery from buildings in Warsaw, including a crowned eagle, Poland's national coat of arms. Rather than destroy the emblem found on the edifice of Warsaw Polytechnic's Chemistry Department, two workers risked their lives to conceal it behind brickwork, resulting in a slight protrusion on the building's surface. Polish Communist authorities then stripped the national eagle of its crown in 1955 (it would eventually return in 1989), an enduring metaphor for the nation's subjugation to the Soviet Union after the war. That same year, on the occasion of the Fifth World Festival of Youth and Students held in the Polish capital, a large dove of peace was painted on the edifice, around and over the concealed eagle. The brickwork that hides the eagle has remained untouched to this day, encapsulating the clash between the desire for independence and the Soviet-mandated terms of peaceful coexistence.[1]

Given birds' enduring association with sovereignty and liberty, and the contrast between South Korean democracy and North Korean authoritarianism, it was impossible not to be reminded of such symbolic connotations upon hearing the airwaves filled with DMZ birdsong. Many pinned their hopes on the 2018 summit as a catalyst for the rebirth for inter-Korean relations. Here, too, the symbolism of spiritual renewal is closely tied to birds, perhaps most commonly represented by the ancient Greek and Egyptian phoenix rising from the ashes. In Korean culture, birds are associated with a spiritual dimension, above all in the figure of the ancient Inmyeonjo, a mythical bird creature with a human face that lives

33

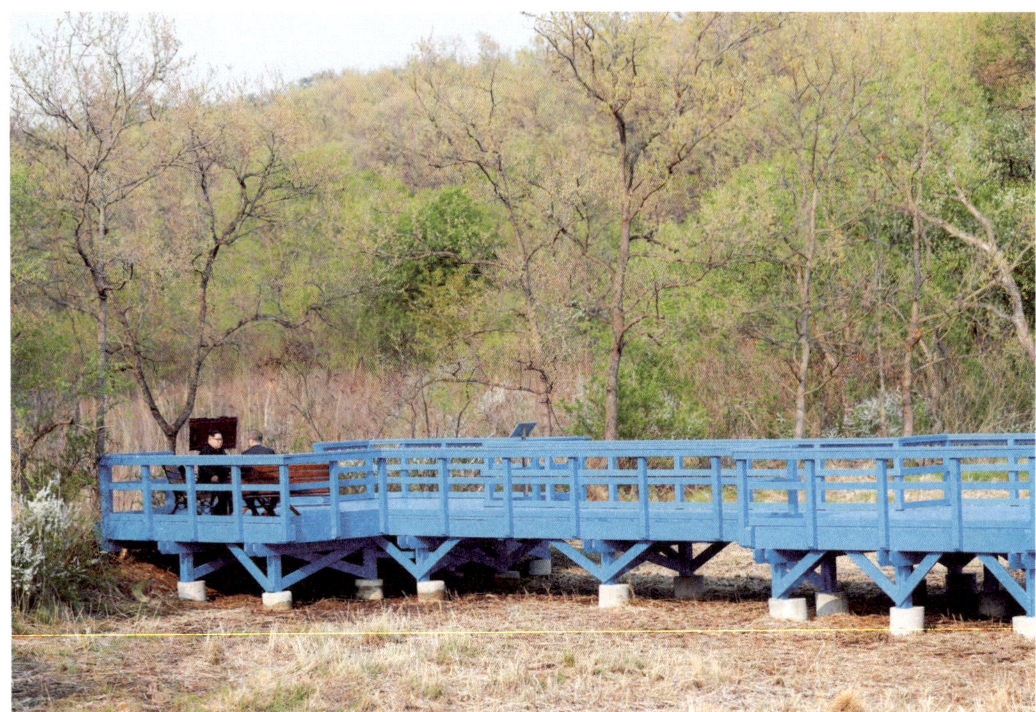

34

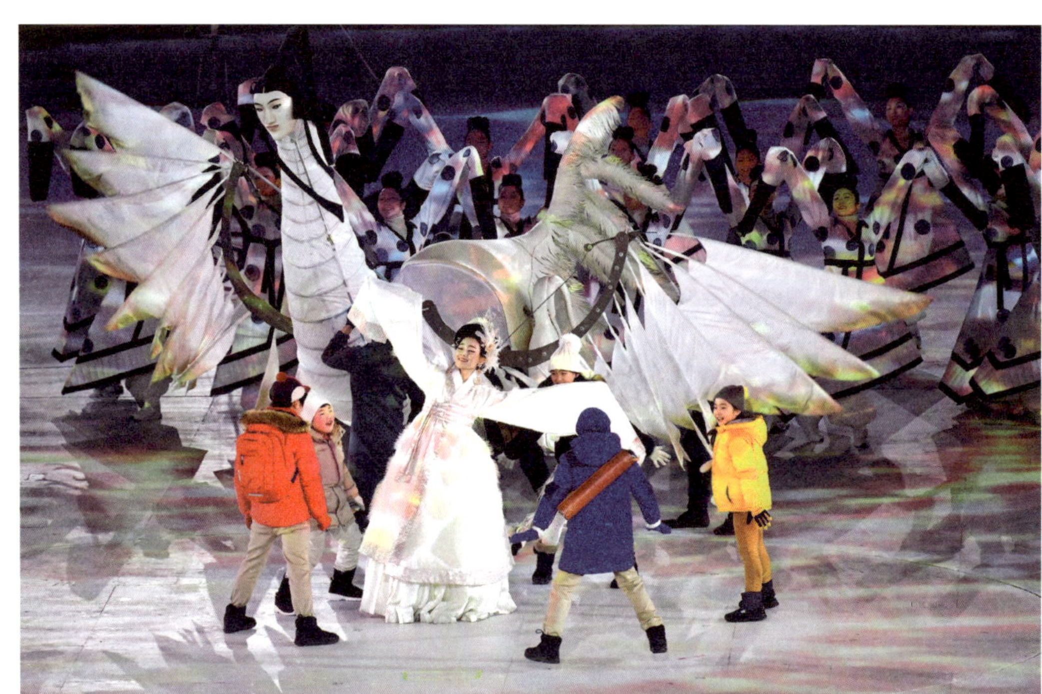

Fig. 33 South Korean President Moon Jae-In (R) and North Korean leader Kim Jong-Un (L) talk while taking a stroll on the Foot Bridge at the Panmunjom in the Demilitarized Zone (DMZ) separating the two Koreas in Paju, north of Seoul, South Korea, 2018. Aflo Co. Ltd. / Alamy Stock Photo

Fig. 34 Dancers perform with a marionette of the ancient Inmyeonjo during the opening ceremony for the 2018 Winter Olympics in Pyeongchang, South Korea. UPI / Alamy Stock Photo

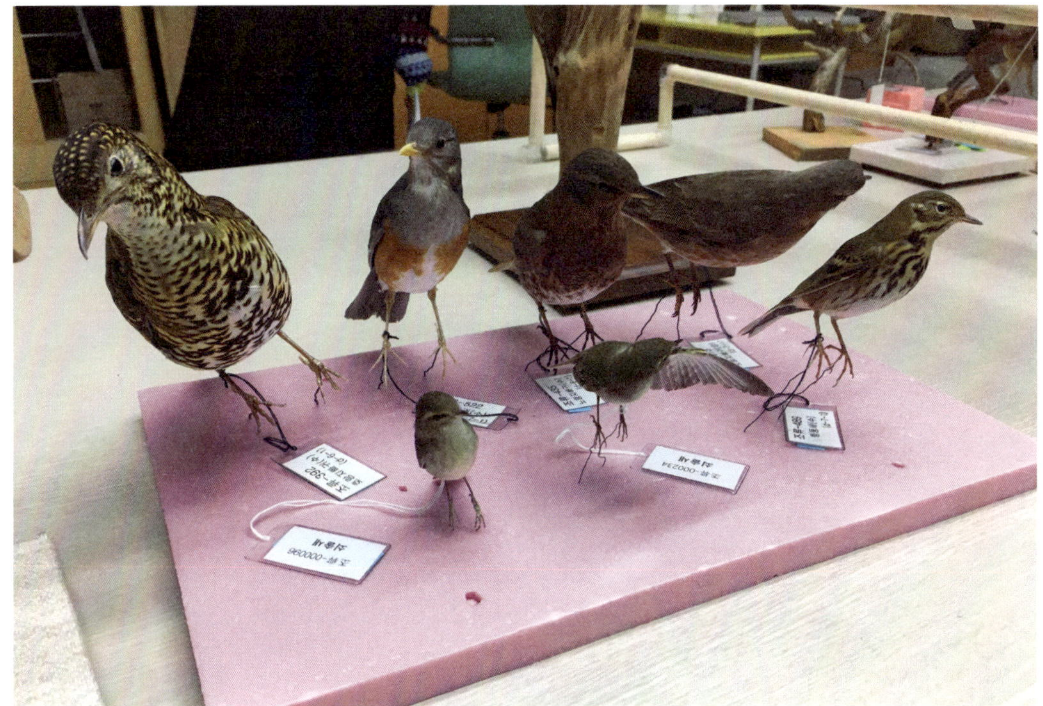

36

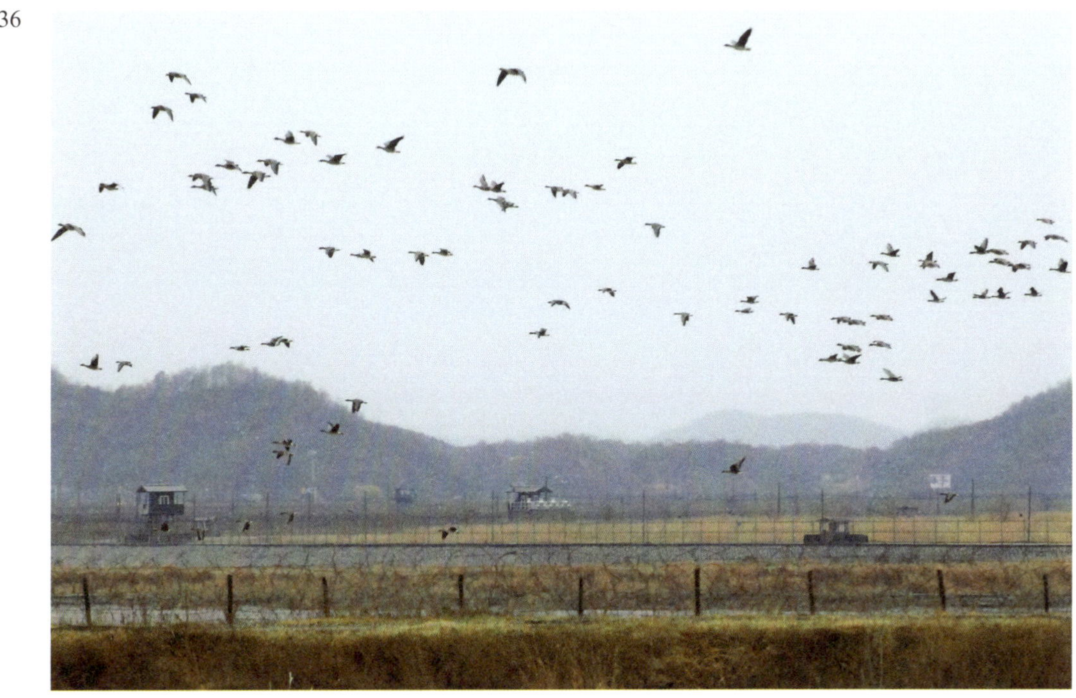

Fig. 35 Taxidermied birds from the collection of the Seodaemun Museum of Natural History, Seoul

Fig. 36 A flock of birds fly over barbed-wire fences near the 2.5-mile wide Demilitarized Zone (DMZ) dividing North and South Korea, 2006. Jung Yeon-Je / AFP

37

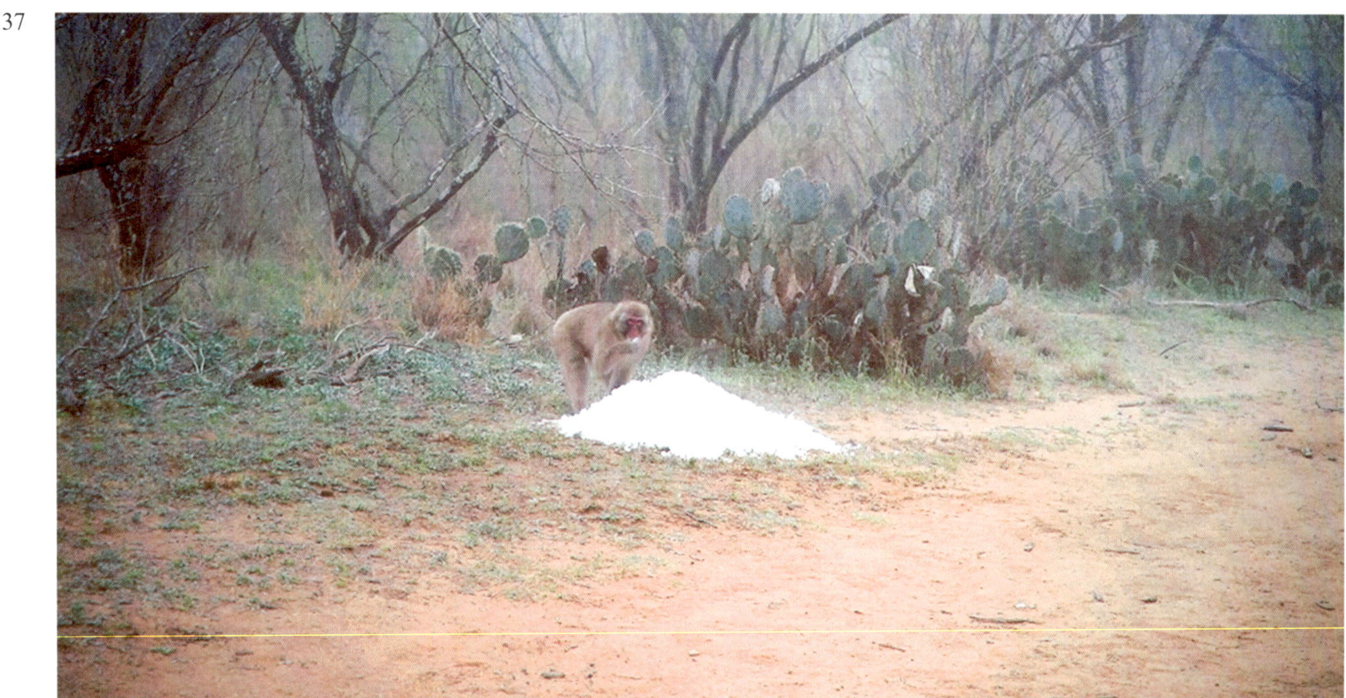

Fig. 37 Shimabuku, *Do snow monkeys remember snow mountains?*, 2016. Video still of HD video projection, vinyl wall text, 20 min., looped, edition of 3 + 2 artist proofs. Courtesy of Shimabuku

between the earth and sky for a thousand years. Symbolizing longevity, the *Inmyeonjo* is said to appear in times of peace as a symbol of unity (it most recently lit up the Twittersphere's puzzled users after appearing during the opening ceremony of the 2018 Winter Olympic Games in Pyeongchang [fig. 34]). The belief that birds are a conduit to an afterlife can be traced as far back as the period of the Three Kingdoms of Korea (57 BCE–668 CE), when mourners would bury their dead with "feathers of large birds; . . . from their desire to make the deceased fly up to heaven."[2] Moreover, in many Korean folktales, humans are reborn as crows, lesser cuckoos, seagulls, and bluebirds, typically after a protagonist's life has been tragically cut short.[3] Folktales posit the bird as a "divine animal that can travel between the celestial and terrestrial worlds, and between the world of gods and the world of humans,"[4] and to this day, it is common for Korean village entryways to be marked with *sotdae* or "spirit poles." These tall, carved wooden pillars are topped with sculpted ducks, which are deemed sacred as they "bridge the heavens and the earth."[5]

Yang's selection of the three DMZ birds was driven not by symbolic connotations specific to their species, but by practicalities: the artist chose her subjects from among those identified by their songs in the summit recording, narrowing the list based on the detail with which the birds could be scanned from taxidermized specimens available at the Seodaemun Museum of Natural History, Seoul (fig. 35) and, critically, the scale at which each could be 3D-printed as a single object, unbroken. Printed in translucent 3D resin, Yang's birds are not solid visual signs but ghostly apparitions. Meaning swirls around them rather than emanating clearly from within through specific readings. Yet, as artifacts of an epochal summit, these birds, and specifically the song that inspired them, can be read as metaphors for the yearning for freedom and healing. Perhaps no one seized upon birdsong as a means to speak of oppression more painfully and acutely than Paul Laurence Dunbar, whose poem *Sympathy* decries the reality of racism in the United States in the powerful and resonant line: "I know why the caged bird sings!"[6]

The *Migratory DMZ Birds on Asymmetric Lens* sculptures relinquish the anthropocentric worldview in favor of the ecocentric, in which our lives—however historic their circumstances might be—are provincialized. In doing so, the three sculptures force us to consider the nature/culture divide and specifically the questions that come to the fore when we privilege the natural over the human. The 2.5-mile-wide sliver of DMZ land that snakes from the Yellow Sea in the west to the Sea of Japan in the east has been virtually untouched for six decades, inadvertently establishing a lush wildlife sanctuary (fig. 36). Almost 160 bird species have been recorded here, accounting for more than fifty percent of the endangered bird species found on the Korean peninsula.[7] Especially important are the flocks of rare red-crowned cranes, considered by Koreans as harbingers of peace, longevity, and unity (their likeness appears on one denomination of the South Korean won coin). Their migrating patterns reflect the intertwinement of human and animal lives: just as North Koreans fled to the South during the famine between 1994 and 1998, so, too, were populations of cranes, vultures, and spoonbills—reliant on leftover crops—forced to the southern side of the DMZ amid the decline of food production in the north.[8] Ironically, while DMZ wildlife has thrived through generations of conflict, today environmentalists fear that peace will drive urbanization that will prove detrimental to the area.

In deprivileging the human narrative, Yang's *Migratory DMZ Birds on Asymmetric Lens* shares an affinity with French artist Pierre Huyghe's *Untitled (Human Mask)*. The film opens with drone footage shot in abandoned Fukushima, Japan, where, in 2011, the Daiichi nuclear power plant was rocked by the Tōhoku earthquake and tsunami, resulting in one of the most severe nuclear accidents to date. In a subsequent scene, a monkey in a girl's dress, its face concealed by a white Noh theater mask and a wig, roams about the interior of a darkened and emptied restaurant where she waits on absent customers, bringing hot towels and beverages. Both Yang and Huyghe tease at the inseparable link between our own and other species, alerting us to the ways in which our affairs play into a shared world.

Reflecting on his works, which have incorporated living things ranging from plants, bacteria, sea creatures, and dogs to humans, Huyghe characterized one of his core aims as not to "exhibit something to someone, but rather the reverse: to exhibit someone to something."[9] Both *Untitled (Human Mask)* and the three *Migratory DMZ Birds on Asymmetric Lens* sculptures surface the question of animal consciousness, and while Huyghe's film ponders the human-animal divide, Yang's sculptures turn to the issue of animal-animal relations. In viewing Yang's sculptures, we are compelled to imagine how they expose birds in the vicinity of the Clark's campus to the likenesses of bird species from the other side of the earth. Each 3D-printed resin element, although whole, comprises two elements: emerging from a cylinder of resin is a bisected bird's upper half, breast to beak, while its lower half, down to feet and tail, is submerged within the resin. While the upper body projects into positive space, the lower body's contours inscribe a negative space, forming a bird-shaped impression in the cylinder where rainwater might pool (see page 116). Describing this element, Yang reflected: "I was imagining [that] the native bird would swim or drink in this birdbath and encounter somehow the shade or transparent shape of the bird from the DMZ."[10] By staggering the bird's top half behind its bottom, Yang compressed its form within a narrow column, ensuring that any birdbath visitors would be face to face with their transparent hosts. Yang's sculptures pose a question: Would a local bird discern the 3D-printed likeness? Local varieties of warblers, tits, and thrushes all appear in Massachusetts, but would they recognize their DMZ cousins?

In probing these concerns with animal consciousness and intelligence, Yang's sculptures bring to mind Japanese artist Shimabuku's project *Do snow monkeys remember snow mountains?*, in which he documented a group of macaques confronted with a pile of ice (fig. 37). The monkeys, which had never experienced snow firsthand, descend from a group of eighty once relocated from around Kyoto to a Texas desert sanctuary in 1972. "Memory is a bridge between animals and people," Shimabuku noted.[11] Similarly to Yang's, his work projects our own preoccupations with cognition, memory, and consciousness into the animal realm. How can we understand reality from a nonhuman perspective? How do birds perceive the world and one another? While mammals (specifically primates, like Shimabuku's macaques) typically rank highest in tests of animal cognitive abilities, a recent series of experiments with ravens proved that some birds rival chimpanzees in their smarts.[12] And while avian species range in their intelligence, only magpies pass the mirror test, which establishes whether an animal is conscious of its own being.[13] Yang's sculptures stage an unknowable encounter, speculating on the meeting between the birds indigenous to Williamstown, Massachusetts, and their DMZ doppelgängers. The dividing line between "domestic" and "alien" Yang invokes gains particular resonance in light of the events that sparked her commission. Whom do we perceive as native or foreign? How do we define citizenship and national belonging? In his brief remarks at the summit, Kim Jong-un declared: "We, who live so close by, are not enemies that must fight against each other, but are more families that share the same bloodline, who must unite."[14]

Between 1965 and 1972, German artist Hans Haacke employed wind, water, plants, and animals in what he described as "systems" generated "with the explicit intention of having their components physically communicate with each other, and the whole communicate physically with the environment."[15] Haacke's systems unfolded before the viewer by demonstrating meteorological events or exploring animal life with chickens, goats, fish, and—in an unrealized work—a mynah bird (fig. 38). It is possible to inscribe Yang and *Migratory DMZ Birds on Asymmetric Lens* within a trajectory of artists including Haacke (as well as his peers Richard Budelis, and Helen and Newton Harrison) whose projects centered on the human/animal divide within an expanded environment. These concerns have recently been revived with renewed vigor by a generation of artists less interested in challenging an artwork's ontology and framing than in examining legacies of economic exchange and colonialism (Candice Lin) or embodiment vis-à-vis queer politics, feminism, and race (Jes Fan, WangShui, Anicka Yi), or in confronting the anthropocentric worldview (Pierre Huyghe, Philippe Parreno). The *Migratory DMZ Birds on Asymmetric Lens* series shares most with the latter and focuses on what French curator and critic Nicolas Bourriaud calls the "crisis of the human scale."[16] Drawing on

38

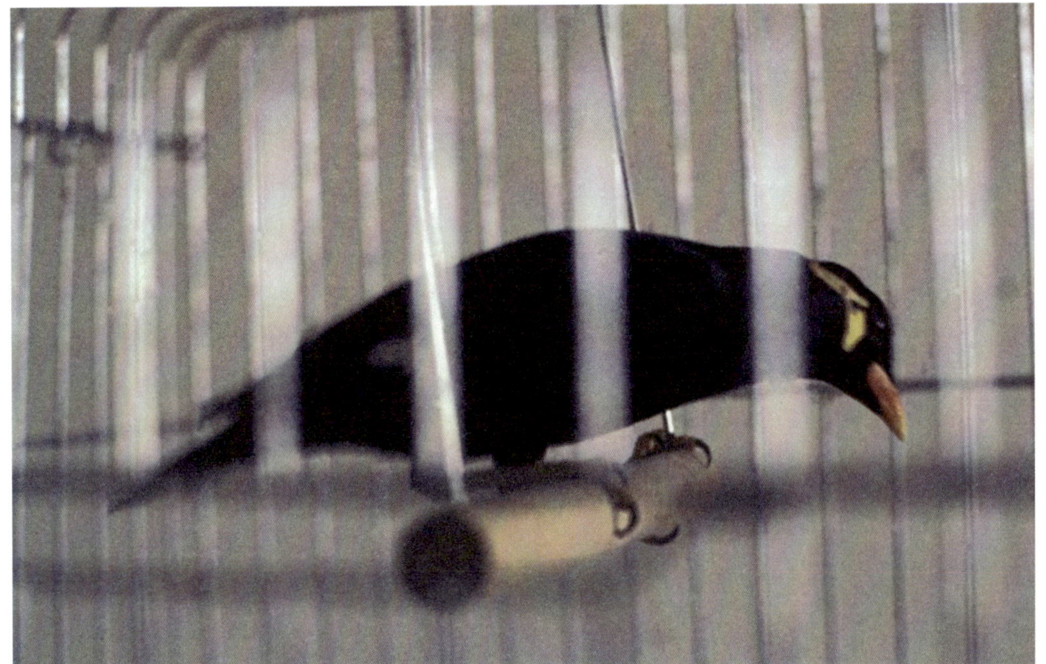

39

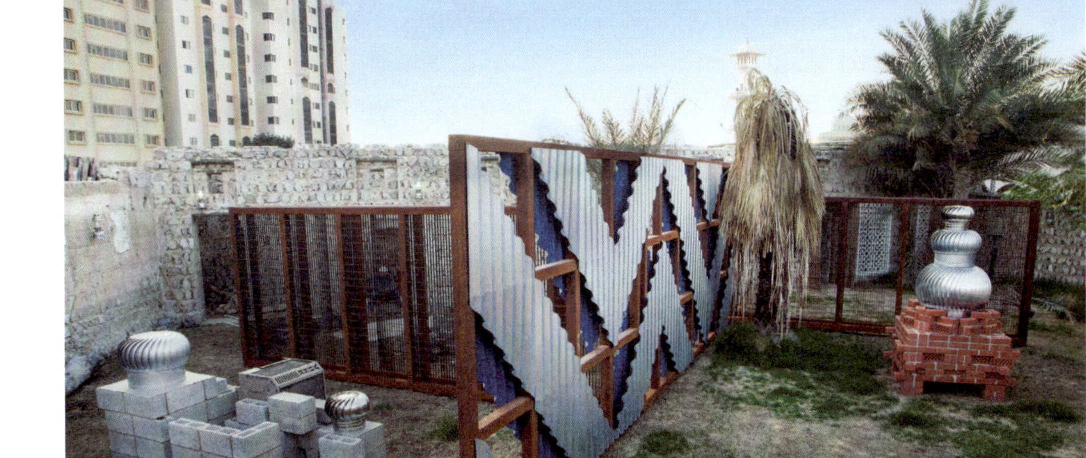

Fig. 38 Hans Haacke, *Norbert: 'All Systems Go'*, 1970–71. Unfinished project, photograph of the mynah bird Hans Haacke attempted to teach to say: "All systems go." © Hans Haacke / VG Bild-Kunst, Bonn. Courtesy of the artist and Paula Cooper Gallery, New York

Fig. 39 Haegue Yang, *An Opaque Wind*. Installation view from *Sharjah Biennial 12: The past, the present, the possible*, 2015. Site-specific installation, dimensions variable. Commissioned by Sharjah Art Foundation. Courtesy of the artist

the writings of philosophers Levi Bryant, Graham Harman, and Bruno Latour, Bourriaud points toward an equivalence forged between the elemental, mineral, plant, animal, and human in the name of "co-activity"[17] that shatters the subject/object divide and removes the human from the privileged center of our worldview. Yang's sculptures force us to question our own role in the natural order, positioning us as mere bystanders to an imagined avian encounter. It is a humbling prospect: to deprivilege our own existence—along with its suffering, conflicts, and wars—in the name of a worldview in which, as Bourriaud notes, relationships are made "horizontal" rather than "unidirectional."[18]

The *Migratory DMZ Birds on Asymmetric Lens* sculptures represent a turn toward new methods of fabrication within Yang's oeuvre, which includes only a handful of outdoor works to date. While always site-responsive and temporary, like the Clark sculptures, Yang's previous works typically combined ready-made materials. *An Opaque Wind*, for example, first realized in Sharjah, United Arab Emirates (2015), and then manifested anew in New York (2016) and Porto, Portugal (2016), consists of industrial vents affixed to bricks and breezeblocks in architectural arrangements that nod toward the Middle Eastern windcatcher towers that had originally inspired Yang (fig. 39). In dwelling on the natural world, the *Migratory DMZ Birds on Asymmetric Lens* are a closer relative to *Tectonic Texture* (2012), made for the outdoor exhibition *Sense and Sustainability* in the quarries of Andrabide in Basque country, Spain. That sculpture consists of a square stack of Ereño marble, Nero crystal, and carved sandstone slabs, each quarried locally and pockmarked with marine molluscs from the Cretaceous period[19]—a meditation on the immeasurability of time, but also our own reliance on nature in service of industry, urbanization, and "progress."

While *Tectonic Texture* employed a degree of mediation, hewn, according to the artist's specifications, with machinery and finished by a mason's touch, the Clark sculptures' production completely replaced the human hand with an automated production process. Each soapstone lens was robotically milled according to a digital rendering, whereby the stone was gradually stripped to give way to its final sculpted shape. Inscribed upon the soapstone—the surface of which changes color depending on the degree of moisture in the air—are a range of references to geographical coordinates (of the Clark Art Institute and the DMZ), sculptural processes, weather events, and bird species. Some words harken back to the inter-Korean summit (unification, resolution), while others veer into the hermetic or poetic (devastation, interlocking, lunar lush). The 3D-printed resin, on the other hand, was generated through the additive process of accumulating layers of biocompatible resin. The relationship between the additive and subtractive modes of fabrication is just one of the many binaries that Yang's three *Migratory DMZ Birds on Asymmetric Lens* sculptures tease at. Chiefly, the commission contemplates the nature/culture divide, yet many other dualities are alluded to: the object and its base, the positive and negative spaces of the 3D resin element, the resonant birdsong and its translation into soundless stone and resin, the deeper versus finer grooves marking each base, as well as the deep geologic time embodied in the soapstone versus the brand-new status of the 3D-printing technology. By embracing the tension between opposites, the sculptures celebrate, as the artist has put it: "coexisting differences."[20] Interspersed among the landscape and never seen simultaneously, the three works speak to fragmentation and plurality, rather than fixed or singular meaning, an emphasis especially relevant to some of the core concerns underscoring the work—particularly identity, nationality, and migration.

Despite their distinctions, underscoring all of Yang's outdoor works is a shared engagement with geometric symbolism. The top slab of *Tectonic Texture* (fig. 40) is carved with hand imprints as well as swirls of a local mason's own choosing, while the layout of *An Opaque Wind* references the role of hexagons in Islamic art and architecture (fig. 41). Similarly, each stone form supporting one of the DMZ birds is an asymmetric take on the *vesica piscis* ("bladder of the fish"), a perfectly symmetrical almond-shaped lens made by overlapping two identical circles (see fig. 17). Yang arrived at a similar form by tinkering with digital rendering software, only to realize afterward its symbolic connotations across cultures. A form of

40

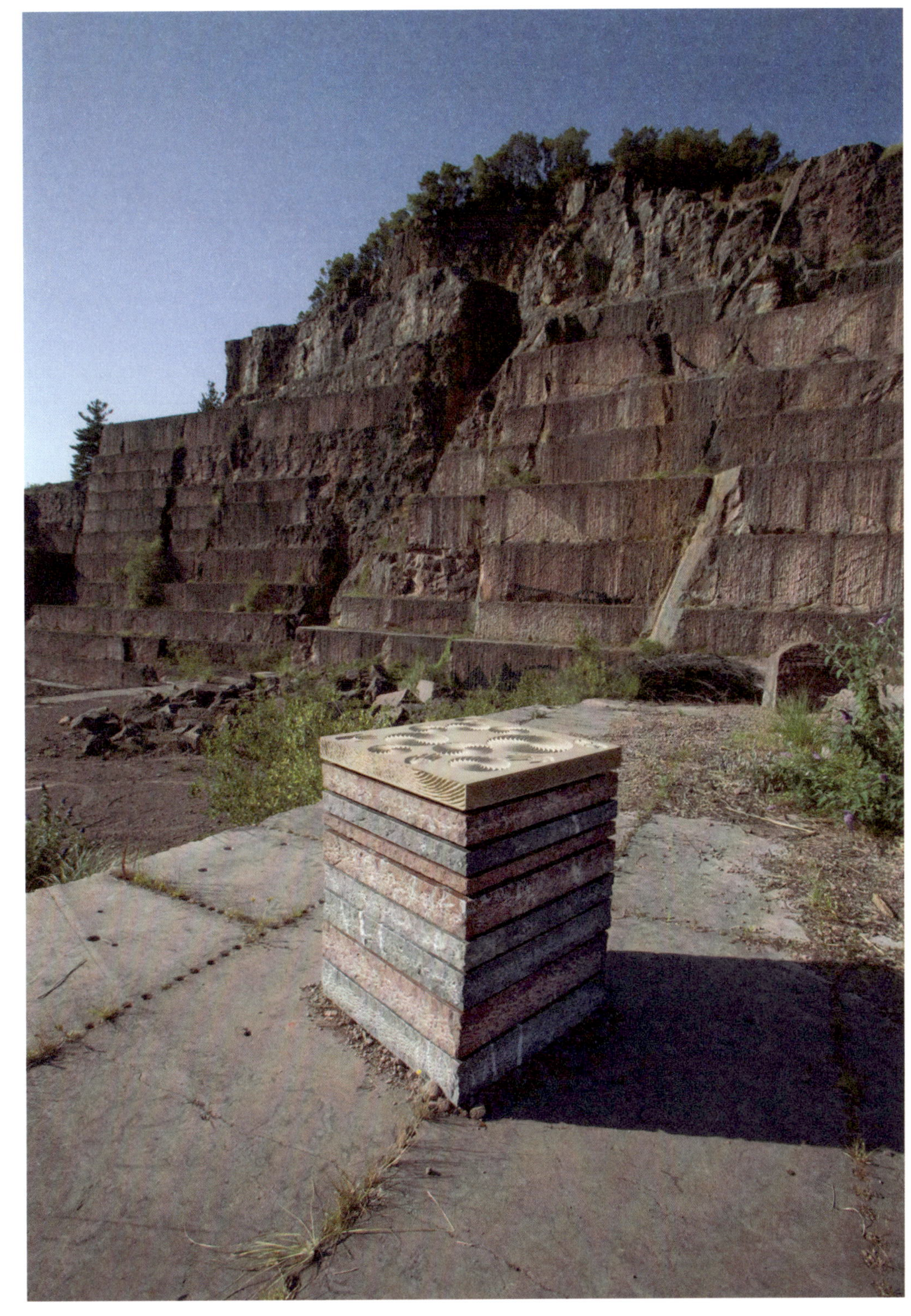

Fig. 40 Haegue Yang, *Tectonic Texture*, 2012. Installation view from *Urdaibai Art 2012: Sense and Sustainability*. Ereño marble, Nero crystal, carved sandstone, 53 1/4 x 31 1/2 x 31 1/2 in. (135 x 80 x 80 cm). Andrabide Quarries, Gautegiz-Arteaga, Basque country, Spain. Courtesy of the artist

sacred geometry, the *vesica piscis* is commonly used in Christian iconography, for example, where it "may signify Christ Incarnate, who mediates heaven and earth, or humanity and the divine."[21] It would seem auspicious that Yang arrived at a shape so rich in spiritual meaning by happenstance. While anchored within our terrestrial reality, her three sculptures, which the artist purposefully scattered across three unique sites on the grounds of the Clark, prod at the limits of our knowledge and experience. They make apparent not only the forces by which we knowingly shape our surroundings, but also the consequence of our actions taken unwittingly. The *Migratory DMZ Birds on Asymmetric Lens* invite us to imagine a reality beyond our familiar one, seen from the perspective of a bird, a migrant, a foreigner.

*Pavel S. Pyś is curator of visual arts at the Walker Art Center.*

1 See "Gmach Technologii Chemicznej Politechniki Warszawskiej" entry on warszawa1939.pl, a website devoted to the history of Warsaw before World War II, published by the Warszawa1939.pl Foundation (available online, in Polish).

2 Inoue Hideo et al., trans., *Seishi tōiden, Higashi Ajia minzokushi*, 1 (Tokyo: Heibonsha, 1974), 273, quoted in Kazuo Matsumura, *Mythical Thinkings: What Can We Learn from Comparative Mythology?* (Frankston, AU: Countershock Press, 2014), 60.

3 For example, in the *jeopdongsae* stories, the lesser cuckoo's sorrowful song is believed to belong to a young woman who met an untimely death.

4 "Legends: Lesser Cuckoo," in Kungnip Minsok Pangmulgwan, *Encyclopaedia of Korean Folk Literature* (Seoul: National Folk Museum of Korea, 2014), 169.

5 "Sotdae," in Myŏng-sŏp Chŏng, ed., *Encyclopaedia of Korean Folk Beliefs* (Seoul: National Folk Museum of Korea, 2013), 186.

6 See Paul Laurence Dunbar, "Sympathy," in *The Collected Poetry of Paul Laurence Dunbar* (Charlottesville: University of Virginia Press, 1993), 102.

7 See John McMahon, "Twitchers at the DMZ: Birdwatching Near the World's Most Dangerous Border," *Remote Lands*, May 23, 2019, http://www.remotelands.com/travelogues/twitchers-at-the-dmz-birdwatching-at-the-worlds-most-dangerous-border/.

8 See Eleana J. Kim, "Flyways," *Society for Cultural Anthropology*, June 27, 2018, http://culanth.org/fieldsights/flyways.

9 Pierre Huyghe, quoted on the exhibition page for *Pierre Huyghe: Uumwelt*, Serpentine Galleries, accessed January 3, 2021, http://www.serpentinegalleries.org/whats-on/pierre-huyghe-uumwelt/.

10 Haegue Yang, "Migratory DMZ Birds on Asymmetric Lens," SoundCloud audio, Clark Art Institute, 5:42, http://www.clarkart.edu/microsites/ground-work/about-the-projects/haegue-yang. Edited from an interview conducted by Molly Epstein and Abigail Ross Goodman, recorded June 23, 2020.

11 Shimabuku, quoted in Kealey Boyd, "In 1972, Snow Monkeys Were Sent to a Texas Desert. Do They Still Remember Snow?," *Hyperallergic*, January 31, 2019, http://hyperallergic.com/482339/shimabuku-do-snow-monkeys-remember-snow-at-denver-art-museum/.

12 See Rachel Nuwer, "Young Ravens Rival Adult Chimps in a Big Test of General Intelligence," *Scientific American*, December 10, 2020, http://www.scientificamerican.com/article/young-ravens-rival-adult-chimps-in-a-big-test-of-general-intelligence/.

13 See Richard Gross, *Being Human: Psychological and Philosophical Perspectives* (Abingdon-on-Thames, UK: Taylor and Francis, 2013), 82.

14 Kim Jong-un, quoted in a transcript from the 2018 inter-Korean summit published within "At Summit, Kim Jong Un *[sic]* Pledges to Not Repeat 'Unfortunate History,'" *PBS New Hour*, April 27, 2018, http://www.pbs.org/newshour/show/at-summit-kim-jong-un-pledges-to-not-repeat-unfortunate-history.

15 Hans Haacke, quoted in the exhibition brochure for *Hans Haacke: 1967*, held at the MIT List Visual Arts Center, October 21–December 31, 2011, accessed January 3, 2021, http://listart.mit.edu/sites/default/files/Haacke_ed_brochure.pdf.

16 Nicolas Bourriaud, "Politics of the Anthropocene: Humans, Things and Reification in Contemporary Art," lecture, Modern Art Museum of Fort Worth, May 15, 2015, SoundCloud audio, 1:20:24, http://www.themodern.org/podcast/politics-anthropocene-humans-things-and-reification-contemporary-art-presented-nicolas.

17 For further context, see Nicolas Bourriaud, "Coactivity: Between Human and Nonhuman," Flash Art, no. 326, June–August 2019, http://flash---art.com/article/coactivity-between-the-human-and-nonhuman/.

18 Bourriaud, "Politics of the Anthropocene."

19 For an analysis of *Tectonic Texture*, see Max Andrews, "Stack of Evidence: Haegue Yang," in *Sense and Sustainability: Reading*, Urdaibai Arte, Fundación 2012 Fundazioa, July 19, 2012, available online, Latitudes website, http://www.lttds.org/assets/Yang_Andrews.pdf.

20 Haegue Yang, "Migratory DMZ Birds on Asymmetric Lens," SoundCloud audio, Clark Art Institute, 5:42, http://www.clarkart.edu/microsites/ground-work/about-the-projects/haegue-yang. Edited from an interview conducted by Molly Epstein and Abigail Ross Goodman, recorded June 23, 2020.

21 Rachel Fletcher, "Musings on the Vesica Piscis," *Nexus Network Journal* 6, no. 2 (2004): 97.

41

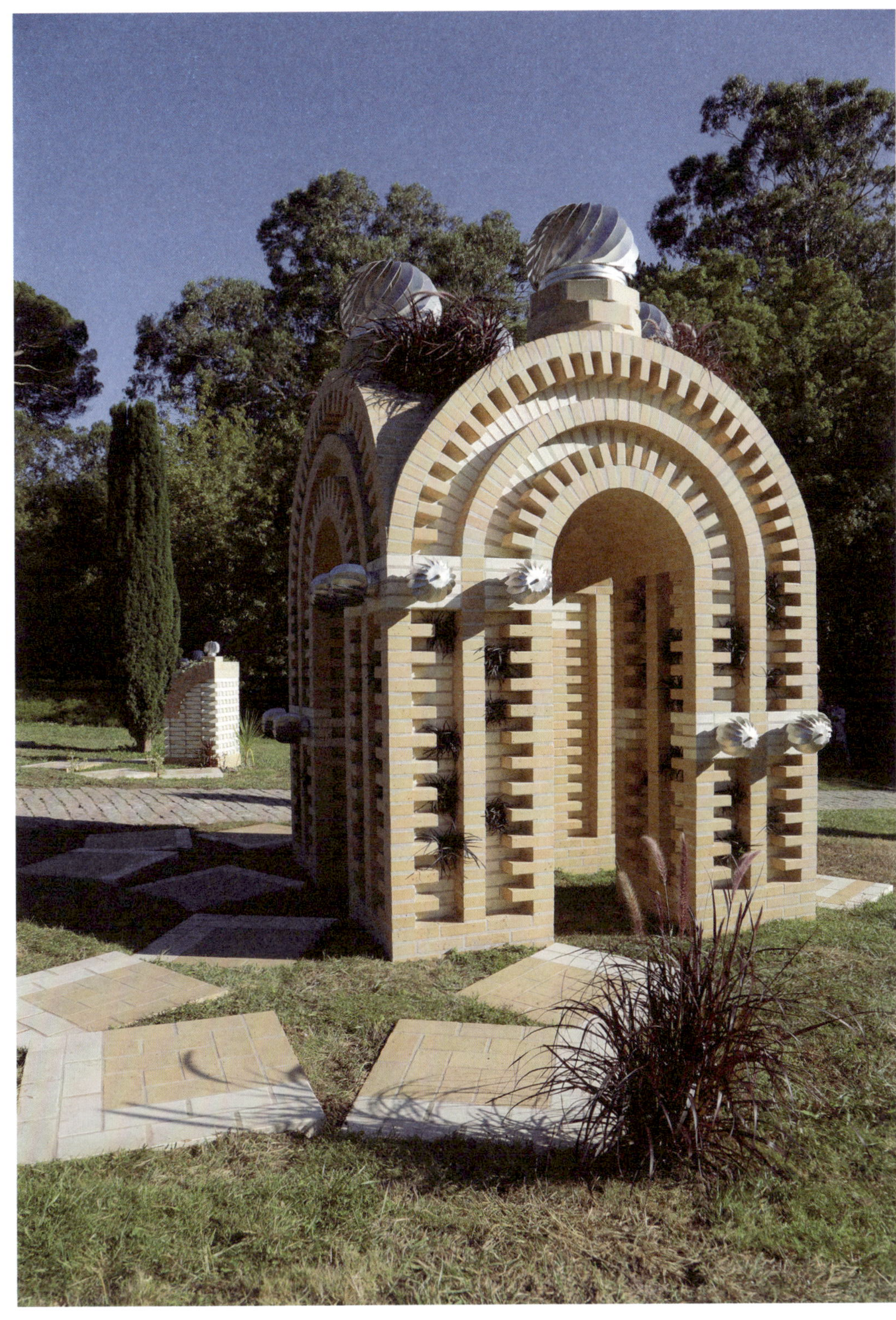

Fig. 41 Haegue Yang, *An Opaque Wind Park in Six Folds* (installation view), 2016. Clay bricks, mortar, turbine vents, steel, soil, stone, cork, various plants, 125 1/4 x 696 1/2 x 485 1/2 in. (318 x 1769 x 1233 cm). Serralves Museum of Contemporary Art, Porto, Portugal

*Migratory DMZ Birds on Asymmetric Lens – Tee-Cher Tee-Cher Vessel (Great Tit)*
pp. 96, 111, 113, 115, 128

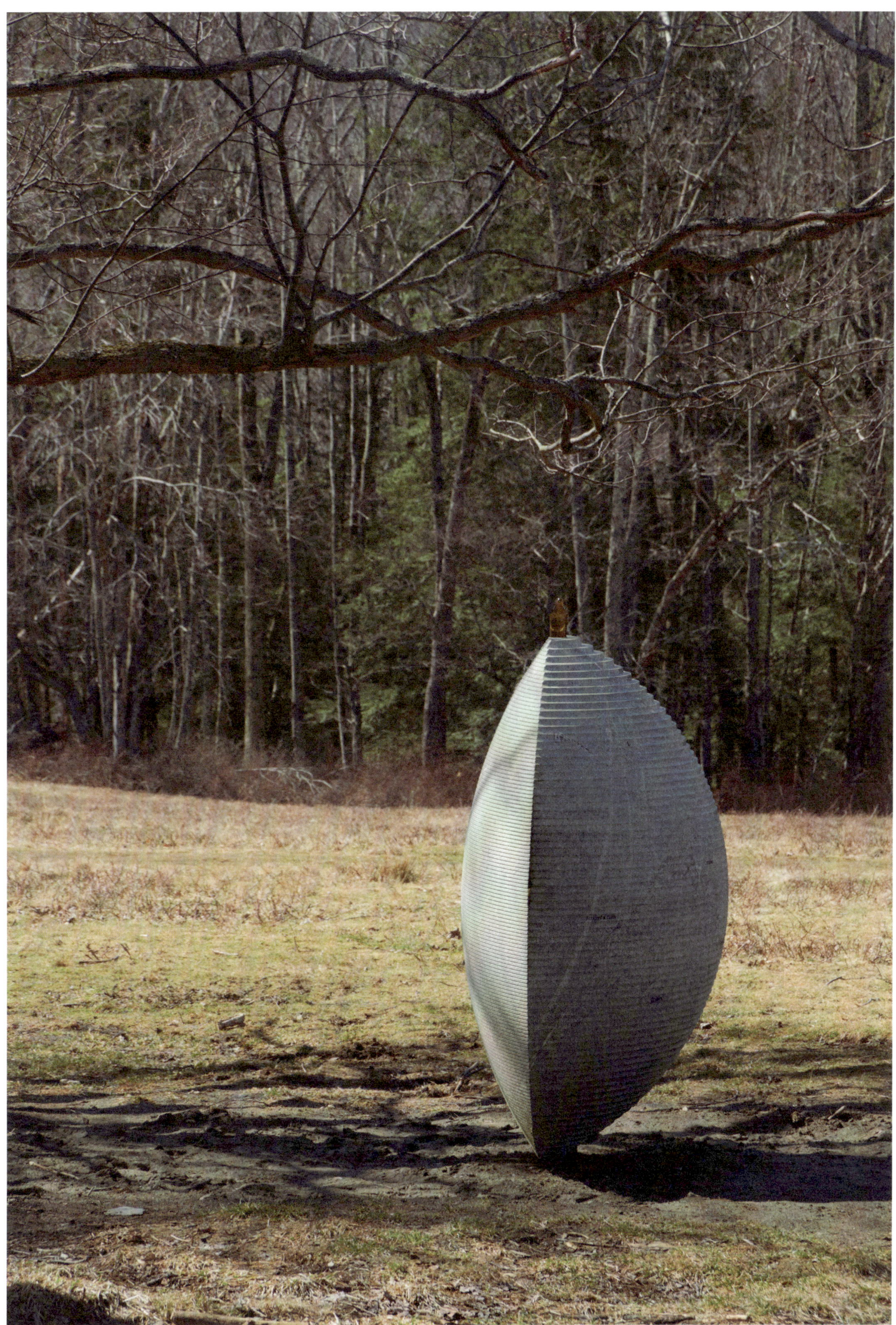

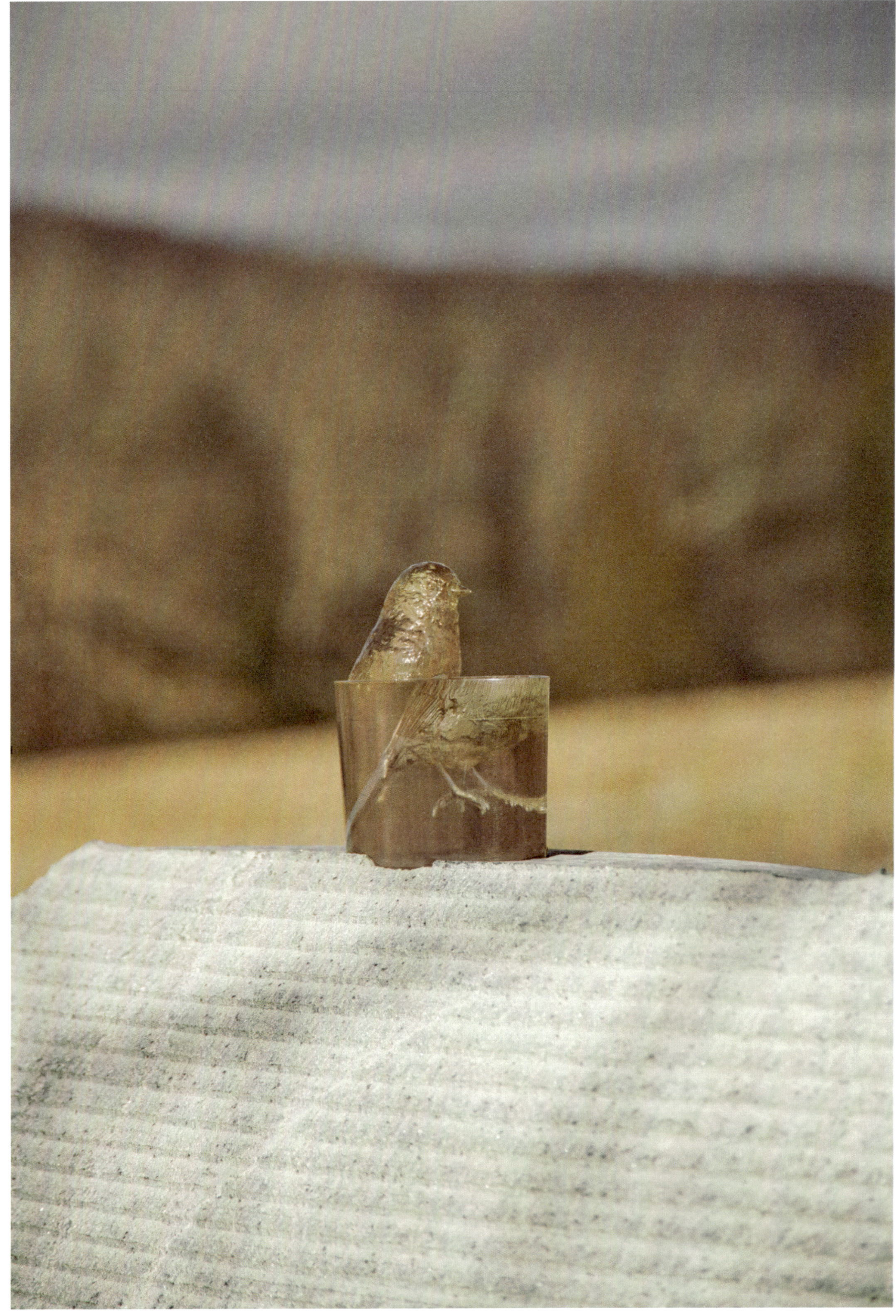

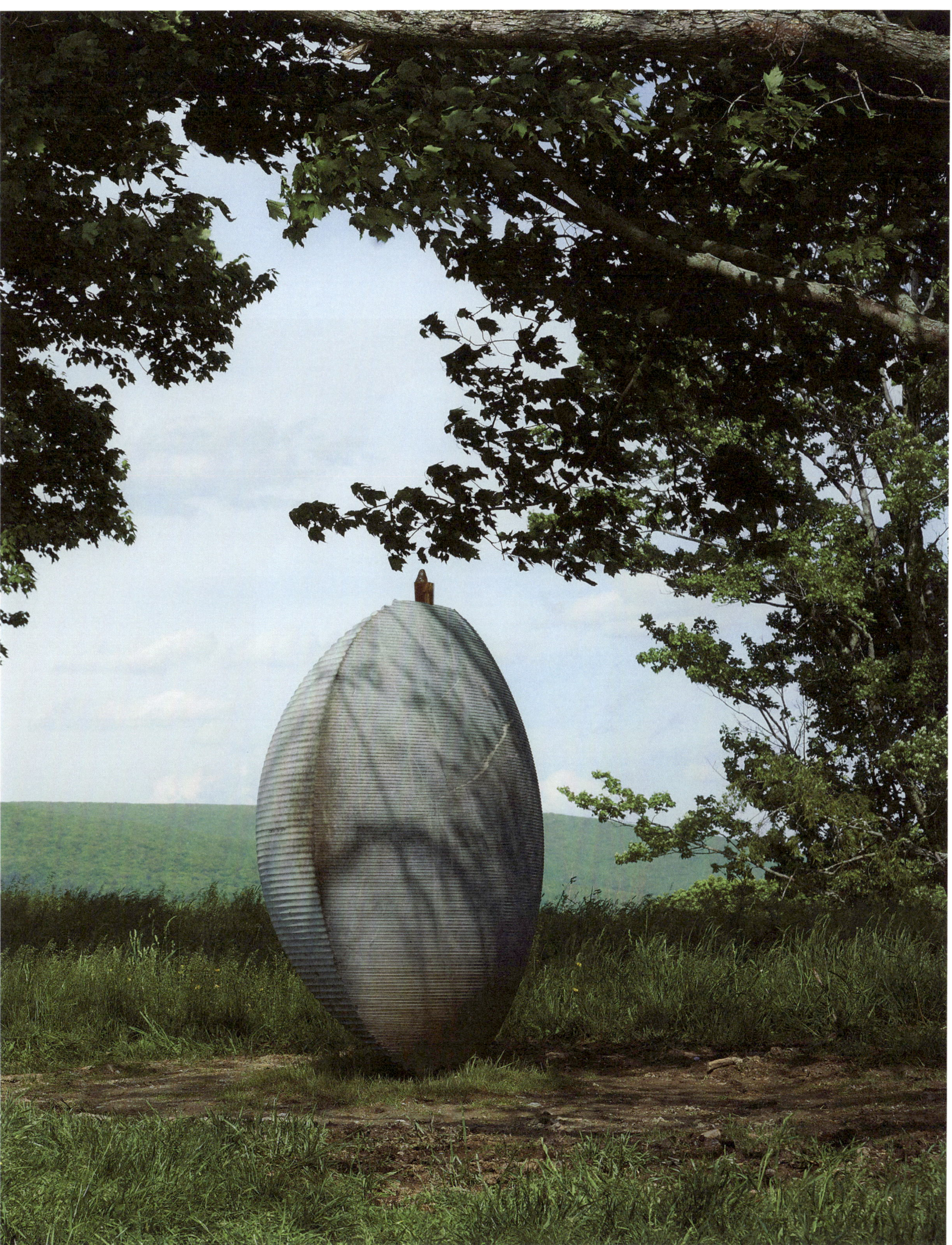

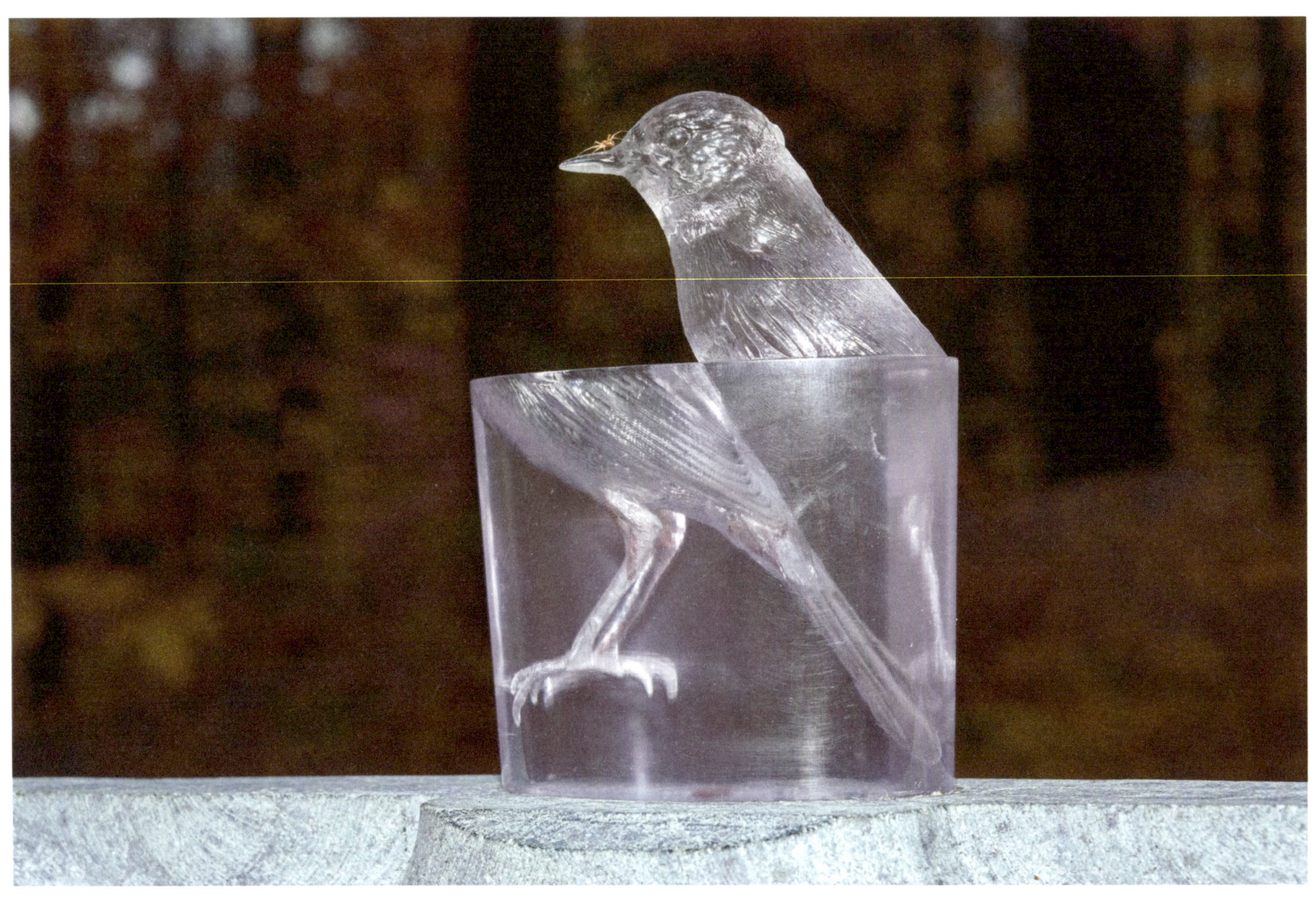

*Migratory DMZ Birds on Asymmetric Lens – Hou-Ke-Kyo Vessel (Japanese Bush Warbler)*
pp. 116–117, 119, 121, 130

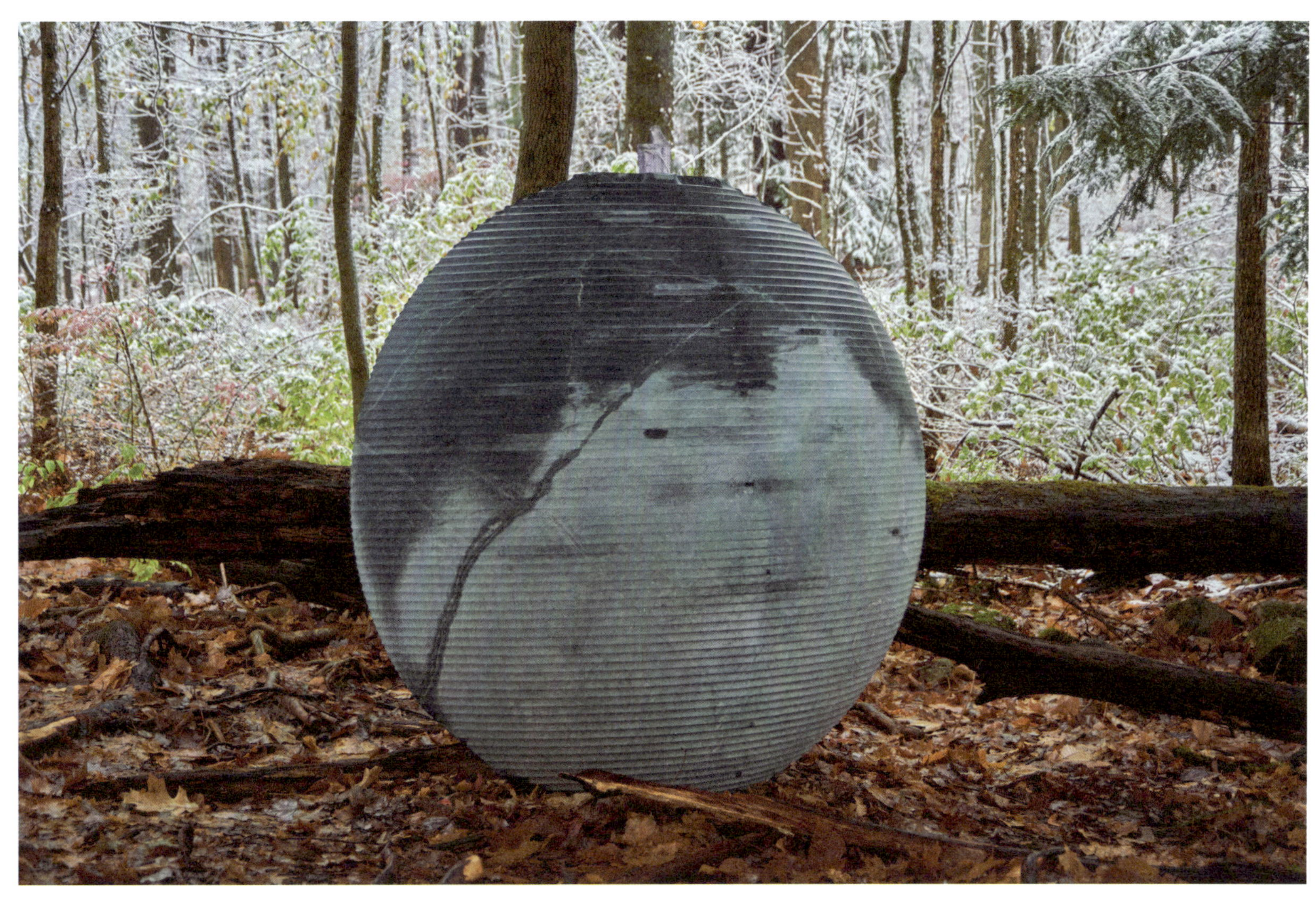

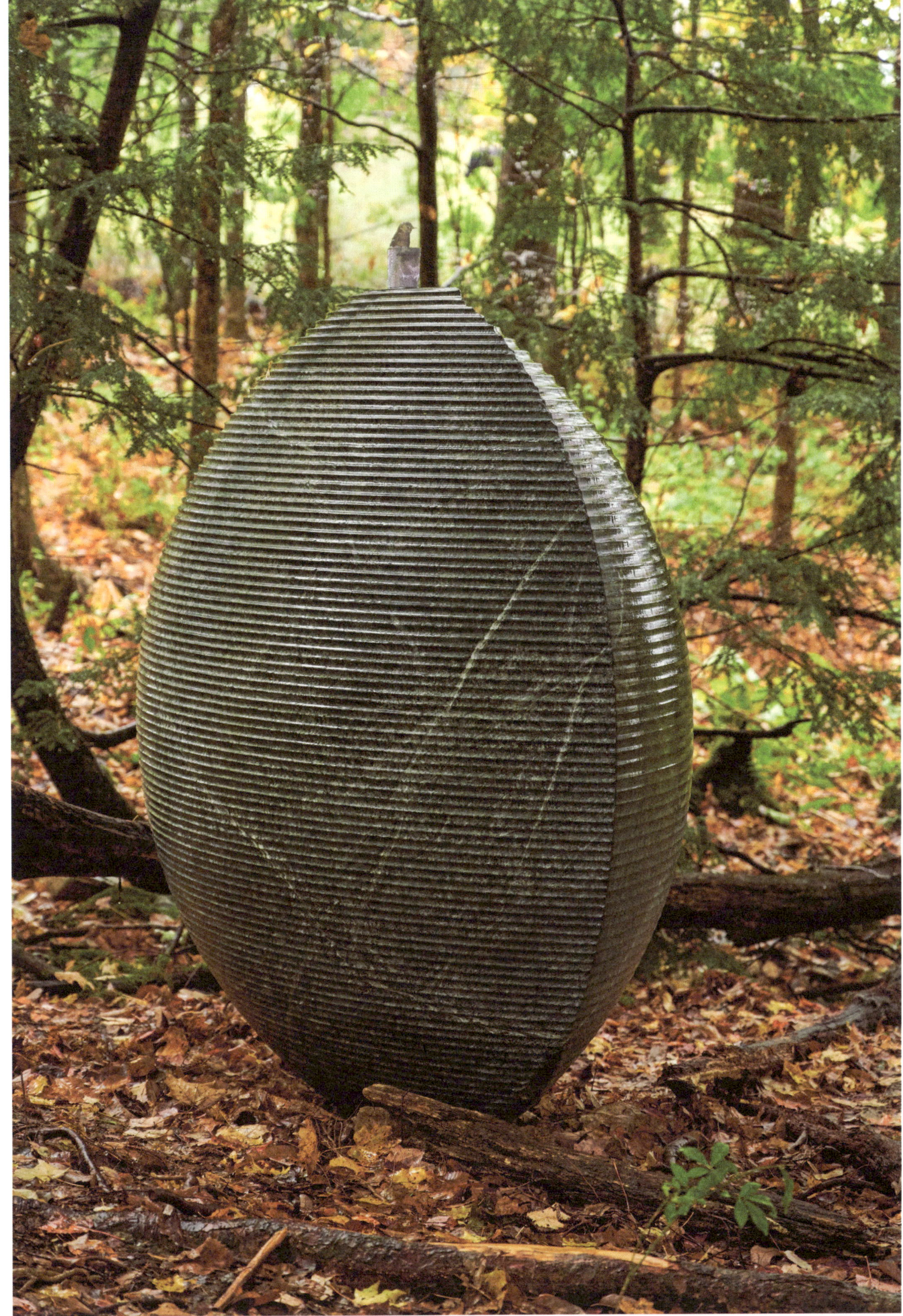

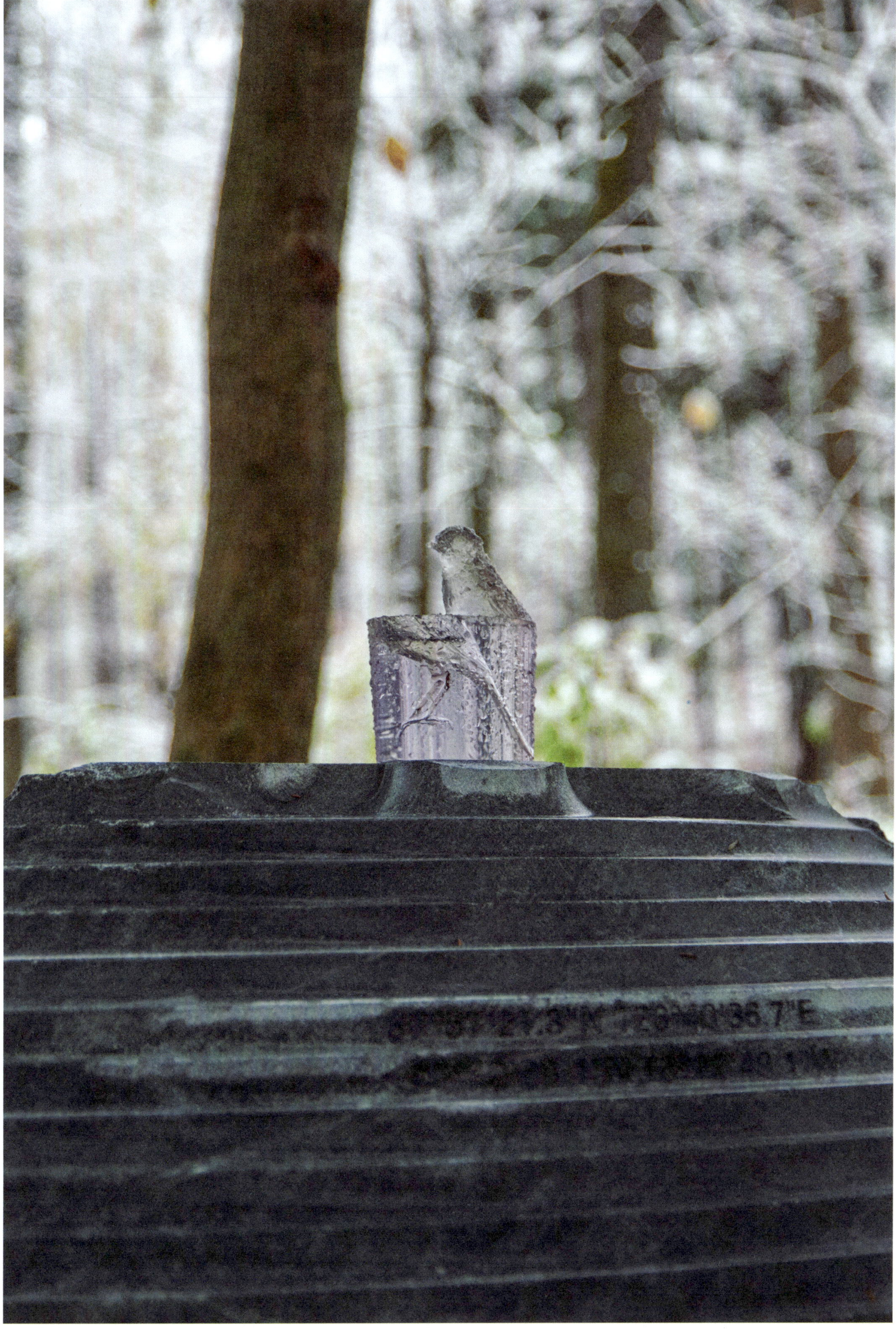

*Migratory DMZ Birds on Asymmetric Lens – Duiitt Duiitt Vessel (Gray-Backed Thrush)*
pp. 123, 125, 127, 132

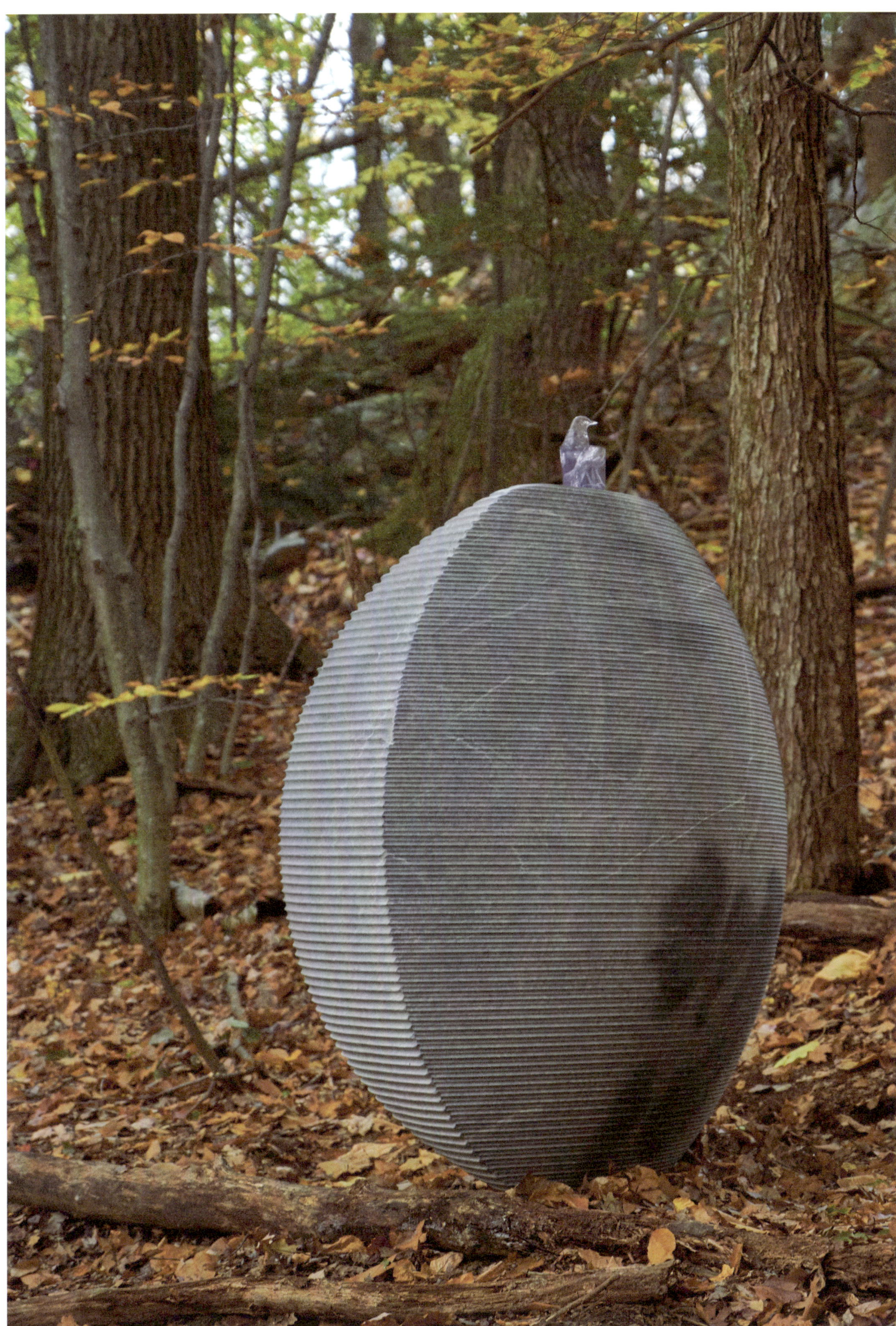

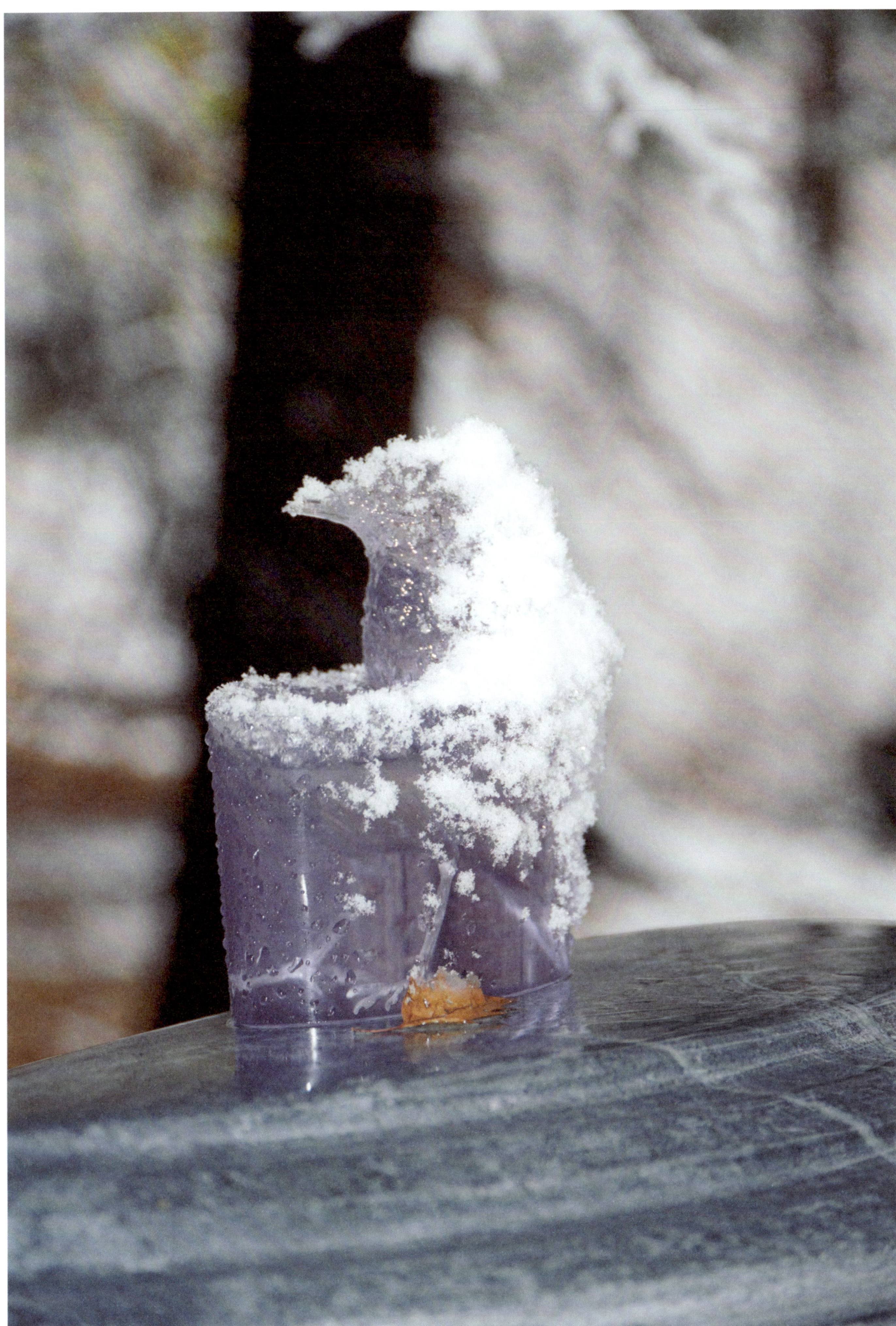

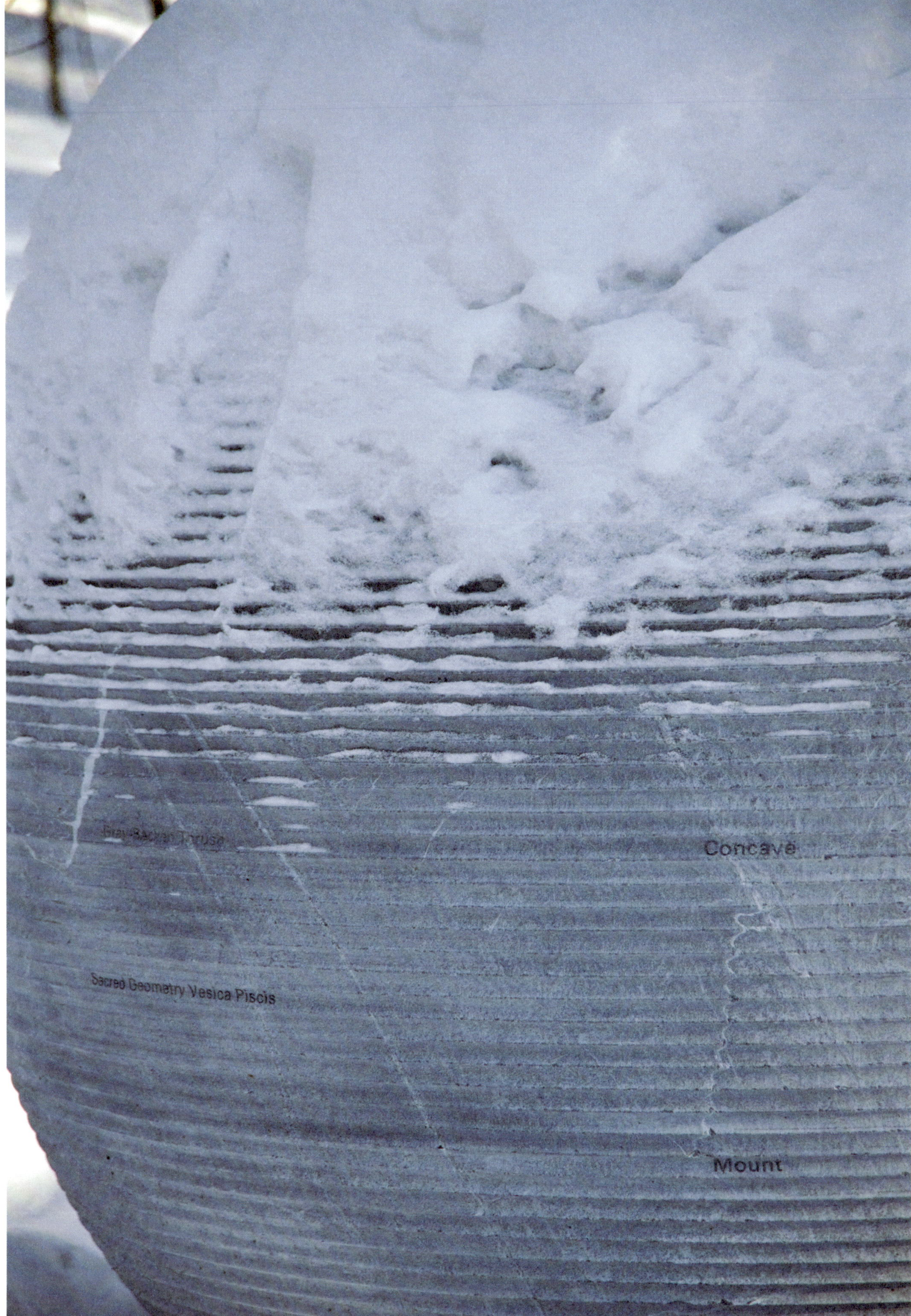
Concave
Sacred Geometry Vesica Piscis
Mount

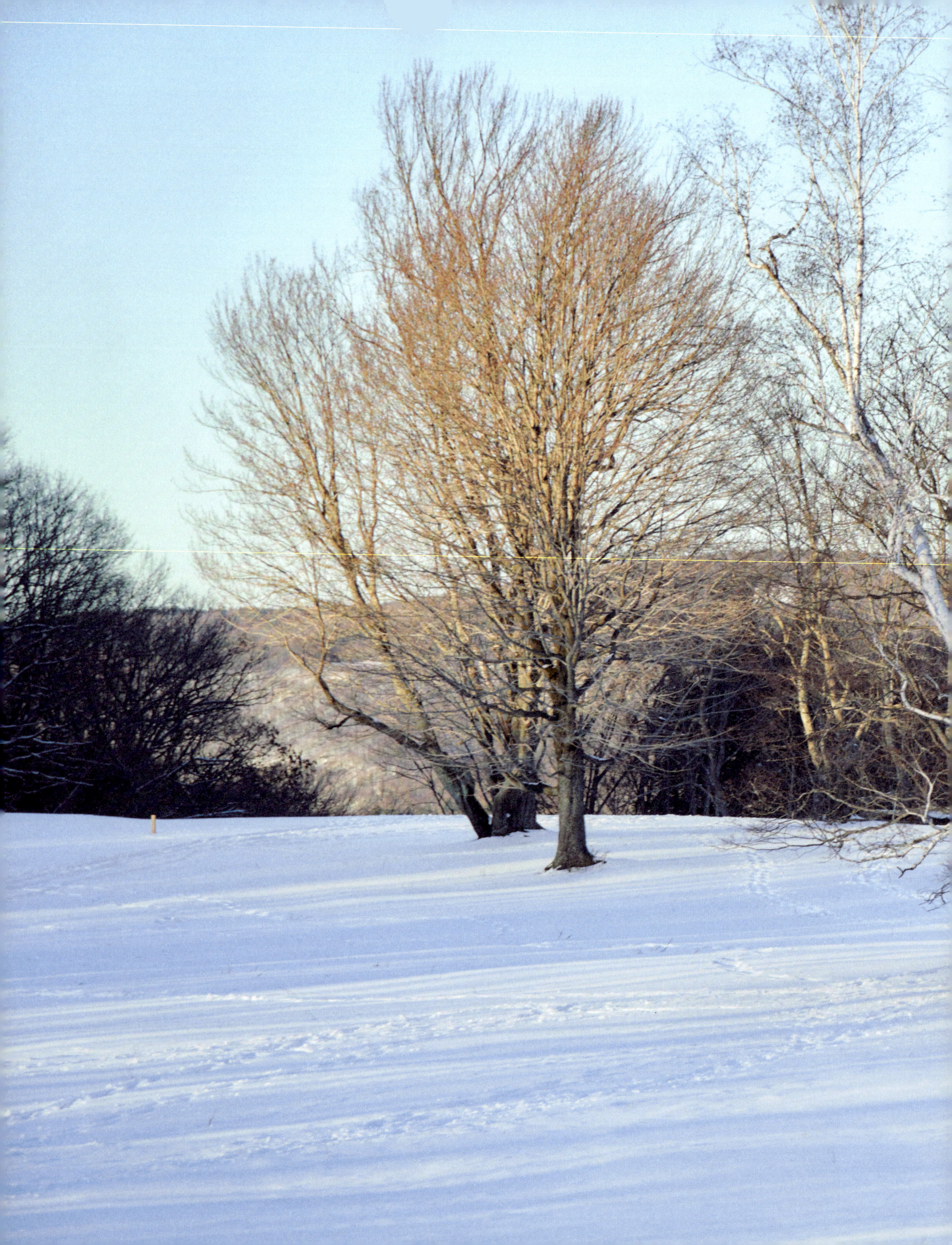

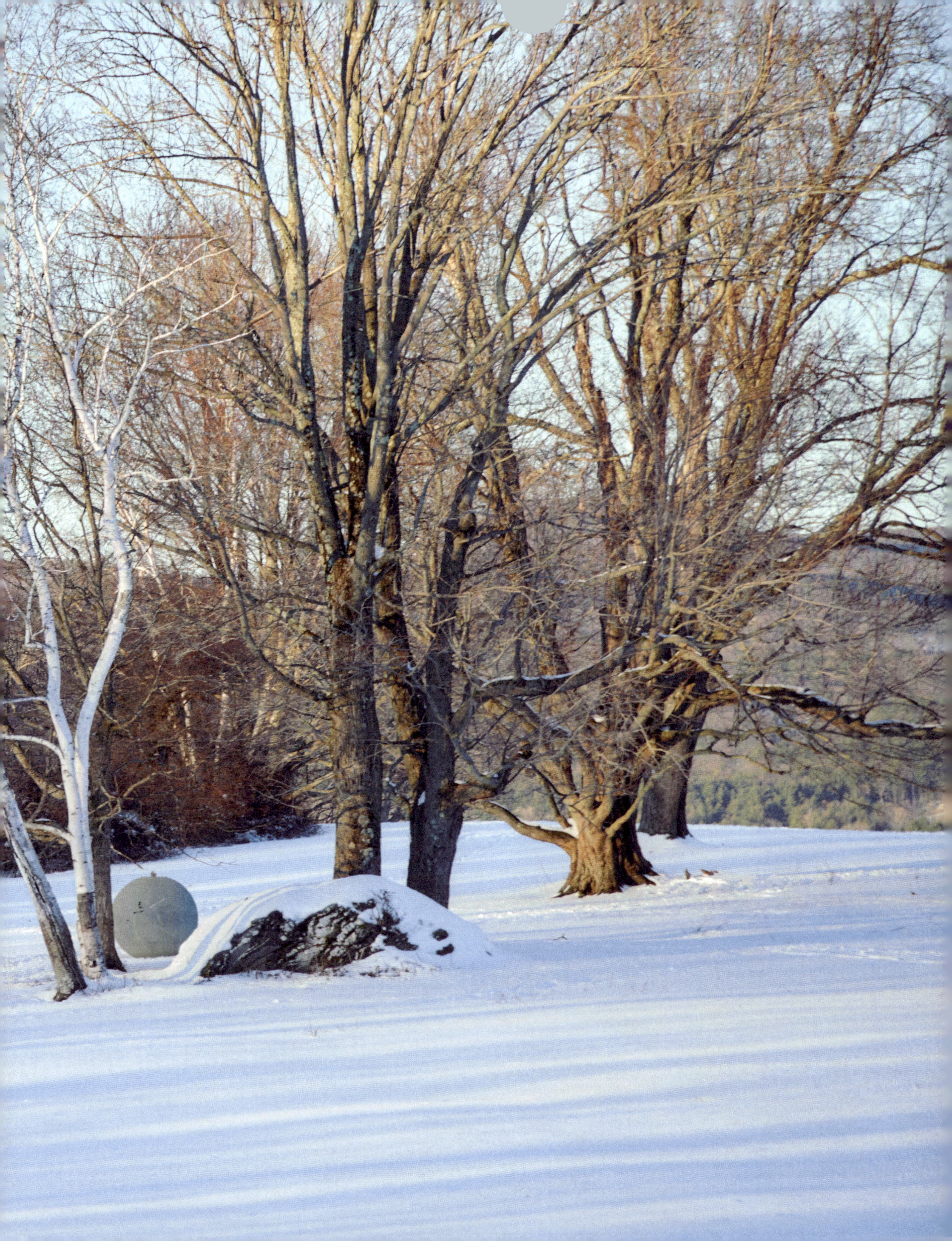

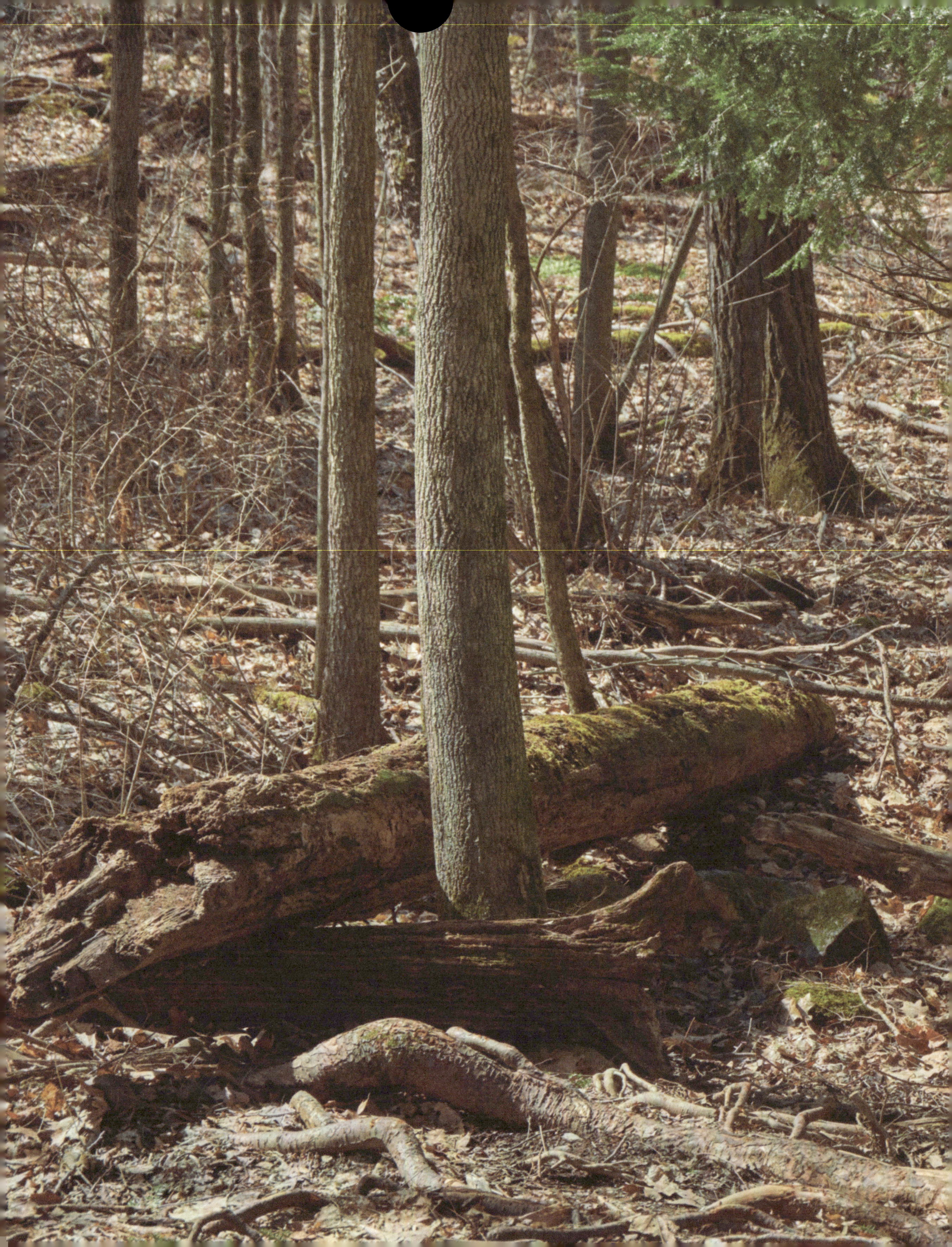

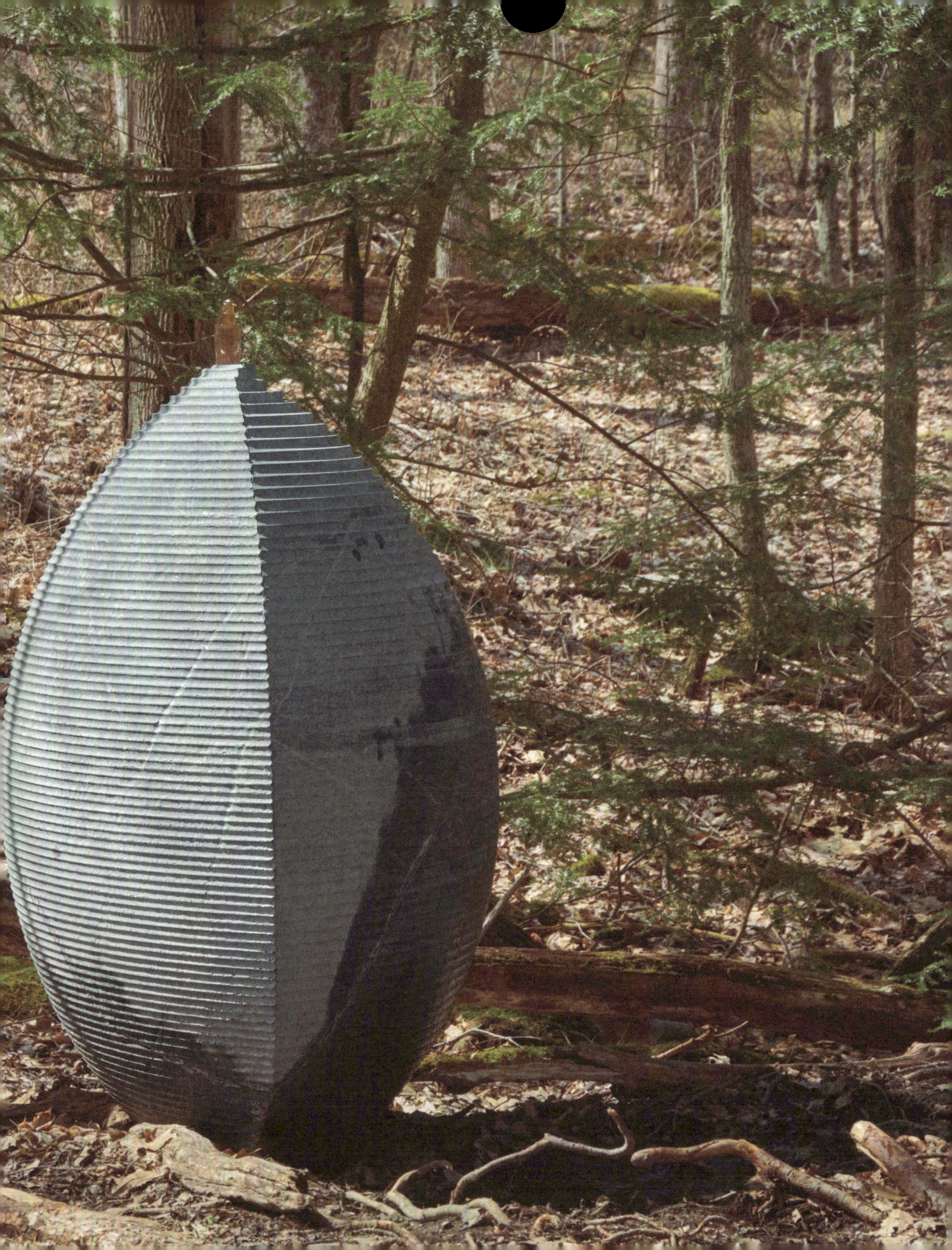

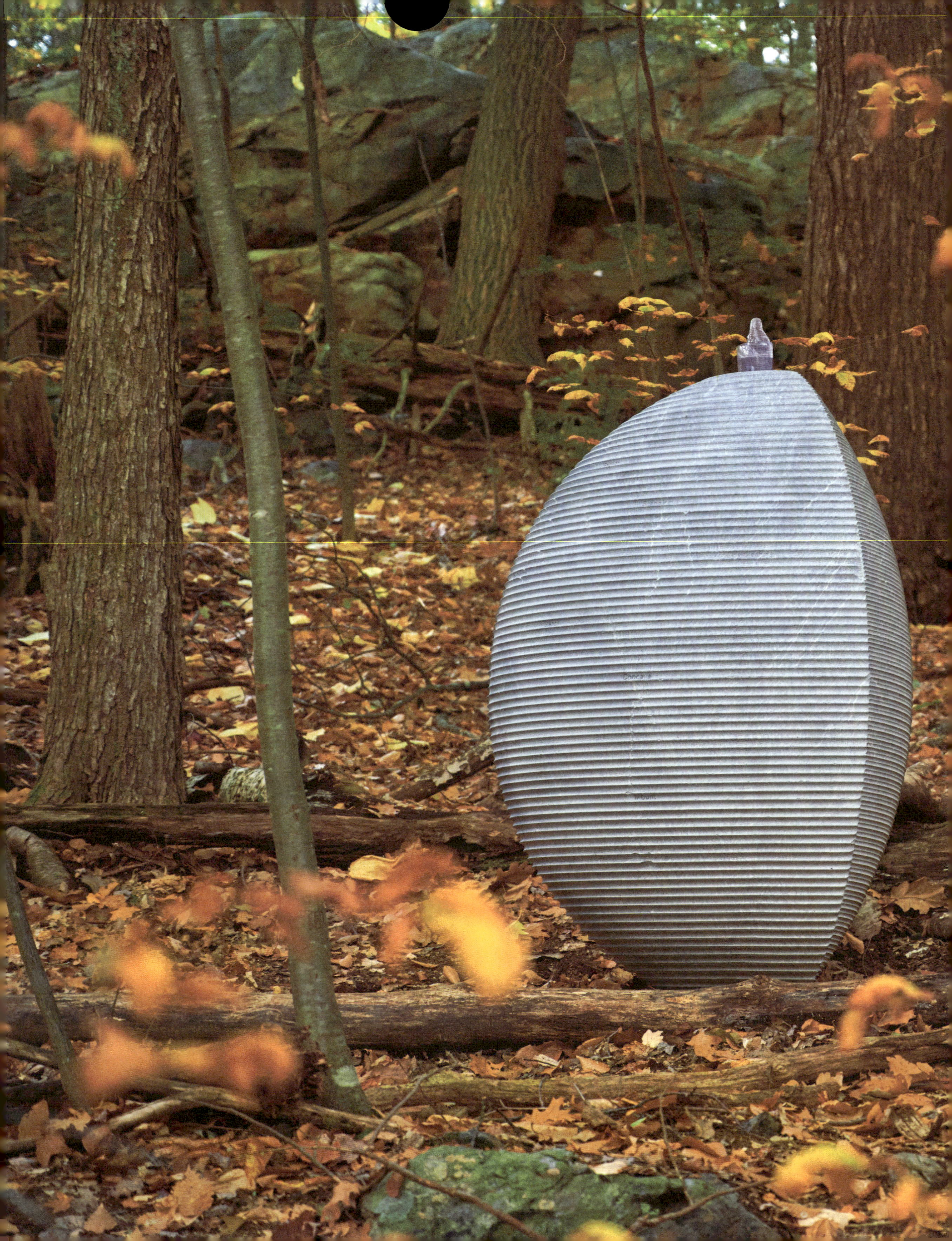

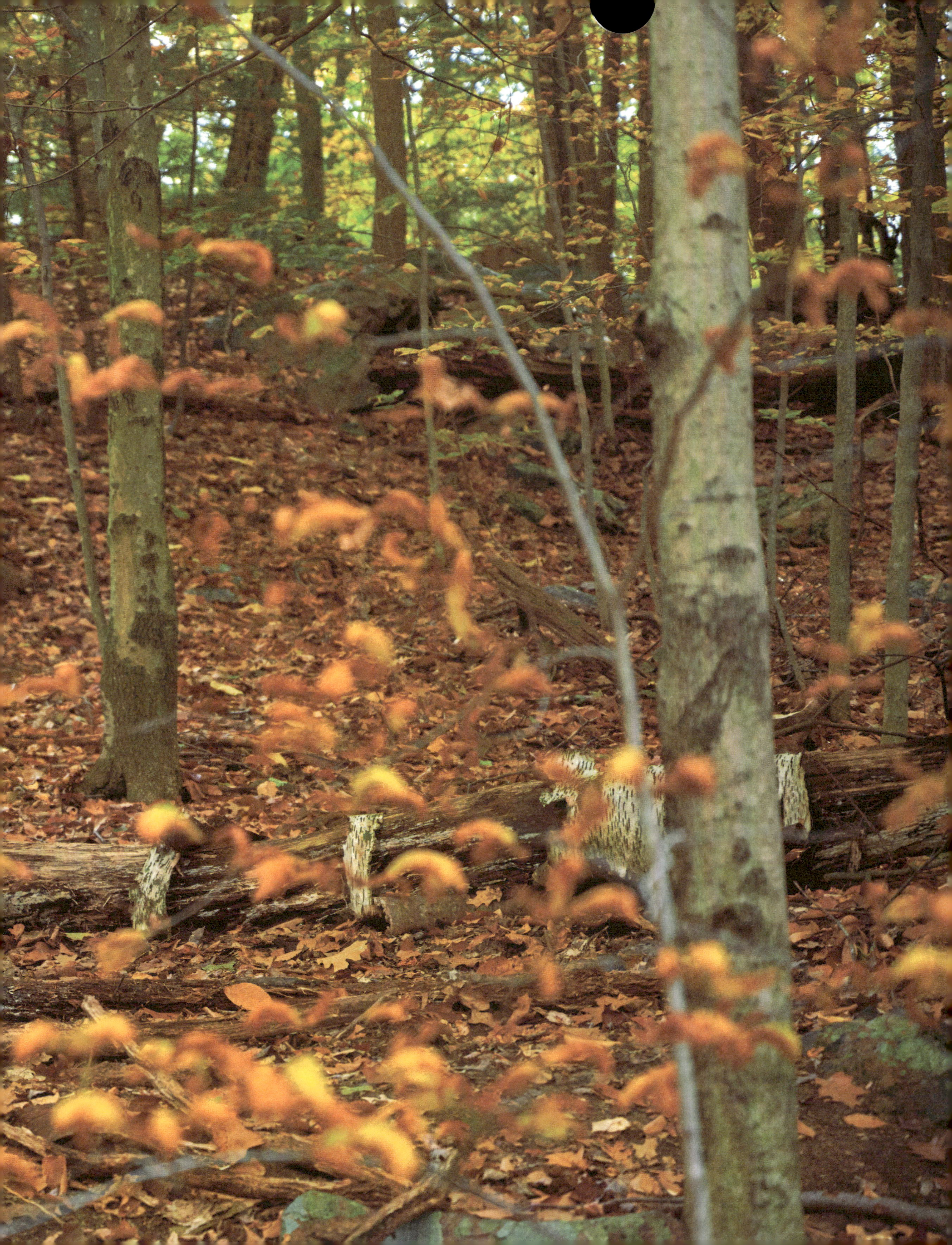

Resin, PVC
128 x 10 x 10 in. (325.1 x 25.4 x 25.4 cm), each column

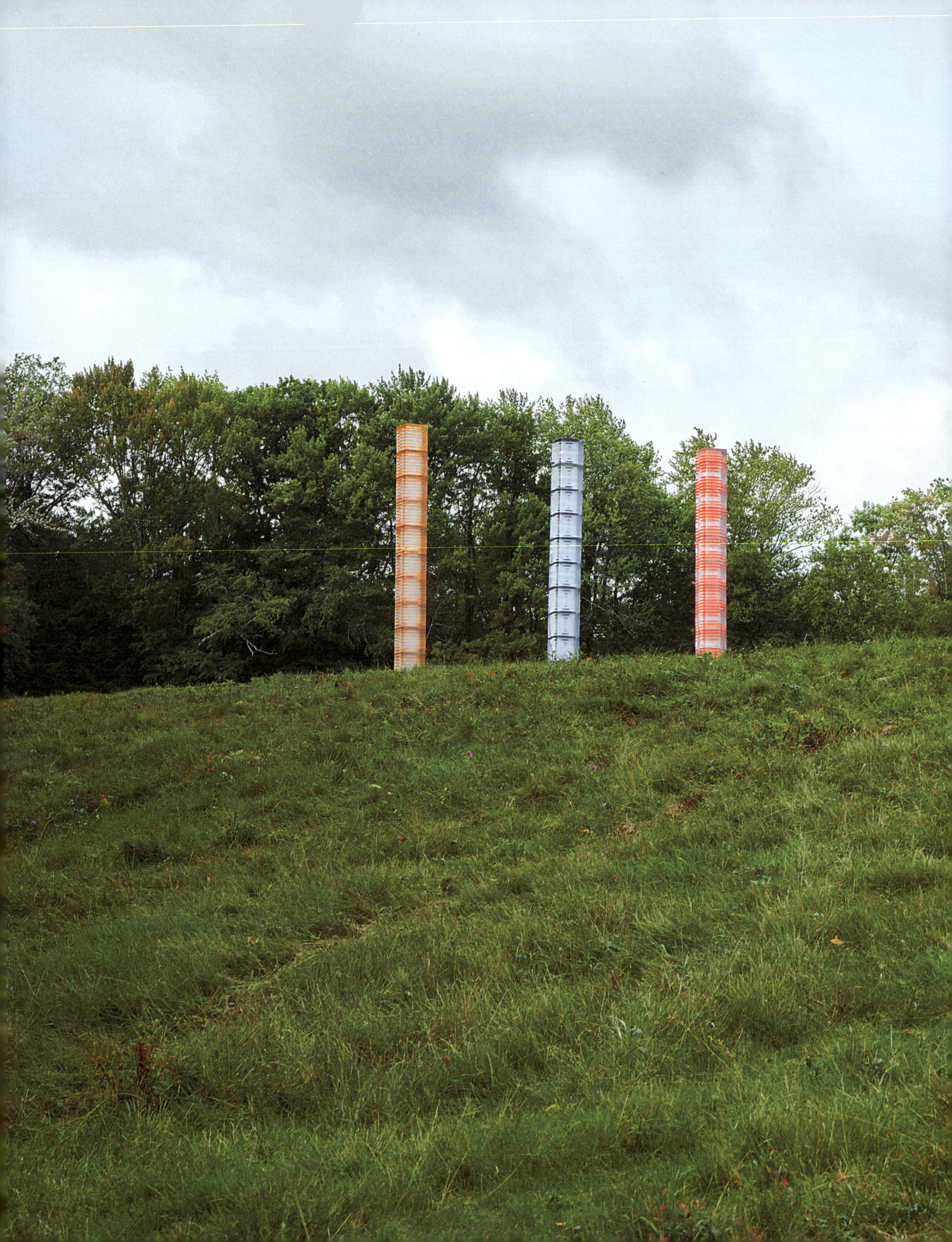

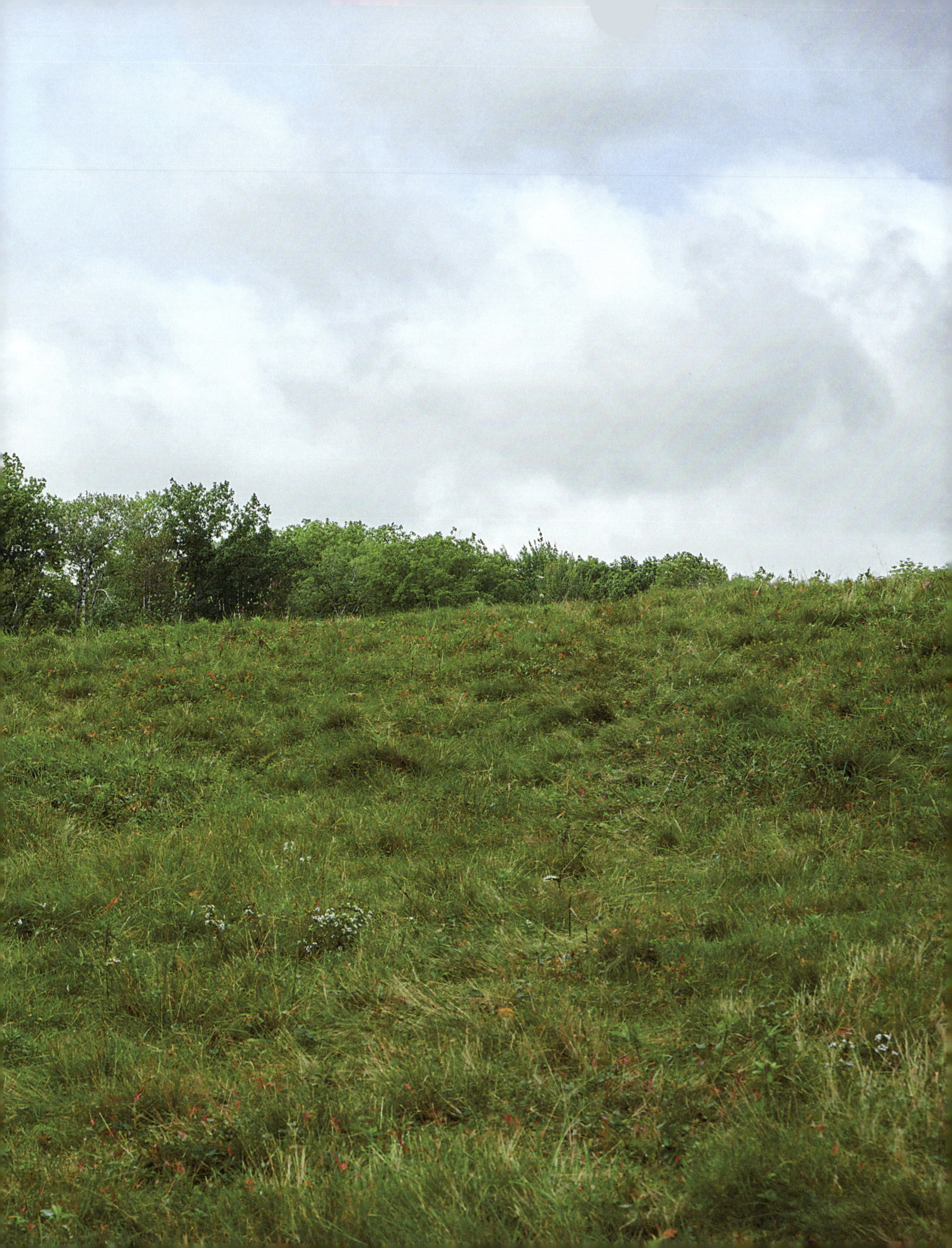

# Post-Industrial: On Eva LeWitt's *Resin Tower A (Orange)*, *Resin Tower B (Yellow)*, and *Resin Tower C (Blue)*

Courtney J. Martin

*The emergence of a kind of sculpture in the last few years that is distinguished from previous sculpture by two main characteristics—that it stands on the ground rather than on a base, and is made of easily available "industrial" rather than expensive conventional materials—raises certain questions about the nature and aims of sculpture, and its relation to reality.*
—William Tucker, 1969

*When I was thinking of conceiving of an outdoor sculpture, what I really wanted it to be was highly visible, not using the traditional outdoor materials of steel and wood. You know those materials that blend in to the environment, which is a beautiful way of making sculpture, but for me I wanted something that really contrasted with nature and stood out against the landscape. I wanted them to be highly encounterable.*
—Eva LeWitt, 2021

## I.
## Entrance / Ascent Up the Hill

In 1969, artist William Tucker described sculpture's shift (as a discipline, not just his practice) from traditional objects—on a base or plinth, hewn from natural materials like stone or wood, crafted by hand—toward what came to define Minimalism, Land Art, and other conceptual methods, noting how this raised "questions about the nature and aims of sculpture, and its relation to reality."[1] More than fifty years later, Eva LeWitt's approach to sculpture reveals how the discipline has shifted once again. If Tucker acknowledged an emerging reality based on the investigation of new materials and placement, LeWitt locates one where sculpture moves away from the industrial, acknowledges its difference from the natural world, and announces itself as a thing apart from rather than a thing of the land. The three sculptures that comprise her project for *Ground/work*—*Resin Tower A (Orange)*, *Resin Tower B (Yellow)*, and *Resin Tower C (Blue)*—stand atop a hill in a pasture overlooking a valley. Roughly eleven feet tall, each translucent resin form is filled with spherical cross-sections of color as denoted by the parenthetical in its title. Completed in 2020, they are LeWitt's first outdoor objects, though they draw on well-known elements of her practice to date and on multiple histories of three-dimensional object making.

Born in Spoleto, Italy, in 1985, LeWitt spent her childhood there, in Manhattan, and in a small town in Connecticut. The contours of each place allowed her to explore different aspects of art and culture that would later shape her studio practice. Where New York offered the downtown art world, commercial galleries, and museums, Spoleto provided something else entirely. It comes alive annually for the Festival dei Due Mondi, a summer music and culture event held since 1958. In 1962, an outdoor sculpture exhibition, *Sculture nella Città*, curated by Giovanni Carandente, ran from June to September and brought an international roster of artists to Spoleto, including Americans Beverly Pepper and David Smith.[2] Underwritten by Italy's largest steel producer, Ilva S.p.A. (previously Italsider), many of the artists invited to the exhibition worked with industrial materials and on a larger scale than they previously had due to access to factory spaces. Pepper, for one, began to use Corten steel in Spoleto.

The 1962 exhibition featured more than 150 works by over 50 living artists, installed alongside the city's ancient and medieval walls to create a dialogue between the two. At the conclusion of the show, some of the works remained, most notably Pepper's *The Gift of Icarus* (1962) and Alexander Calder's *Teodelapio* (1962, fig. 42). The Calder, which stands over 58 feet tall and is nearly as wide, rises in a city square. Completed in August of 1962, the painted-steel stabile is a kind of monument both to the show and to the period when experimentation with industry via materials, craftsmanship, and funding moved sculpture away from traditions that had remained largely intact since the Renaissance, specifically hand carving marble. LeWitt's experience as an artist, however, is at a remove from the fascination with industry among postwar artists like Calder and Pepper. When she speaks of seeking to create a work in "contrast to the landscape,"[3] LeWitt seems to reference the kinds of public art that would have populated her childhood in both Italy and the United States, works like Calder's, Smith's, and Pepper's. Yet in describing "looking at a lot of outdoor sculpture and not being able to find it immediately," LeWitt acknowledges the ways that these midcentury public sculptures now blend into the background precisely for the reasons that they once seemed so defiant and radical.

Perhaps LeWitt's disinterest in sculpture's immediate past reflects the scope of her training. She attended Bard College, where she made a serious effort to study the history of art across a range of time periods and cultures, including antiquity and pre-Columbian art, in addition to training as a sculptor. LeWitt is drawn to history and to biography, but not art criticism or theory. After Bard, she worked for sculptors Tom Sachs and Tara Donovan. If either left an imprint on LeWitt, Sachs may have imparted the sense of whimsy evident in her embrace of vibrant colors, while Donovan encouraged her toward organic and inorganic material play as well as seriality and repetition. LeWitt notes having come to sculpture early in her life out of a sense that she wanted to make art that gave energy rather than took it away; she could only figure out how to do so in three-dimensional making.[4]

Over the last five years, the artist has created a series of installations that mine the flexibility of artificial materials—foam, latex, mesh and plastic—through handmade objects. The resulting wall-based and free-hanging structures, like the curtain *Untitled (Mesh Circles)* (2021, fig. 43), a site-specific work created for the Institute of Contemporary Art / Boston, have a semi-inorganic feel. This aligns with other seeming incongruities in LeWitt's approach to art making, such as her disengagement with computers and digitization, as well as her hope that her public works stand out in the environment, rejecting the generational pretense that large-scale industrially made sculpture should somehow be made indistinct.

Minimalism was industrial because it was proximate to the production means that it used. Land Art, in turn, was anti-industrial because its critique of the built environment, including art, was a reaction to the mechanized turn in art making. One might describe LeWitt's ethos as post-industrial—meaning that she is well aware of what can be done with new materials, and even more so of how to employ mechanized processes, and she chooses to use both as she pleases. For example, she does not rely solely on the computer for communication or for creation, despite the prevalence of computer-aided design tools for modeling and for imaging objects in space (fig. 44). For someone of her generation who makes three-dimensional and installation art, LeWitt's low-fi approach is notable. From a sociological perspective, the post-industrial is a turn away from the mechanized and factory labor (which itself marked a shift from the handmade and agrarian) toward the service sector. In a sense, not making, just providing.

By 1969, a number of theorists, including Daniel Bell, David Reisman, and Alain Touraine, had come to use the term to describe a way of working outside of making, which is both bodily and idea driven. For Touraine, in particular, the post-industrial allows for new social movements levied around protest to take shape.[5] Thus, Minimalism is to industrial as land art is to anti-industrial, which is explicitly *not* post-industrial. The post-industrial alignment of LeWitt's practice, then, relies not only upon industrial materials or production but also upon the artist's willingness to use industry's bi-products, like the clear resin, in an idea-driven manner. To do so without critique and with an effortless lack of fanfare also speaks to her having successfully moved on from the discussions that charged sculpture before the end of the twentieth century.

## II.
## Out in the Field

LeWitt's three resin sculptures, standing like totems on the hilltop meadow above the Clark Art Institute, are reached by a network of intersecting trails that lead into and out of the woods that surround the museum. The artist chose this site during her initial visit, which followed an overnight snowstorm that left several feet of snow on the ground. Despite the climatic interruption, she felt drawn to that specific spot on top of the hill.

Originally, she planned to place several objects across the field. She envisioned them as a scattering of monoliths that might, from a distance, resemble a ring of trees, evocative of an intimate meeting place like those among the actual tree groupings nearby. She reduced the number of elements to three once she realized she needed to make each form as tall as possible, perhaps a further nod to distinguishing them from the

42

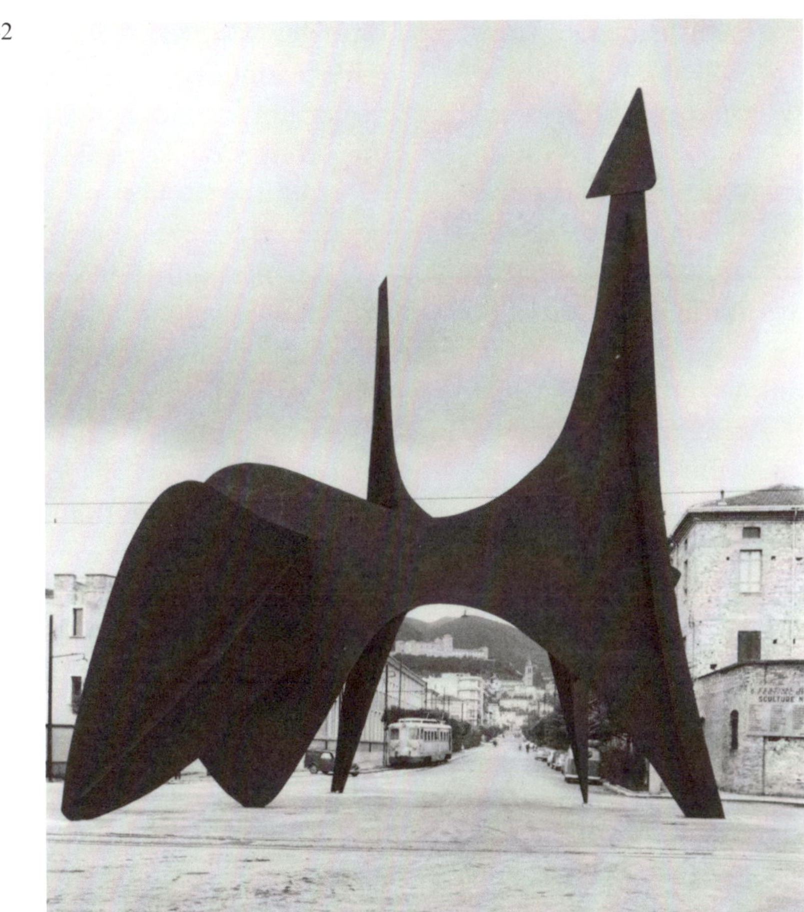

43

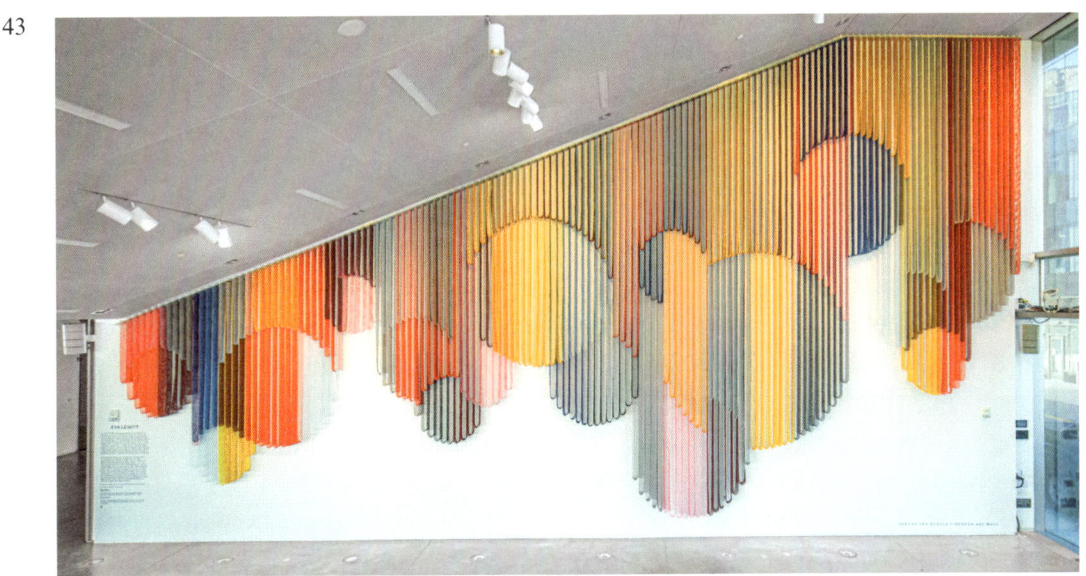

Fig. 42 Alexander Calder, *Teodelapio*, 1962. Sheet metal and paint, 702 x 554 x 554 in. (1,783.1 x 1,407.2 x 1,407.2 cm). Galleria Civica d'Arte Moderna, Spoleto. © 2021 Calder Foundation, New York / Artists Rights Society (ARS), New York. Photo by Ugo Mulas © Ugo Mulas Heirs

Fig. 43 Eva LeWitt, *Untitled (Mesh Circles)*, 2021. Installation view from *Eva LeWitt*, the Institute of Contemporary Art/Boston, 2021. Courtesy of the artist and VI, VII, Oslo, Norway

landscape. That distinction is drawn primarily from the elements of vivid color for which each column is named: *Orange*, *Yellow*, and *Blue*. As an avowed colorist, LeWitt wanted the colors to stand out, to call attention to themselves, and to drive the reception of the towers in relationship to the landscape. Each column is constructed of individual layers of clear resin interspersed with and surrounding colorful, flat PVC shapes in graduated sizes, hand cut by LeWitt: orange and blue disks, and yellow squares inscribed with cut-out circles (fig. 45). Arranged in expanding and contracting sequences within each column, the shapes appear to form a series of spheres or spindles, as if dissected laterally to resemble an expanded cross-section. To view each object up close is to see the slivers of viscous color in the clear space. From afar, it is as if the slices are tinted lenses through which to view the rest of the landscape.

In this project, as in others, LeWitt activates a celebration of color by foregrounding it in the construction of the object. She came to resin as a material because of its clarity; because it is transparent, color can be seen within and through it. Light then becomes a physical component in each of the sculptures. The polymer base of resin makes it subject to infinite variations dependent on light, another characteristic that drew the artist to resin as a material. The towers are formally familiar, resonating equally with ancient stele, found from Africa to Europe to islands across the Pacific, and with geometric modernism. Standing higher than human height, but lower than the tree line, the trio feels less imposing because of the transparency of the resin. Their potential for imposition is undone by their ability to transmit light and color, but this transmission also sets them apart from the opaque colors of the trees, flowering plants, ground, and sky that surround them.

During my visit to the Clark in the fall of 2020, the sky was clear and bright and the day unseasonably warm. The blue column mimicked the appearance of the sky in the middle of the day, while the yellow burned so bright in the reflection of the sun that it took on a range of tones from saffron to burnt orange. LeWitt intentionally cultivated this possibility of environmentally driven tonal variance to reflect the palette of New England's seasons, the yellows, oranges, and reds of fall and blue of the winter sky. Her instinctive responsiveness to this environment is, no doubt, an outgrowth of having lived in neighboring Connecticut.

Outdoor sculpture is a challenge to the environment and for the object. While LeWitt's *Resin Towers* are her first outdoor work, she acclimated quickly to the challenge of siting work in the landscape, likely as a result of having worked through a number of material types in previous projects and the experience of co-executing large-scale projects by other artists. She first laid out her ideas for the towers in a hand-drawn schematic of grids that became what she calls "little sculptures," hand-made scale models or maquettes of the final works (fig. 46). LeWitt experimented with the resin in her studio, making the color inserts at a small scale. She then cut the PVC by hand before passing the material off to her fabricator, Karen Atta, who poured all of the resin and embedded the PVC components within the layers of each tower (fig. 47). Even working with a fabricator, it was important for the artist to have a primary relationship with the labor involved in the creation of the work. For LeWitt, that relationship is not so much performative as it is experimental and experiential. From this experience, she developed some sense of what the amorphous, semisolid resin is capable of doing. Having never worked with resin on this scale prior to this project, LeWitt has now added it to her material vocabulary. When working with a fabricator in the future, LeWitt will know the material's limits and will be able to gauge her own parameters for object making based on that understanding.

Since the *Ground/work* exhibition is temporary, LeWitt is even more sanguine about the towers' afterlives. She has thought of "chopping them up and putting them back together" or "mixing the colors," to create new objects of differing heights and tonal values.[6] The artist is open to the idea that they might move indoors and be shown in a space without the added environmental interactions. She is not invested in the towers remaining as they were first shown, but rather in their "modularity" or "adaptability." What LeWitt describes here is not so much site-specificity as site-responsiveness. In the former, the object's realization is tied to place, but the latter allows for both the temporality of the towers in the exhibition and

44

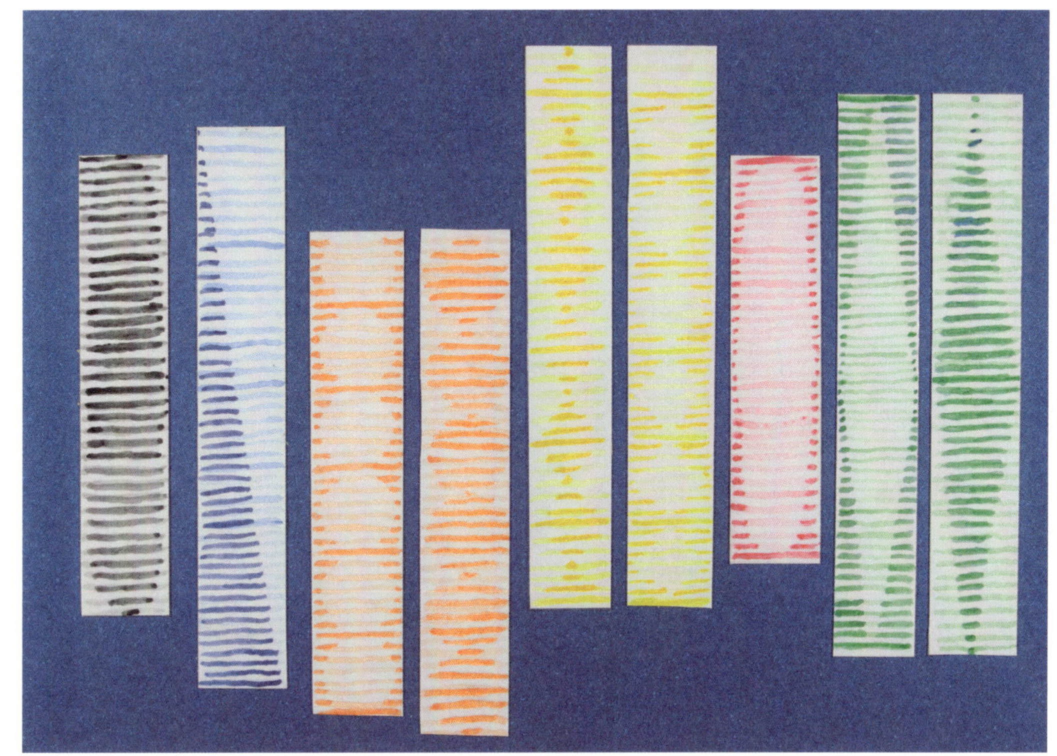

45

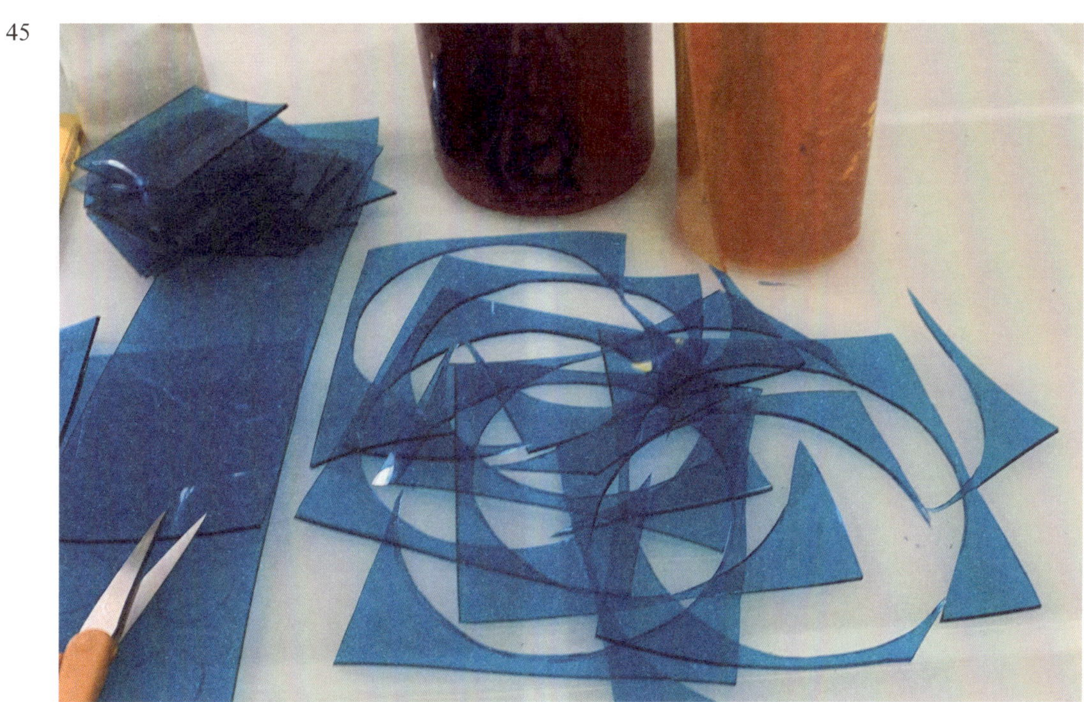

Fig. 44 Preparatory sketch for Eva LeWitt's *Resin Towers*
Fig. 45 Hand-cut materials in Eva LeWitt's studio

46

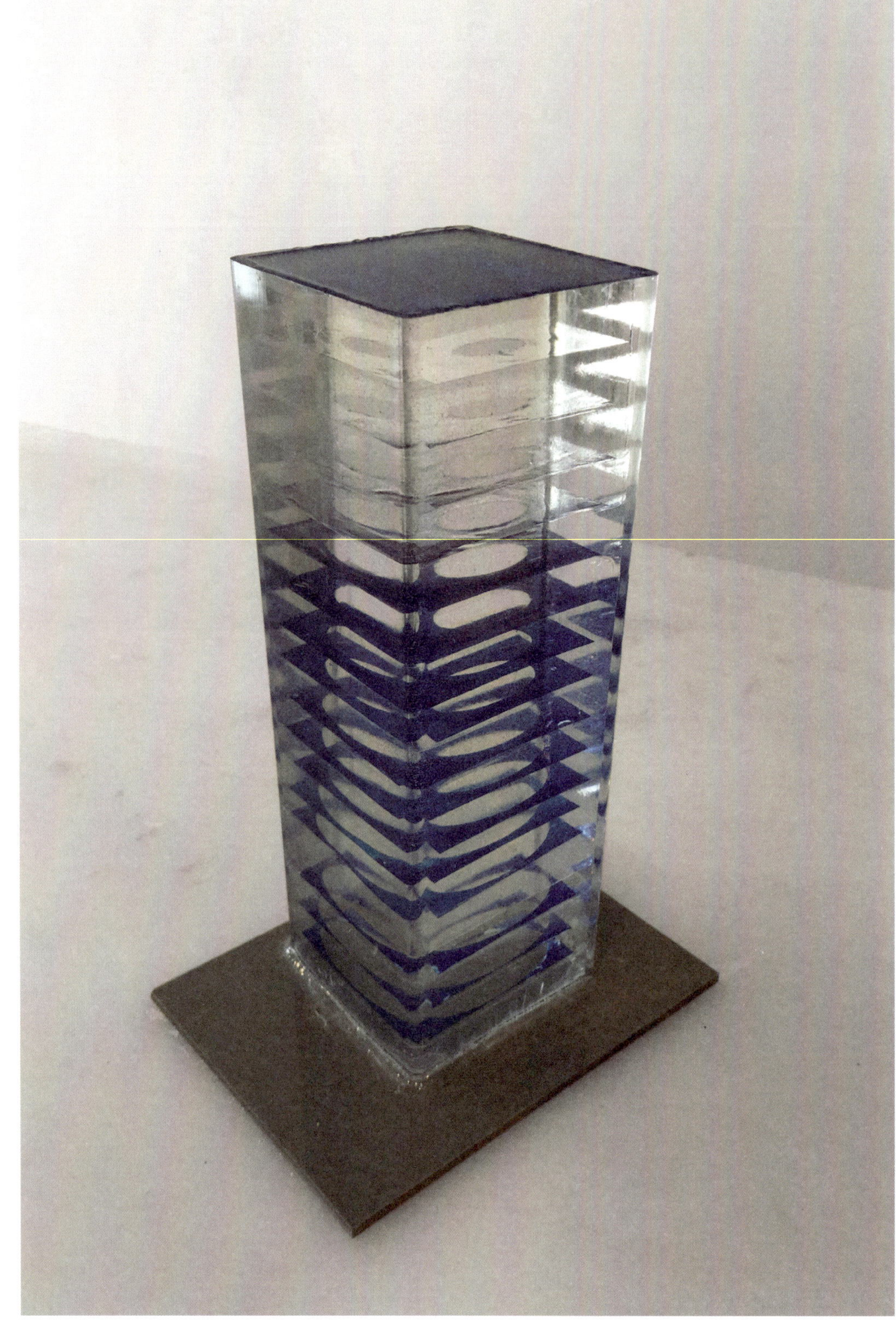

Fig. 46 Early maquette for *Resin Towers* in LeWitt's studio, 2019

their afterlife at the end of the show. The conditions will inevitably change, in ways not so dissimilar to the dramatic shifts of light, weather, and atmosphere throughout the run of the show. LeWitt thinks that the towers need to be together, though she is not wedded to the idea that they have to be. "They are all describing the same thing from a different point of view," she notes, but "they say it better when they are all together." While site-specific works reference and rely on a particular location, the three towers' relationship to one another is their immutable specificity.

## III.
## Exit / Descent Down the Hill

Though *Ground/work* is the Clark's first outdoor exhibition, it is premised on a number of interrelated ideas with which LeWitt's towers are also entangled. The Clark is best known for its European paintings, rather than for its sculpture holdings; most of the three-dimensional works in the Clark's permanent collection are of the traditional register (equestrian bronzes, portrait busts, marble groups, and decorative ornaments), which William Tucker identified as sculpture's point of departure in the late 1960s. However, when visiting the institute's campus, LeWitt saw Thomas Schütte's *Crystal* (2015), a zinc-coated copper and wooden structure that can be entered into and physically explored. On long-term loan to the Clark and sited in a pasture near the halfway point to the top of Stone Hill, the sculpture sits evenly between the ambitions of large-scale sculpture and that of habitable architecture, in the manner of a folly. For LeWitt, it has particular resonance as a referent to the ways that built form—here asymmetry taken from naturally occurring crystalline structures—can work with the landscape without folding into or oppressing it. LeWitt was not building an actual tower, but the architectonics of her objects enliven the ability of three-dimensional sculpture to stand in—both literally and physically—as, for, and in place of other concepts. Thus, her towers are totemic as much as they are naturalistic and relational, if not also commemorative and serial.

When Tucker heralded the emergence of a new kind of sculpture in January 1969, preparations were underway for one of the most significant early exhibitions of sculpture in the landscape, *Earth Art*, held in Ithaca, New York, at Cornell University's Andrew Dickson White Museum of Art over the following months. It was the first museum exhibition to show site-specific works; all were commissions, and nearly all were made on site, many of them spread throughout the city and into its semi-rural borders. As the title suggests, it set a precedent, if not also a definition, of and for Earth Art, with its near synonymic term, Land Art. Both would be defined largely by what had been realized in Ithaca and in individual projects elsewhere in the United States where art was made directly in the landscape using natural materials. As *Earth Art*'s curator Willoughby Sharp opined in the catalogue, "With a tremendous vocabulary of means at its disposal, the new sculpture manifests itself in an infinite variety of configurations."[8] Of these configurations, density, opacity, and rigidity were the most common and profound.

There is a reason that I keep returning to the ideas of mid-twentieth-century sculpture to position what LeWitt is doing now, fifty-odd years later. The periodization of sculpture often sees Tucker's pithy remarks on tradition as galvanizing, and the incorporation of nontraditional sculpture by midcentury makers like Eva Hesse, Nancy Holt, Richard Hunt, Robert Irwin, Donald Judd, Robert Morris, Martin Puryear, David Smith, or Robert Smithson into the art historical canon was revolutionary. As LeWitt points out to us, that sculpture provided a base, a ground, from which she grew, but to which she did not have to conform. She adeptly borrows from the generation of makers that preceded her, yet without close adherence to a formal discipline or to an ethos. For the curators of *Ground/work* to introduce a temporal sculptural project to the Clark's landscape is to exercise this history. It speaks to the ways in which LeWitt's towers belong to a new generation of making, one that might be marked by the environmental, civic, and social turn that the world seemed to be inching toward in the second half of 2020, just as she was releasing them out into the landscape. (Indeed, few curatorial ideas seem more prescient in 2020 than an outdoor exhibition that allowed for visual and experiential engagement without contact.) These are quiet, significant forms whose publicness will be charged and changed as they move from this landscape to wherever else the artist decides to take them.

*Courtney J. Martin is the sixth director of the Yale Center for British Art.*

Epigraphs: William Tucker, "An Essay on Sculpture," *Studio International* 177, no. 907 (January 1969): 12; Eva LeWitt, conversation with the author, January 29, 2021.

1 See Tucker epigraph.
2 For a contemporary perspective on the exhibition, see David Sylvester, "The Spoleto Experiment," *Sunday Times (London)*, December 9, 1962. For a historical take, see Marin R. Sullivan, "Activating Sculpture: The Curatorial Program of *Sculture nella città*," *Journal of Curatorial Studies* 2, no. 3 (2013): 356–82.
3 Eva LeWitt, conversation with the author, January 29, 2021.
4 LeWitt, conversation with the author.
5 Alain Touraine, *La société post-industrielle: Naissance d'une Sociente* (Paris: Seuil, 1969).
6 LeWitt, conversation with the author.
7 LeWitt, conversation with the author.
8 Willoughby Sharp, "Notes Toward an Understanding of Earth Art," *Earth Art* (Ithaca, NY: Andrew Dickson White Museum of Art, Cornell University, 1970), n.p.

47

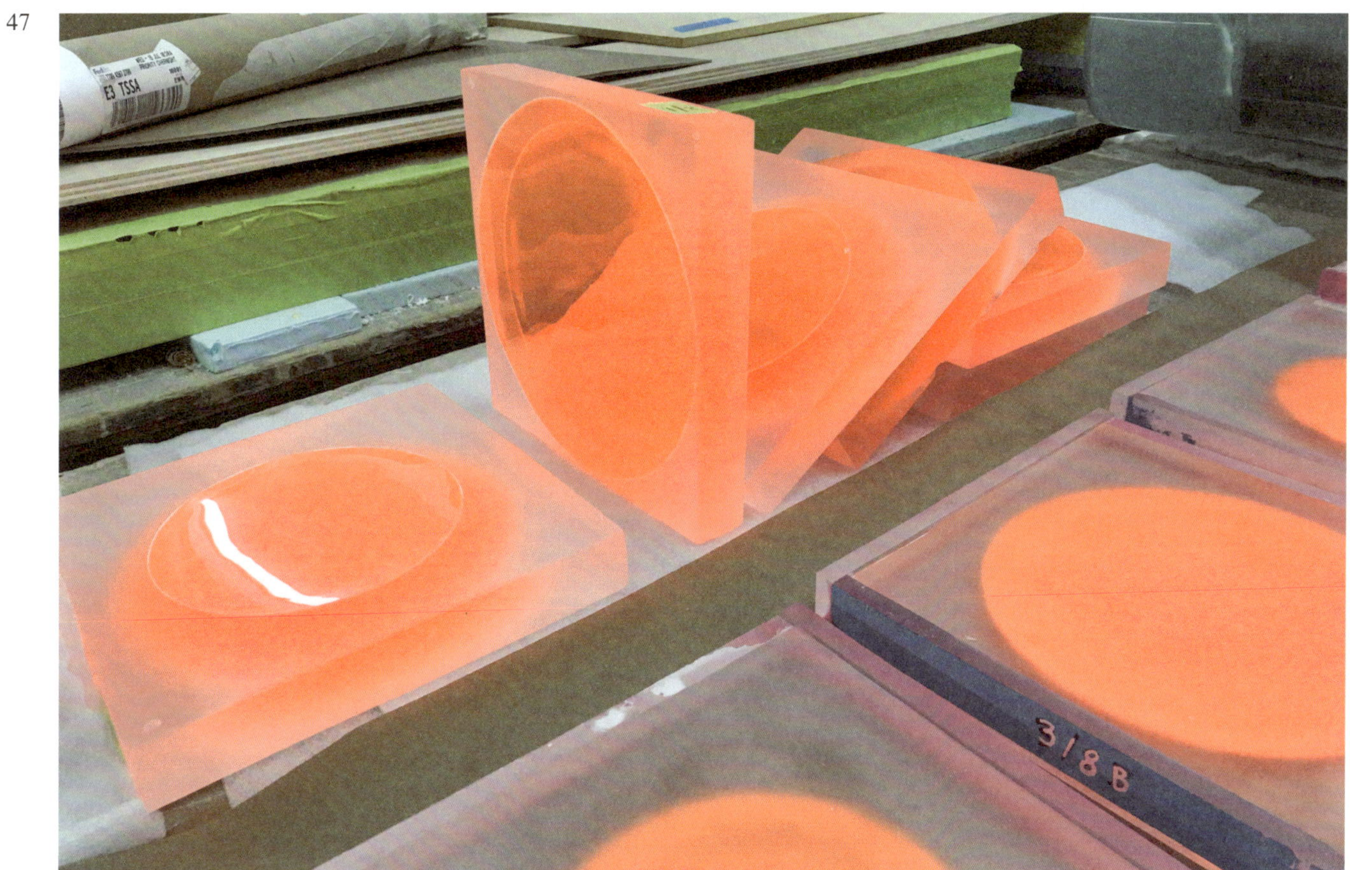


Fig. 47 *Resin Tower A (Orange)* in production

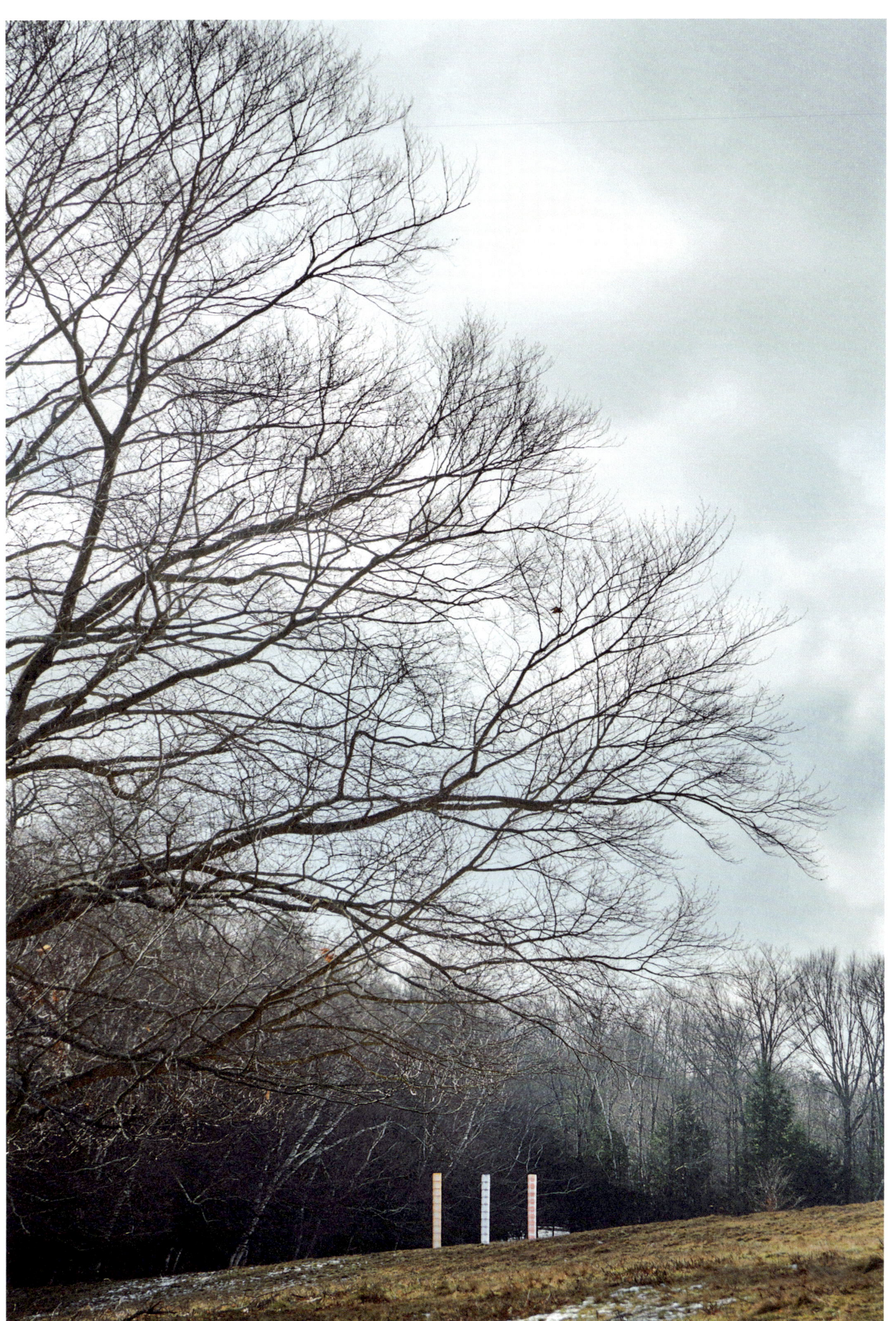

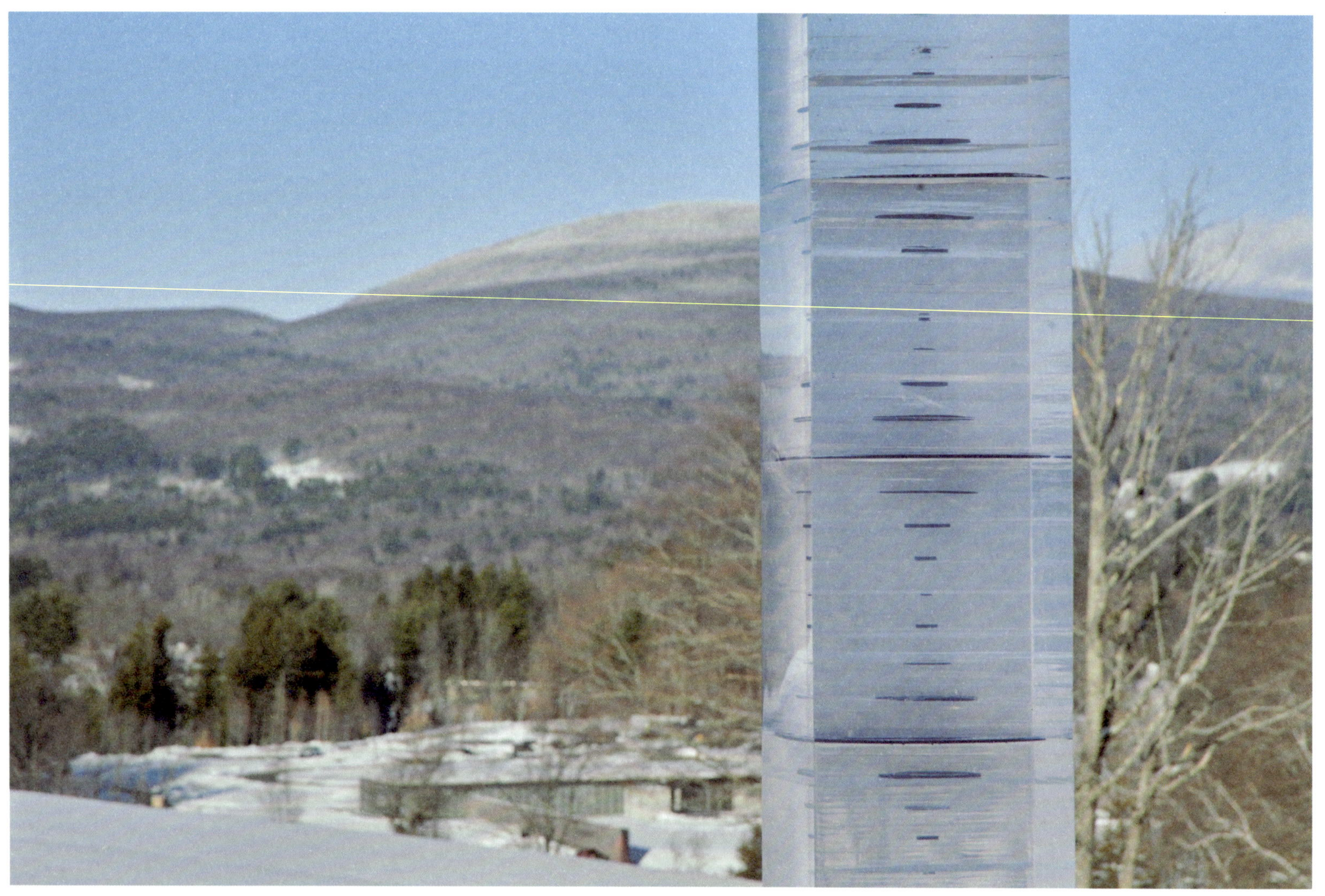

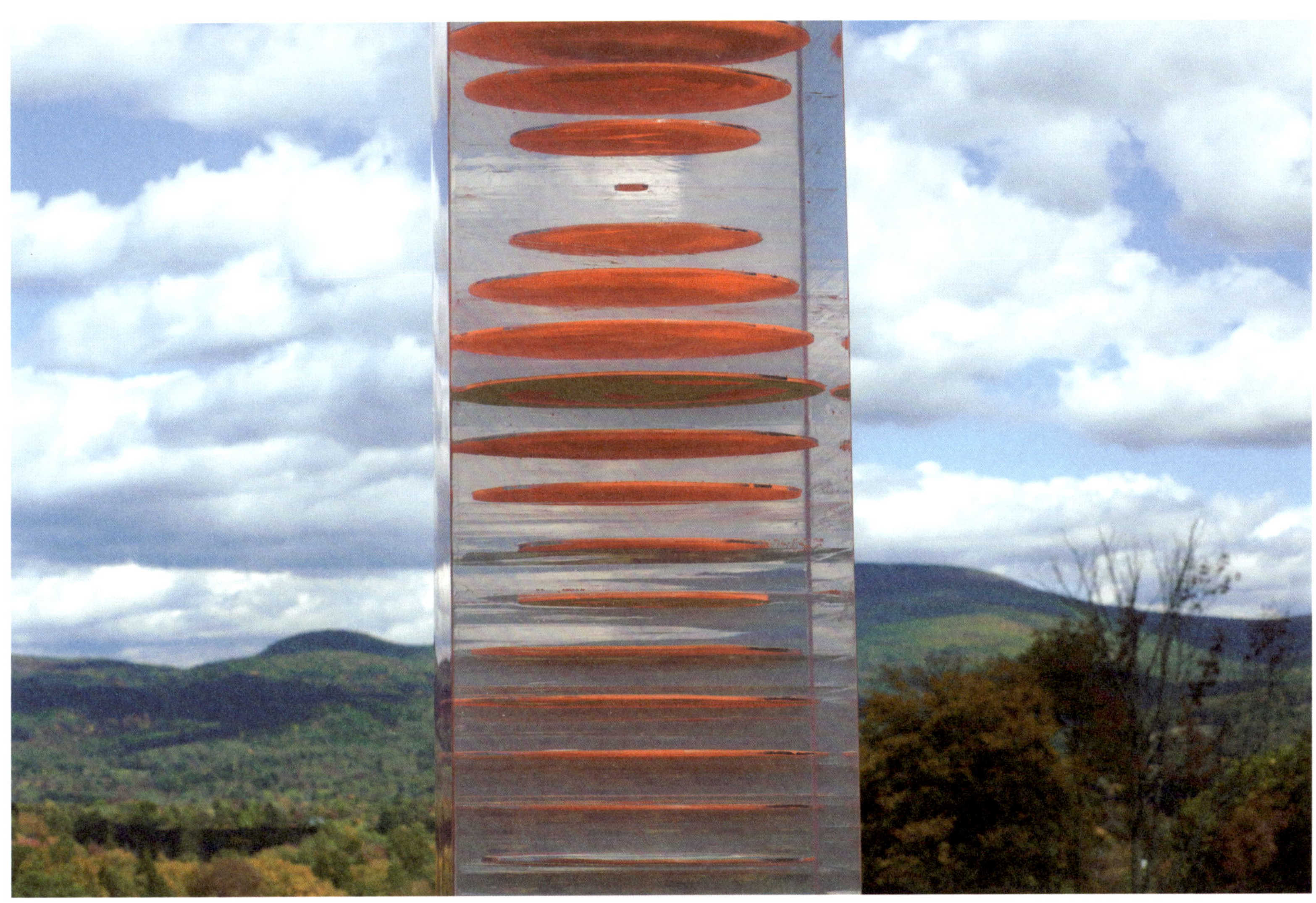

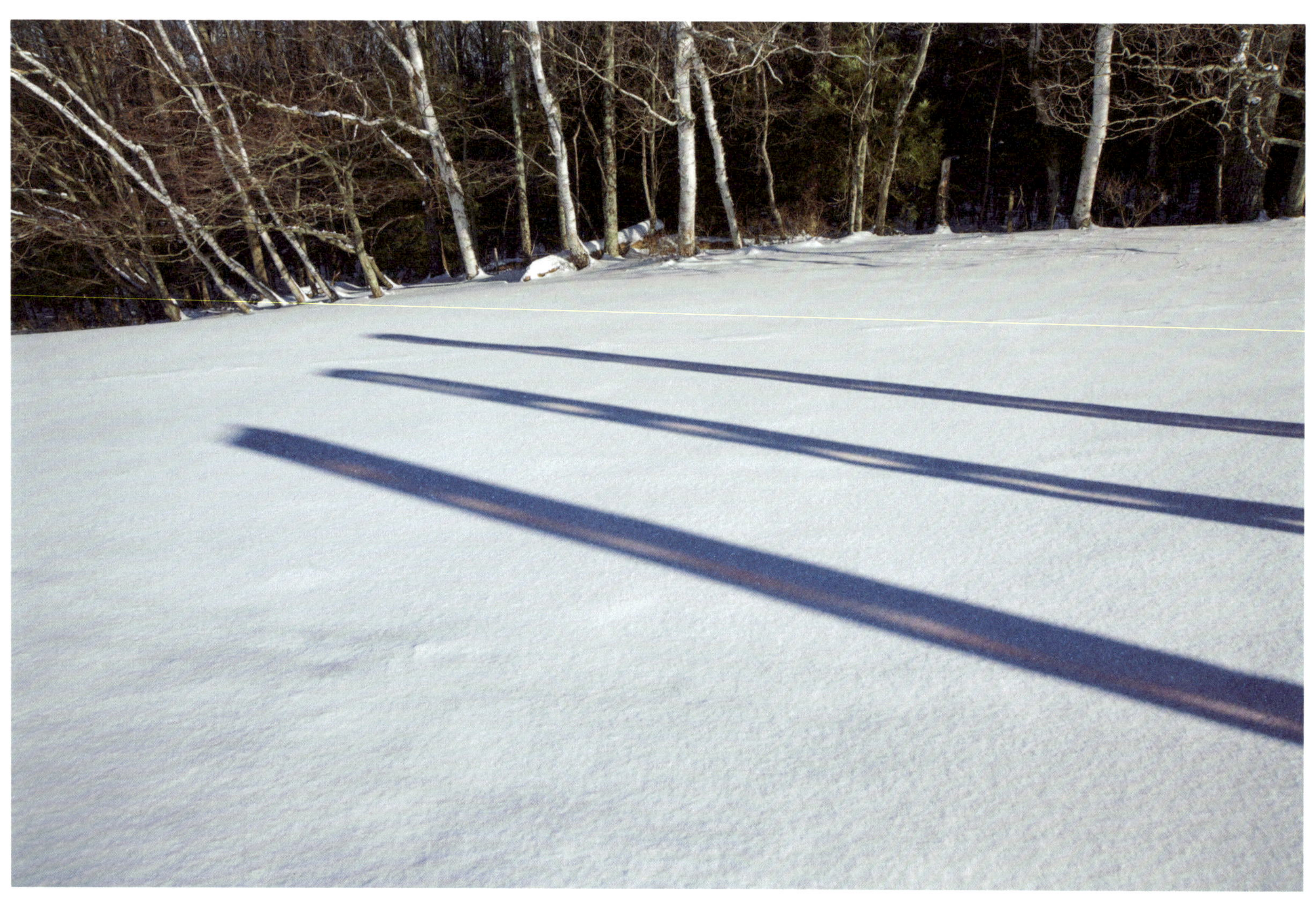

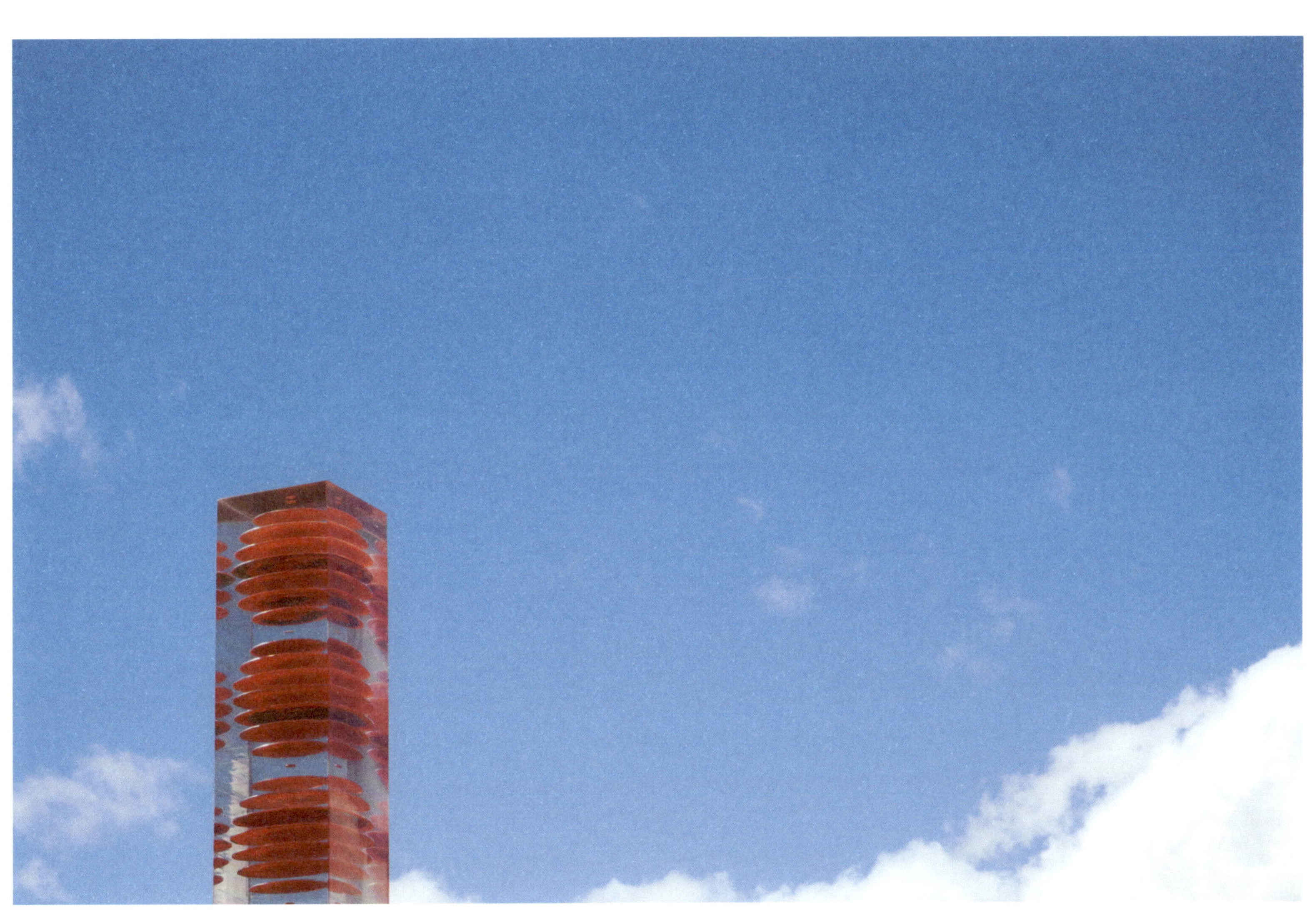

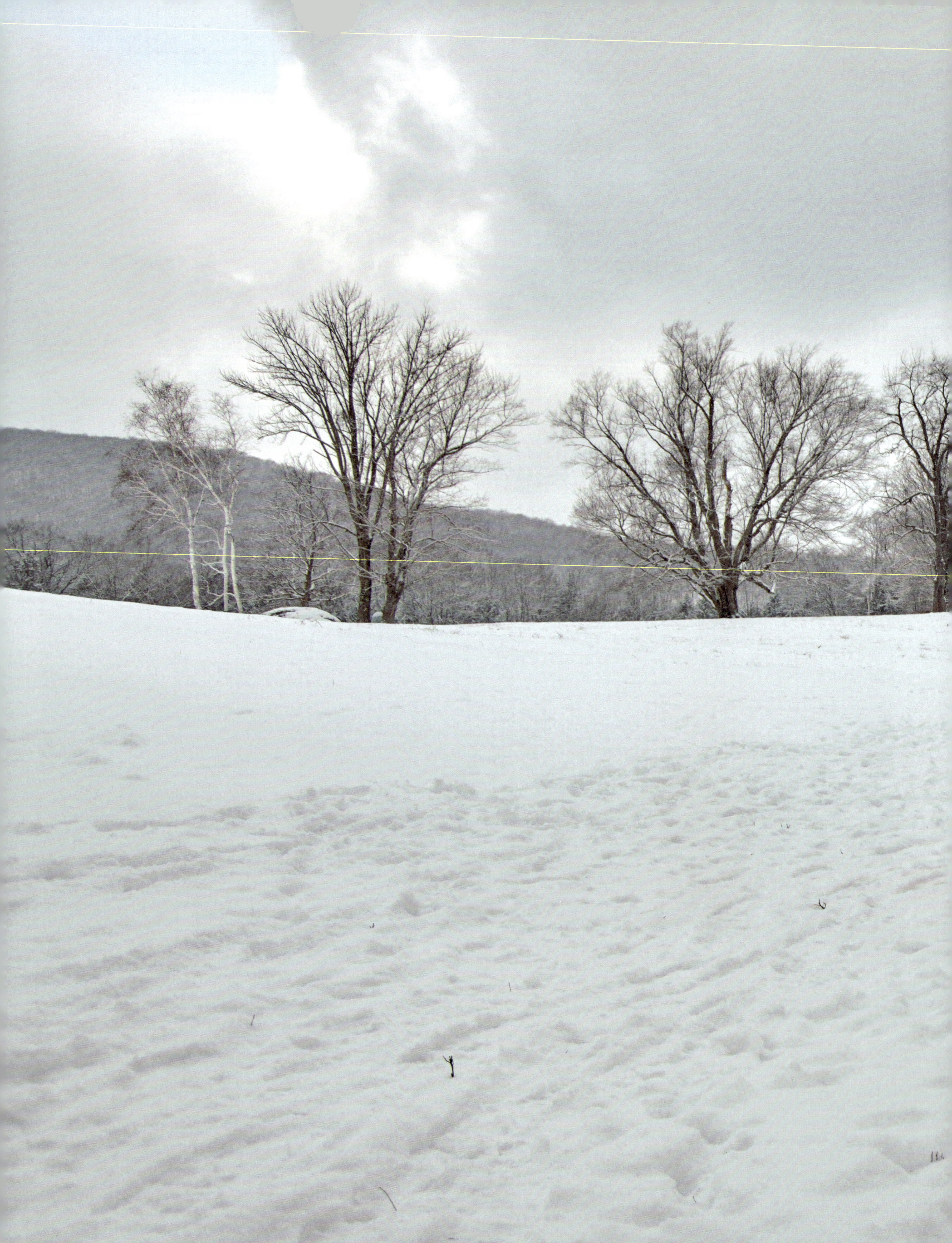

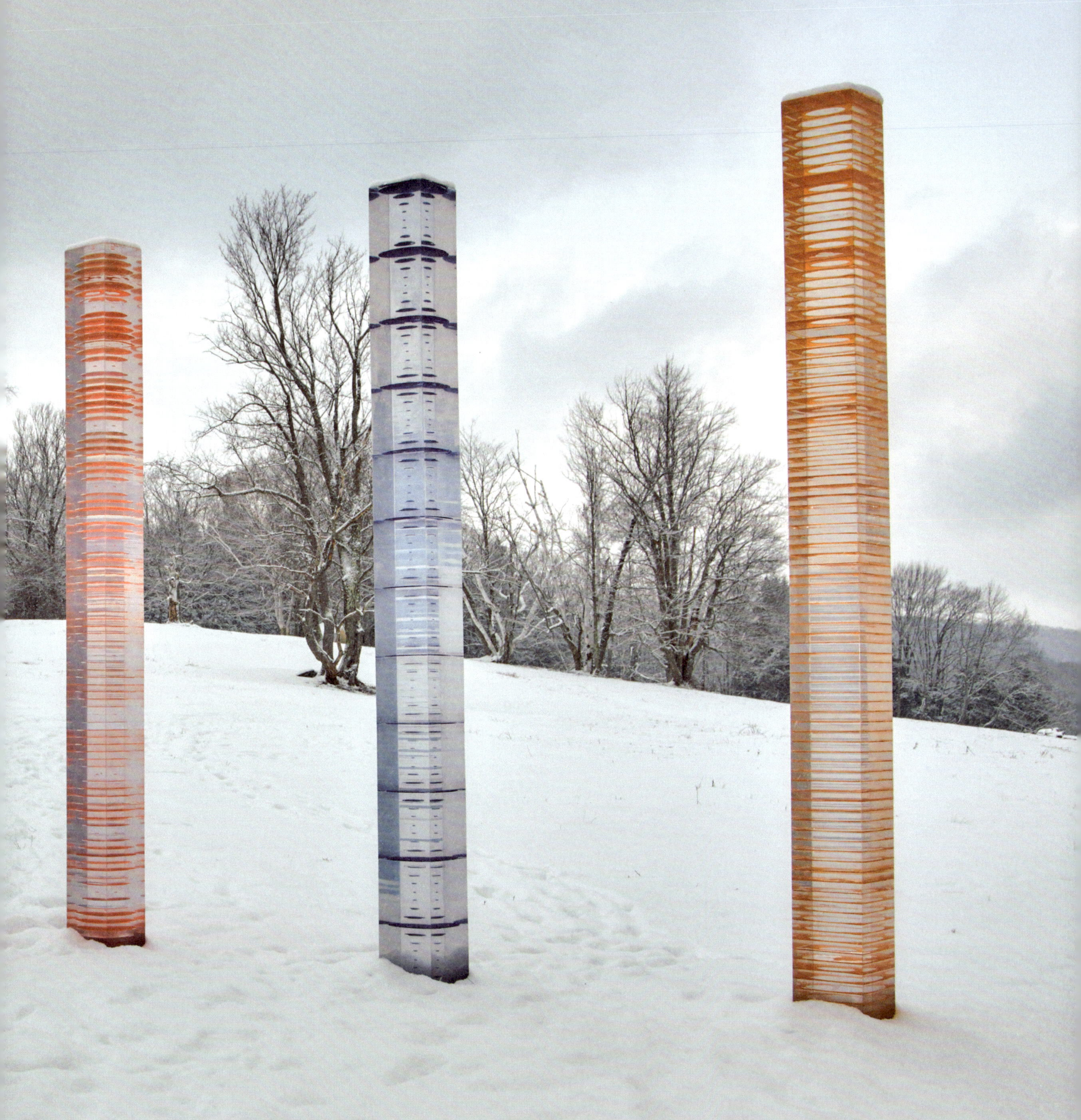

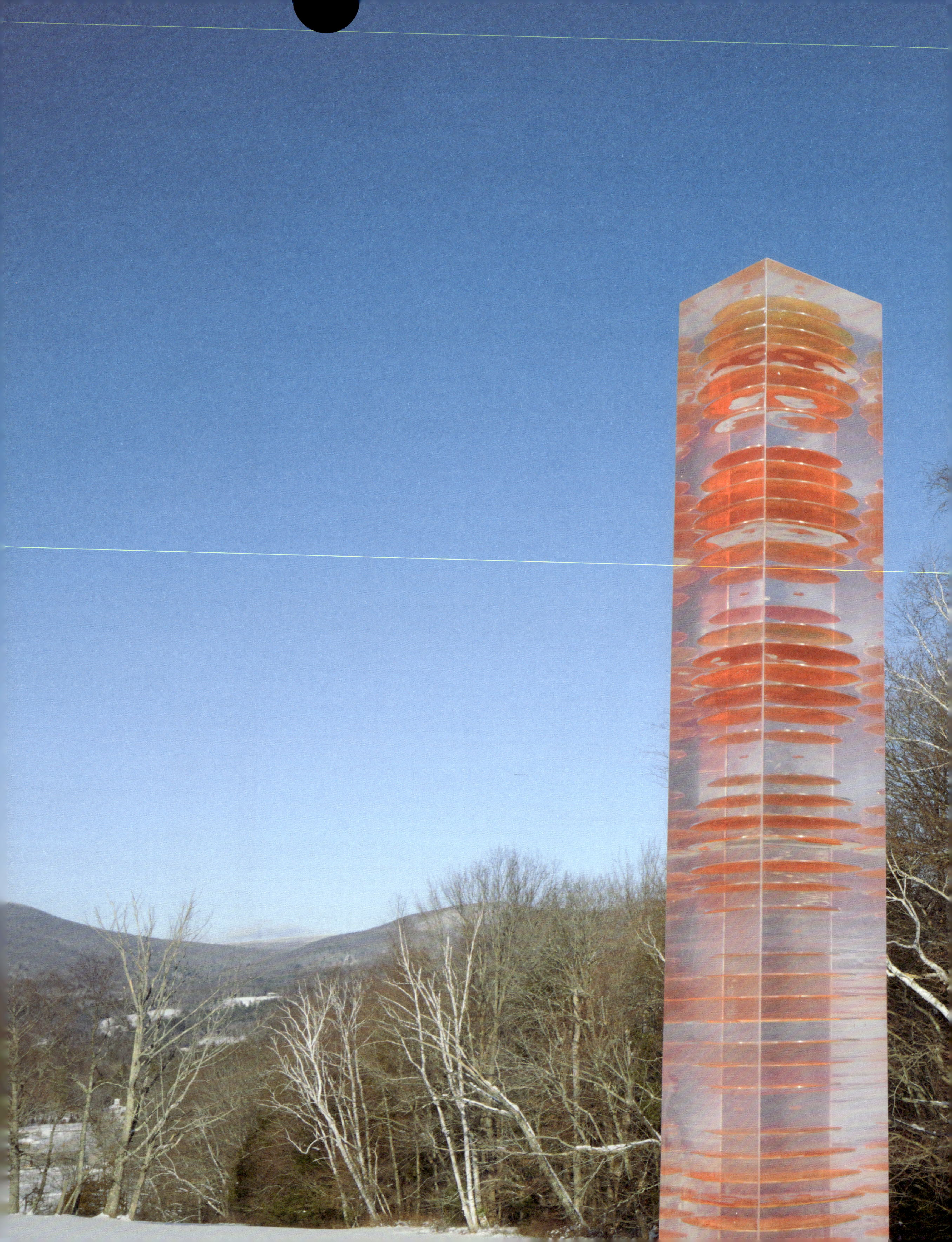

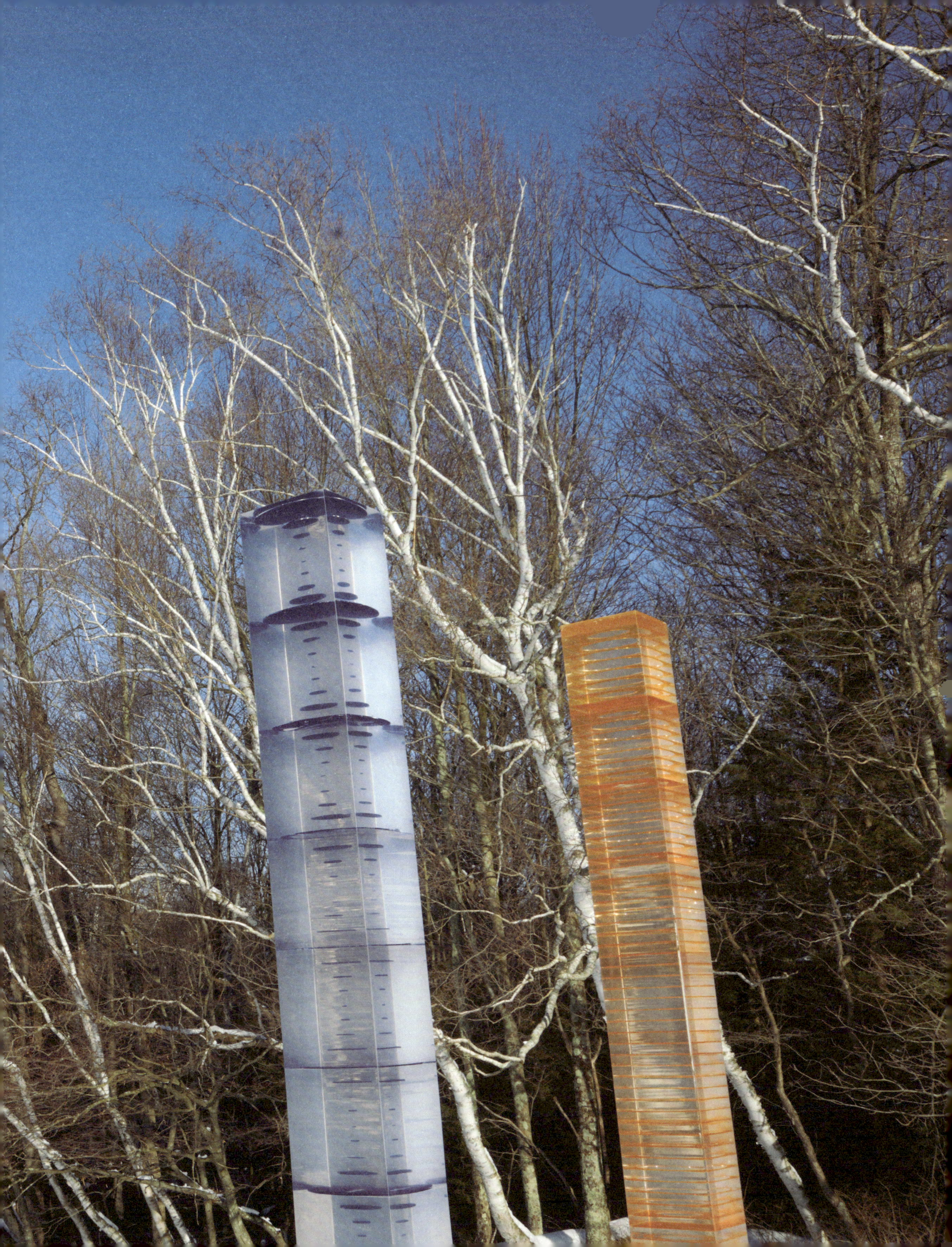

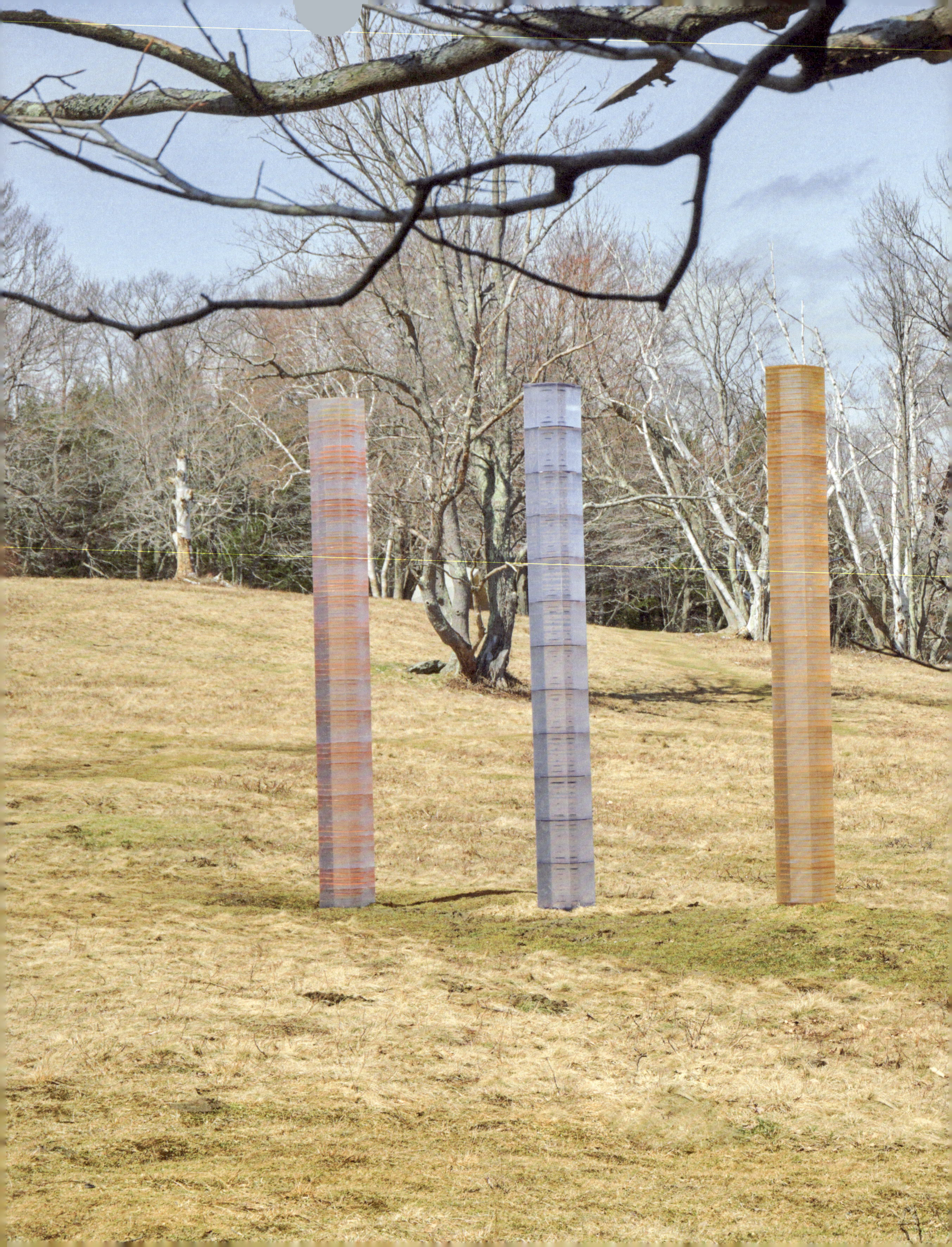

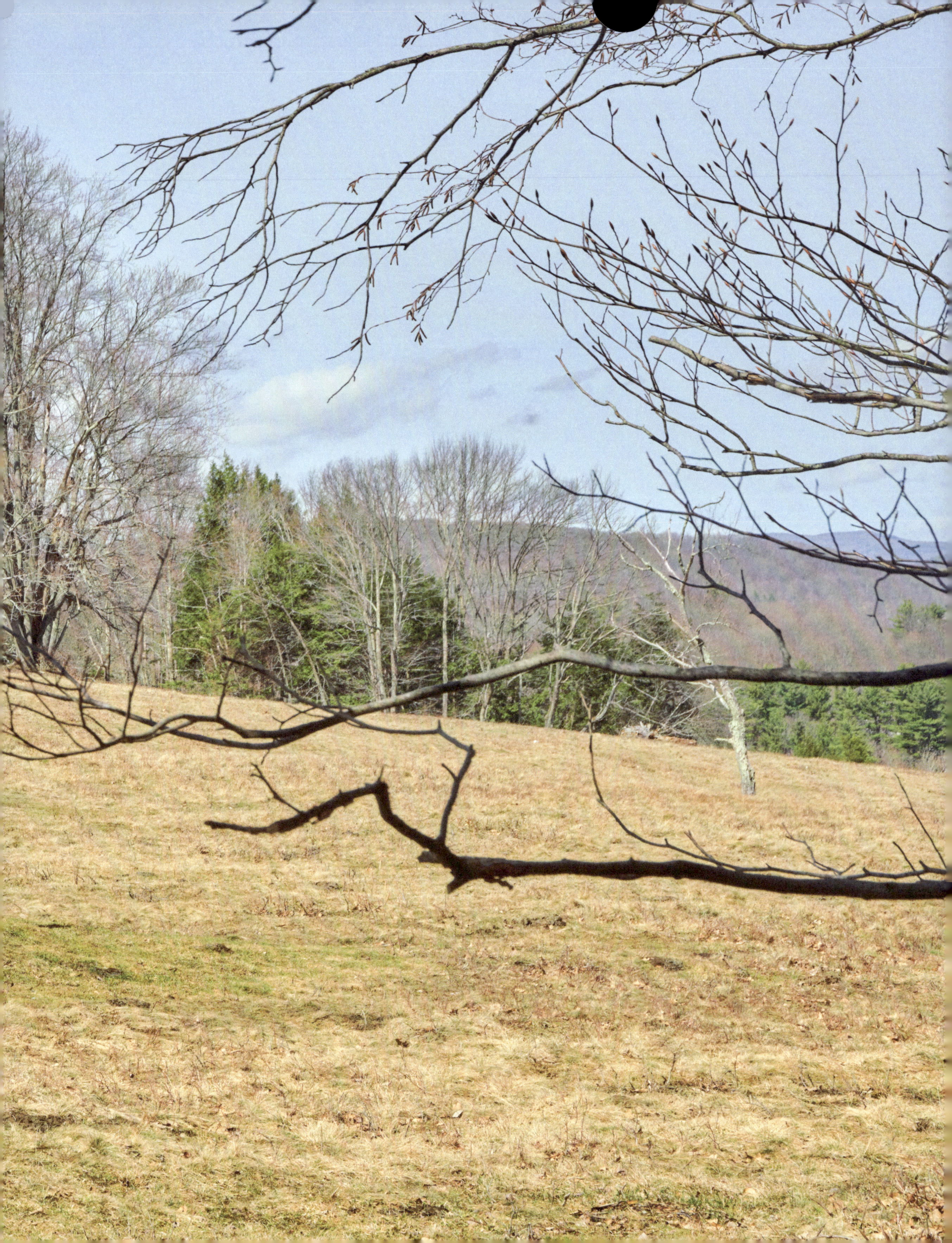

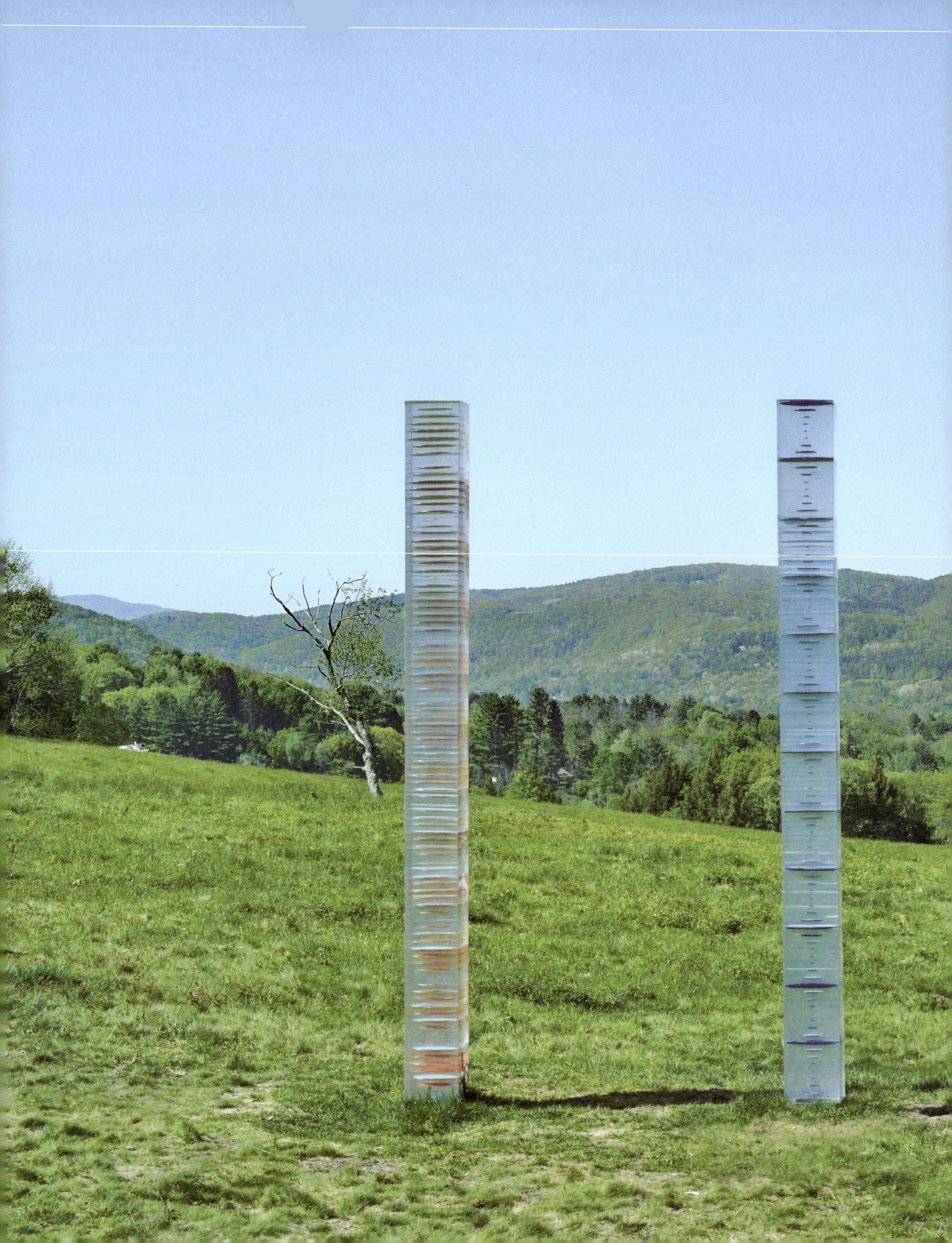

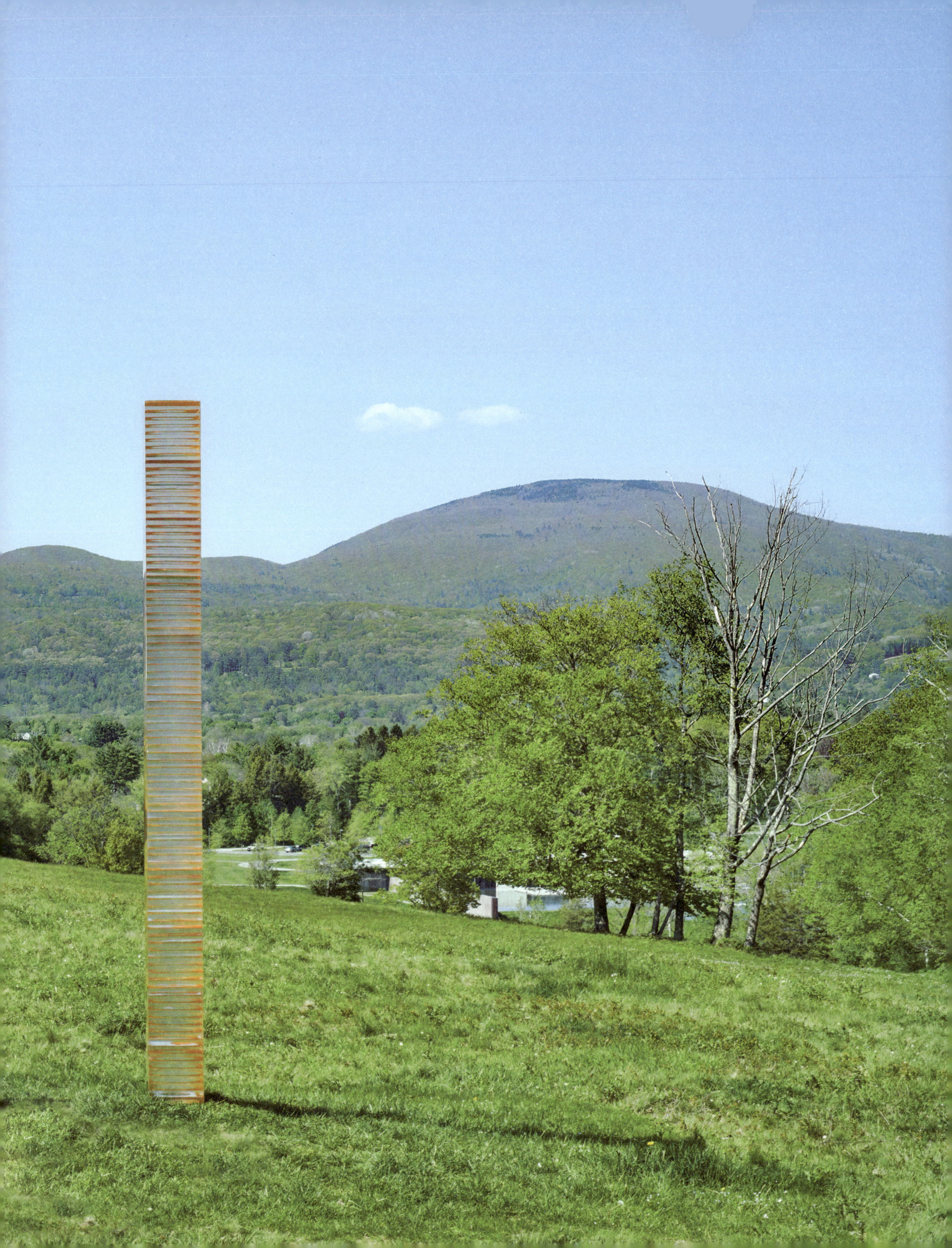

Marble, stainless steel
61 5/8 x 77 3/4 x 115 1/2 in. (156.5 x 197.5 x 293.4 cm)

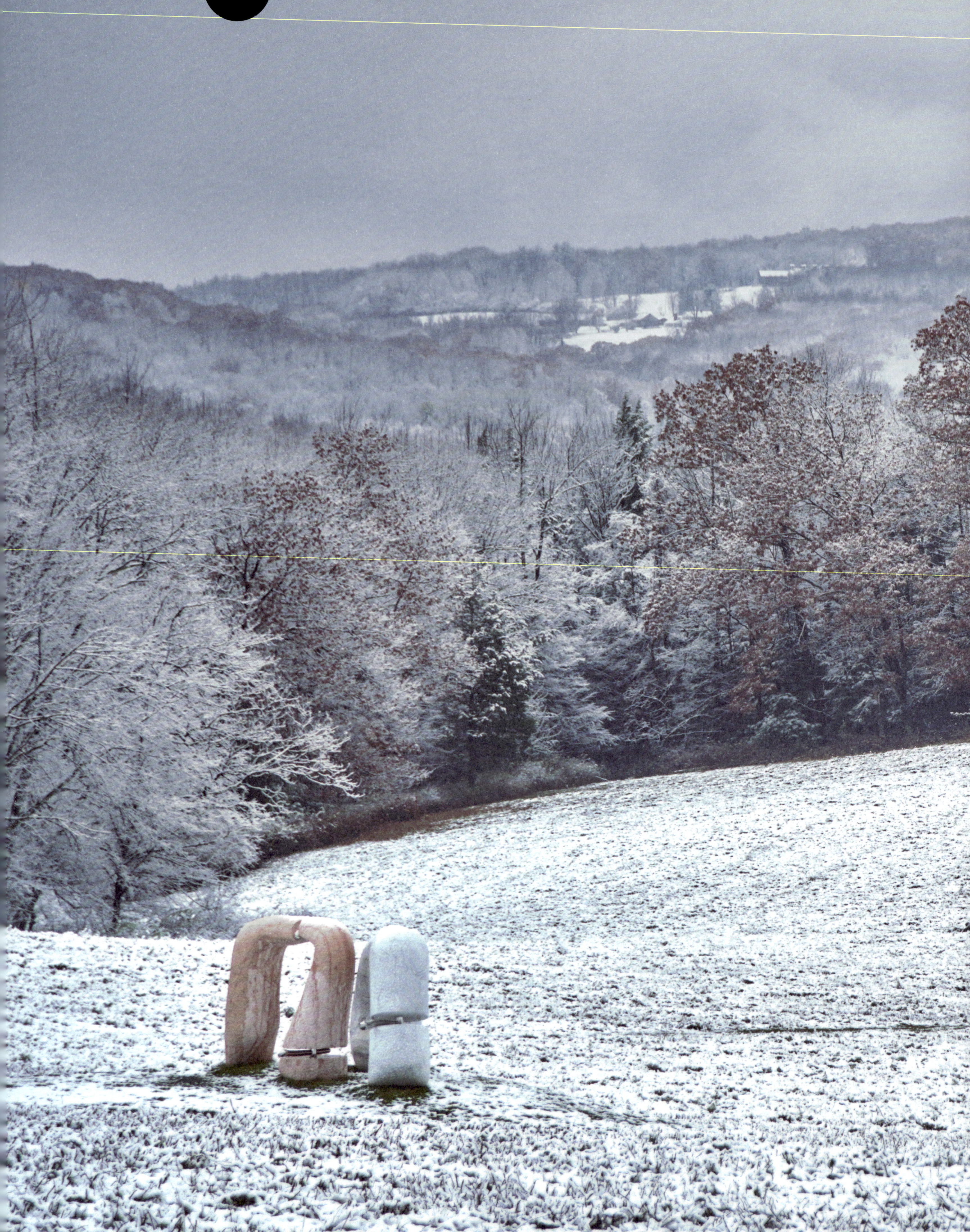

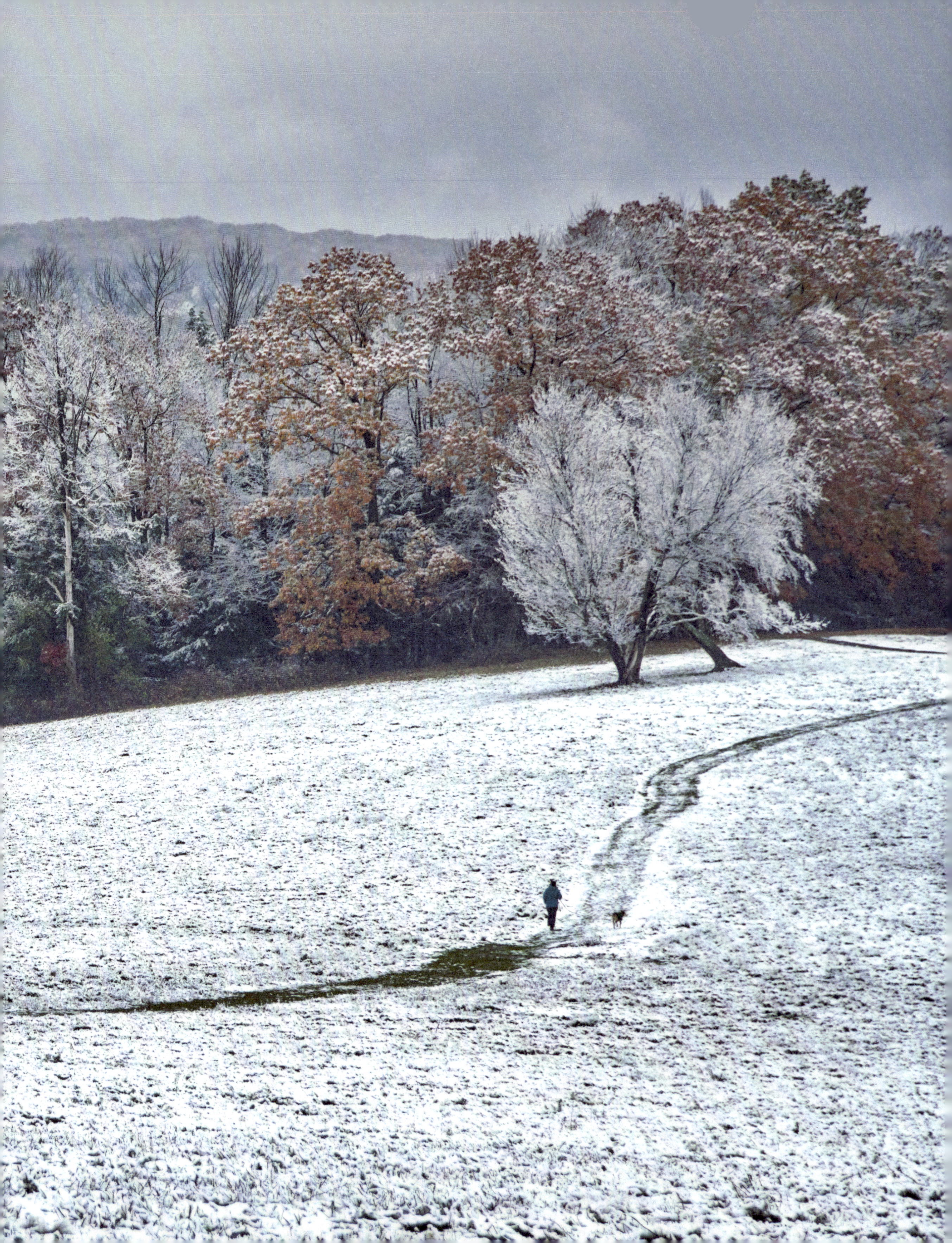

# Adoration of the Joint: Nairy Baghramian's *Knee and Elbow*

Robert Wiesenberger

On a recent spring day, two cows acquainted themselves with the arched stone forms of Nairy Baghramian's *Knee and Elbow*. One, squeezed into the aperture of the pink marble, seemed comforted by the even pressure on its body, leaning in for support. The second nuzzled the first. Upon hearing of this, Baghramian was pleased with the interest her work had elicited, the expanded sculptural ensemble formed, and the fact that her nearly cow-sized marbles were well-anchored below ground, able to withstand such affections.

*Knee and Elbow* (2020) is a suspiciously straightforward title for an artist who often names her work in allusive, even cryptic ways (recent examples include *Piff Paff*, 2015; *Peeper*, 2016; and *Portrait (The Concept-Artist's Smoking Head, Stand-In)*, 2016). But the two abstracted forms—the larger, white one the knee and the smaller, pink one the elbow, according to the artist—spring from Baghramian's interest in the human body's poses and postures in art, dance, and everyday life, and in the load-bearing anatomy that undergirds them.

While Baghramian's sculptural practice has long been concerned with the vulnerabilities of bodies—in evocative, but never illustrative ways[1]—*Knee and Elbow* might be her most explicitly figurative work yet. Its precise subject matter also suggests an important dimension of Baghramian's art, namely one of articulation, attuned to the joint as both an agent of mobility and a meeting of materials. Architect Louis Kahn's observation that "the joint is the beginning of ornament," and "ornament is the adoration of the joint,"[2] applies, though differently than he intended, in Baghramian's case. With *Knee and Elbow*, the artist's attention to joints, which she also adorns, is a kind of adoration; so, too, is the particular form of care implied by how her bodies are held, supported, and sustained.

## Pose

Contemporary dance is a frequent reference for Baghramian, who has collaborated with choreographers on exhibitions of her sculpture.[3] In the context of *Knee and Elbow*, she considers Yvonne Rainer, who once said of her breakthrough performance *Trio A* (1966), in which she passed smoothly through a series of everyday movements, that it was "about a kind of pacing where a pose is never struck."[4] Baghramian evokes a similar fluidity in *Knee and Elbow*, and the possibility of countless configurations. Her elbow appears, so to speak, en pointe, and both it and the knee seem to sit lightly on the earth, unmediated by a plinth. Baghramian also cites Simone Forti, who explained her 1960 Dance Constructions—for example *Huddle* (fig. 48), in which six or seven performers enact the title formation while taking turns climbing over the mutually supporting mass—by saying that they are "dance[s] but [they] also can be seen as sculpture[s] made of people."[5] Baghramian's proposition, conversely, is that sculptures might appear as performative as people.

For dancers, joints are always the first thing to go, a literal kind of "professional deformation," to borrow the title of Baghramian's 2016–18 career-spanning solo exhibition—a French expression for the ways in which one's job tends to shape one's outlook (an "occupational hazard," but with a plastic dimension).[6] If wear, tear, and weight tax the *Knee and Elbow*, Baghramian's figures are relieved of their burdens by disembodiment. These nonspecific subjects—ungendered, unraced, and otherwise unmarked—rest and recover, as one might after the steep climb up Stone Hill to see them. We contemplate them in their own moment of proprioception, before the next move.

## Pain

For an artist whose practice over the past two decades has been resolutely sculptural, the decision to finally use marble, the discipline's most noble material, was not taken lightly. It was inspired, Baghramian says, by her visit to the Clark, whose founding building, completed in 1955, is a squat temple in white marble and whose collection traffics heavily in Neoclassicism. This visit also put her in mind of portraiture and its poses. In the Clark's permanent collection, Baghramian encountered bodies ranging from the sturdy, almost columnar figures of Piero della Francesca, disposed formally in space, to the young ballerinas of Edgar Degas, stretching and resting in their classroom.

48

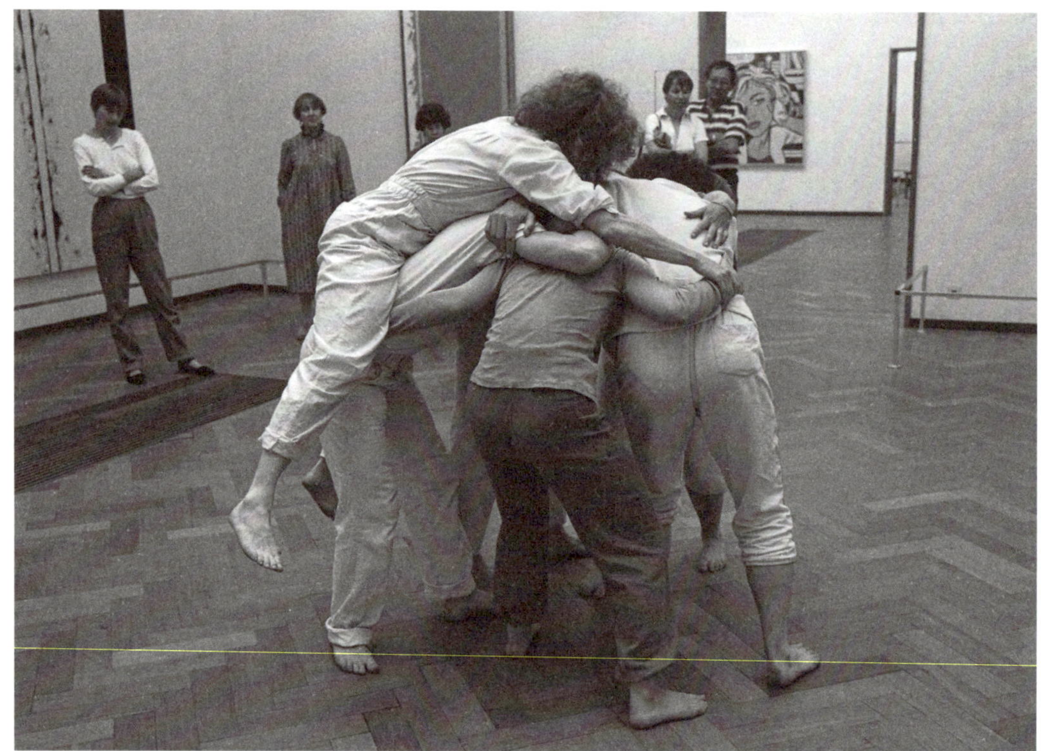

49

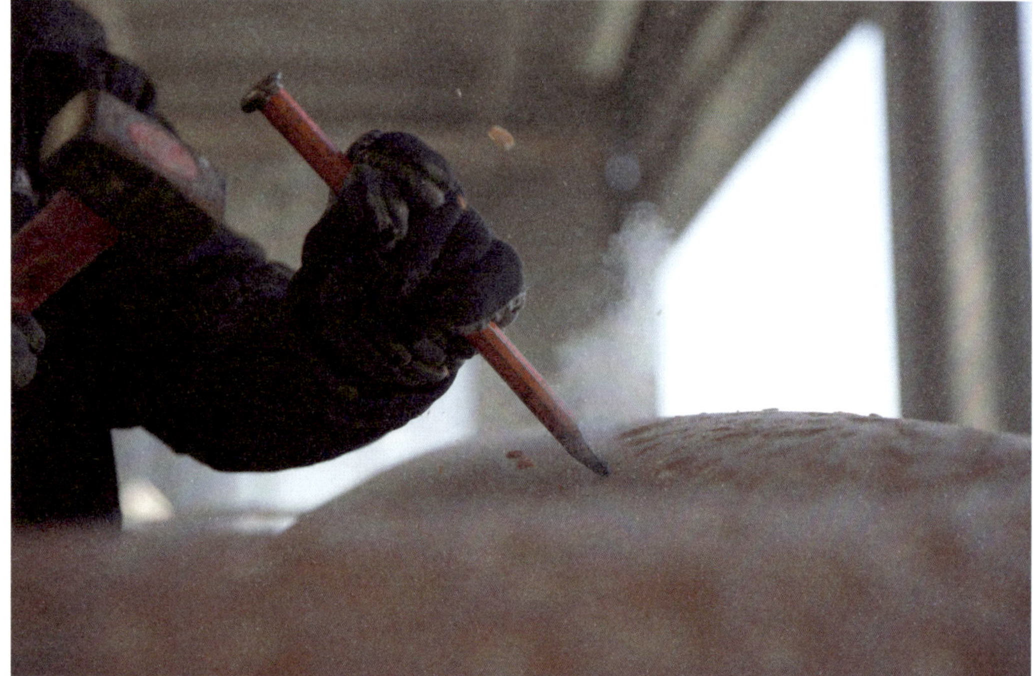

Fig. 48 Simone Forti, *Huddle*, 1961, performance, May 16, 1982. Stedelijk Museum, Amsterdam
Fig. 49 A craftsperson chisels marble according to Baghramian's instruction

50

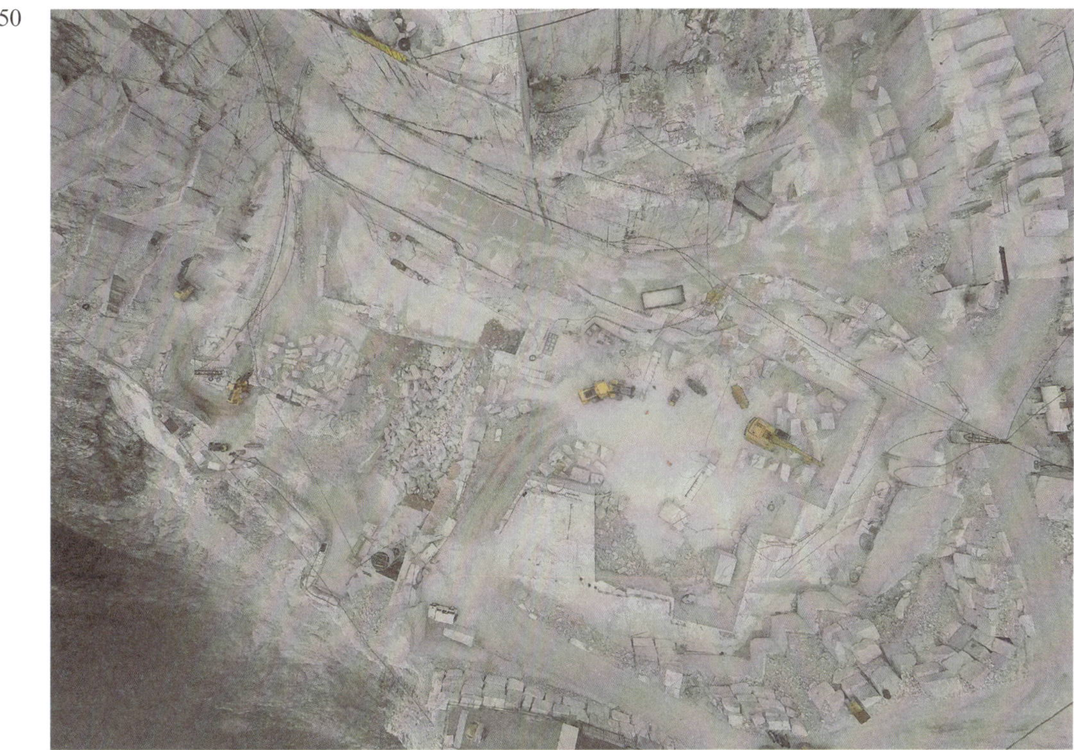

51

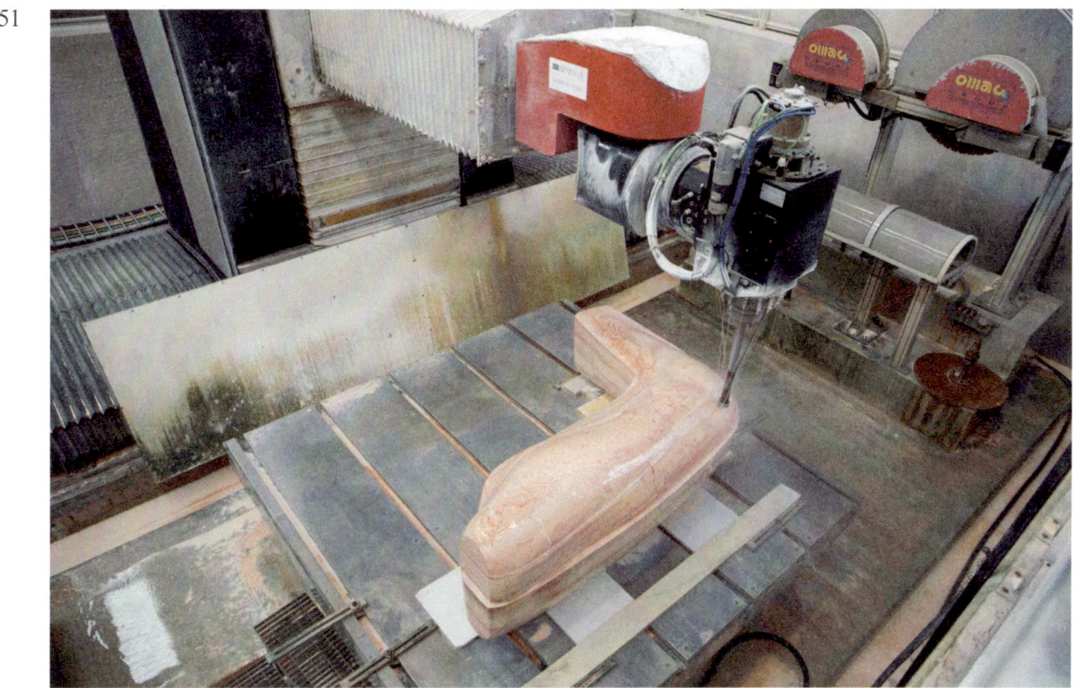


Fig. 50 The Henraux quarry in Carrara, Italy, as seen from above
Fig. 51 A computer-controlled (CNC) milling machine at work on Baghramian's sculpture

52

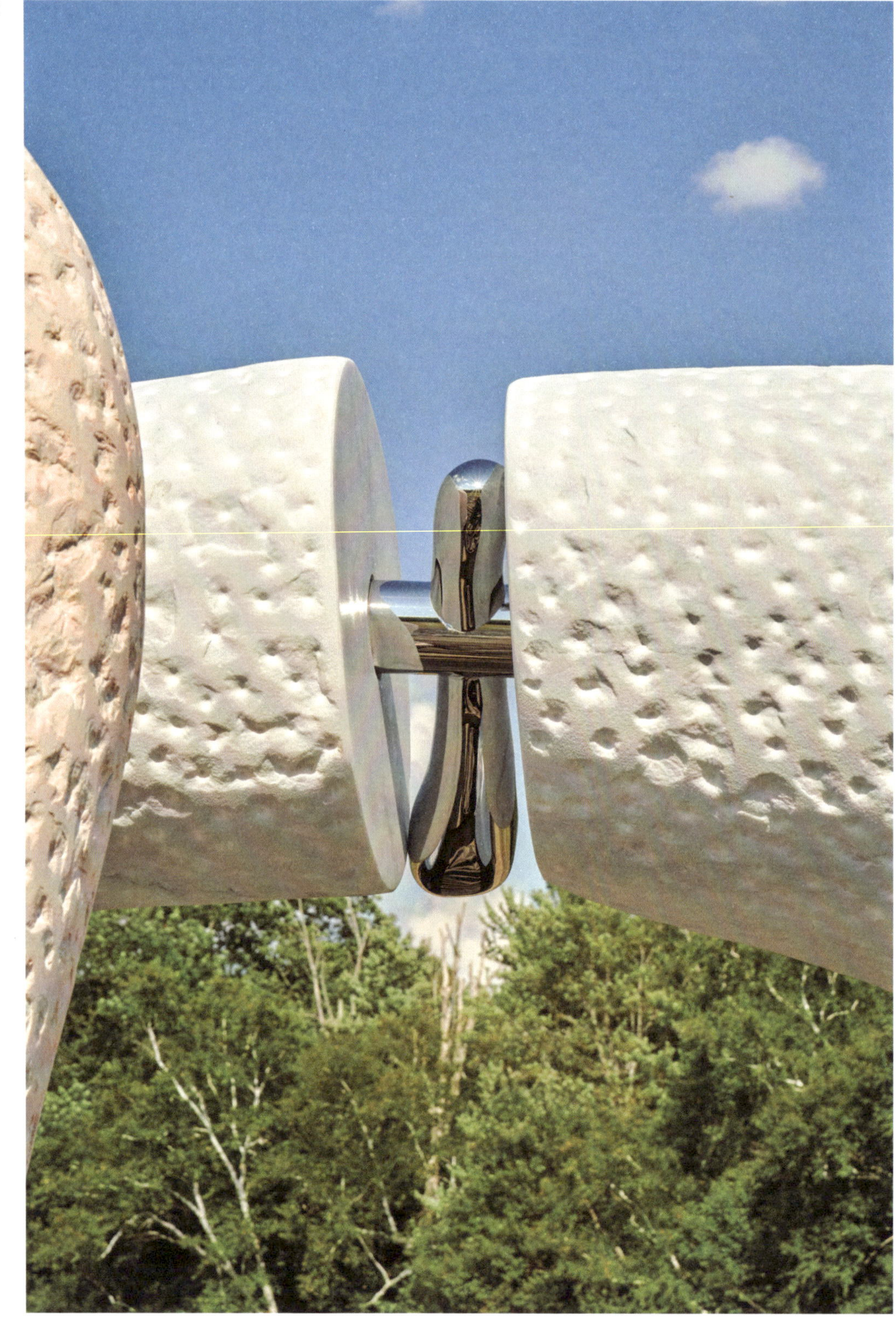

Fig. 52 Nairy Baghramian, *Knee and Elbow* (detail), 2020

In April 2018, when the artist visited the famed Henraux quarry in Carrara, Italy, their stonemasons helped her find the finest blocks of white and pink marble, veined by the fewest mineral imperfections.[7] The eldest quarrier, in his eighties, had worked with some of the twentieth century's preeminent sculptors, including Hans Arp, Louise Bourgeois, Barbara Hepworth, Henry Moore, and Isamu Noguchi—all of whom, in their way, had also navigated the fluid boundaries between figuration and abstraction. What Baghramian asked the craftspeople to do with these pristine pieces of stone, however, surprised them. The marbles were not to be polished, she instructed, but pitted all over by bush hammering and chiseling—a trial by a thousand blows (fig. 49).

Baghramian has consistently made a virtue of facture, or the marks of an object's making, for example by retaining the telltale seams after casting aluminum, or in the uneven brushing of paint on glass. Besides visually softening hard surfaces and attracting touch, these details register a material's earlier states. For her, pockmarking the marble was a way of acknowledging the pain she sensed in it on her visit to the vast, faceted pit at the base of Monte Altissimo (fig. 50). Perhaps the stone had registered the ordeals of deep geological accumulation (primordial marine life sedimenting into limestone), metamorphic transformation (heat and pressure making marble), and sudden extraction (with chains or explosives). Or maybe the artist sensed the melancholic ways in which marble, with its classical connotations, is always already a kind of pre-ruin. In any case, she thought these traumas should be surfaced on the stone and present as symptoms do, rather than be polished away in denial.

This putative finish cannot, however, necessarily be restricted to the surface; any chisel blow might drive fissures to the stone's center, making the treatment a new kind of violence. The divots accentuate, and exacerbate, the marble's inherent porosity which, along with its chemical reactivity and the fragilities traced by its veining, belies its associations with timelessness and durability. As always, Baghramian parlayed these deficiencies into a form that is at once elegant and ungainly. Our responses to it might range from aesthetic enjoyment to embodied empathy (*Einfüllung*, or feeling into), as we identify our own somatic contingencies and vulnerabilities.

If *Knee and Elbow* surfaces the stone's pain, that pain is also reciprocal. The job of quarry worker has historically been one of the most arduous and dangerous in Italy. Carrara has had quarries since Ancient Rome, and generations of workers have identified with the Roman slaves who once toiled there. In the late nineteenth century, the region became the birthplace of anarchism in Italy, and quarriers clashed violently with local government, demanding self-rule and an end to the class and wage system. The labor movement in Italy, and the country's first unions, emerged from Carrara, which remains known as the unofficial capital of anarchism in Europe.

Today the job of quarry worker is considerably safer and better organized.[8] The most grueling work, of shaping blocks into their initial form, has been outsourced to a computer-controlled (CNC) milling machine whose robotic arm, in Baghramian's project, resembles the forms it was programmed to carve, as if the machine appendage were sculpting in its own image (fig. 51). Still, the masons will not be redundant any time soon. Not only is the final finishing a precise job that resists mechanization, but so too is the initial quarrying: during the selection process, senior masons "read" a stone's vulnerabilities from the spidery network of its veins.

## Prosthesis

Bulbous forms are not new in Baghramian's sculptural vocabulary, but the sheer mass of the material in *Knee and Elbow* is (past lumps—in foam, wax, rubber, or polyurethane—have appeared pillowy). Baghramian lightens her *Knee and Elbow* by dissecting them: each has been severed at two points, revealing both the smooth interior faces of the marble and a skeletal structure sheathed in stainless steel, polished to a mirror finish. The steel rods have been embellished by irregularly shaped, somewhat Arp-ian protuberances in the same material, projecting out at various points (fig. 52). Collectively, these operations refuse any conceit of organic wholeness—a presumption that

53
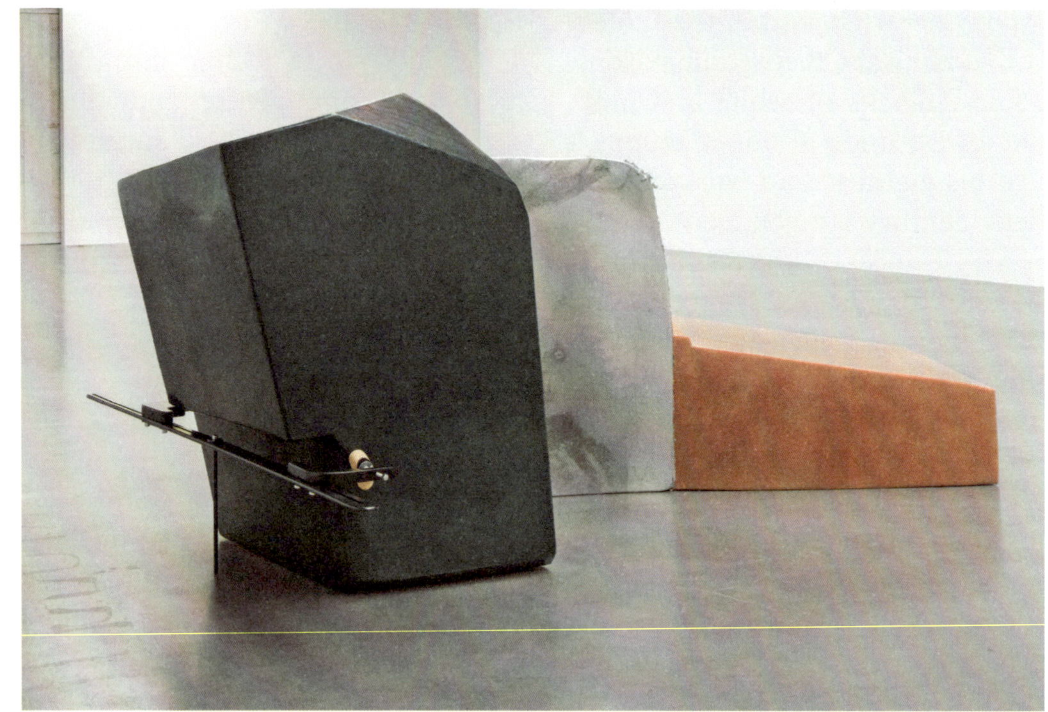

54
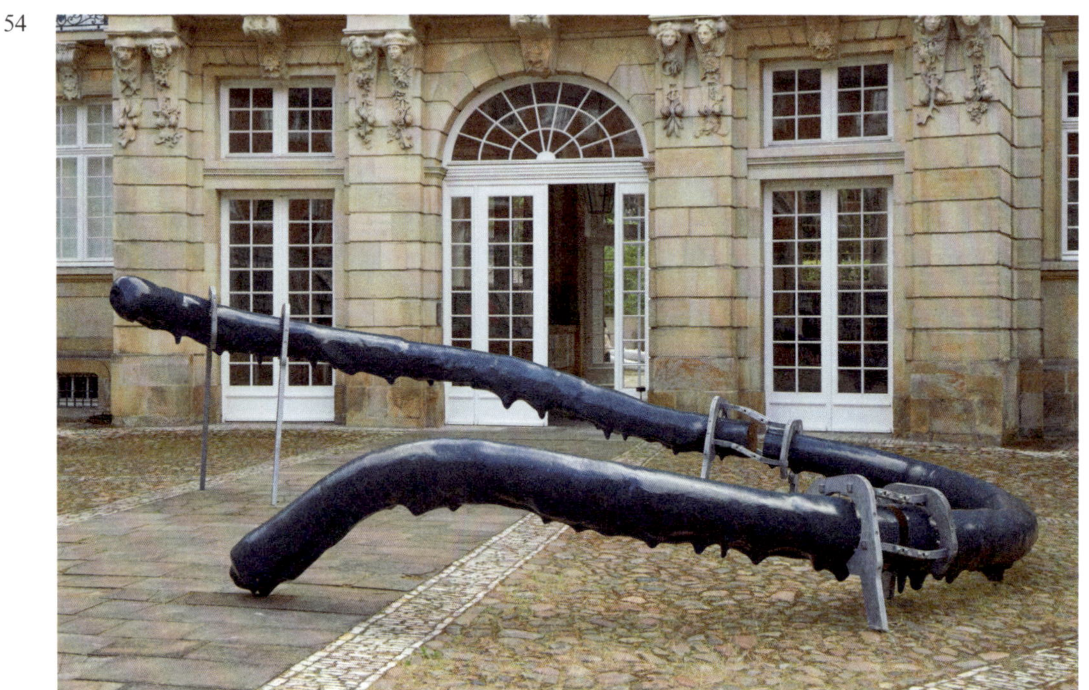

Fig. 53 Nairy Baghramian, *Maintainers A*, 2018. Cast aluminum, painted aluminum, cork, styrofoam, pigmented paraffin wax, overall: approximately 64 9/16 x 145 11/16 x 90 9/16 in. (164 x 370 x 230 cm). Museum of Modern Art, New York

Fig. 54 Nairy Baghramian, *Beliebte Stellen / Privileged Points*. Installation view from Skulptur Projekte Münster, 2017. Lacquered bronze, metal, lashing chain, tensioning devices, rubber

underlies most monolithic sculpture, from ancient statuary to modernist, biomorphic forms (even when they are also invisibly structured).

Depending on how one reads the work—and Baghramian readily indulges in such speculation—the steel couplings are bone or perhaps marrow, the cratered marble flayed or freshly epilated flesh. The steel protuberances (whose phallic aspect, it must be said, is prominent) could be instruments holding the body open; handles presenting themselves for torqueing; jewelry-like body modifications; the emergent signs of a compound fracture; medical implants of a kind; or, with their mercurial sheen, the electrical impulses of nerves, and their shooting pains, made visible. The techno-futuristic finish might also evoke the posthuman body of a cyborg, albeit in classical garb. All this metal could also call to mind the tools of two seemingly distant trades: the stainless steel saws, drills, and mallets used by orthopedic surgeons are not so different from those of the stonemason, and "surgical precision" often entails quite forceful interventions on the body.[9]

The joints Baghramian works on, however, are not just between femur and tibia/fibula—indeed, the bends here are monolithic—but between stone and steel, natural and synthetic, rough and smooth. In masonry or carpentry, the meeting of two materials is a joint, whether or not it moves (and it usually does, even if imperceptibly). When Louis Kahn called the joint the start of ornament, he meant the precise and restrained juxtaposition of materials, rather than the application of decoration. Baghramian's applied steel elements exceed this standard, whether they are structural or ornamental, prosthetic or decorative, or the first as a form of the second—articulations of a vulnerability usually meant to be concealed. In British English, "articulation" is another word for a physiological joint. In *Knee and Elbow*, Baghramian articulates her subject, its surfaces, and its component parts, calling out and differentiating them in their attributes and affordances and emphasizing their interrelations.

In her practice, generally, Baghramian does not so much assemble her diverse palette of materials—which includes aluminum, glass, polyurethane, resin, rubber, silicone, steel, and wax—but rather allows them to hold one another up. Gravity is rarely taken for granted here. In *Maintainers A* (2018, fig. 53), for example, two large, wax-covered foam masses sandwich an upright, roughly cast aluminum plate between them. The plate is additionally propped up by two aluminum wedges, like doorstops, and the larger of the foam masses, which could certainly support itself, is hugged by a handmade clamp fixed with cork pads that meets the floor in a single, under-structured leg, like a kickstand. Each site of connection is a joint, or a "privileged point," to use the title of another of Baghramian's sculptures (fig. 54), whether suggesting wear (between the rough aluminum and wax) or care—the wax block, cushioned by cork bumpers.

## Place

In a recent interview, when asked how she would explain her art to someone who had never seen it, Baghramian's first response was: "My work depends very much on the place from which it emerges."[10] These places are usually architecturally defined; Baghramian has, for example, had a longstanding interest in the domestic interior, both spatially and ideologically.[11] In the *Ground/work* exhibition, however, *Knee and Elbow* appears in an open field, on a part of Stone Hill that overlooks the Clark's buildings below, the college campus and church steeples of Williamstown beyond, and Vermont's Green Mountains on the horizon. There is no clear spatial or architectural enclosure here, and yet *Knee and Elbow*, for all its strangeness, also appears to fit—connected with rather than oblivious to its surroundings.

Visitors who take the Pasture Trail up from the museum to see the piece will have first encountered Thomas Schütte's 2015 installation *Crystal*, a zinc-clad wood structure that is equal parts architectural folly and observatory (Baghramian's interest in a sculptural dialogue with the Schütte was one factor in siting her work where she did). *Crystal* has become a fixture of the Clark campus, but it is not permanent—in keeping with the museum's practice of not acquiring contemporary art. Rather, it is on long-term loan from the artist, yet built so sturdily that it is unlikely to disappear anytime soon. Baghramian's piece, like all those in *Ground/work*, is also only a temporary visitor, scheduled to leave Williamstown after the exhibition's run. The artist wishes to be honest about these conditions, however sensitive to site *Knee and Elbow* may be.

Asked to further explain her work and its hallmarks in the same recent interview, Baghramian observed: "What often bothers me about sculptures is this enormous self-confidence. I work on everything that goes into making a sculpture feel so confident. My sculptures should help to formulate doubts about them."[12] With *Knee and Elbow*, the artist operates on assumptions about the fixity, stability, and signification of sculpture; its autonomy or relation to site; and the inertness, durability, and historicity of its materials. Baghramian went on to acknowledge her doubt that any artistic genre or medium had a special claim to political commitment and offered that "'ambivalent abstraction' might be a better way to describe my work."[13] The ambivalence, then, is of both the sculptor and the sculpture, which appears here at once of its place and on the move, august and also somewhat awkward.

## Postscript

From its promontory, *Knee and Elbow* mimes the double-humped, tree-dappled contours of the mountain range beyond. And perhaps the material senses some family relation: Stone Hill was, some half-billion years ago, Alpine height—Matterhorn, more or less—before being ground down to hill status. But Baghramian's sculpture isn't the archetypal Romantic wanderer, surveying the land from on high. Rather, its forms remind me of Philip Guston's parodic, textured lumps, in all their ambivalence. Guston's white and pink are the cowardly cloth of Ku Klux Klan hoods and the swollen, raw skin beneath (marble statuary, it should be said, has also long been willfully misread through, if not animated by, white-supremacist ideology).[14] His canvases abound with appendages, evoking either classical fragments or carnage (fig. 55). Guston, like Baghramian, felt ambivalence about his abstraction before turning, or rather decisively returning, to figuration, which he believed had a stronger claim on the political exigencies of everyday life.

Baghramian's figures are more refined, and less dopey, than Guston's, and she also seems to have more empathy for them. In the course of a recent interview, Baghramian made a passing remark about our new COVID world that might illuminate her aesthetics as much as it does her politics. She lamented "the fact that in 2020, we are not able to find other words to describe social distancing, such as 'careful closeness,' which would mean the same thing but would have a different effect, rather than the ultimate goal being to protect just yourself. Isolation follows from social distancing."[15] We never, in other words, hold only ourselves up. These conditions of support, both material and social, matter deeply to the artist.

*Robert Wiesenberger is associate curator of contemporary projects at the Clark Art Institute.*

The author would like to thank Williams College Rodgers Intern Kaira Mediratta for her research assistance and Catherine Damman and Sophie Nichols for reading a draft of this essay.

1 In approaching Baghramian's work, André Rottmann observes, "The beholder is . . . faced with carcasses, surrogates, segments, and rudiments that, precisely in their reduced physicality, both evoke and withhold bodily presence and phenomenological abundance; yet by virtue of (and not, as one might think, despite) the principled negation of figuration, gestalt, and volume, Baghramian's works, which might be described as disfigured sculptures, possess a precarious bodily presence." See André Rottmann, "Nairy Baghramian: The Matrix of the Sculpture," in *Nairy Baghramian: Déformation Professionnelle*, ed. Martin Germann and Vincenzo De Bellis (Munich: Prestel, 2018), 67. "Prosthetic formalism" is Kerstin Stakemeier's term for Baghramian's work. Kerstin Stakemeier, "Nairy Baghramian: Stedelijk Museum voor Actuele Kunst, Ghent, Belgium," *Artforum* 55, no. 8 (April 2017): 200–201.

2 Louis Kahn, *Light is the Theme: Louis I. Kahn and the Kimbell Art Museum*, ed. Nell E. Johnson (New Haven, CT: Yale University Press, 2012), 43.

3 Baghramian collaborated with the William Forsyth company in 2008, Adam Lindner in 2012 and 2015, and Maria Hasabi in 2019.

4 Yvonne Rainer, "Interview with Lyn Blumenthal," in *A Woman Who . . . : Essays, Interviews, Scripts* (Baltimore: Johns Hopkins University Press, 1999), 64.

5 Simone Forti, quoted in "High Line Art Performance: Simone Forti, Huddle, May 24, 2012," Friends of the High Line YouTube Channel, http://www.youtube.com/watch?v=pf3Xo6xPjrE.

6 *Nairy Baghramian: Déformation Professionnelle* appeared at the Stedelijk Museum voor Actuele Kunst (S.M.A.K.), Ghent, November 26, 2016–February 19, 2017, and the Walker Art Center, Minneapolis, September 8, 2017–February 5, 2018.

7 The specific types of white and pink marble Baghramian selected are Bianco Altissimo and Rosso Verona, respectively.

8 As of the time of writing, Baghramian was relieved to learn that, despite being hard hit by the COVID-19 pandemic, Henraux had nevertheless avoided layoffs during the crisis.

9 I am indebted to Kristin Swan for this observation.

10 Johanna Adorján, "Nairy Baghramian im Interview," *Süddeutsche Zeitung*, August 29, 2020. (Translation by the author.)

11 See Robert Wiesenberger, "Janette Laverrière: Evocations," in *Question the Wall Itself*, ed. Fionn Meade and Jordan Carter (Minneapolis: Walker Art Center, 2017), 126–35.

12 Adorján, "Nairy Baghramian im Interview." (Translation by the author.)

13 Nairy Baghramian, "Nairy Baghramian: Ambivalent Abstraction" (in conversation with Paulina Pobocha, organized by the Museum of Modern Art, New York), *Ocula*, August 28, 2020, http://ocula.com/magazine/conversations/nairy-baghramian-on-ambivalent-abstraction/. This coinage resonates with Lucy Lippard's term "eccentric abstraction," which she used as the title for a 1966 exhibition that featured the sculpture of Louise Bourgeois, Eva Hesse, and Yayoi Kusama—each to some degree a precursor to Baghramian's practice. See Lucy R. Lippard, "Eccentric Abstraction," in *Changing: Essays in Art Criticism* (New York: E. P. Dutton, 1971), 98–111.

14 Sarah E. Bond, "Why We Need to Start Seeing the Classical World in Color," *Hyperallergic*, June 7, 2017, http://hyperallergic.com/383776/why-we-need-to-start-seeing-the-classical-world-in-color/.

15 Baghramian, "Ambivalent Abstraction."

55

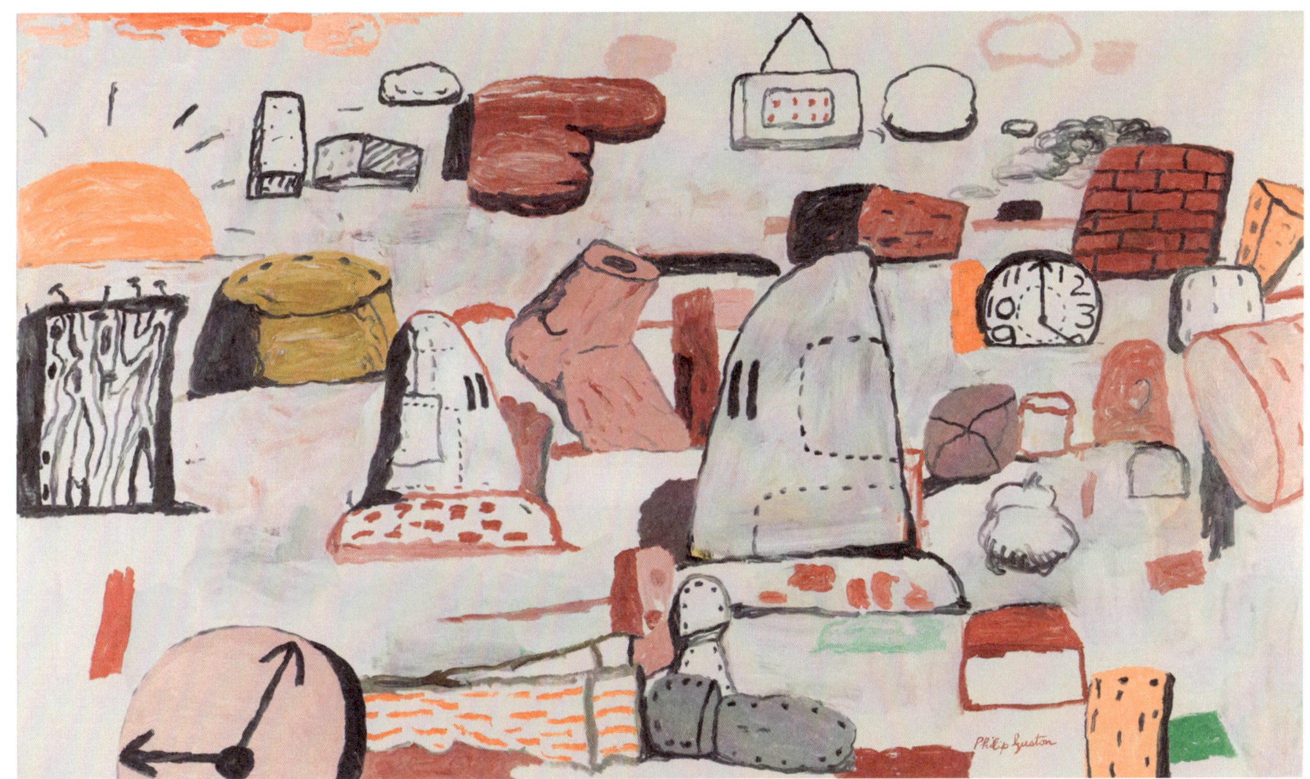


Fig. 55 Philip Guston, *Flatlands*, 1970. Oil on canvas, 70 x 114 1/2 in. (177.8 x 290.8 cm). San Francisco Museum of Modern Art, gift of Byron R. Meyer. © The Estate of Philip Guston, courtesy of Hauser & Wirth

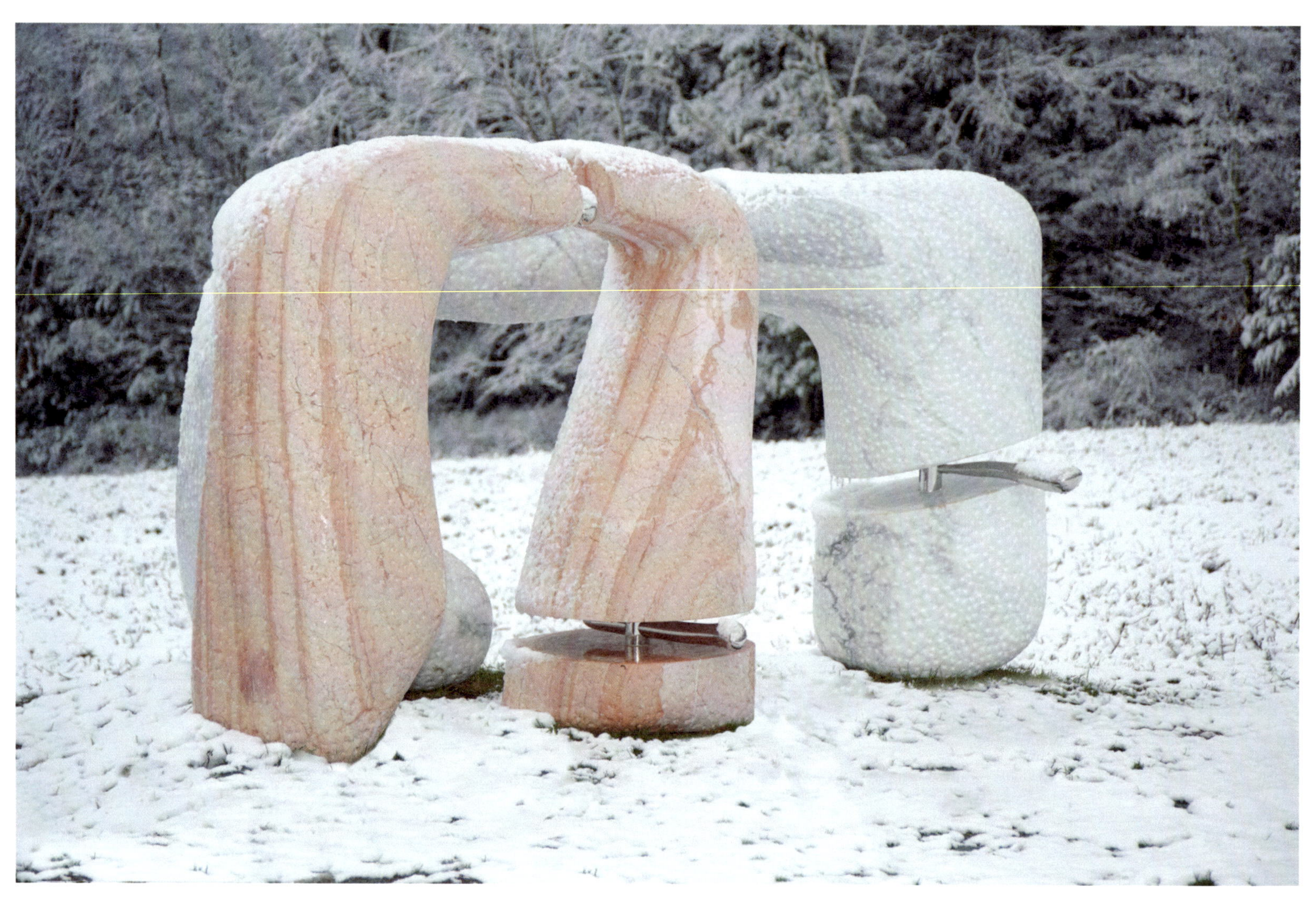

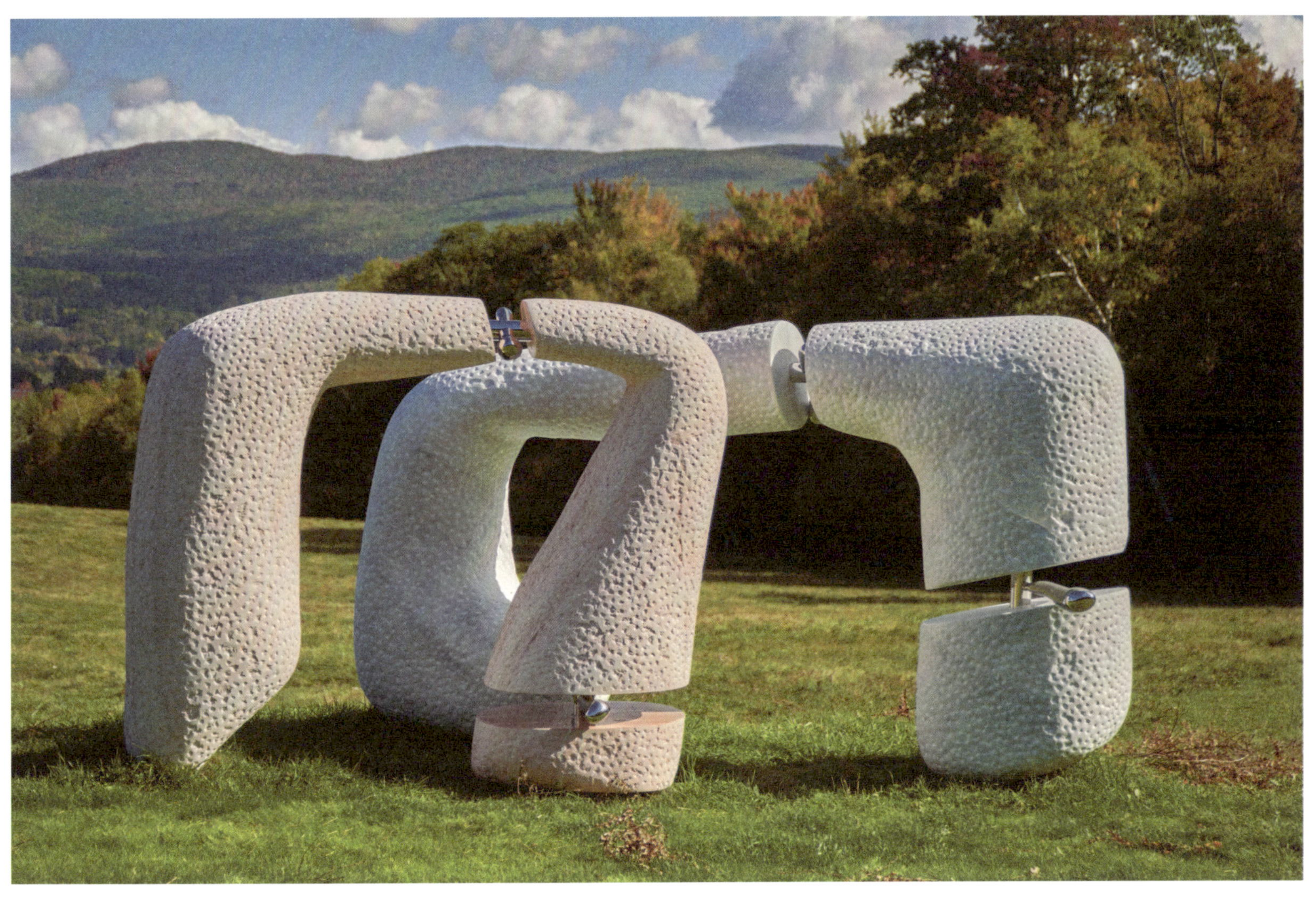

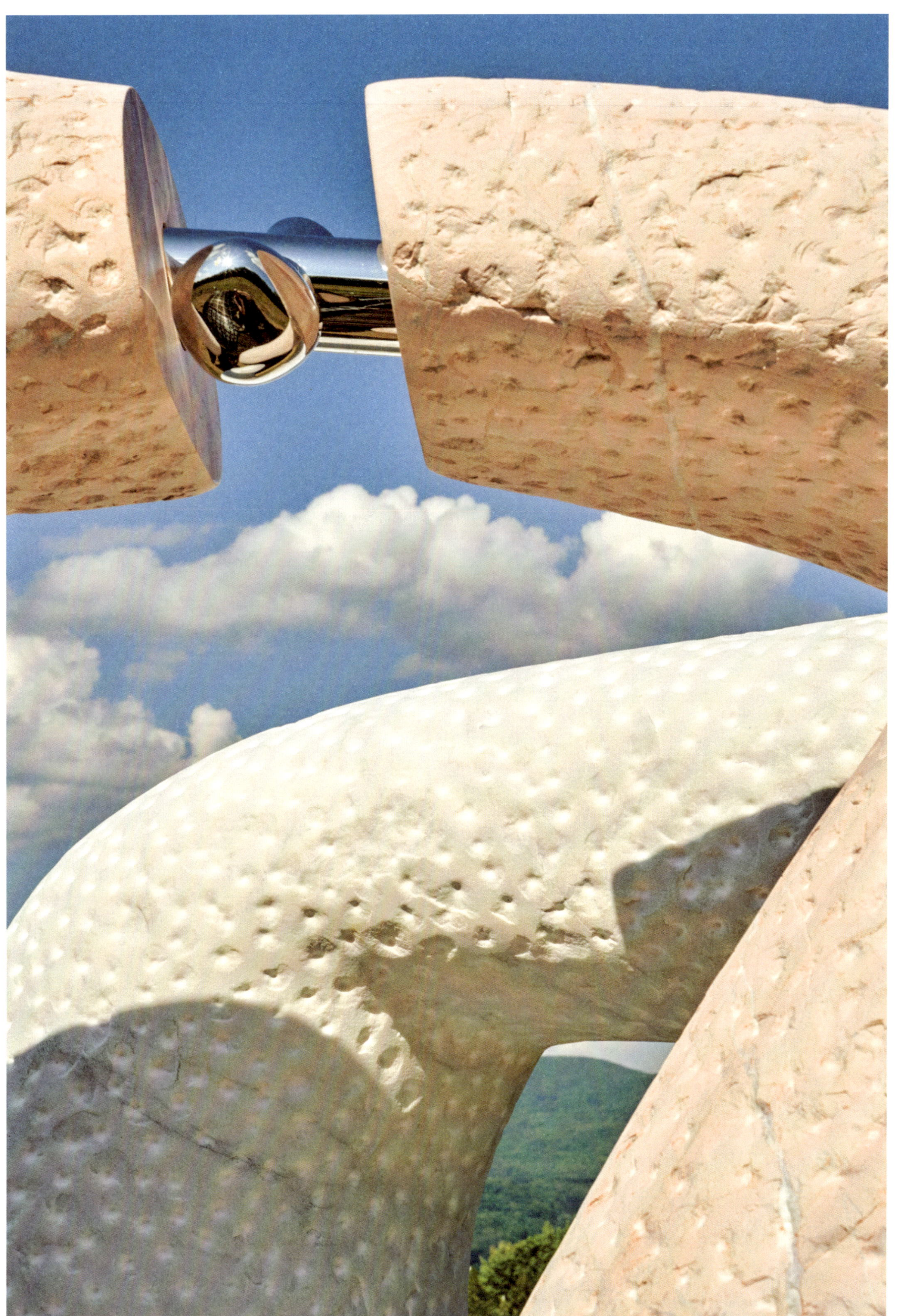

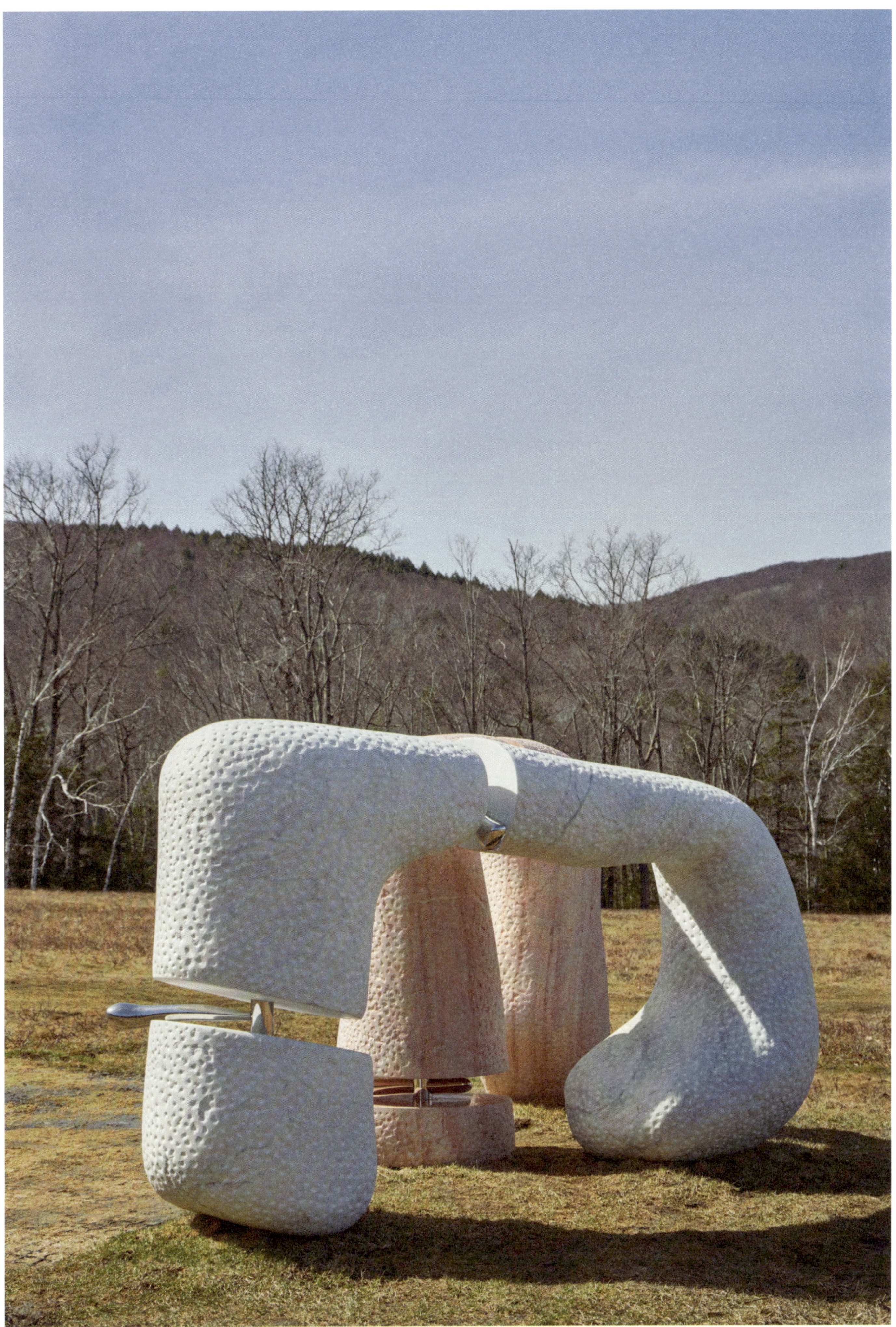

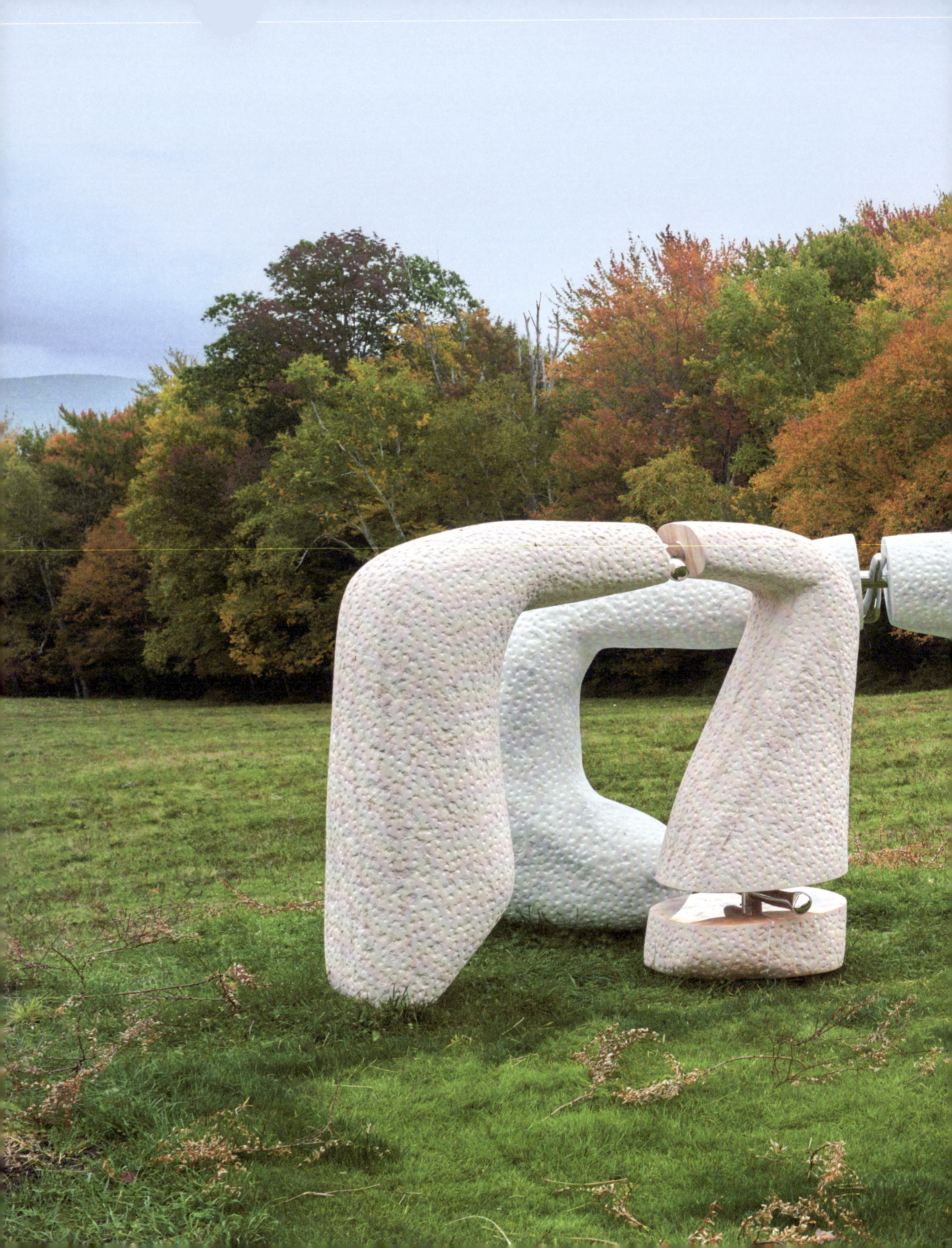

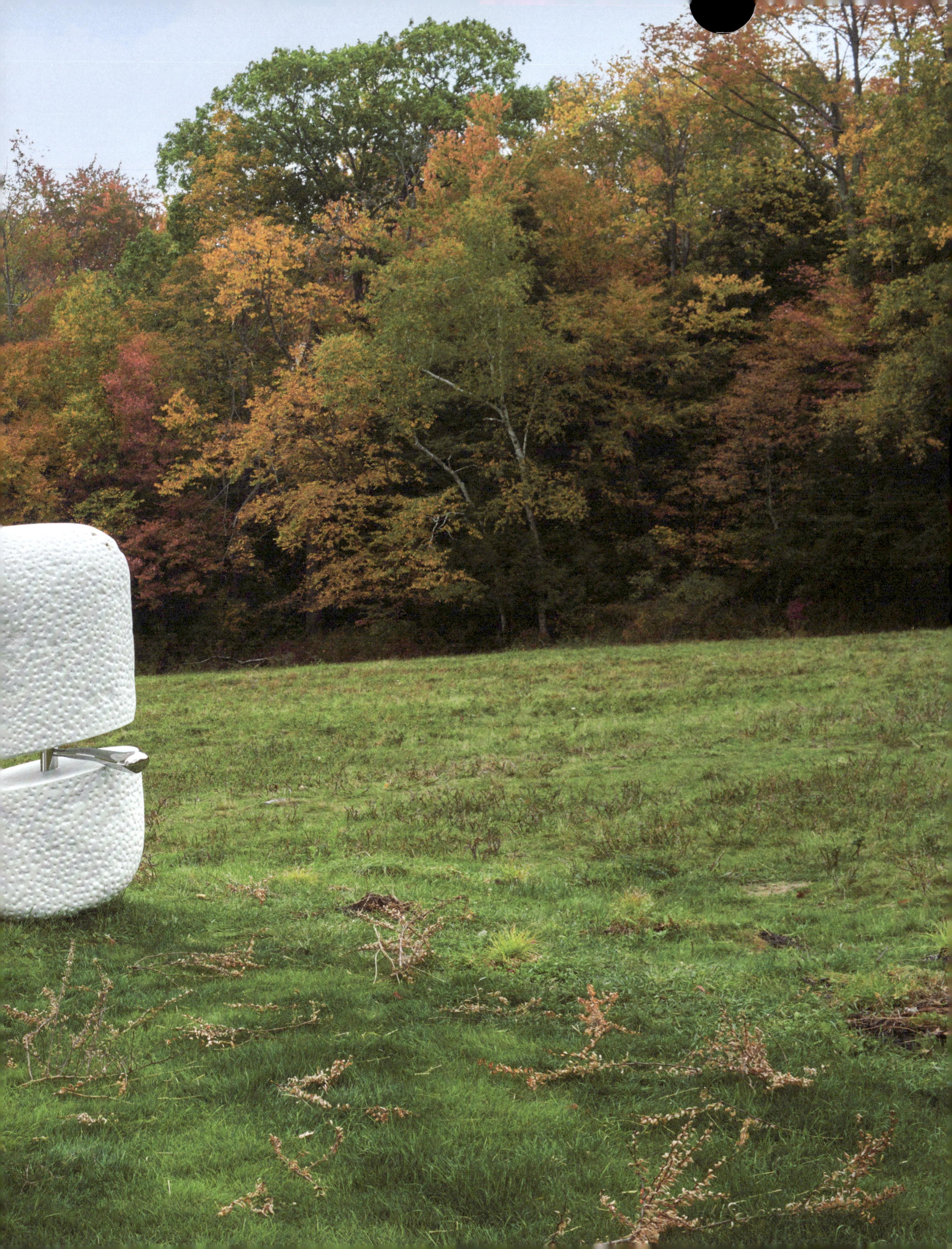

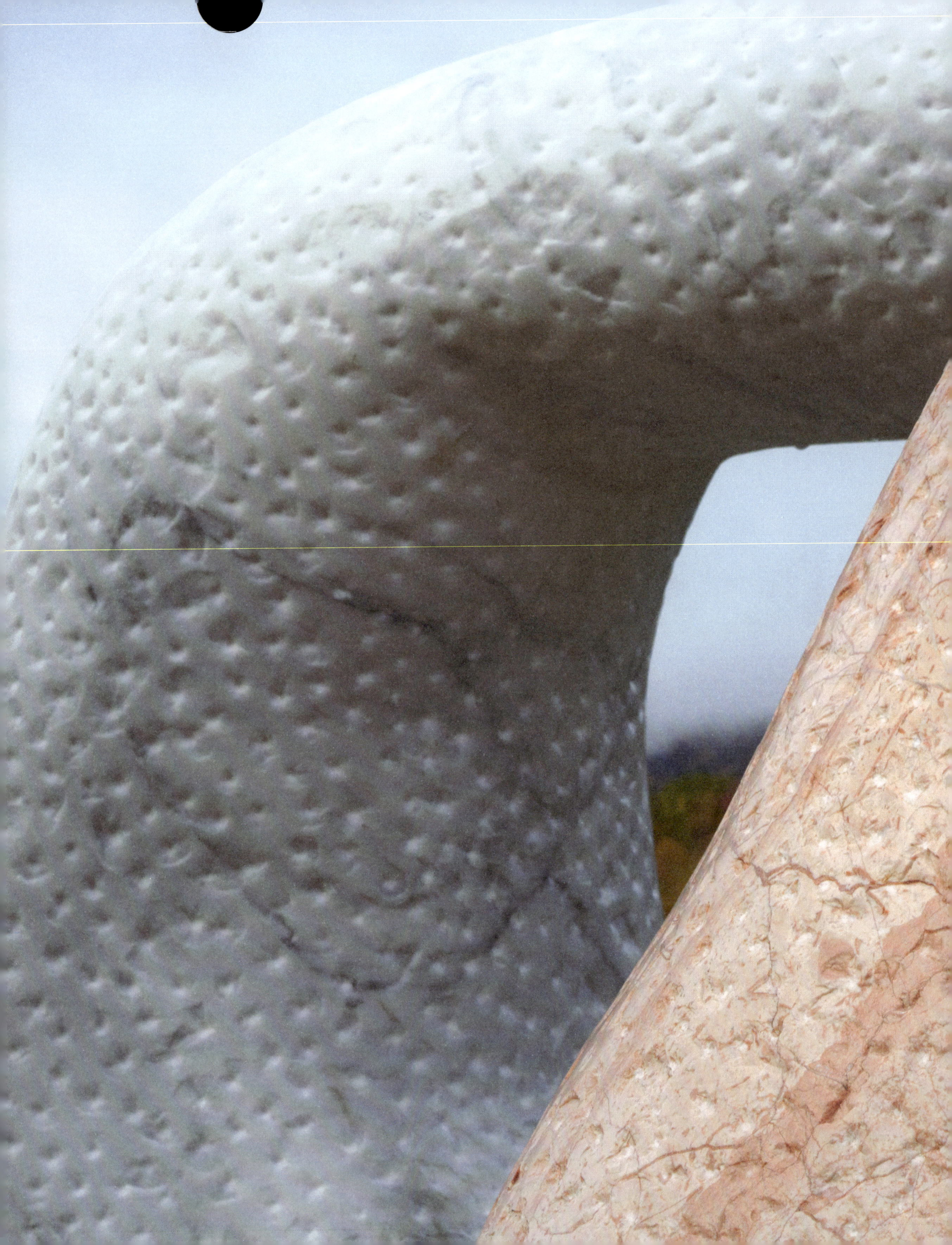

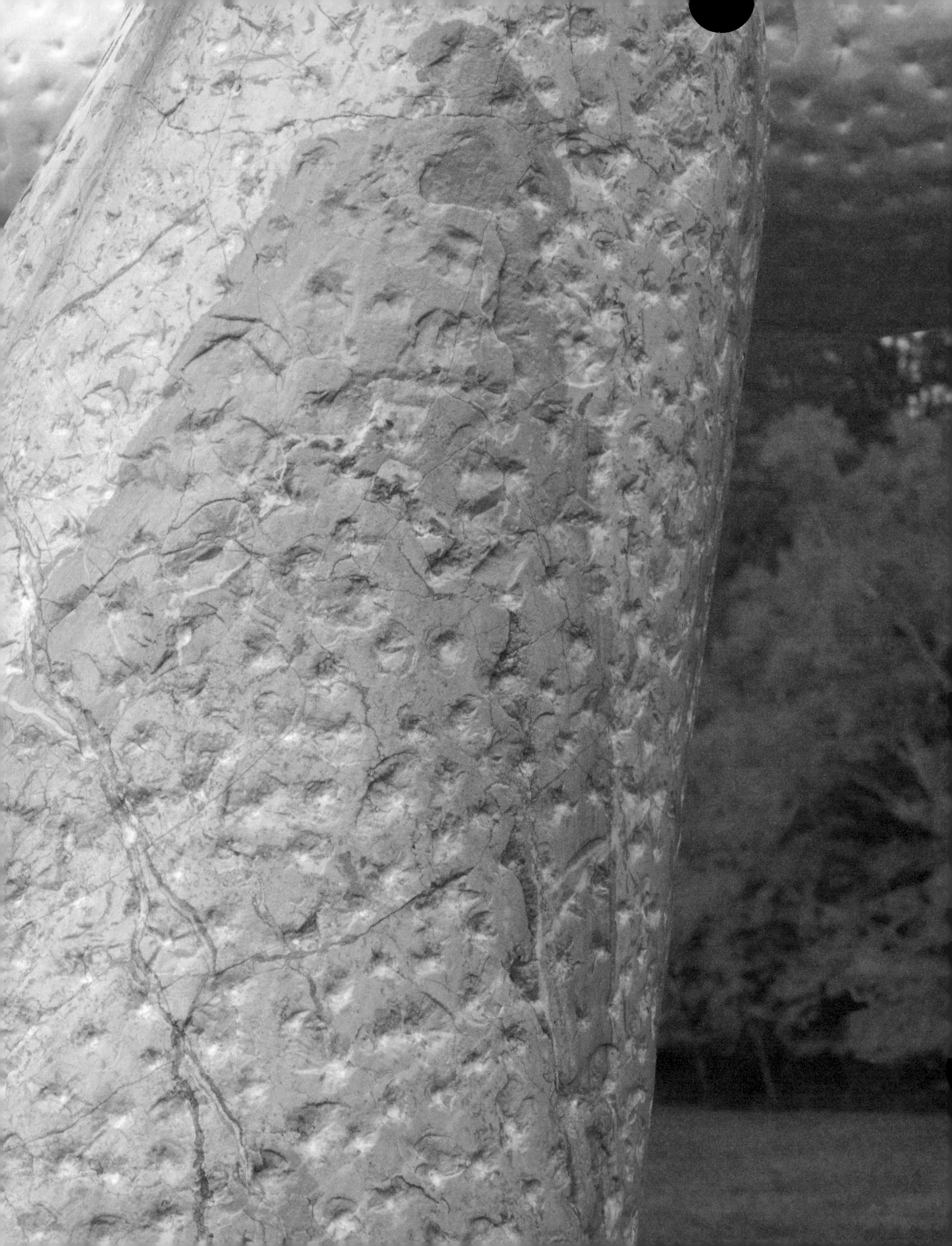

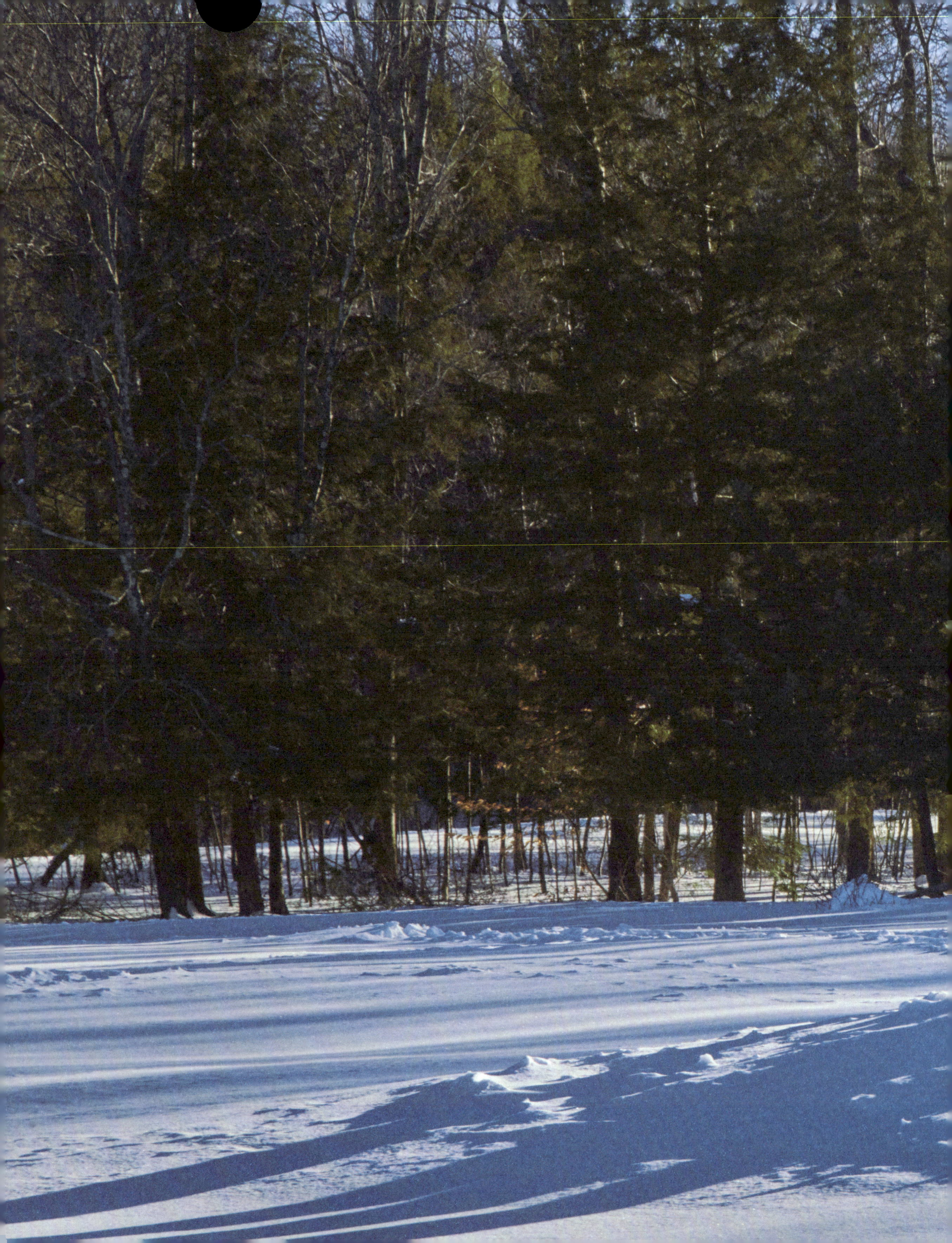

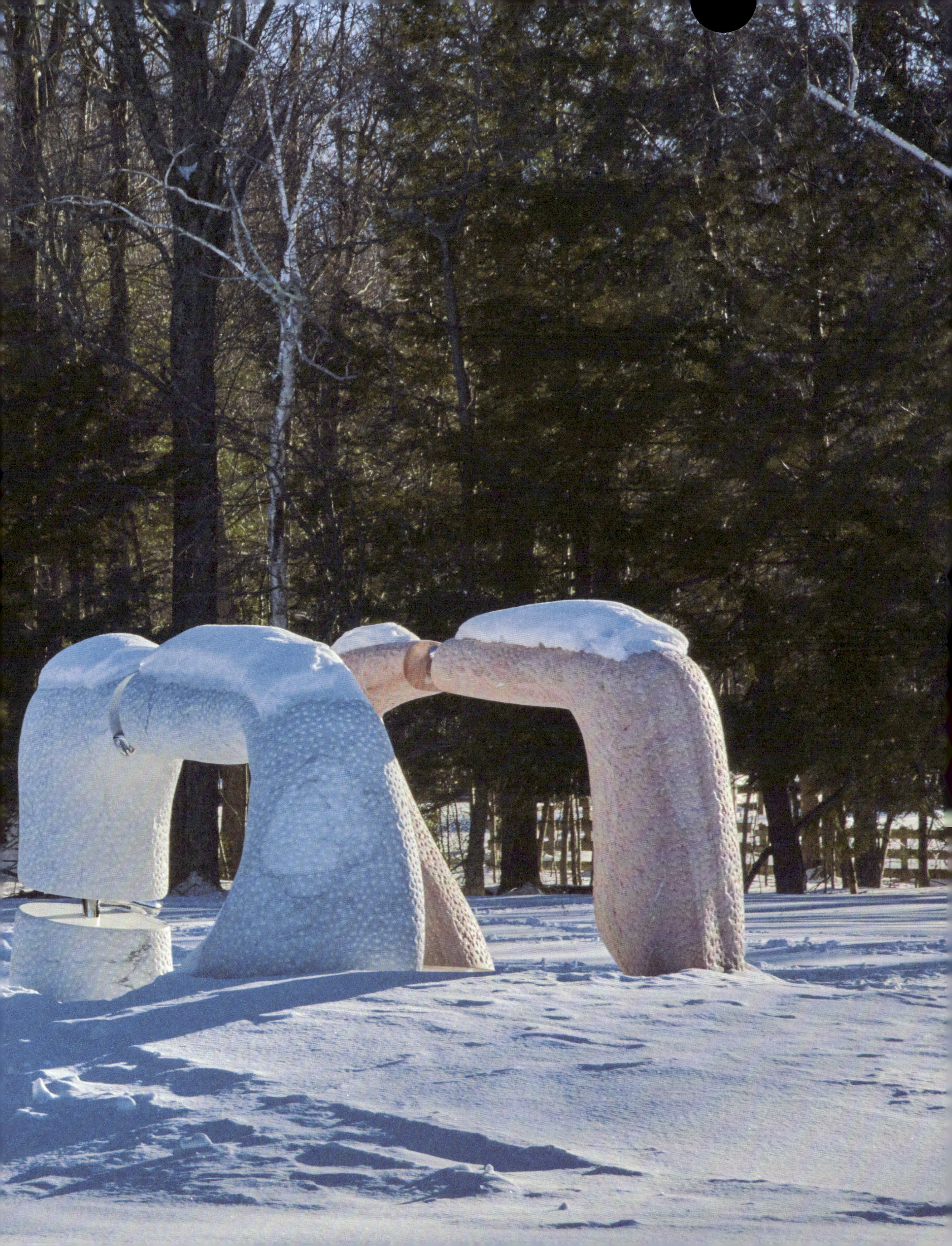

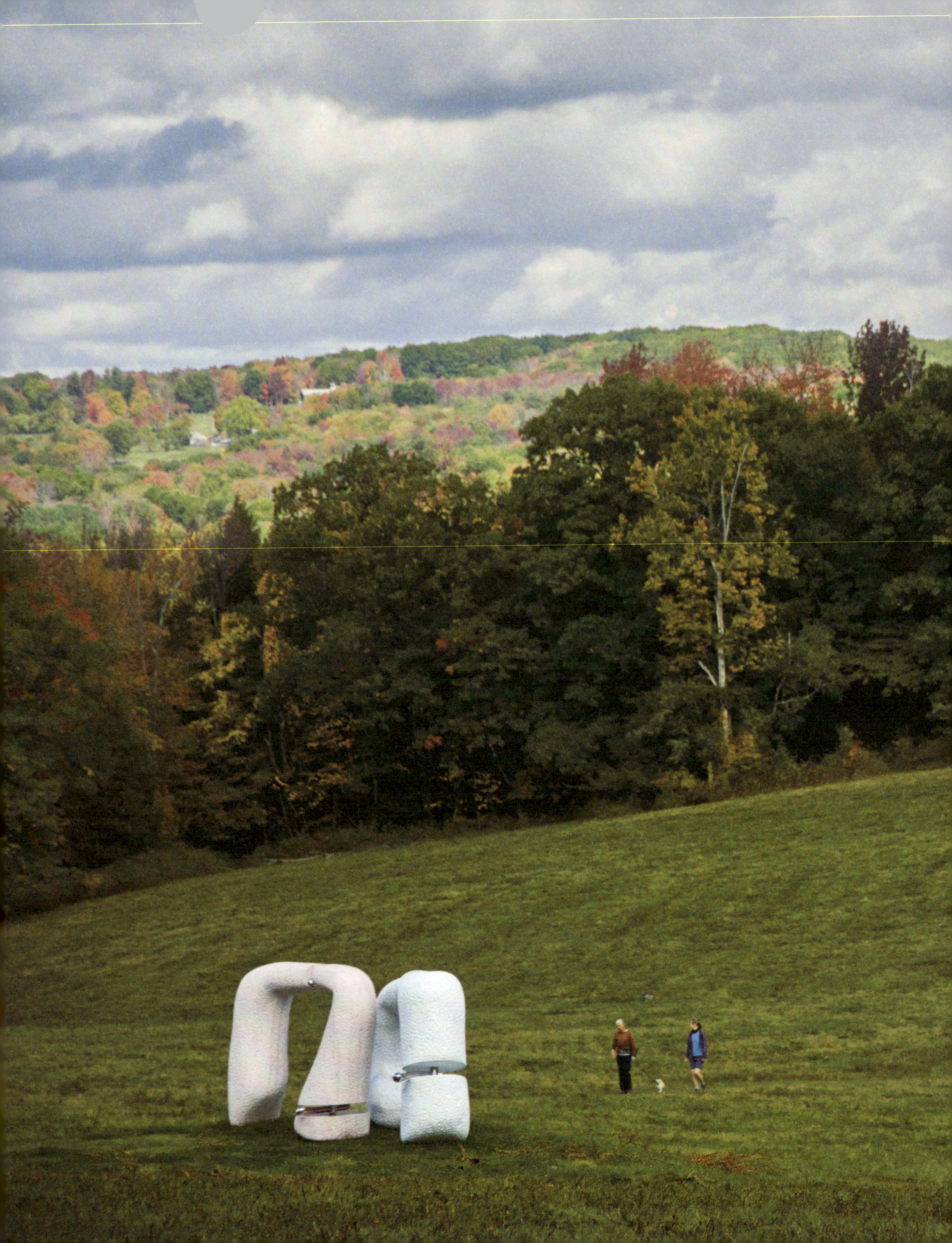

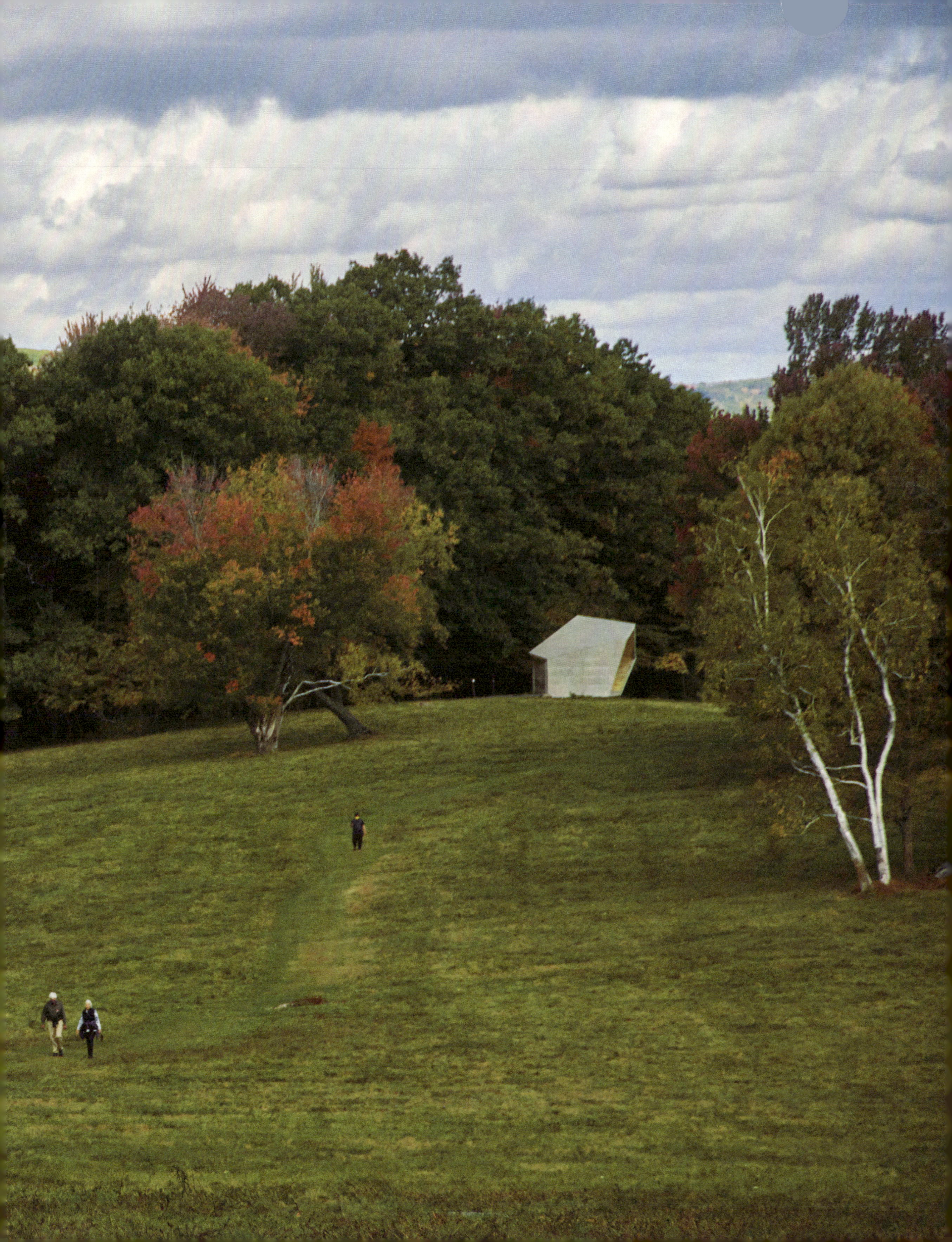

Optical acrylic, bronze, rope
84 x 48 x 42 in. (213.4 x 121.9 x 106.7 cm)

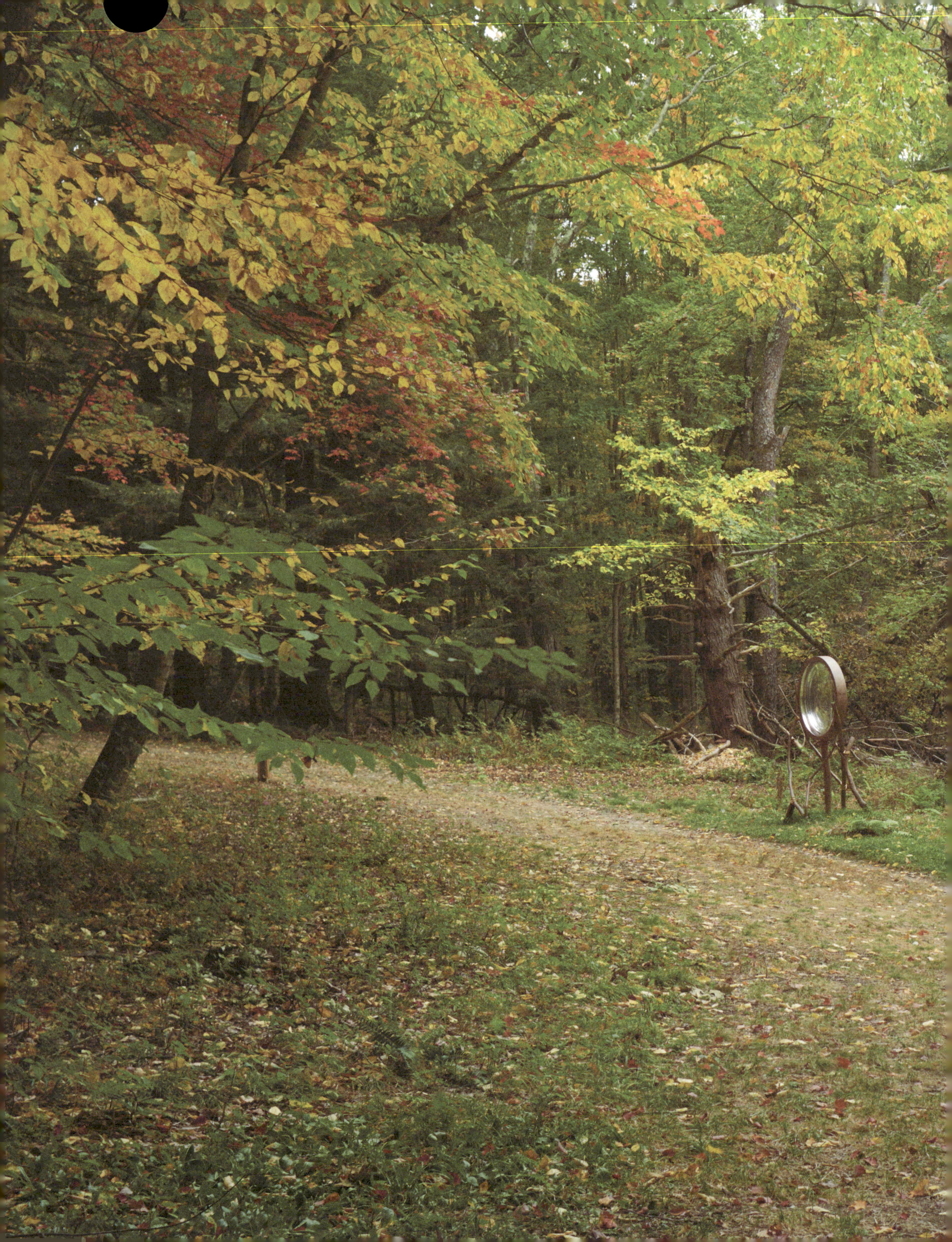

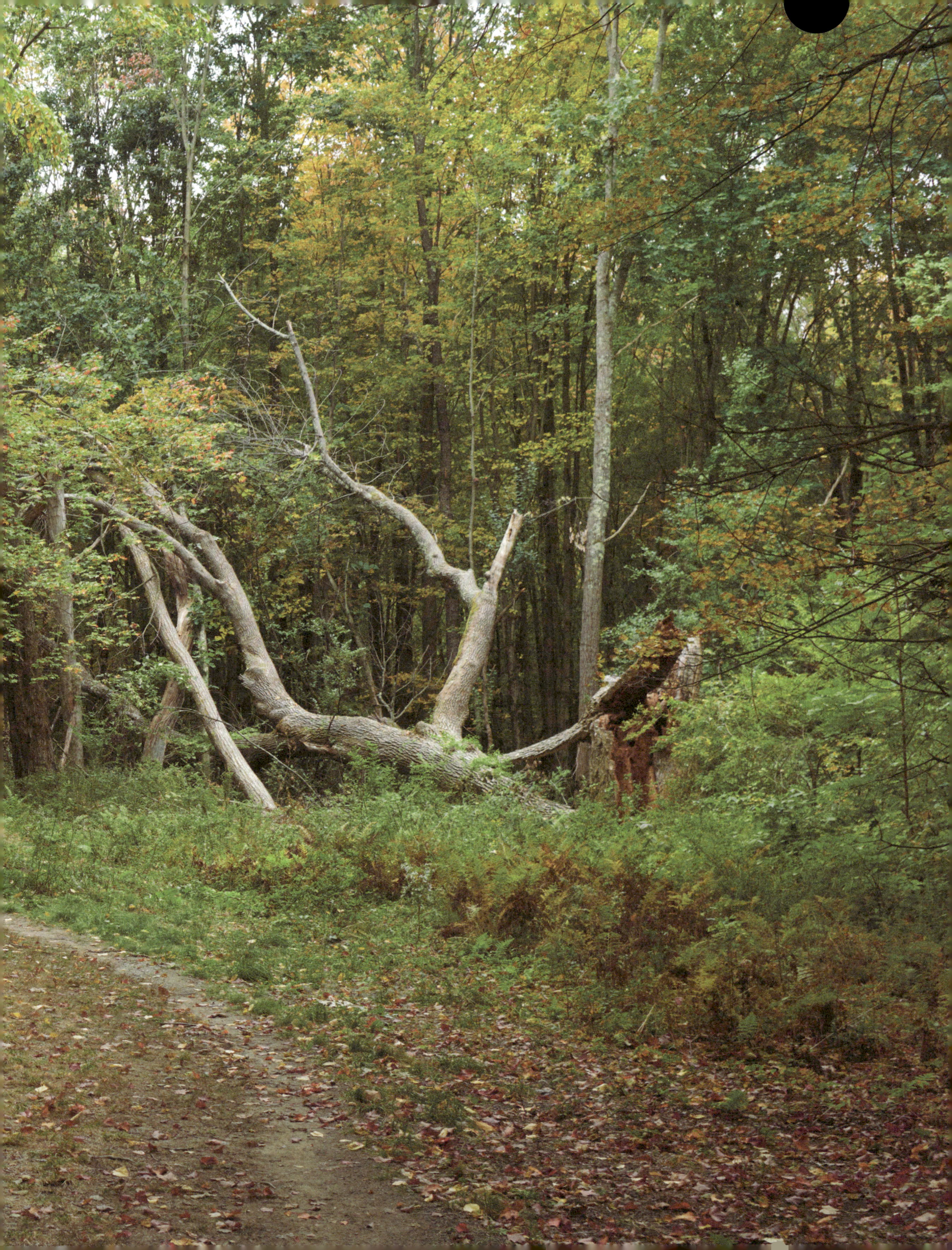

# Pushing against Certainty: Kelly Akashi's Expansive Vision in *A Device to See the World Twice*

Lumi Tan

To find Kelly Akashi's *A Device to See the World Twice* (2020), you follow a trail leading away from the open pasture of the Clark Art Institute, up the incline of Stone Hill. You enter a wooded area, aware of leaving behind the idyllic view of the Berkshire mountains, the backdrop against which the campus of the Clark is set. Trees cloak the open sky as you cross through a utility gate. If you approach Akashi's piece in the same way I did, in the same late-afternoon light that I did, a bend in the trail reveals a dramatic shaft of sunlight before you come upon the sculpture. A canopy of slender trees at the entrance to a clearing frames a view of an enormous fallen ash tree. In a phone conversation, Akashi reveals that, due to travel restrictions during the COVID-19 pandemic, she has seen the site only in winter. I have seen it only once, on an unusually warm September day, and I dwell on this difference in perception; the distance between our memories of the site might be less dramatic if it were in another geographic region where the seasonal changes weren't so pronounced, or if the exhibition were less accessible to the public. My encounter was contingent on these conditions, and many others. What happens when you don't feel confident that you are on the correct path? I felt validated only once I happened upon two hikers who seemed familiar with the trails. How long, I wondered, have those hikers been walking these trails? Do they come every day, every week? How does Akashi's sculpture affect their routine? How was my experience altered through first observing their interaction with the work before inspecting it myself? How long have these trails existed? What non-human life is affected through our navigation of this land? What organisms live in parallel to our decisions?

Throughout its yearlong installation, *A Device to See the World Twice* will remain a steadfast witness to the kinds of temporal and material change that Akashi has continually sought to document in her work as a sculptor. The label of "sculpture" and its traditionally unalterable status is something Akashi concedes to, even as she pushes against its certainty. As its name indicates, Akashi's "device" has a usefulness that distinguishes it from sculpture made merely to be observed and admired. Her work is a tool for seeing something else: "the world," its title tells us. That day I visited the work, the world in this niche of the woods was brilliantly verdant, on the cusp of a seasonal shift, a contracting of daylight and the ensuing transition of leaves into warmer tones. Akashi had originally planned to focus her viewing device on the monumental ash tree when it stood upright; however, three months after her second visit to the Clark, the tree collapsed from a break just a few feet above its roots, its long trunk now parallel to the ground, its fallen branches interwoven with others. In its severe reorientation, the ash tree unapologetically remains the center of attention, seen through the lens reaching *out* rather than up. The work's responsiveness to this type of entropic event is a testament to Akashi's long interest in the vast, incomprehensible simultaneity between geological and mortal timelines.

As a landform, Stone Hill emerged 500 million years ago, when colliding tectonic plates crumpled into mountains more than 14,000 feet high. Over 400 million years, the mountains subsided, glaciers turned into lakes, and the peaks of Stone Hill became islands. The glacial lake drained into the Hudson River about 16,200 years ago, forming the landscape we now see from the trails of the Clark. The Mohicans inhabited this land for centuries prior to European colonists, who assigned its current name in the mid-1800s, converting much of the land for agriculture. In the twentieth century, these agricultural areas gave way to development steered by Williamstown, Williams College, and the Clark. Despite this more recent reshaping of the land, when I look at a color lithograph by Williams student George Yeomans from 1855–56 (fig. 56),[1] I feel an uncanny connection to the view he captured from the peak of Stone Hill—the same view we leave behind as we enter the woods to approach Akashi's work. I understand the framing of the vantage point—likely without anything else in common with Yeomans—and this confirms how I position myself in the landscape, that I can still potentially see the same way someone did 150 years ago, that I'm looking the "right" way. In contrast, topographical maps of the area from the period cannot convey this sense of shared perspective with those mapmakers as they stood on that same land, potentially among some of the same trees that now surround Akashi's sculpture (the average lifespan of an ash tree is 200 to 300 years). Without the presence

56 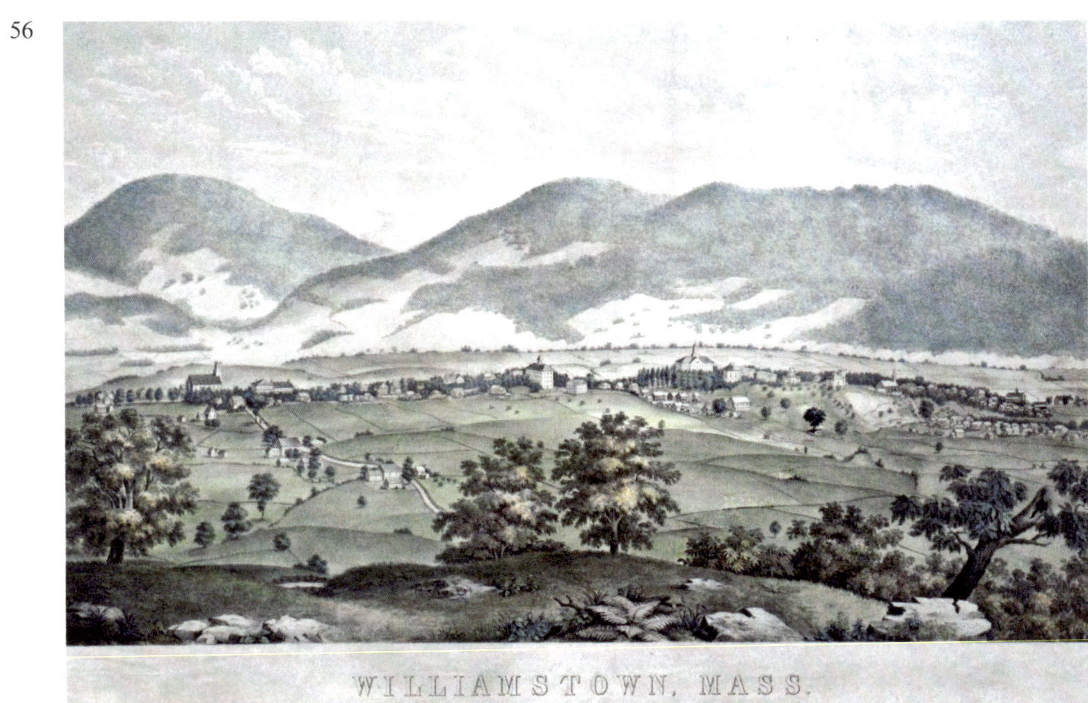


57 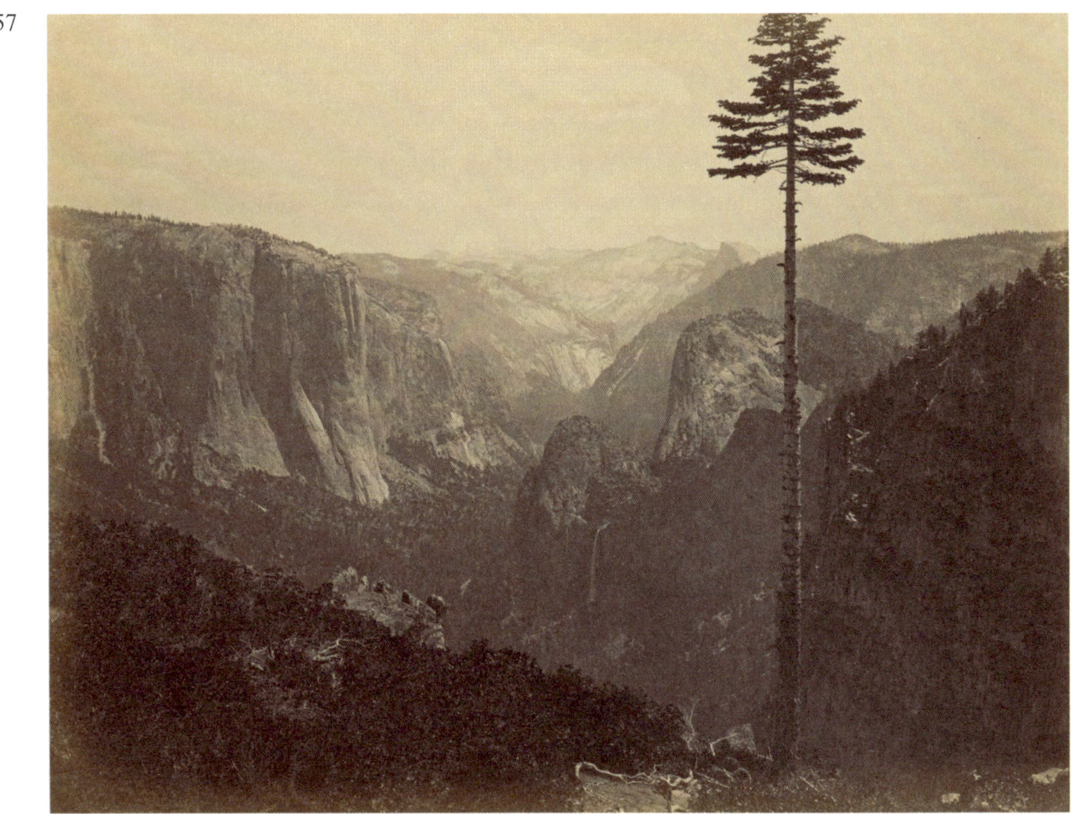

Fig. 56 George Yeomans, printed by P. S. Duval Co., Philadelphia, *Williamstown, Mass. as Seen from Stone Hill*, 1855–56. Hand-colored lithograph, 15 3/8 x 26 in. (39.1 x 66 cm). Flynt Family Collection

Fig. 57 Carleton Watkins, *Yosemite Valley from the Best General View*, 1866. Albumen silver print, 16 1/8 x 20 9/16 in. (41 x 52.2 cm). The J. Paul Getty Museum, Los Angeles

of her work, the deterioration of this particular ash would be a routine marker of the forest's life cycles; Akashi's device allows us to see it as an exceptional landmark that unifies our positions as viewers.

Akashi began making art as an analogue photographer, working in a medium where both process and phase change are highly tangible. By choosing a viewpoint for *A Device to See the World Twice* that is devoid of static architecture, Akashi guarantees that transformations ranging in scale from the copious operations of imperceptible microbes to the slow-motion descent of the imposing ash tree will be enclosed within its frame. This embrace of change becomes a potent critique of photography's entangled relationship with nature and possession, particularly in the early history of the medium. In the expansionist history of the United States, one can look to the famed example of Carleton Watkins's 1866 *Yosemite Valley from the Best General View* (fig. 57) to see how photography played a crucial role. As an employee of the California Geological Survey, Watkins undertook a photographic expedition in Yosemite Valley in the decades following the California gold rush and the Mariposa War between Native Americans, including the Ahwahneechee and Chowchilla Yokut, and Euro-American miners, backed by a California state militia. His most celebrated image from this trip brought together four impressive landforms—Bridalveil Falls, Cathedral Rock, Half Dome, and El Capitan—and went on to define the "best general view" of the valley for preservationists and developers alike. This engineered "objectivity" belies a specifically settler-colonialist gaze, adopting an omnipotent, godlike position from the landscape's highest vantage points, in contrast to the perspective of the Ahwahneechee and Miwok who lived and worked on the land, viewing it from a human scale. In "Overexposed: Whiteness and the Landscape Photography of Carleton Watkins," Martin A. Berger compares the authoritative perspective of photography to the hand-drawn maps of the local Indigenous people: "Ideologies were not made real merely through their inclusion in photographs, but rather photographs were made real to the extent that they contained ideologies in accordance with audience values. It is thus the images that a society takes as true which possess a unique potential to reveal its values."[2] Watkins's photography of Yosemite Valley, which began in 1861, was used to support legislation that first allocated the land to the state of California in 1864, and then reclassified it as a national park in 1890 after the state could no longer handle the volume of tourists it attracted.

Undoubtedly, these spectacular views of nature remain the dominant images in our collective consciousness of the American West. Photography, and its use through social media, has become an ever more powerful force in our desire to obtain the "best" view—one that dramatizes our ability to dominate nature rather than exist in harmony alongside it. These images accumulate value once they are emulated and replicated by others. In eschewing the inert, iconic vista from Stone Hill once captured by Yeomans, the view framed by *A Device to See the World Twice* stands in direct opposition to this historical impulse to command the landscape, which can ultimately destroy the nature it celebrates. It is a work that creates images of nature in relation to its conditions, rather than against them, and refutes the often-violent photographic terminology and ideology of shooting and capturing its living subjects. Images such as those created by Yeomans and Watkins persist in a vision that encourages an illusion of nature being shaped by the human eye; Akashi encourages the potential for our sight to be reshaped by nature. One of Akashi's early ideas for her *Ground/work* commission was to create a camera obscura with which she would continually make prints as the seasons changed, in accordance with the format's capacity for simultaneously seeing and making images. Beyond the challenges this would have presented for a Los Angeles–based artist who would have had to travel across the country continually, even before the pandemic, the strategy still felt too fixed for Akashi. Instead, through the use of a double-concave lens that slightly compresses the image, the final sculpture accomplishes novel ways of seeing without the artist having to intervene to edit or crop the images. The framing—and thus production—of images is therefore continuous, as is our own consciousness of which details we focus on or ignore.

This is a concept that Robin Kelsey, in *Photography and the Art of Chance*, recognized within the practice of photography pioneer Henry Fox Talbot: "Talbot construes the real artistry of all pictorial art as an opportunism of sight. In his scheme, discovering a picturesque subject requires aesthetic sensibility and inspiration; transposing it to a surface, whether canvas or photographic paper, is merely a matter of mechanical industry."[3] Kelsey sees this lineage continuing into the twentieth century with Edward Weston, once the aesthetics of photography have become more defined and thus more available for experimentation: "[Weston] carries on Talbot's project of shifting the locus of creativity to the eye, but with a new emphasis on the capacity of that eye to anticipate what the photographic appartus will record. Affirming the revelatory powers of that apparatus, Weston asks in his daybooks: 'Why limit yourselves to what your eyes see when you have such an opportunity to extend your vision?'"[4]

While Akashi's lens is far larger than what we are accustomed to seeing on a camera—a proper opportunity to "extend our vision"—the sculpture is deliberately human in scale. Akashi's title informs us that the work affords two ways of looking, both through the lens and beyond it. She leaves room for the eyes to drift, for our bodies to respond not exclusively to the sculpture but also to everything that surrounds it. Through its scale, the work acts as a proxy for one's own body: with distance, it gives us a concrete understanding of how diminutive and passive we are within the landscape. Alternatively, when I came right up to the work, my own image was reflected and repeated, and I'm unsure if what I saw of the landscape was also a reflection (a world seen twice), or if the sculpture, in fact, collapses what is visible on both sides of the lens. I didn't turn around to confirm what the truth might be; instead, I trusted the lens, Akashi's own looking glass, to communicate an alternative view from what appeared to me before I arrived at the sculpture. While the lens does not provide a portal into a distorted reality, it prods us toward new perspectives while simultaneously enabling us to reflect upon our own bodies with more clarity. At a time when technology is conflated with digitality, it is easy to forget that eyeglasses, too, are technology. In speaking about the work, Akashi references her own acrylic lenses, a device she relies upon to see. Indeed, many of us fall completely out of relation to the world without this mediation.[5] The device is in plain sight, but it does not undermine the authenticity of individual experiences.

While the sculpture's lens presents as a technology to enhance our vision, photographic analogy applies as strongly to the armature that holds the acrylic discs. Made of bronze casts of branches that Akashi collected while in residency at Headlands Center for the Arts in Sausalito, California in 2019, the armature brings together two landscapes with entirely different ecosystems. Though these two disparate sites are not necessarily identifiable within the work, Akashi concentrates on this doubled image of the branches themselves, between permanent cast object and the decaying, always in motion, natural world that surrounds it. A generative challenge for Akashi is the attempt at portraying the "present moment," a concept that has traveled further from photography as the everyday digital images we now encounter are more associated with persuasive manipulation than evidential veracity. She thus finds in bronze casting more affinity with the notion of preserving impressions of time. In an age when photography's relationship to memory and accountability, through the ubiquity of smartphones and ease of digital editing, seems more tenuous than ever, the facility of pushing a button may feel at odds with the labored process of bronze casting. But Akashi considers bronze a relic that creates a "parallel to nature, rather than a representation."[6] The casting process also creates dependencies between the materials' developing states of being that resonate with analogue photography; the bronze cast grants us a clearer view of the form, again drawing attention to details—unique knobs, ridges, and furrows—that we might overlook on an actual tree branch. While the lens is a scalable object that Akashi has sized for human bodies, the branches remain one-to-one embodiments, relating to the landscape and the surrounding trees on their own terms. A synthetic rope with a golden sheen, which Akashi uses frequently in her sculpture in both formal and utilitarian ways, ties the branches together, a simple gesture that plays on the perceived fragility of these forms, manifested in the visible decomposition along the trails. Through the structure of the lens, the armature

58

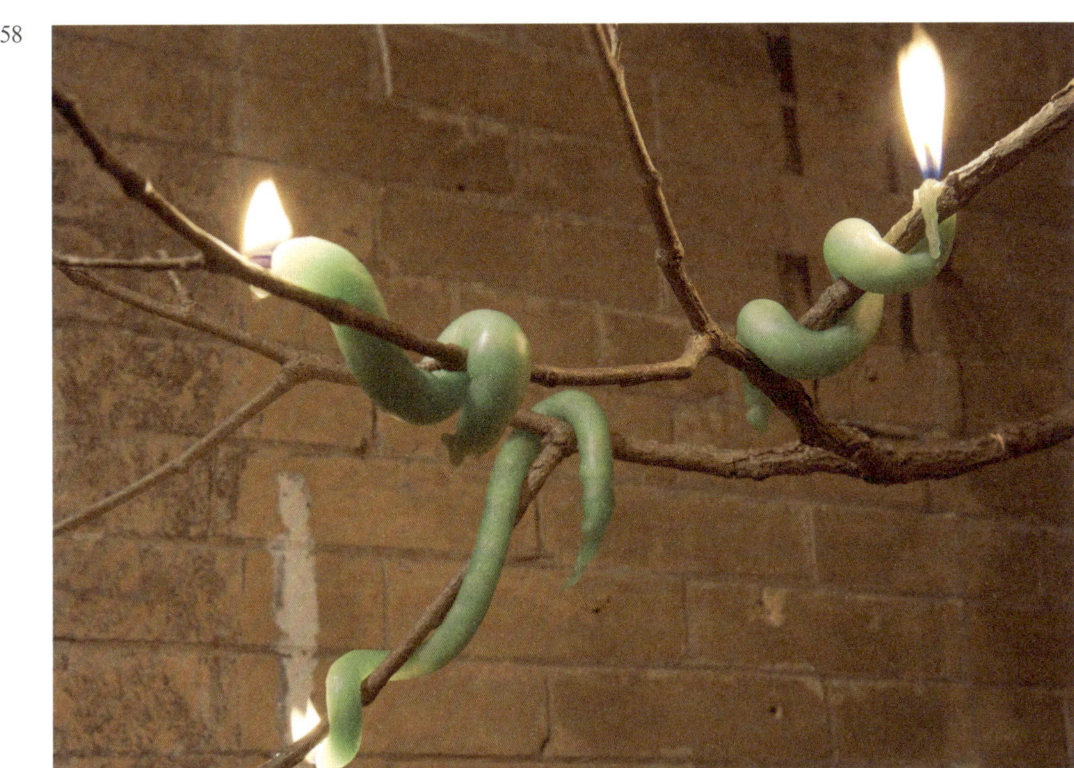

59

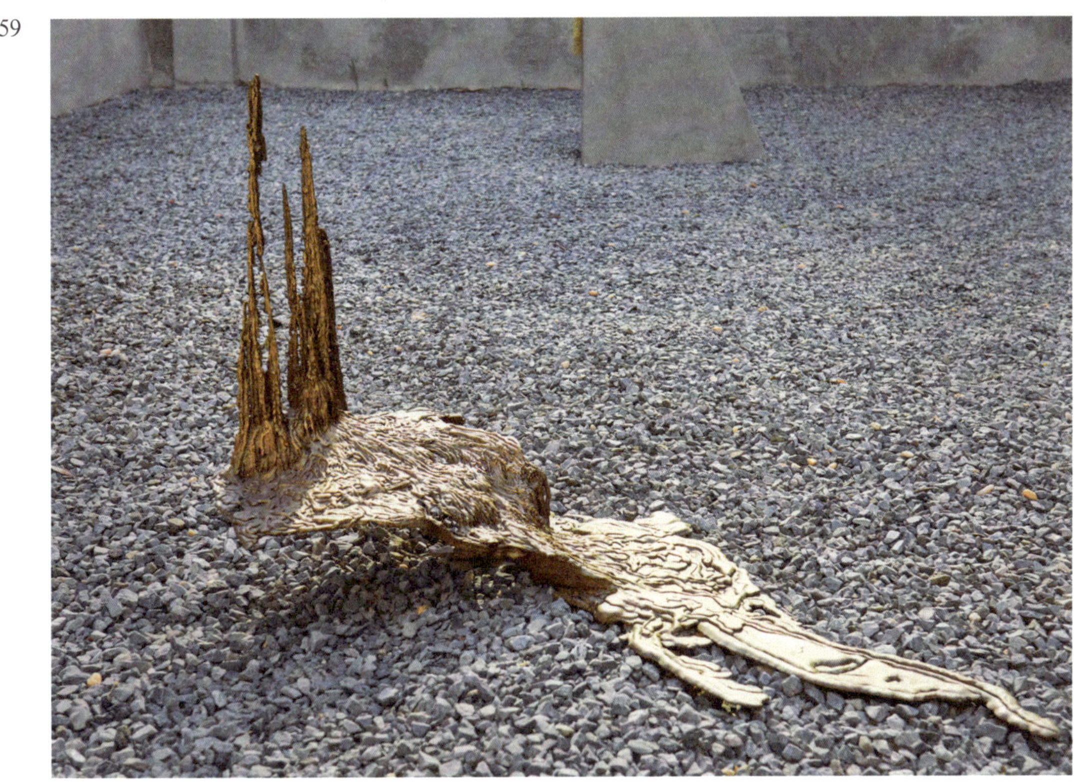

Fig. 58 Kelly Akashi, *Carbon Copy*, 2017 (detail). Installation view from *Long Exposure*, SculptureCenter, New York, 2017. Bronze, wax, cotton wick, bronze wire, dimensions variable.

Fig. 59 Kelly Akashi, *Big Drip*, 2016–17. Installation view from *Long Exposure*, SculptureCenter, New York, 2017. Bronze, 28 x 58 x 45 in. (71.1 x 147.3 x 114.3 cm).

of branches, and the rope, the viewer is pulled in and out of the present moment—and in and out of assumptions about the natural world.

These varying gestures of materiality cohere through Akashi's understanding and acknowledgment of both the limits and potential of sculptures and photography, as well as the perceived stability of each medium. Substances that experience profound changes of state such as a glass and wax feature prominently in the artist's work; as in photographic methods, these materials allow for impressions, malleability, and effects made by light and heat. And despite their ability to shape-shift, the artist's chosen materials all carry vivid, individualized haptic memories within their chemical makeup and physical form. While the metamorphosis of glass from sand to liquid to sculptural object occurs in a foundry, out of sight, Akashi's candle works transmogrify in full view throughout their display, without the artist herself there to light or witness them. By transferring that responsibility to the exhibition space in which they are displayed, the artist therefore shares the authorship of these works, and the sculptural form of the candle is constantly made and remade. In *Long Exposure*, Akashi's 2017 solo show at SculptureCenter, New York, the aspect of time's relationship to legibility and information is immediately put forth in the title—the longer the camera's exposure, the more movement it captures, often creating blurs or other obscurities instead of images we can clearly "see." Yet the blurring of textures, of temporalities, of comprehension is precisely what Akashi directs us to in works such as *Carbon Copy* (2017, fig. 58), in which lit green candles are coiled around delicate bronze branches hung from above in the dim, narrow passageways of the SculptureCenter's basement galleries. The fusing of the two elements—one mutable and ephemeral, one fixed in time—becomes more pronounced as the exhibition progresses. The title of the work points to the impossibility of such an outcome; the candles, even if reproduced, will never behave in exactly the same fashion. In this way, Akashi's dual form appears analogous to other examples of organic cohabitation, such as self-feeding Spanish moss that attaches itself only to other plants and trees as substrates.

The outdoor sculpture *Big Drip* (2016–17, fig. 59) is a bronze cast of a landscape of melted wax that travels vertically, sideways, and pools on the ground in a dexterous balance. The anomalous directions in which the wax flowed underscore how Akashi consistently shifts our expectations of how materials serve one another. While wax is an essential part of the bronze casting process, its function is to melt away as an ephemeral mold that gives way to (and shapes) a metal object. Here, what is usually disregarded and discarded as the utilitarian remains of the fabrication process instead becomes permanent and hypervisible, its manifold ripples and pools accentuated. The once-liquid bronze allows the wax patterns to be repeated, arresting a "present moment" that would otherwise pass and disappear, undocumented.

Akashi's agile use of glass throughout her practice similarly highlights the physical presence of the medium, despite its transparency; this is also an essential quality of *A Device to See the World Twice*, which presents not only a lens to look through but also an object to navigate around. In another manifestation of her fluid treatment of materials, Akashi created a series of photograms by placing hand-blown glass forms on the surface of photo paper, creating images of materiality itself. In *Lenses* (2018, fig. 60), these forms are recast from a technology to a subject; instead of rendering the glass invisible, Akashi lends each of the glass forms a physical presence, revealing their individual compositions, their variation in surface, shape, and edge, their thing-ness. Through this presentation, glass undergoes yet another transformation, taking on the anatomical complexity of an organism—a connection that Akashi made more explicit in the 2019 exhibition *Figure Shifter* at François Ghebaly, where she used fossils of ancient shells from the Natural History Museum in Los Angeles for reverse crystal casts. The casts were displayed alongside hand-blown glass, tomographic images, and photograms, among other approaches to seeing and creating images (fig. 61). Rather than using these direct photographic techniques to convey information or proof, Akashi allows these images—and her viewers—to continually build upon other associations.

Theorist Kaja Silverman's "The Miracle of Analogy" provides an important counterpoint to the indexicality of photography as discussed in Roland

Barthes's *Camera Lucida*. Silverman writes: "If a photograph can prove 'what was,' then it is the royal road to certainty—the means through which we know and judge the world. . . . Indexicality wrings all of the futurity out of the photographic image, extinguishing our last principle of hope."[7] Instead of understanding photography as always existing as artifact, Silverman liberates the photographic image—and thus knowledge conjured from the image—from merely existing in the past. "Not only is the photographic image an analogy, rather than a representation or an index, analogy is also the fluid in which the so-called 'medium' of photography develops—and often in unexpected directions. This process does not begin when we decide that it should, or end when we command it to. Photography develops, rather, *with us*, and *in response to us*."[8] Despite coming thirty years after *Camera Lucida*, Silverman's response to Barthes is not restricted to digital photography's ephemerality and its iterative abilities. We have built much of our understanding of the world through images as evidence; Silverman provides a framework to look at both a history and a future built on evolving relations rather than solely on what can be represented in a single moment.

"With us and in response to us" is an apt characterization for Akashi's work as a whole and for the expansive definitions she brings to the media ascribed to her practice. However delicate or impermanent the material deployed, the artist's works never read as precious objects that need distance from their viewers. Instead, they compel us toward intimate readings, to draw on embodied knowledge, to understand their mutability even without being witness to it. One of the last sculptures I experienced in person before New York City shut down to prevent the spread of COVID-19 was Akashi's *Weep* (2020, fig. 62), a centerpiece of her solo exhibition *Mood Organ* at Tanya Bonakdar Gallery. It is a large bronze orb that slowly emits tears, which stream down its surface. Akashi asks us to do something unusual here; to have empathy with an inanimate object that has no anthropomorphic form, made of a material that does not visibly tarnish during the duration of the exhibition but takes its time, accumulating texture and patina over the years to come. Through this relatively simple mechanism, she leaves

60

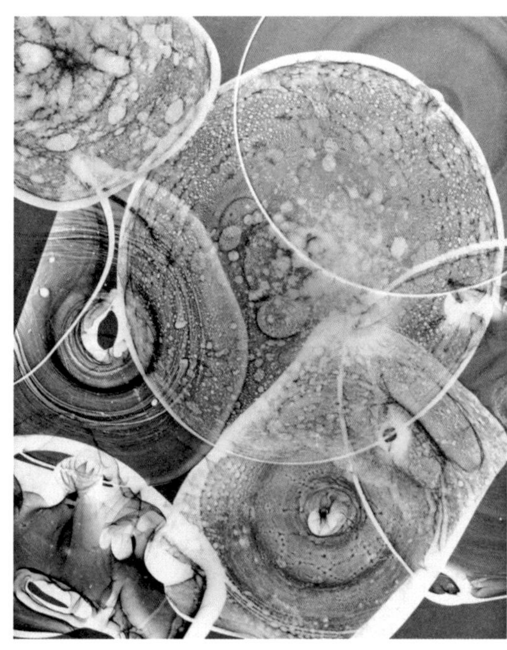

Fig. 60 Kelly Akashi, *Lenses*, 2018. Silver gelatin photogram, walnut frame, unique, 19 1/2 x 15 1/2 x 1 1/2 in. (49.5 x 39.4 x 3.8 cm)

space for the audience to take on emotions, to experience empathy, by refusing to define the experience for us in the moment of viewing. The scale of *Weep* confronts our own bodies; it does not overwhelm us. This orb somehow becomes as fragile as the tabletop glass sculptures that convene around it in the exhibition, as slippery as our own sensibilities and as transitory as a century-old ash tree. It declares an independent lifespan outside of the values of preservation.

Several months after I shared space with *Weep*, Akashi's *Device to See the World Twice* became one of the first artworks I was able to experience firsthand, even as the ongoing pandemic undeniably continues to reshape every physical encounter. This work grants us time to reflect on the restless world within and beyond the frame, positioning us as image makers in our own right and releasing us from the confines of a single image as authority. With hope, we hold onto this freedom of sight, allowing this experience to fluidly transform into other senses and relations so that we can continue to see anew. A device's function is by definition a particular one, but Akashi's device is overtly generous, giving us just enough structure not only to see but to feel differently.

*Lumi Tan is senior curator at The Kitchen.*

1 All information on Stone Hill from the exhibition website for *Sensing Place: The Clark and Stone Hill*, Clark Art Institute, July 4–October 16, 2016, accessed October 4, 2020, http://www.clarkart.edu/microsites/sensing-place/history/exhibition.
2 Martin A. Berger, "Overexposed: Whiteness and the Landscape Photography of Carleton Watkins," *Oxford Art Journal* 26, no. 1 (2003): 3–23.
3 Robin Kelsey, *Photography and the Art of Chance* (Cambridge, MA: Harvard University Press, 2015), 21.
4 Kelsey, *Photography and the Art of Chance*, 27.
5 Kelly Akashi, "A Device to See the World Twice," SoundCloud audio, Clark Art Institute, 4:26, http://www.clarkart.edu/microsites/ground-work/about-the-projects/kelly-akashi. Edited from an interview conducted by Molly Epstein and Abigail Ross Goodman, recorded April 27, 2020.
6 Kelly Akashi, phone conversation with the author, October 2, 2020.
7 Kaja Silverman, "The Miracle of Analogy," *non-site.org*, March 14, 2014, http://nonsite.org/the-miracle-of-analogy/.
8 Silverman, "The Miracle of Analogy," italics original.

Fig. 61 Installation view of *Figure Shifter*, François Ghebaly Gallery, Los Angeles, 2019
Fig. 62 Kelly Akashi, *Weep*, 2020. Bronze, stainless steel, water, 62 x 96 x 96 in. (157.5 x 243.8 x 243.8 cm)

61

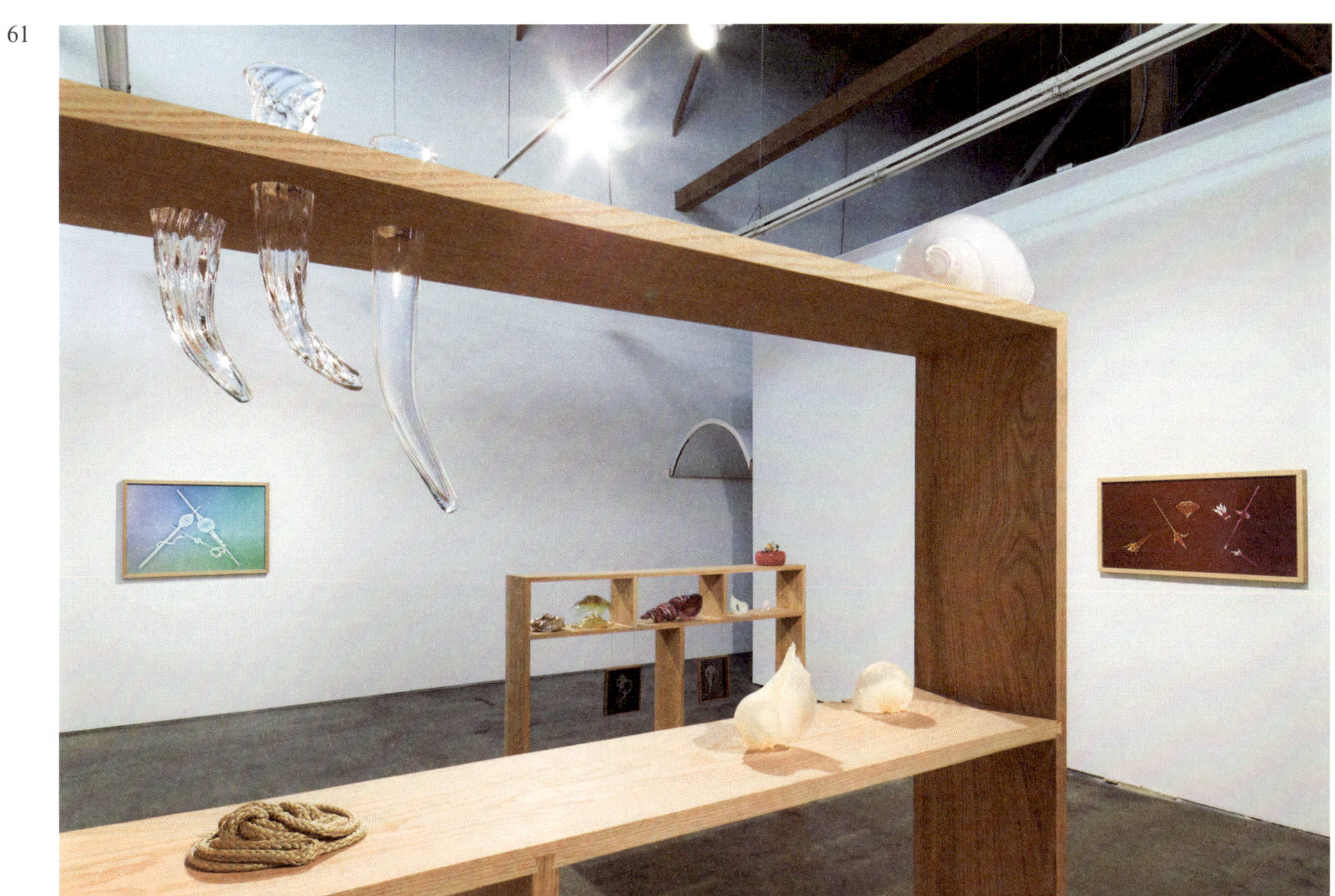

62

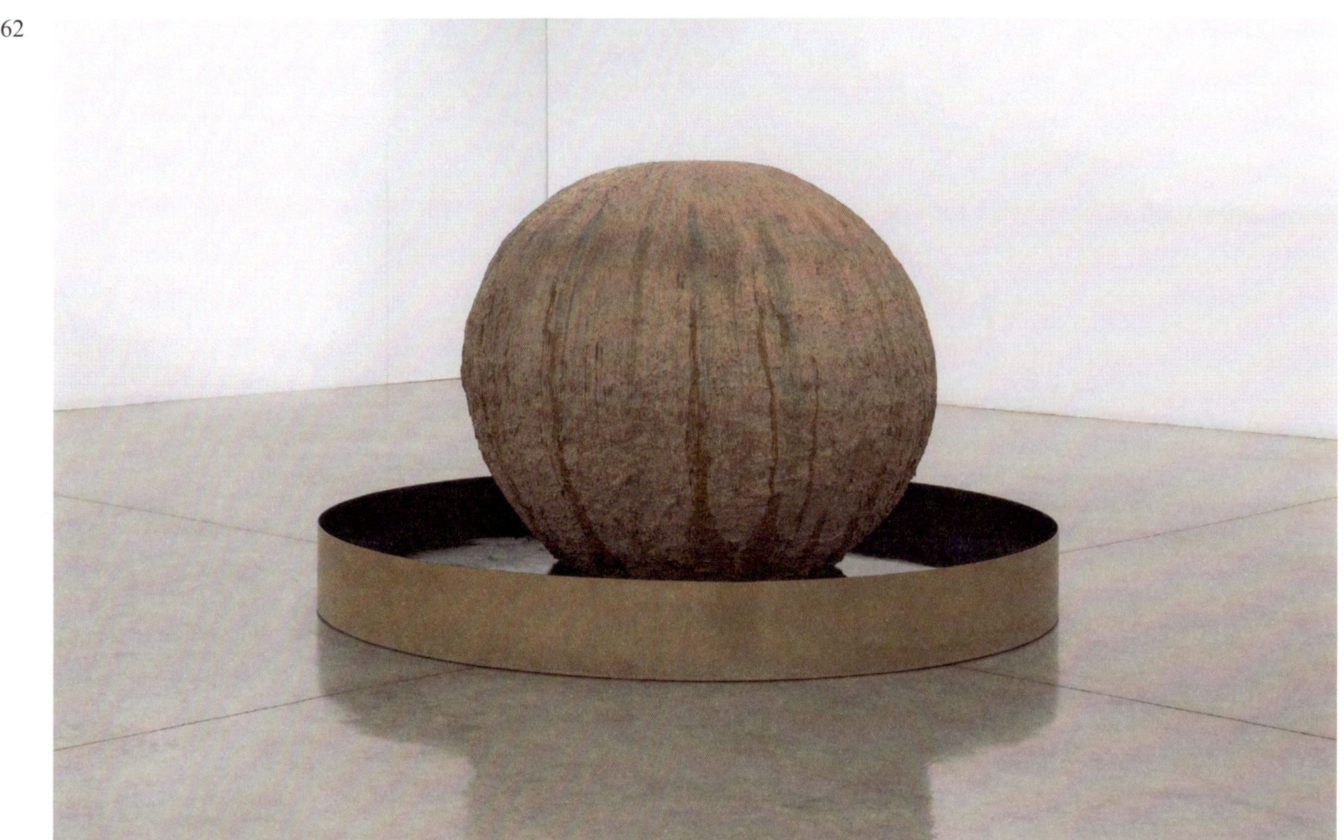

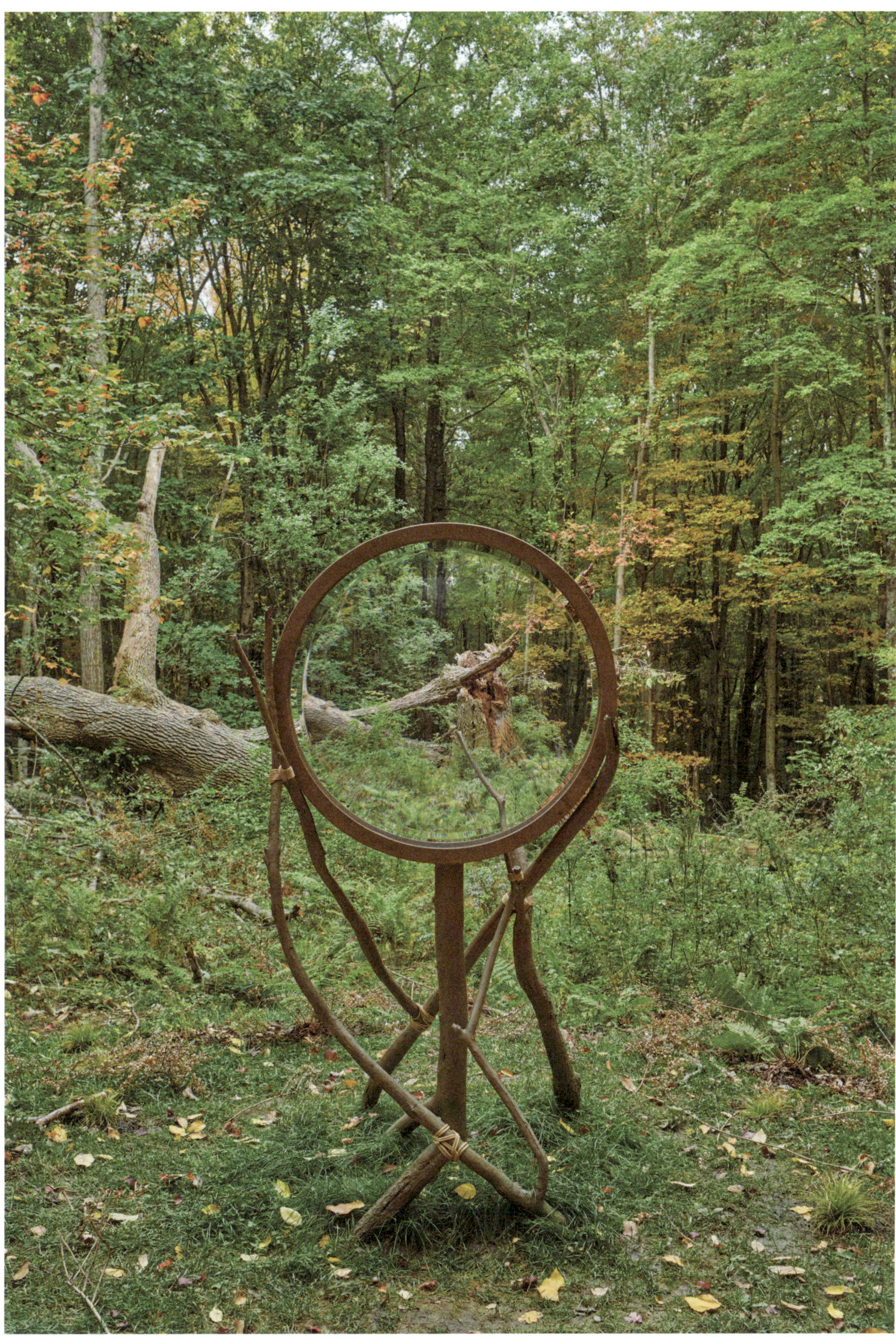

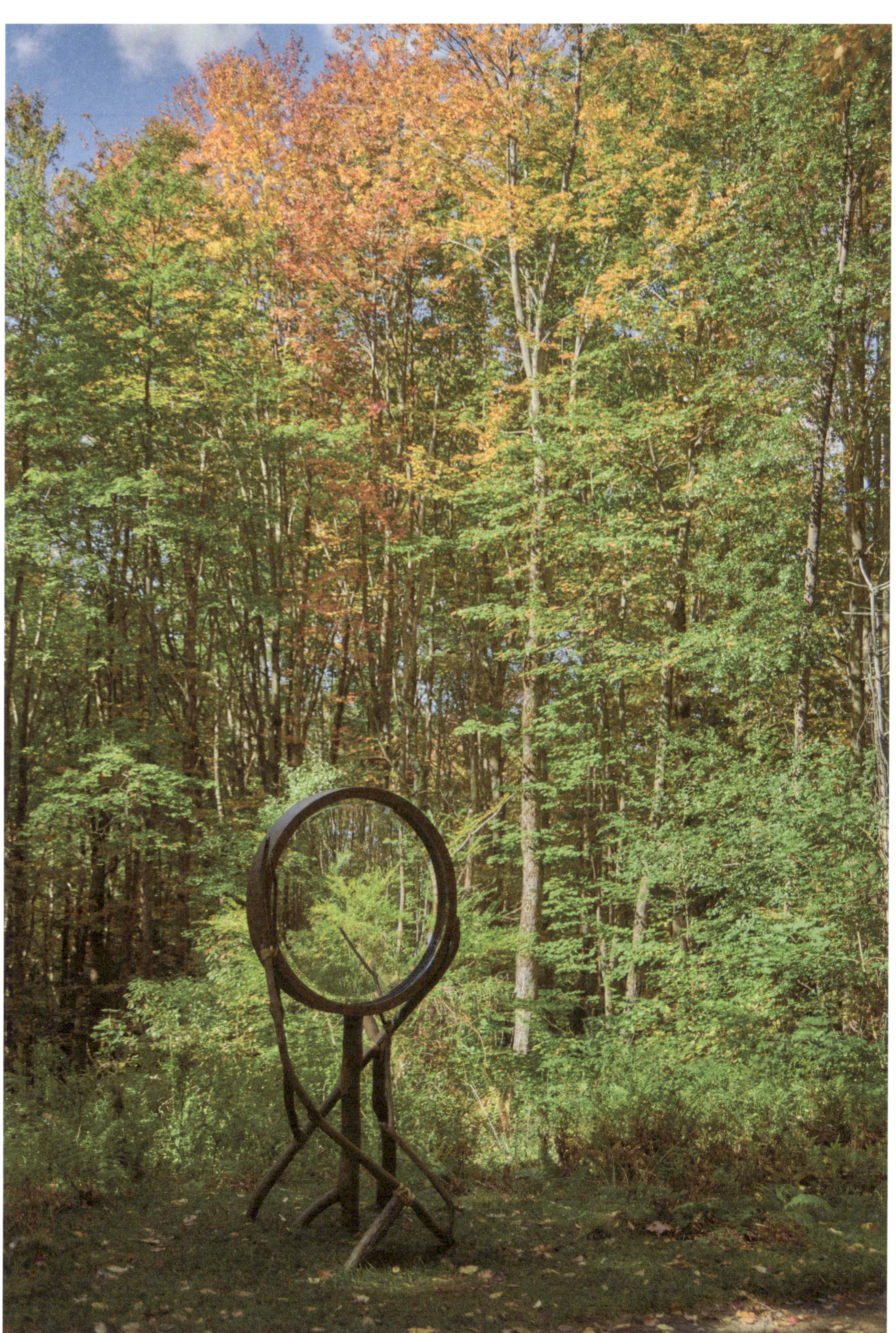

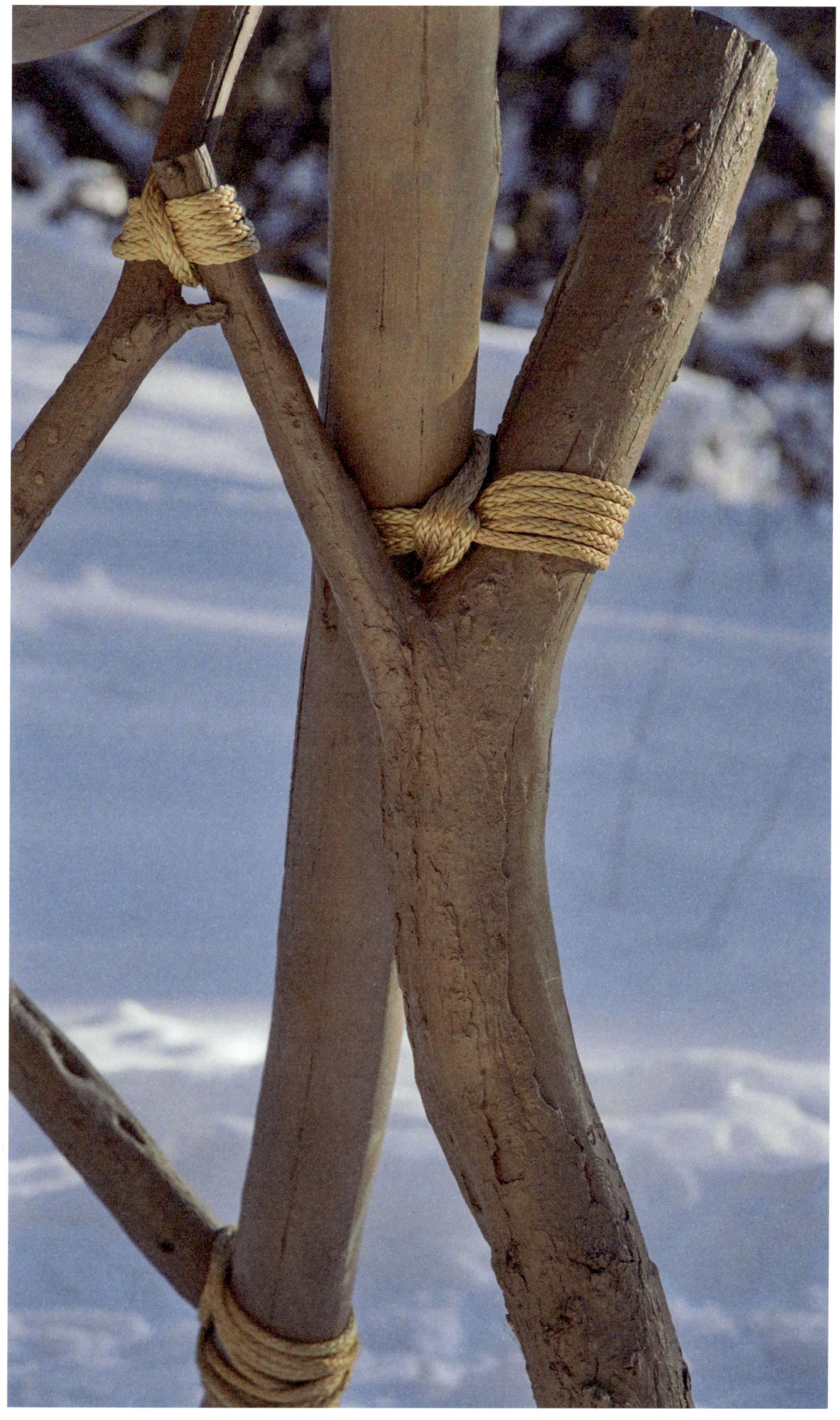

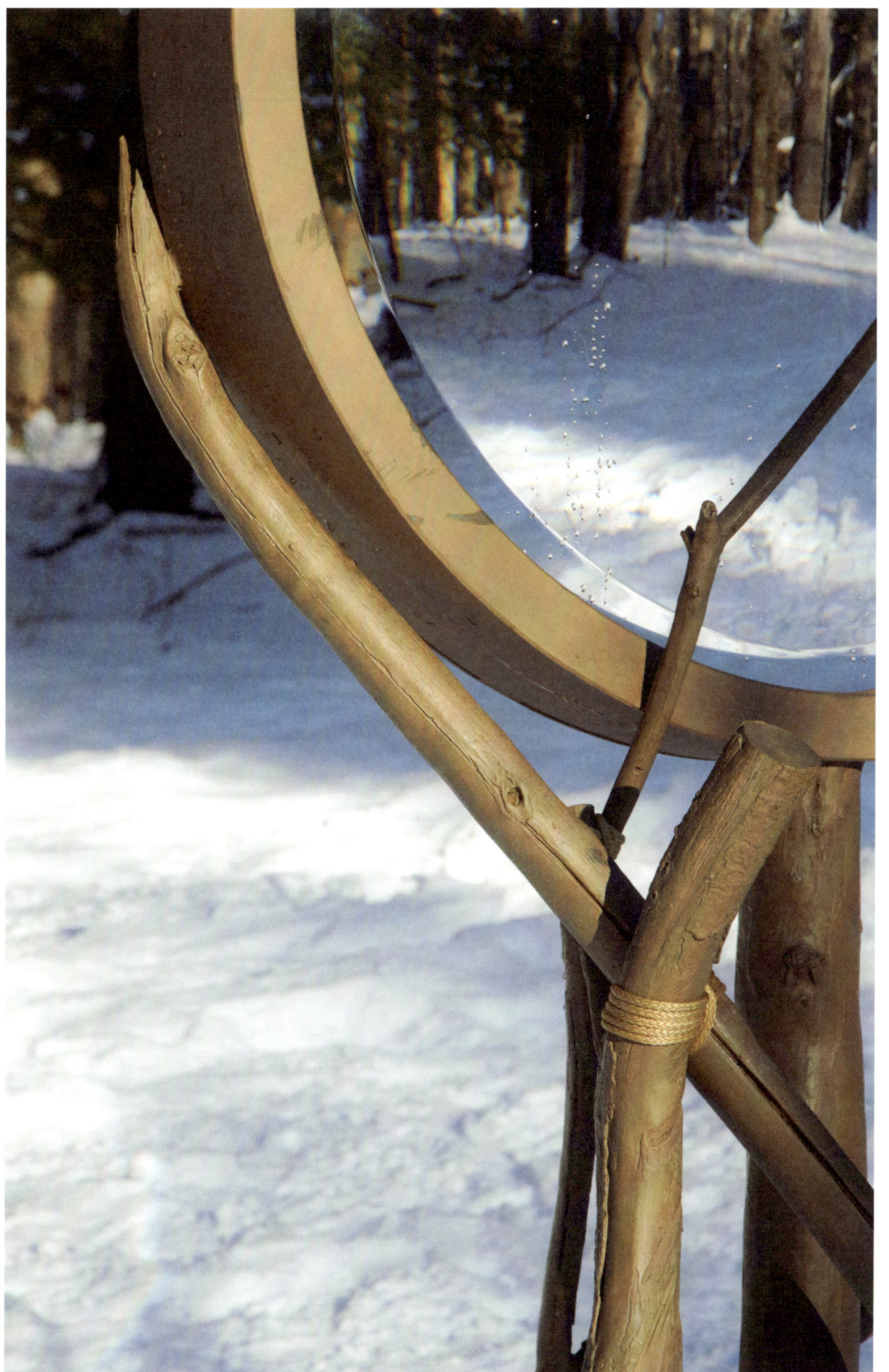

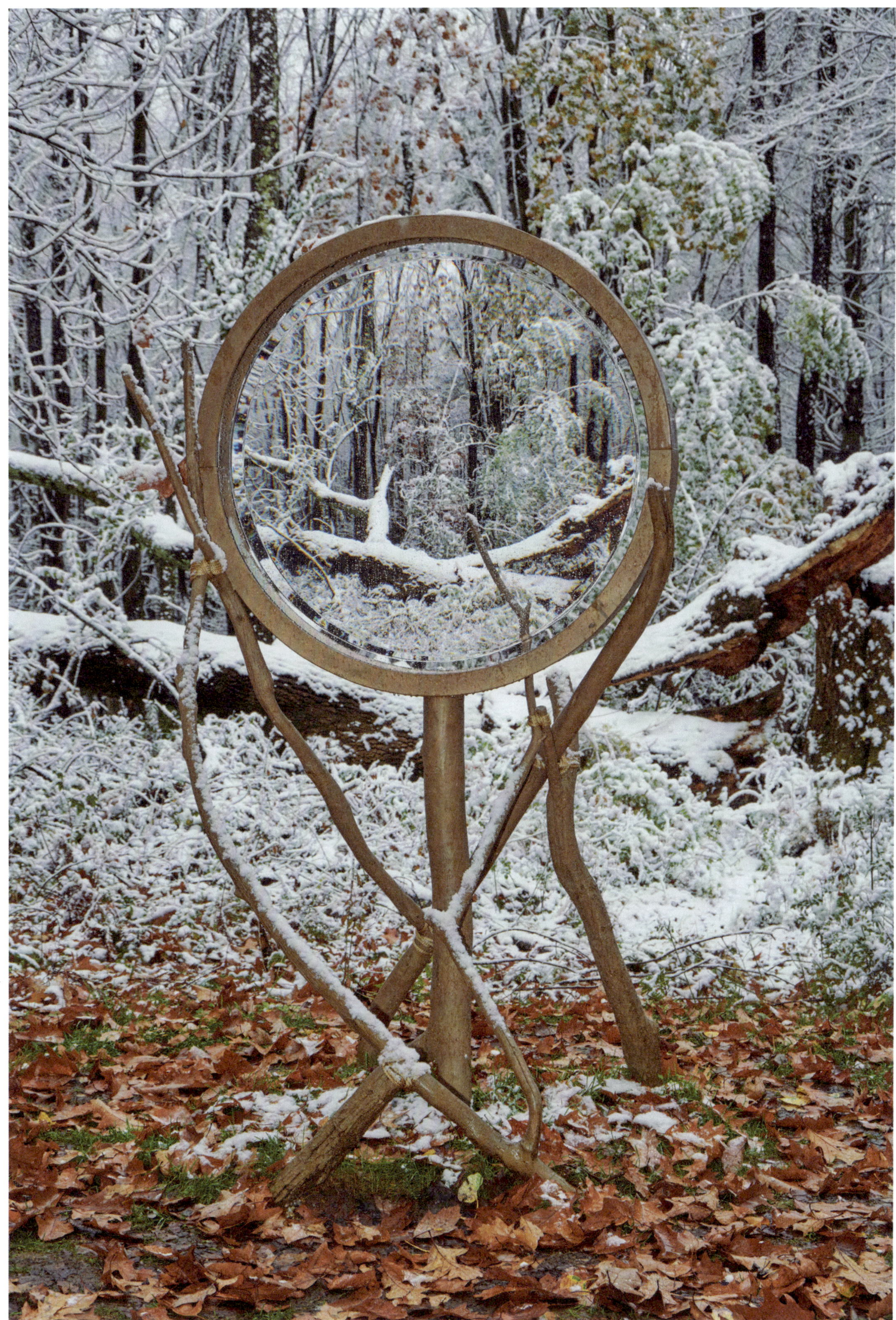

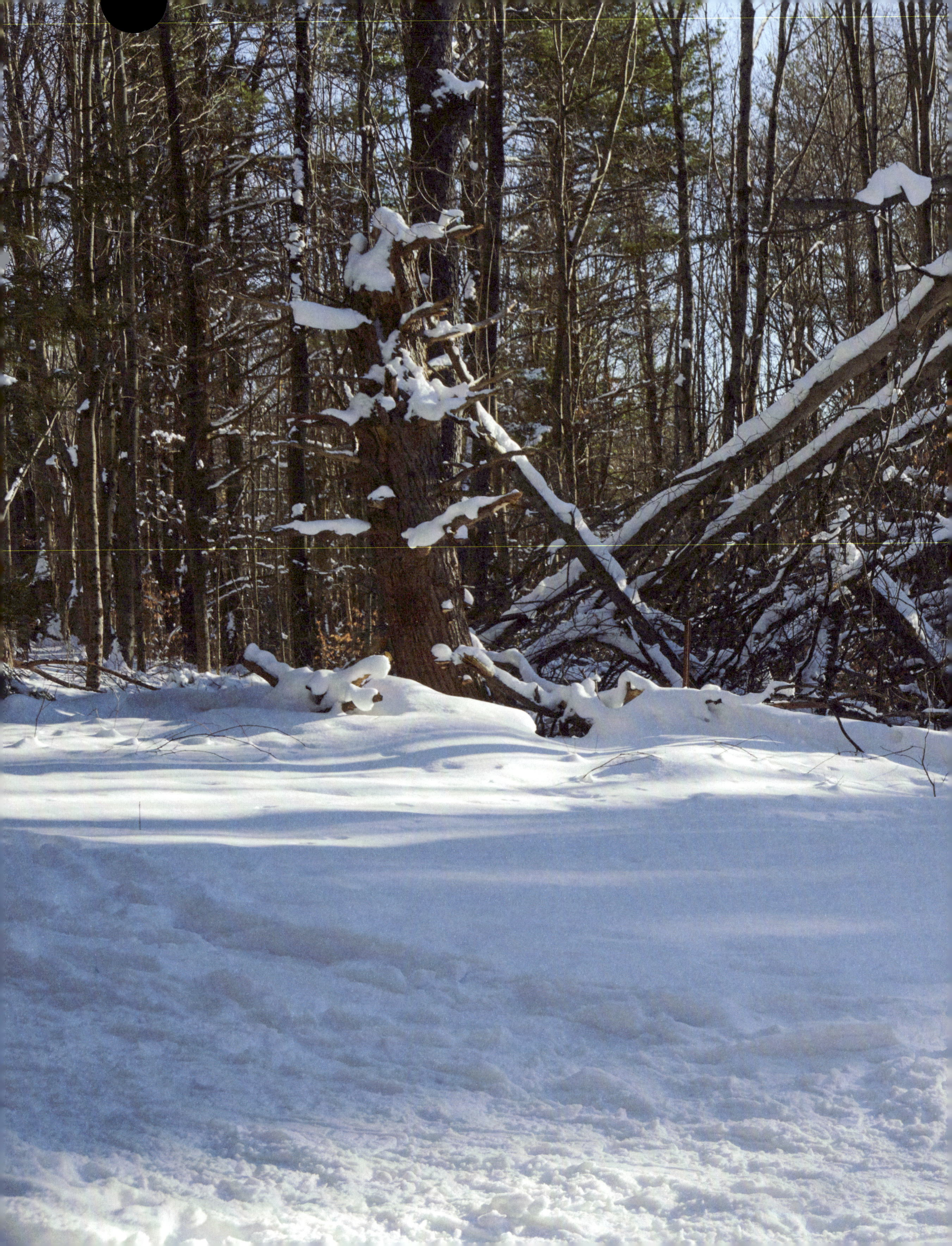

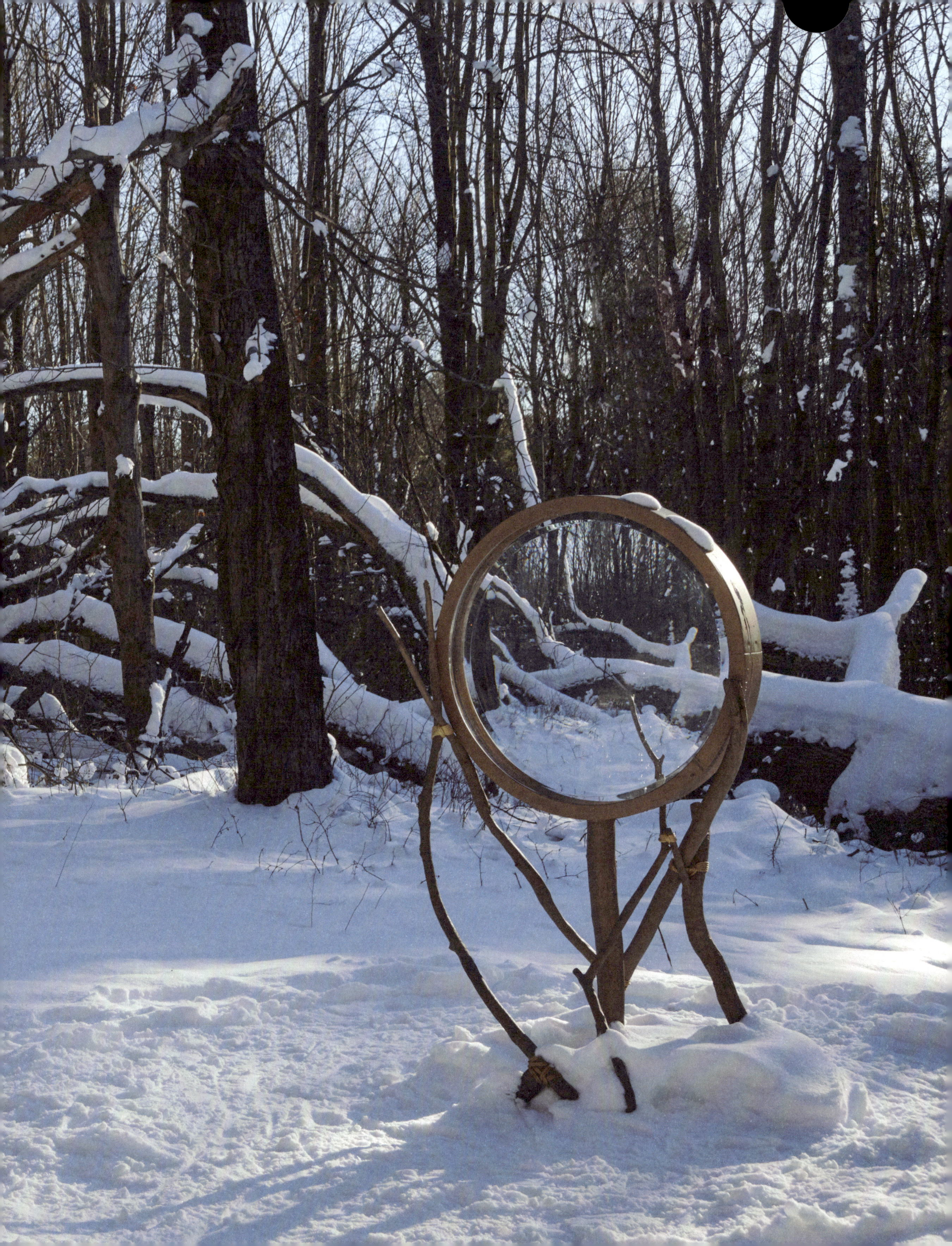

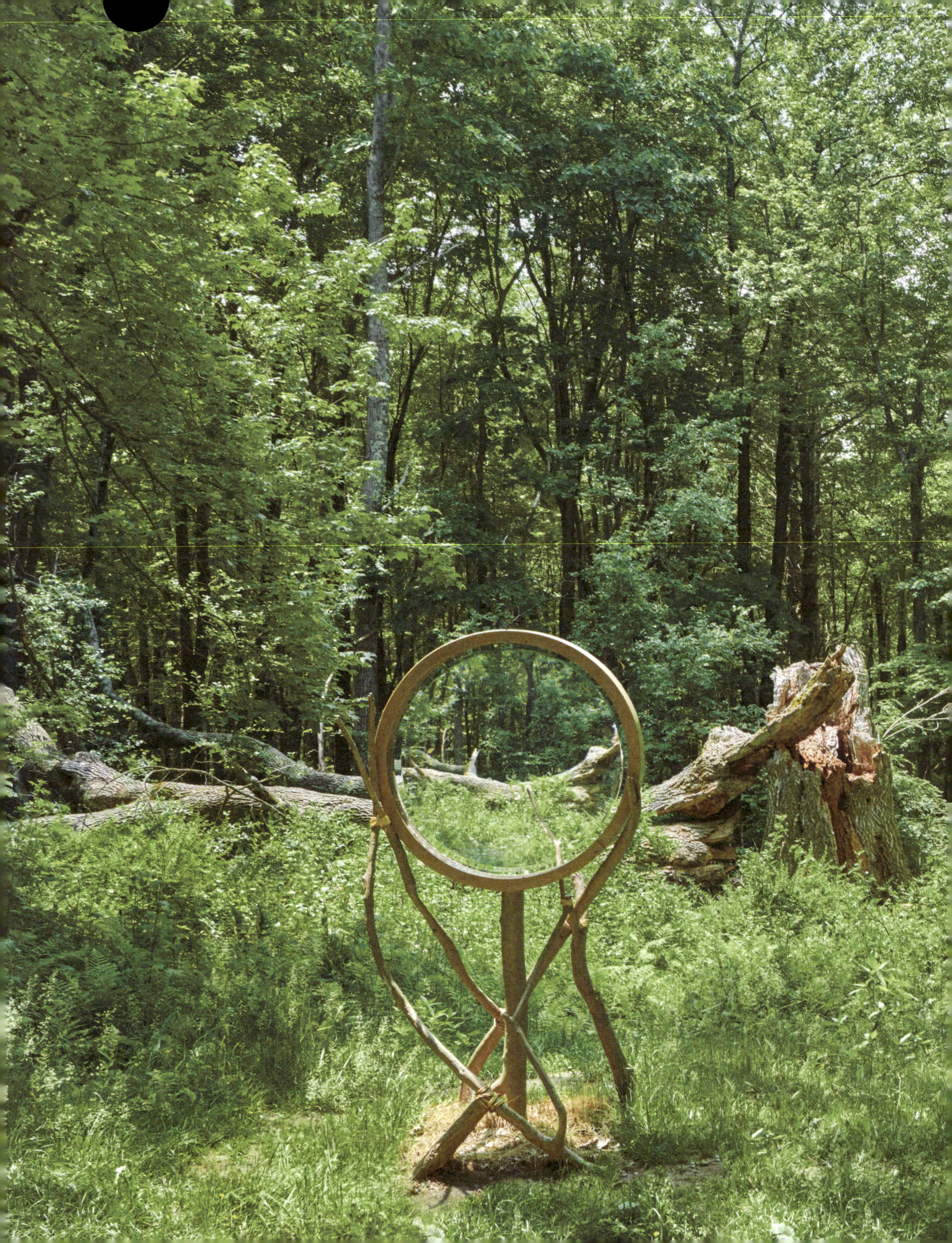

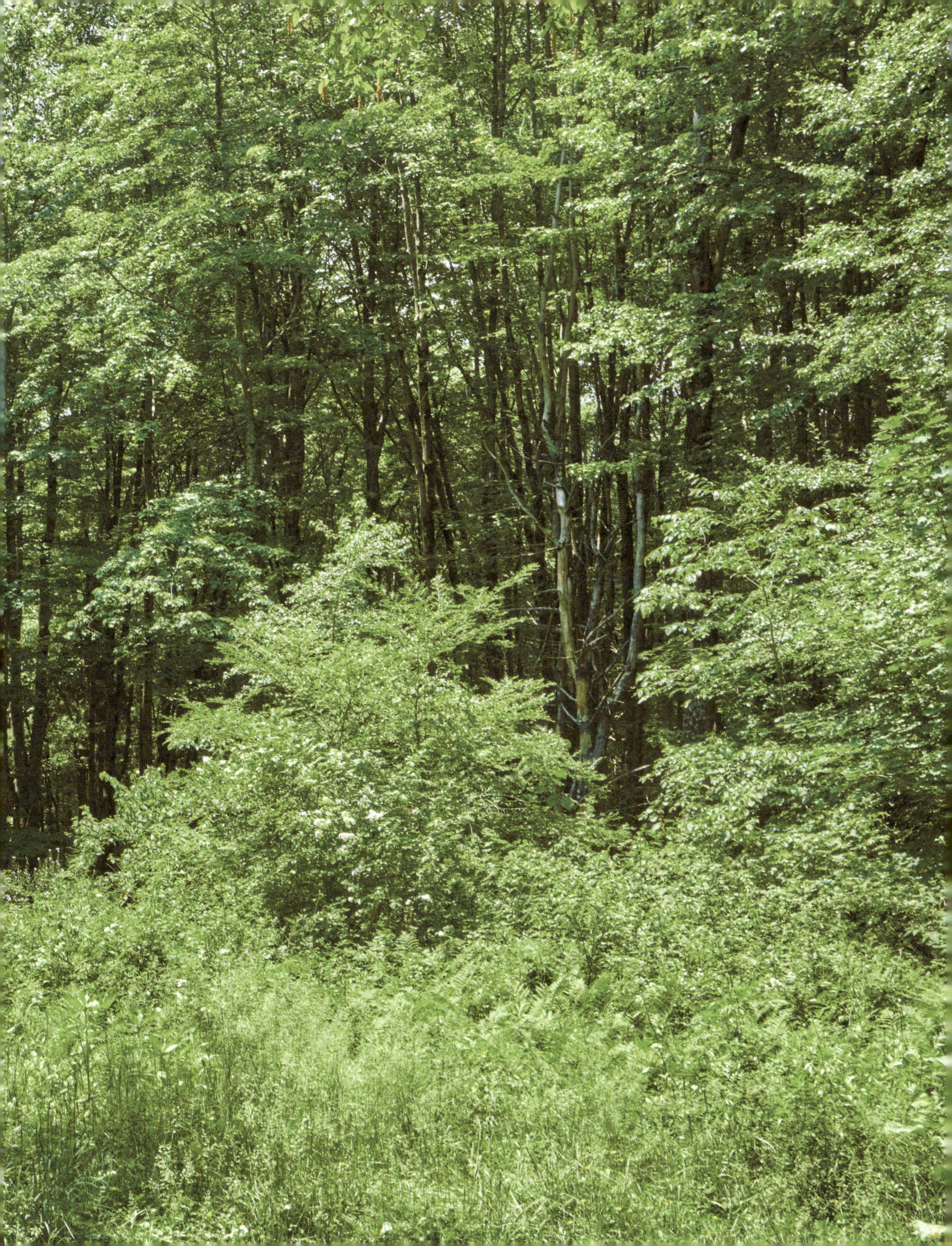

# Seasonal Index

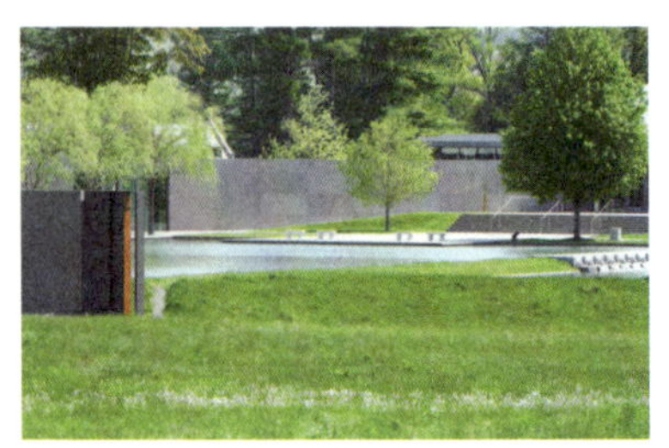

pp. 60–61

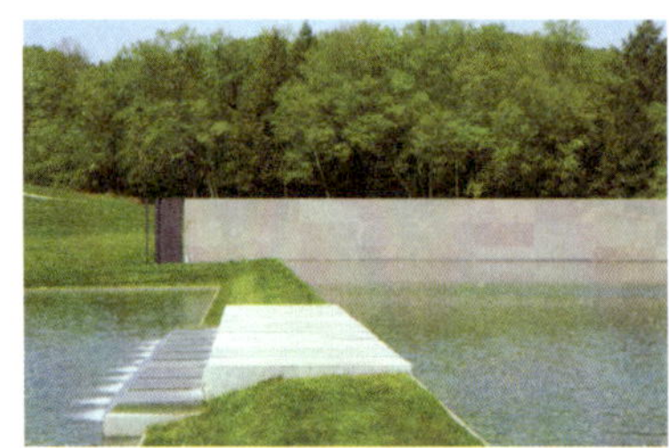

pp. 62–63

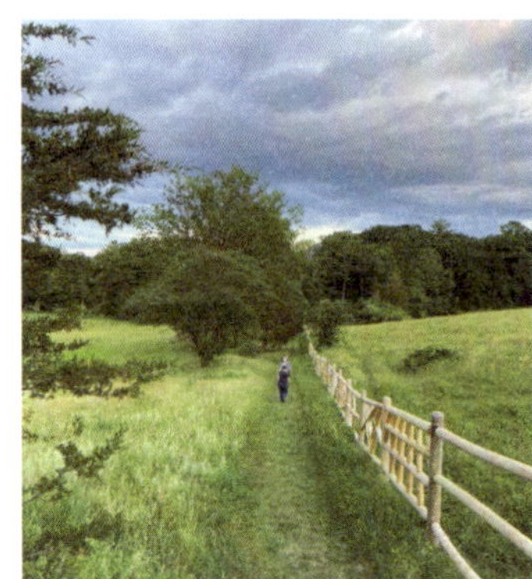

p. 26

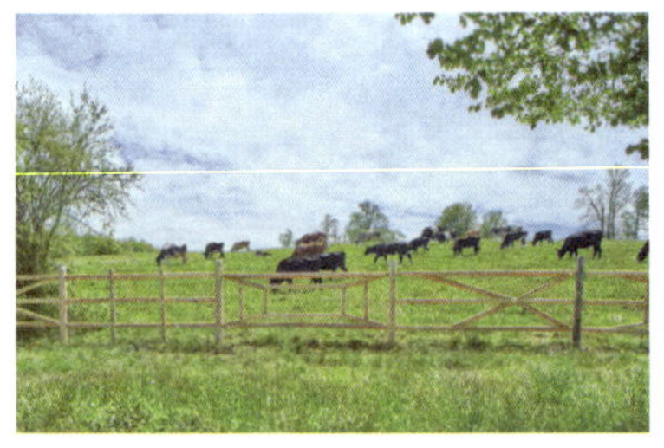

p. 82

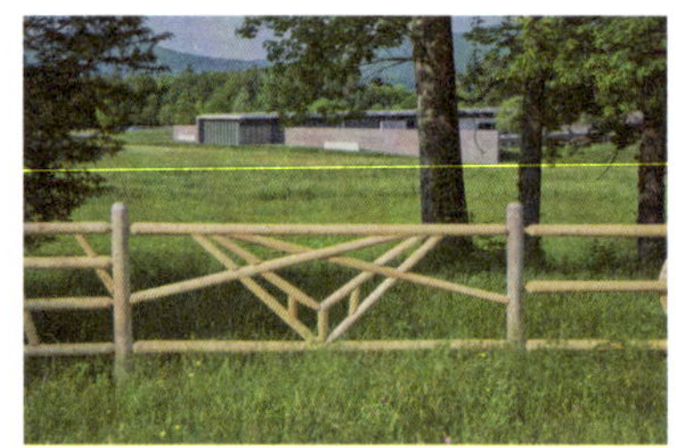

pp. 88–89

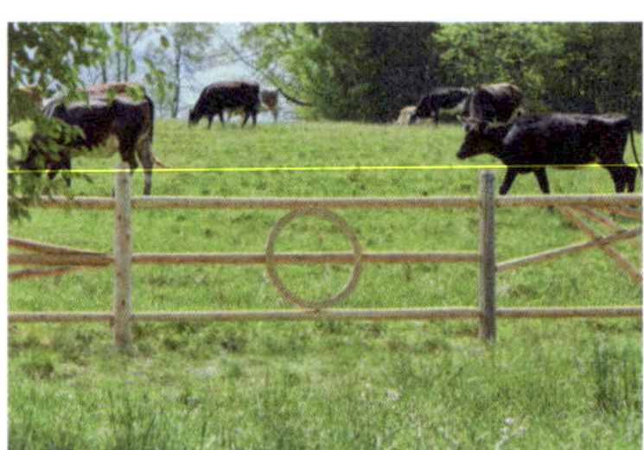

p. 83

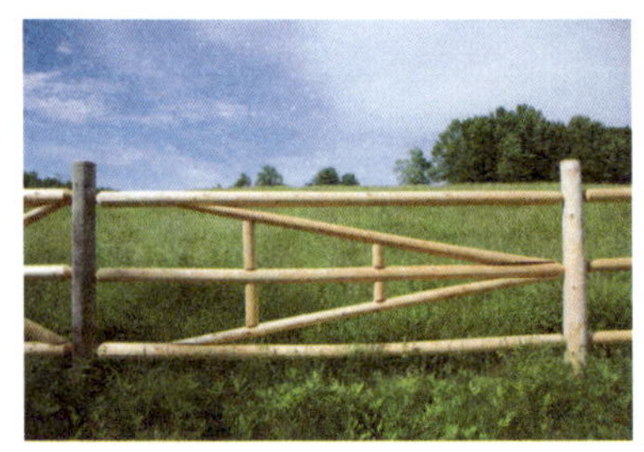

p. 81

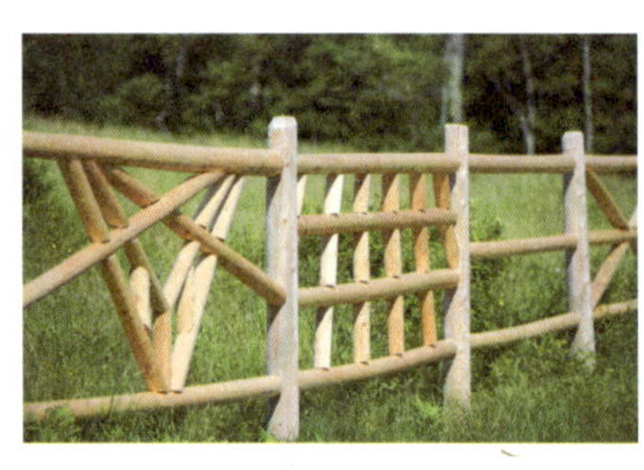

p. 80

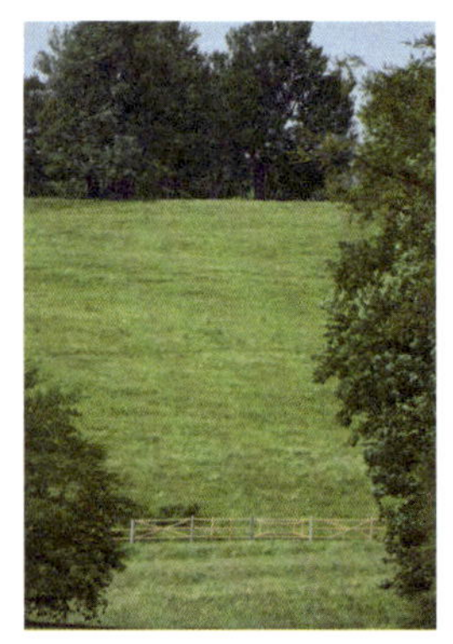

p. 85

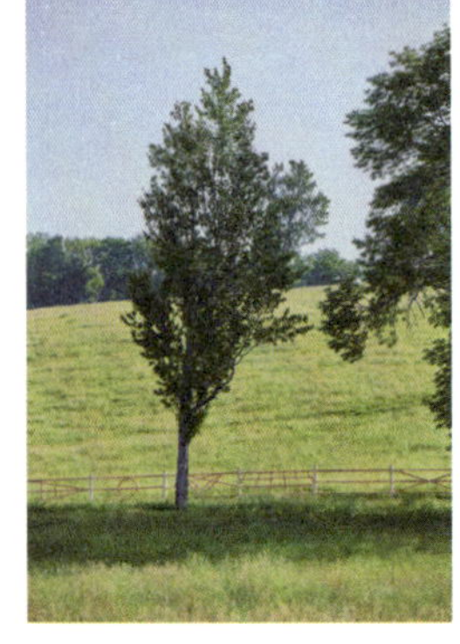

endpaper

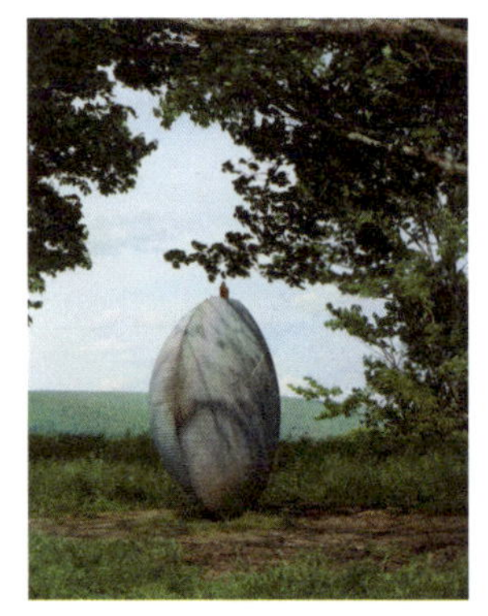

p. 115

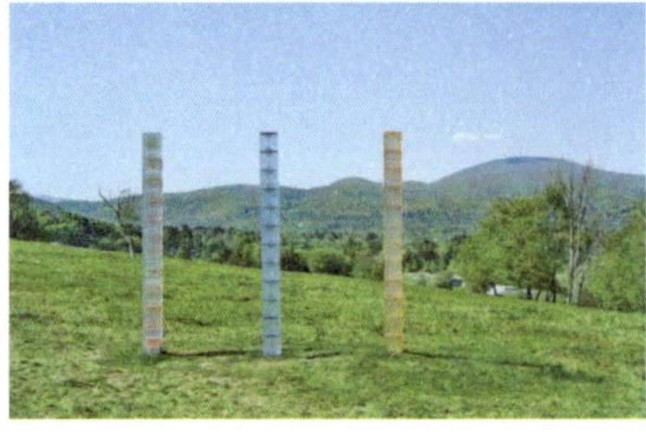

pp. 160–61

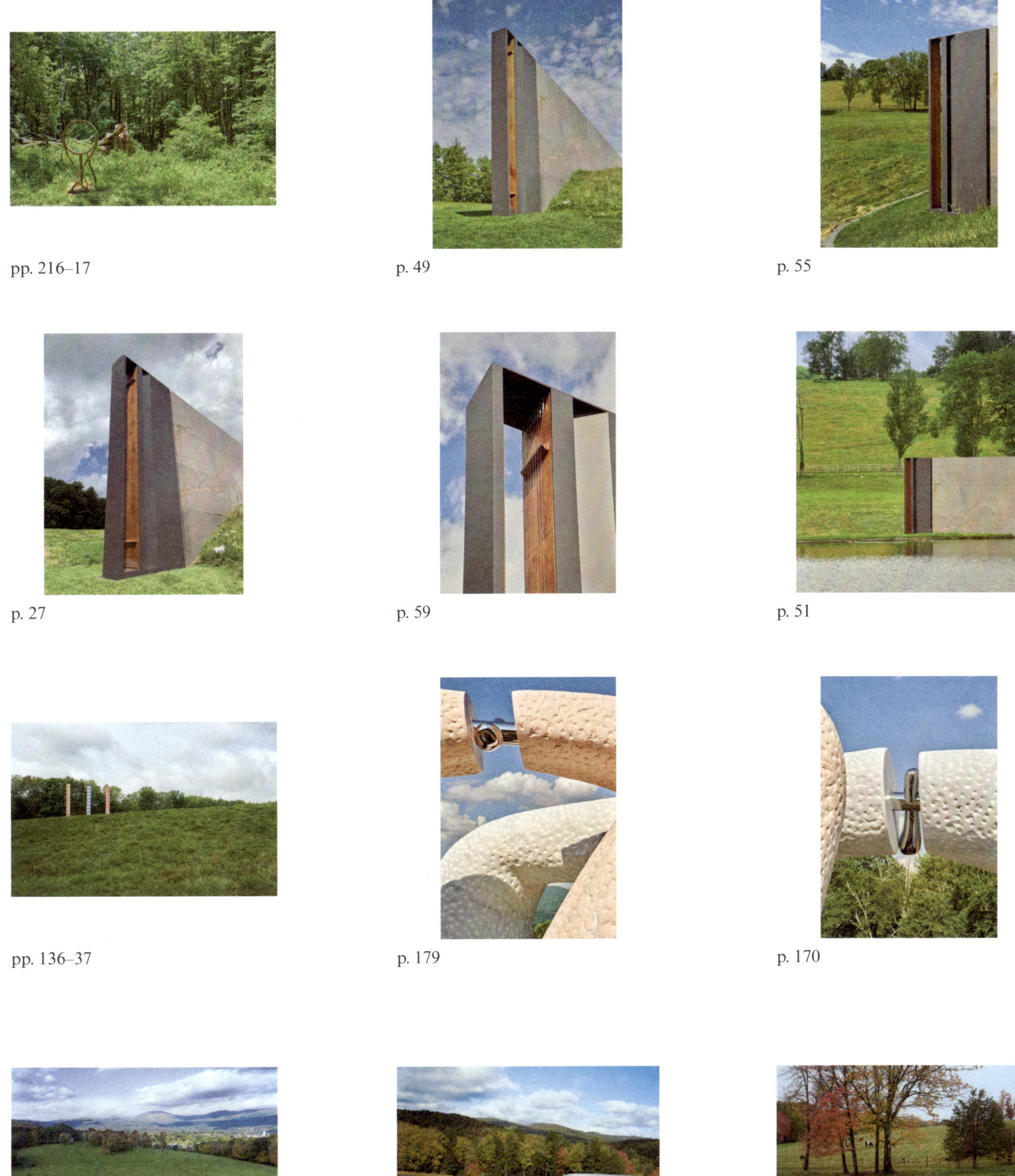

pp. 216–17

p. 49

p. 55

p. 27

p. 59

p. 51

pp. 136–37

p. 179

p. 170

endpaper

pp. 36–37

pp. 86–87

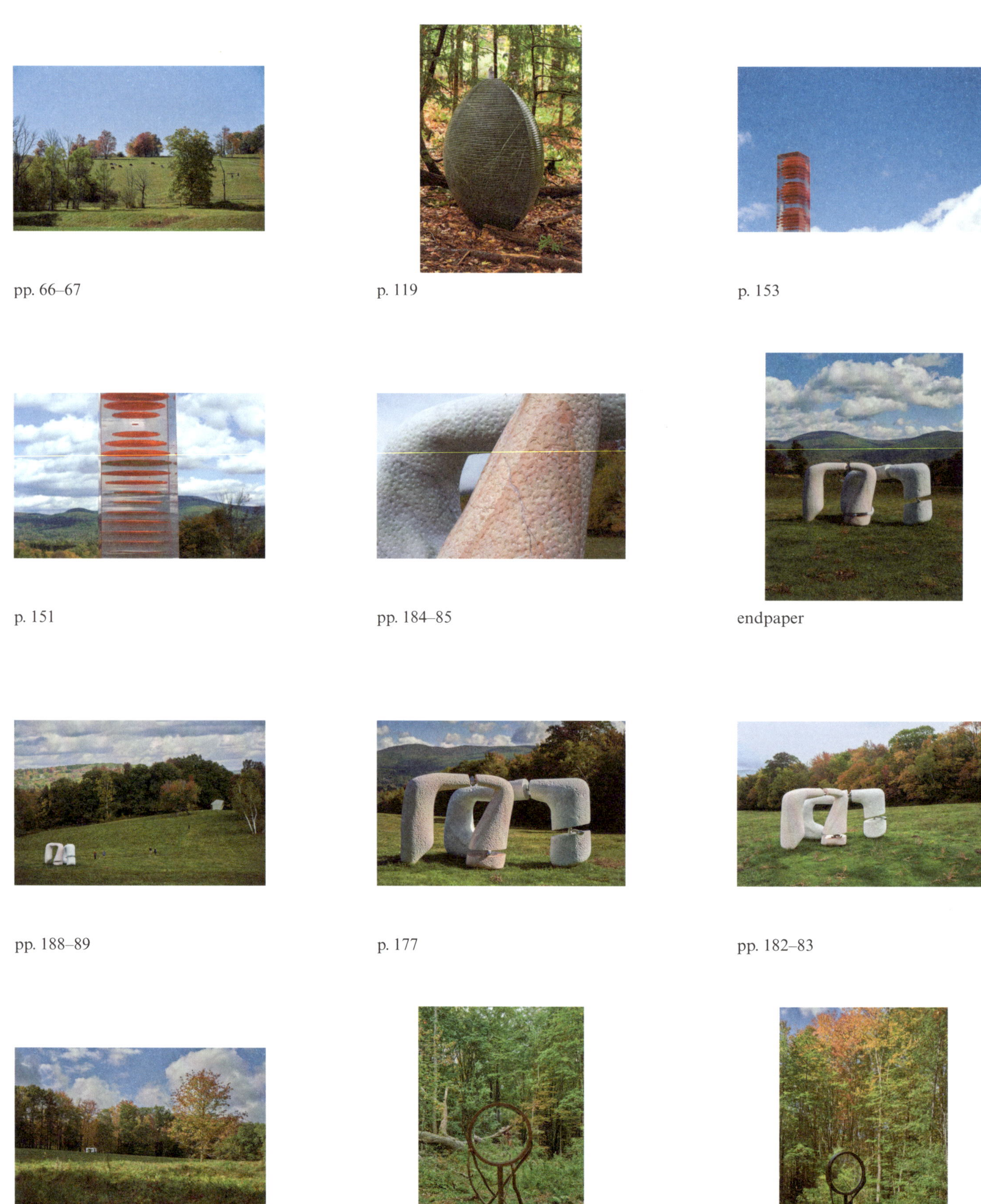

pp. 66–67

p. 119

p. 153

p. 151

pp. 184–85

endpaper

pp. 188–89

p. 177

pp. 182–83

p. 11

p. 205

p. 207

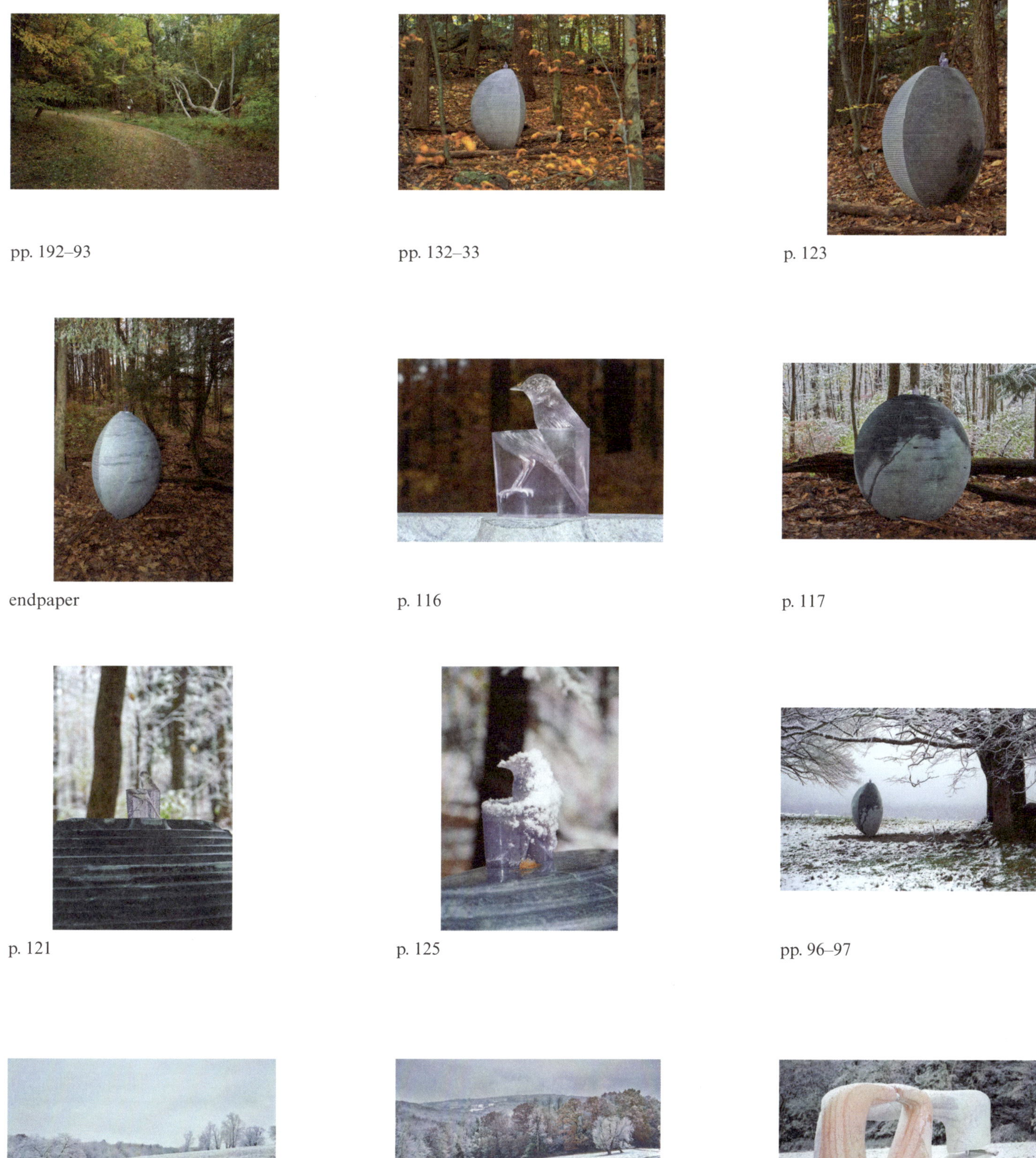

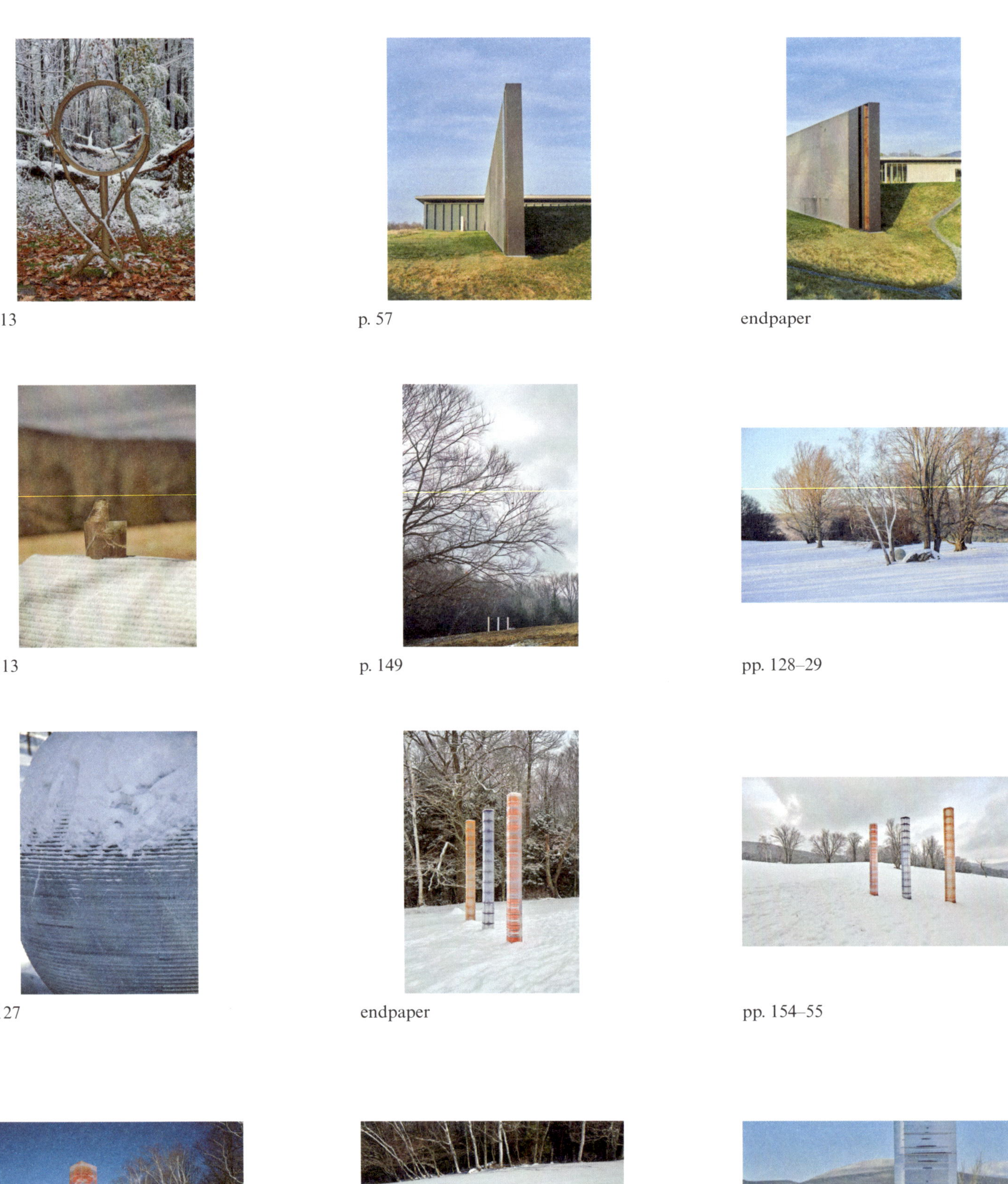

p. 213

p. 57

endpaper

p. 113

p. 149

pp. 128–29

p. 127

endpaper

pp. 154–55

pp. 156–57

p. 152

p. 150

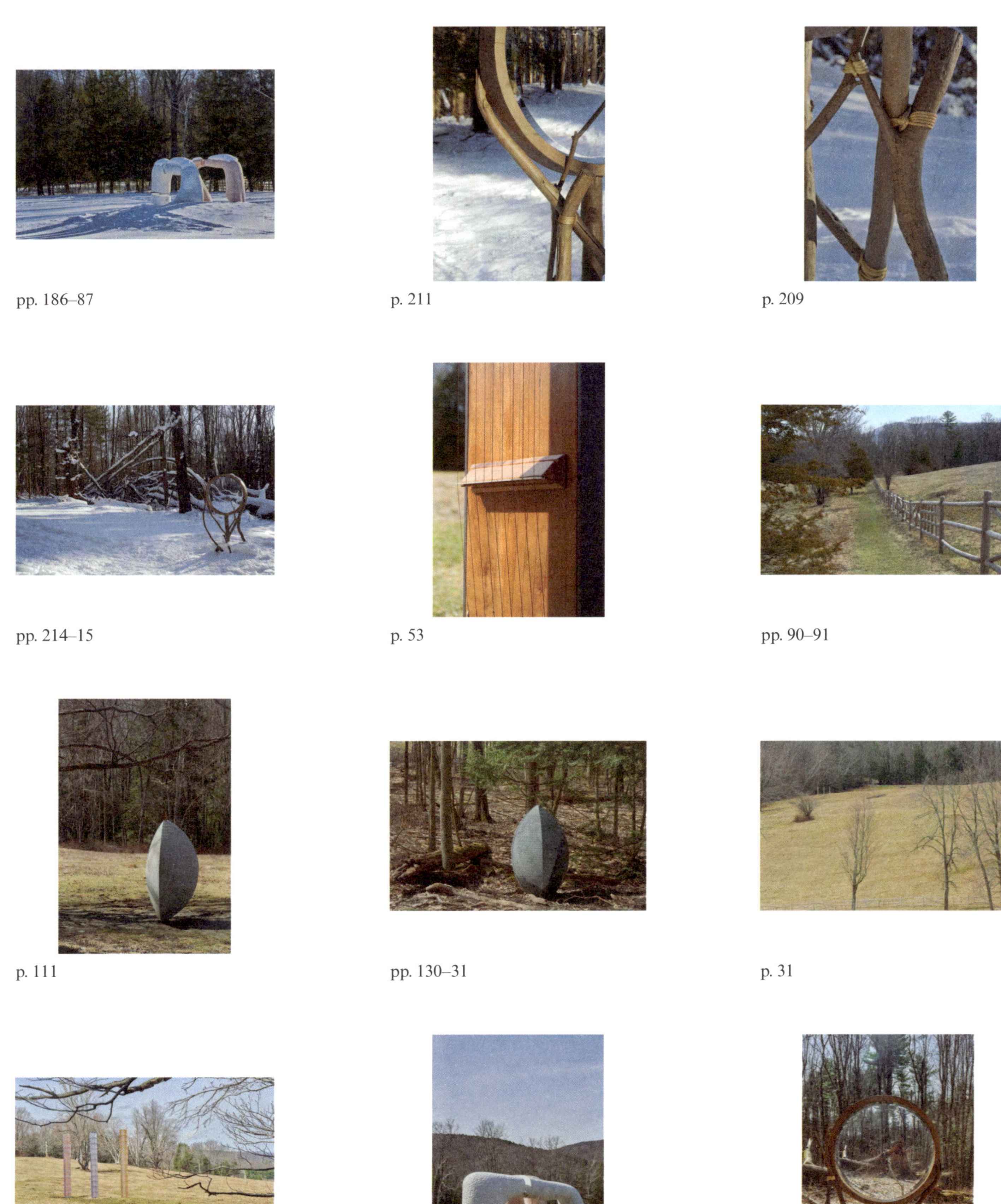

pp. 186–87

p. 211

p. 209

pp. 214–15

p. 53

pp. 90–91

p. 111

pp. 130–31

p. 31

pp. 158–59

p. 181

endpaper

# About the Artists

## Kelly Akashi

Kelly Akashi (b. 1983, Los Angeles) trained as an analog photographer and brings a documentarian's instincts and curiosity to a practice that embraces a range of diverse materials and age-old processes. Her work is included in the permanent collections of the Los Angeles Museum of Contemporary Art; the Hammer Museum, Los Angeles; the Brooklyn Museum; and the Sifang Museum, Nanjing, China, among others. Recent solo exhibitions include presentations at the Aspen Art Museum (2020); Tanya Bonakdar Gallery, New York (2020); Headlands Center for the Arts, Sausalito, California (2019); Carolyn Glasoe Bailey Foundation, Ojai, California (2019); ARCH Athens (2019); François Ghebaly Gallery, Los Angeles (2019 and 2016); and SculptureCenter, New York (2017). Akashi lives and works in Los Angeles.

## Nairy Baghramian

Nairy Baghramian (b. 1971, Isfahan, Iran) grapples with issues of vulnerability and authority as she deconstructs and reassembles the human form, ever mindful of the forces of history, material, and context. Baghramian's work is held in the permanent collections of the Centre Pompidou, Paris; the Art Institute of Chicago; the Museum of Modern Art, New York; the Solomon R. Guggenheim Museum, New York; the S.M.A.K. Museum of Contemporary Art, Ghent, Belgium; the Stedelijk Museum, Amsterdam; Tate Modern, London; and the Walker Art Center, Minneapolis, among others. Baghramian's recent solo presentations include projects at Fondazione Furla/Galleria d'Arte Moderna, Milan (2021); PERFORMA-19, New York (2019), Palacio de Cristal del Retiro, Madrid (2018); the Walker Art Center (2017); and the S.M.A.K. Museum of Contemporary Art (2016). Baghramian has also participated in the Venice Biennale (2019 and 2011); the Yorkshire Sculpture International (2019); *documenta* 14 in Kassel and Athens (2017); Skulptur Project Muenster (2017 and 2007); the Lyon Biennale (2017); the Glasgow International Festival of Visual Art (2012); and the Berlin Biennale (2014 and 2008). Baghramian lives and works in Berlin, Germany.

## Jennie C. Jones

Jennie C. Jones (b. 1968, Cincinnati) employs strategies of collage and assemblage in her ongoing project of translating sound into physical matter, reframing the contributions of African Americans to include a modernist, minimalist vernacular. Her work is included in the permanent collections of the Museum of Modern Art,

New York; the Solomon R. Guggenheim Museum, New York; and the Hirshhorn Museum and Sculpture Garden, Washington, DC, among others. Recent solo presentations include projects at the Arts Club of Chicago (2020); the Philip Johnson Glass House, New Canaan, Connecticut (2018); Contemporary Arts Museum Houston (2015); the Hirshhorn Museum and Sculpture Garden (2013); The Kitchen, New York (2011); Yerba Buena Center for the Arts, San Francisco (2011); and Atlanta Contemporary Art Center (2009). Jones lives and works in Hudson, New York.

## Eva LeWitt

Eva LeWitt (b. 1985, Spoleto, Italy) leverages the forces of color, gravity, suspension, and volume with a sensitivity to space, an interest in repetition and variation, and a reconsideration of materials and their inherent properties. Her work is held in the permanent collections of the Hirshhorn Museum and Sculpture Garden, Washington, DC; Kistefos Museum, Jevnaker, Norway; and X Museum, Beijing, among others. Recent solo exhibitions include presentations at the Institute of Contemporary Art / Boston (2021); the Aldrich Contemporary Art Museum, Ridgefield, Connecticut (2019); the Jewish Museum, New York (2018); and VI, VII Gallery, Oslo (2018). LeWitt lives and works in New York.

## Analia Saban

Analia Saban (b. 1980, Buenos Aires) explores the intersections and overlap between traditional media and new technologies, disrupting conventional techniques of drawing, painting, weaving, and sculpture to probe the capacity of an object and the myriad meanings found within its form. Her work is in the permanent collections of the Los Angeles County Museum of Art; the Centre Pompidou, Paris; the Israel Museum, Jerusalem; the Hessel Museum of Art at Bard College, Annandale-on-Hudson, New York; Fonds regional d'Art contemporain (FRAC) d'Auvergne, France; the Hammer Museum and the Museum of Contemporary Art, Los Angeles; and the Albright-Knox Art Gallery, Buffalo, among others. The Modern Art Museum of Fort Worth (2019) and the Blaffer Art Museum, Austin, Texas (2016), have both presented solo exhibitions of Saban's work. Saban lives and works in Los Angeles.

## Haegue Yang

Haegue Yang (b. 1971, Seoul) explores themes of social and political histories in her work, extricating familiar objects and materials from their primary functions and environments and repurposing them in a new framework of abstraction. Yang's work is held in the collections of the Museum of Modern Art, New York; M+, Hong Kong; Seoul Museum of Art; Tate, London; the Solomon R. Guggenheim Museum, New York and Abu Dhabi; Walker Art Center, Minneapolis; and Centre Pompidou, Paris, among others. Recent solo exhibitions include projects at the Art Gallery of Ontario, Toronto (2020); MMCA Seoul (2020), MCAD Manila (2020), Tate St. Ives (2020), the Bass Museum of Art, Miami Beach (2019); South London Gallery (2019); and her first European survey show, mounted by Museum Ludwig, Cologne (2018). A new commission by the artist, titled *Handles*, was recently on view at the Marron Atrium of the renovated Museum of Modern Art, New York, from 2019 to 2021. Yang lives and works between Berlin and Seoul.

# Works in the Exhibition

Kelly Akashi
b. Los Angeles, 1983; lives and works in Los Angeles
*A Device to See the World Twice*
2020
Optical acrylic, bronze, rope
84 x 48 x 42 in. (213.4 x 121.9 x 106.7 cm)
Courtesy of the artist; François Ghebaly Gallery, Los Angeles; and Tanya Bonakdar Gallery, New York

Nairy Baghramian
b. Isfahan, 1971; lives and works in Berlin
*Knee and Elbow*
2020
Marble, stainless steel
Overall: 61 5/8 x 77 3/4 x 115 1/2 in. (156.5 x 197.5 x 293.4 cm); Knee: 61 1/2 x 107 3/4 x 26 1/2 in. (156.2 x 273.7 x 67.3 cm); Elbow: 61 5/8 x 75 3/4 x 26 1/2 in. (156.5 x 192.4 x 67.3 cm)
Courtesy of the artist and Marian Goodman Gallery, New York, London, and Paris

Jennie C. Jones
b. Cincinnati, 1968; lives and works in Hudson, New York
*These (Mournful) Shores*
2020
Powder-coated aluminum, wood, harp strings
197 1/16 x 72 x 18 in. (500.5 x 182.9 x 45.7 cm)
Courtesy of the artist; PATRON Gallery, Chicago; and Alexander Gray Associates, New York and Germantown, NY

Eva LeWitt
b. Spoleto, 1985; lives and works in New York
*Resin Tower A (Orange)*
*Resin Tower B (Yellow)*
*Resin Tower C (Blue)*
2020
Resin, PVC
128 x 10 x 10 in. (325.1 x 25.4 x 25.4 cm), each column
Courtesy of the artist and VI, VII, Oslo

Analia Saban
b. Buenos Aires, 1980; lives and works in Los Angeles
*Teaching a Cow How to Draw*
2020
Cedar wood
620 ft. (189 m)
Courtesy of the artist and Tanya Bonakdar Gallery, New York / Los Angeles

Haegue Yang
b. Seoul, 1971; lives and works in Berlin and Seoul

*Migratory DMZ Birds on Asymmetric Lens – Tee-Cher Tee-Cher Vessel (Great Tit)*
2020
Soapstone, 3D-printed resin
62 x 58 1/4 x 28 3/4 in. (157.5 x 148 x 73 cm)
Courtesy of the artist and kurimanzutto, Mexico City / New York

*Migratory DMZ Birds on Asymmetric Lens – Hou-Ke-Kyo Vessel (Japanese Bush Warbler)*
2020
Soapstone, 3D-printed resin
62 x 58 1/2 x 33 1/2 in. (157.5 x 148.6 x 85.1 cm)
Courtesy of the artist and kurimanzutto, Mexico City / New York

*Migratory DMZ Birds on Asymmetric Lens – Duiitt Duiitt Vessel (Gray-Backed Thrush)*
2020
Soapstone, 3D-printed resin
62 x 58 x 35 in. (157.5 x 147.3 x 88.9 cm)
Courtesy of the artist and kurimanzutto, Mexico City / New York

The Clark would like to extend its sincere gratitude to all the donors whose contributions made this exhibition possible.

Susan Adler
Lee and Bob Albern
Robert Aliber
Kristen and James Allen
Therese Allen
Robert Alter and Lisa DeLima
Shirley Anderson and Robert Fisher
Edward Baptiste and Wendy Philbrick
Karl Barbir and Cathleen Barrett
Frank Barrie
Molly and John Beard
Elizabeth Beaudoin
Linda and Charles Becker
Jill and Ned Benedict
Joan Benjamin and Laurence Cherkis
George Bergen
Amy Bernstein
Irene Bernstein
Elmer and Olga Bertsch
Linda and Robert Bicknell
Joan Blair
Sydelle and Lee Blatt
Carolyn and Nelson Bonheim
Jeannene Booher
Maureen Fennessy Bousa and Edward P. Bousa
Kathleen Braden and Gerald Keusch
Gayl Braisted
Shirley Brandman and Howard Shapiro
Jane Briggs
Gaye Brown
Ronald Brown
Susan and Stephen Brown
Lynn Buckner
Robert Buckwalter
Judith and Frederick Buechner
Helen and Warren Buhler
Stephen Bullock
Madeline Burke-Vigeland and Nils Vigeland
Rinda and Lewis Burleigh
Betsy Burris and Brad Wells
Mary Virginia Burrus
Margaret Byrnes
Joshua Cantor-Stone
John Carroll
John Carver
Kay and Elliot Cattarulla
Rebecca and Daniel Cellana
Carolyn Truesdell and John Cheney
Kate and Lynn Christianson
Kathy and Stanley Cichanowski
Susan Stetson Clarke
Libby and Philip Clay
Carl Clemente
Richard and Robin Clutz
Lori Cohen and Christopher Rothko
J. D. Cole and Sheila McElwaine
Michele Cole and Brendan Rafferty
Ralph Colin, Jr.
Carol Cone
Karen Conlin and Raymond McGarrigle
Ann and Thomas Connolly
Françoise and Joseph Connors
Linda G. Conway
Liz and Tom Costley
Pamela Cothey
Countryside Landscaping & Design Inc.
Tom and Melissa Cragg
Dianne Cutillo and Bernard Pinsonnault
Pamela and Peter D'Ambrosio
Emily Daunis and Daniel Wallis
Paul J. David, MD
Elizabeth de Rham
Michael Deep
Christian Dewailly and Elizabeth Garger
Deborah and Edward Dickinson
Maureen and Jack Dietze
Jay E. Dubé
Kathryn and Gerald Dudding
Francesca Eastman and Edward Goodstein
Julia Eddy and Dan Mayer
Robert Eddy
Barbara and Michael Eisenson
Dede Emerson
Mary Jo and Walter Engels
Ellen and Thomas Ennis
Kathleen Erickson and Robert Grace
Ellen Gail and Rhon Ernest-Jones
Maribeth and Philip Eugene
Gintare Everett
Suzanne and Richard Farley
Deborah Fehr
Cornelia and Robert Ferguson
Jay Fisher
Juliet Flynt
Sarah Foehl
Diane Forsyth and William Frazier
Mary M. Fuqua
Thomas Fynan and William Loutrel
Magda Gabor-Hotchkiss
Janet Gain
John and Virginia Gajewski
Peter Gale
Nancy Gaudette
Claire Geller-Kolchetski
Michelle Gersen and Michael Zweig
Anne and Michael Gershon
Susan Gold
Janice and David Golden
Ellen and Alan Goldner
Jill Goodman
Michael Gordon
Cheryl Gowie and Daniel Schmidt
Philip Gray and Janet Travers
Wendy and Joel Greenberg
Walter and Carla Gunn
Christel Hagen
Carmela and Paul Haklisch
Ellen and Scott Hand
Mary Ellen and Gates Hawn
Anne and Thomas Haxo
Ughetta Hirsch
Diane and Robert Hitter
Patti and Daniel Holland
Margaret Hornick and Brian Conolly
Susan and Joseph Horton
Jennifer Howlett and Mark Stevens
Nicholas Hruch
Joan and James Hunter
Christopher Huyck and Jane Perkins-Huyck
Charles Ihlenfeld and William Packard
Anne Isbister and Christopher Ballog
Barbara and Alan Jacobs
Phyllis and Joseph Jaffe
Monique Jalbert
Stephen and Lisa Jenks
Stephanie Johnson and Charles Bonenti
L. Katherin Jones
Eric and Laura Jordahl
Rachel and Mike Judlowe
Sue and Dennis Kaufman
Jane Keener and Paul Janssens
Anne Kelly and Mark Van Wormer
Sandy Kelly and Marjorie Chamberlain
Patricia and William Kenney
Elaine Kersten and Laurence Cadorette
James Kettlewell
Diana and Thomas Killip
Debbie and Tony King
Del and Georgette Kinney
Gay Klaus-Scarborough
Gloria and Eric Koster
Margaret and Richard Kronenberg
John Kurkland
Laurie LaChapelle and David Leach
Terry Lamb
Kate and Chet Lasell
Patricia Leach
Elizabeth Lee
Natalie and George Lee
Robert Lee
Julie and Benedict Leerburger
Alan Lesser
Andrew Levin
Howard and Barbara Levine
Marion and Peter London
Kathy and David Lord
Mary Ann and Ralph Lowen
Constance and Nancy Luther
William Macanka
Turi MacCombie and David Neelon
Sarah Marshall
Mass MoCA
Nancy J. McIntire
Kathy and Philip McKnight
Ruth and Stephen Melville
Anne Melvin and Daniel Sullivan
Faith Menken
Carol Messerschmitt
Susan Miller
Ann and John Milliman
Patricia Mion
James and Barbara Moltz
Jacqueline Moran and Megan Karlen
Judy Moss
Anne and Charles Mott
Melanie Mowinski and Douglas Molin

Mary and Stephen Muller
Katherine Nahum
Lisa and Tony Nasch
Carol and Steven Nash
Regina Nash
National Endowment for the Humanities: Exploring the human endeavor
Pauline and Richard Nault
Paul Neely
Brenda Nelson
Beth and Richard Nesbitt
Dana and Lukasz Niedzielski
Robert Nottke
Matt and Greta Noyes
Lisa and Charles O'Brien
Ana Maria Olivo and James Hoch
Angela and Joseph Orsene
Harmon Pardoe
Chrystina and James Parks
Patricia and Stephen Peters
Rosamond and Ronald Pietras
Margot and Leonard Platt
Vsevolod Popov
Carla Procaskey and Anthony Falanders
Ramelle and Michael Pulitzer
Mary Ann and Bruno Quinson
Judith and Lawrence Raab
Margaret and Jay Rachfal
Janet and John Rausch
Cornelia and Wallis Reid
Donnie Richman
Janet Romano and Theodore Jadick
Lyn and Allen Rork
Linda Rose
Karen Rosenberg
Sabina and Alex Rosenblum
Georgeanne and Jean Rousseau
Ann and Alfred Ruesch
Cecelia and George Rufo
A. William Rutter, Jr.
Vicki Safram
Vicki and Scott Saltzman
Carl Samuelson
Elizabeth Sayman
Amy and Charlie Scharf
Mary Beth Schiffman and David Tochen
Cynthia and Wayne Schneider
Rosalie and David Schottenfeld
Nan Schow
Karen and Robert Scott
Harriet Seeley
Monica and John Shanahan
Lynn and Daniel Shapiro
Molly O'Meara-Sheehan and Joseph E. Sheehan III
Irene Shen
Judith Shepherd and Larry Silver
Jo-Anne Sherburne
Sally and Robert Silberberg
Cynthia and William Simon
Anne Skinner and Gordon Squire
Anthony and Anne Smeglin
Barbara Smith
Mitchell and Alison Smith
S. Wylie Smith
Janis Smythe
Denise Littlefield Sobel
Stefanie Solum and Peter Starenko
SPC Print. Integrated
Deborah and Wayne Sprague
Carol and Bob Stegeman
Tamanika Steward
Jonathan Swartz
Roberta Sweet and Amanda Greenwood
Frederic Taylor
Diane and Michael Taylor
Richard Tedoldie
Terra Foundation for American Art
Joseph C. Thompson
Laurie and Peter Thomsen
Jane and William H. Told, Jr.
Jesse Tran and Loren Brink
Paul Trela
William Verry
Royall Victor III
Hedda W. von Goeben
Susy and Jack Wadsworth
In honor of Marilyn and Ronald Walter
Beth and Dustin Wees
Carolyn and Helge Weiner-Trapness
Candace Weir
Londa Weisman and Sidney Knafel
Alleson White
Anne and Alexander White
Maryalice Widness and Philip Schenck
Hannelore Wilfert and Karl Moschner
Dr. and Mrs. Harold A. Wilkinson
James Wilson
Paul Wing
Eileen Wolff
Susan Wolfthal
Cynthia Wood and Edward Perry
Thomas Woodward and David LePere
Lillian Woodworth
Sharon and Harvey Yorke
Kathi Young and Andy Masetti
Anonymous (3)

# *Ground/work*

Published by the Clark Art Institute on the occasion of the exhibition *Ground/work*, Clark Art Institute, Williamstown, Massachusetts, October 6, 2020–October 17, 2021.

*Ground/work* is organized by the Clark Art Institute with guest curators Molly Epstein and Abigail Ross Goodman.

Major support for *Ground/work* is provided by Karen and Robert Scott, Denise Littlefield Sobel, and Paul Neely. Additional funding is generously provided by the Terra Foundation for American Art; the National Endowment for the Humanities: Exploring the human endeavor; Maureen Fennessy Bousa and Edward P. Bousa; Amy and Charlie Scharf; Elizabeth Lee; MASS MoCA; Chrystina and James Parks; Howard M. Shapiro and Shirley Brandman; Joan and Jim Hunter; James and Barbara Moltz; and a gift in honor of Marilyn and Ron Walter.

Any views, findings, conclusions, or recommendations expressed in this exhibition do not necessarily represent those of the National Endowment for the Humanities.

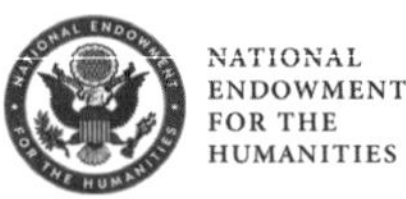


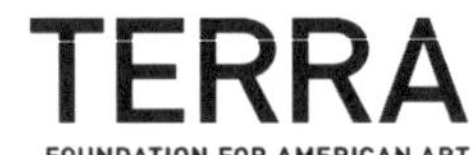


Produced by the Publications Department of the Clark Art Institute
225 South Street
Williamstown, Massachusetts 01267
clarkart.edu

Anne Roecklein, managing editor
Kevin Bicknell, editor
Samantha Page, assistant editor
David Murphy, rights and licensing associate
Gabriel Almeida Baroja, publications intern
Copyedited and proofread by Kristin Swan

Design by Laura Coombs
Printed on Munken Polar Rough 120gsm
Printed and bound in Belgium by die Keure



ISBN 978-0300257601

Distributed by Yale University Press
302 Temple Street
P.O. Box 209040
New Haven, Connecticut 06520-9040
yalebooks.com/art

ISBN 978-0-300-25760-1

10 9 8 7 6 5 4 3 2 1
Library of Congress Cataloging-in-Publication Data

Names: Sterling and Francine Clark Art Institute, author, organizer, host institution. | Epstein, Molly, editor. | Goodman, Abigail Ross, editor. | Martin, Courtney J. | Porter, Jenelle. | Pyś, Pavel S. | Tan, Lumi. | Umolu, Yesomi. | Wiesenberger, Robert.

Title: Ground/work / edited by Molly Epstein and Abigail Ross Goodman; with essays by Courtney J. Martin, Jenelle Porter, Pavel S. Pyś, Lumi Tan, Yesomi Umolu, Robert Wiesenberger. Other titles: Ground work

Description: Williamstown, Massachusetts : Clark Art Institute, [2021] | Includes bibliographical references. | Summary: "Published by the Clark Art Institute on the occasion of the exhibition Ground/work, Clark Art Institute, Williamstown, Massachusetts, October 6, 2020–October 17, 2021. Ground/work is organized by the Clark Art Institute with guest curators Molly Epstein and Abigail Ross Goodman. Building on a history of collaboration with contemporary artists, the Clark commissioned Kelly Akashi, Nairy Baghramian, Jennie C. Jones, Eva LeWitt, Analia Saban, and Haegue Yang to create new works of art in active dialogue with this specific environment. This book contains eight essays that address the significance of these artworks and artists from curators and writers Courtney J. Martin, Jenelle Porter, Pavel S. Pyś, Lumi Tan, Yesomi Umolu, and Robert Wiesenberger"-- Provided by publisher.

Identifiers: LCCN 2021018377 | ISBN 9780300257601 (hardcover)

Subjects: LCSH: Sculpture, Modern--21st century--Exhibitions. | Outdoor sculpture--Massachusetts--Williamstown--Exhibitions. | Site-specific sculpture--Massachusetts--Williamstown--Exhibitions. | Sterling and Francine Clark Art Institute--Exhibitions.

Classification: LCC NB198.6 .S73 2021 | DDC 730.9744/1--dc23
LC record available at https://lccn.loc.gov/2021018377

Images of Kelly Akashi's work are courtesy of the artist; François Ghebaly Gallery, Los Angeles; and Tanya Bonakdar Gallery, New York. Images of Nairy Baghramian's work are courtesy of the artist and Marian Goodman Gallery, New York, London, and Paris. Images of Jennie C. Jones's work are courtesy of the artist; PATRON Gallery, Chicago, and Alexander Gray Associates, New York and Germantown, NY. Images of Eva LeWitt's work are courtesy of the artist and VI, VII, Oslo. Images of Analia Saban's work are courtesy of the artist and Tanya Bonakdar Gallery, New York / Los Angeles. Images of Haegue Yang's work are courtesy of the artist and kurimanzutto, Mexico City / New York

Unless otherwise noted, all photographs are taken by Thomas Clark. Additional photography credits include:
Mike Agee: figs. 3, 23, and 24; Joe Aidonidis/Great Sky Media: cover and endpaper; Ueli Alder: fig. 29; Tucker Bair: figs. 4, 5, and 9; Filipe Braga © Fundação de Serralves: fig. 41; Cathy Carver: fig. 19; Kevin Dietsh/UPI: fig. 34; Marten Elder: fig. 61; Molly Epstein: fig. 8; Ernesto Galan: fig. 43; Abigail Ross Goodman: fig. 14; Pierre Le Hors: fig. 18; Kyle Knodell: figs. 58 and 59; Kitmin Lee: fig. 60; Jason Madella: fig. 16; Bob Matheson and the Art Gallery of Greater Victoria: fig. 7; Charles Mayer: fig. 26; Henninh Rogge: fig. 54; Deema Shahin: fig. 39; Studio Haegue Yang: fig. 35; Katherine Du Tiel: fig. 55; Benjamin Westoby, fig. 54; Jason Wyche: fig. 21; Eva Zubero: fig. 40

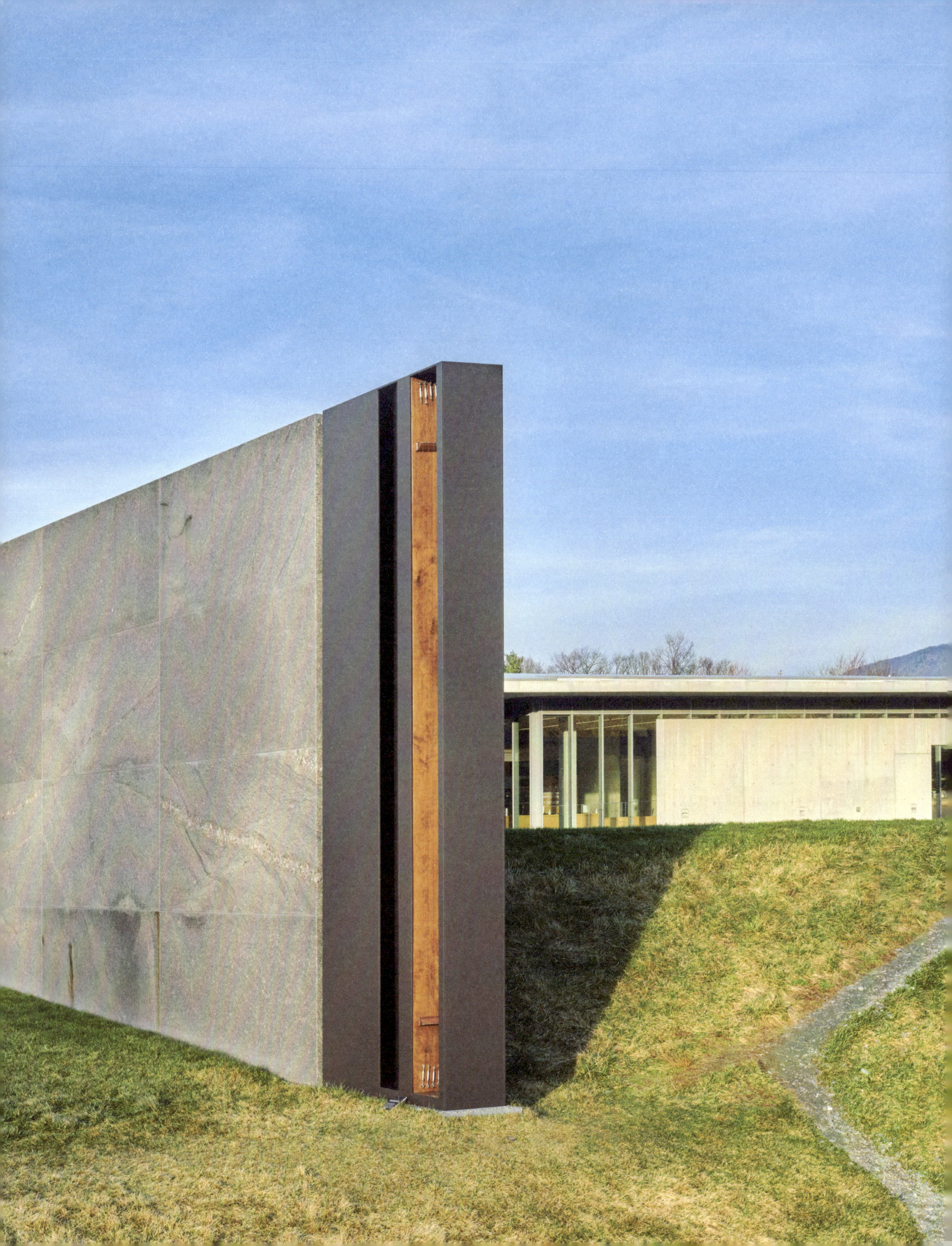

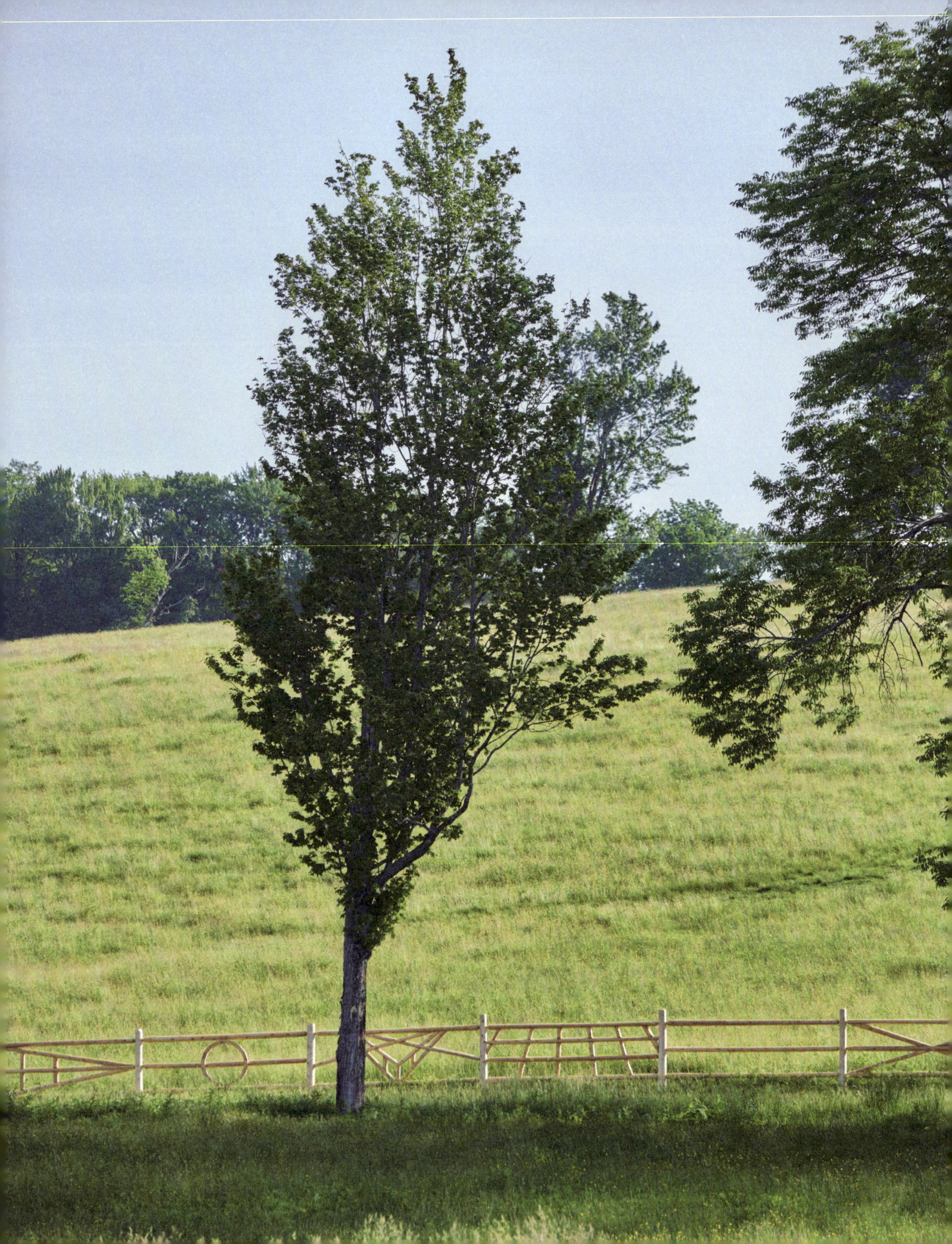

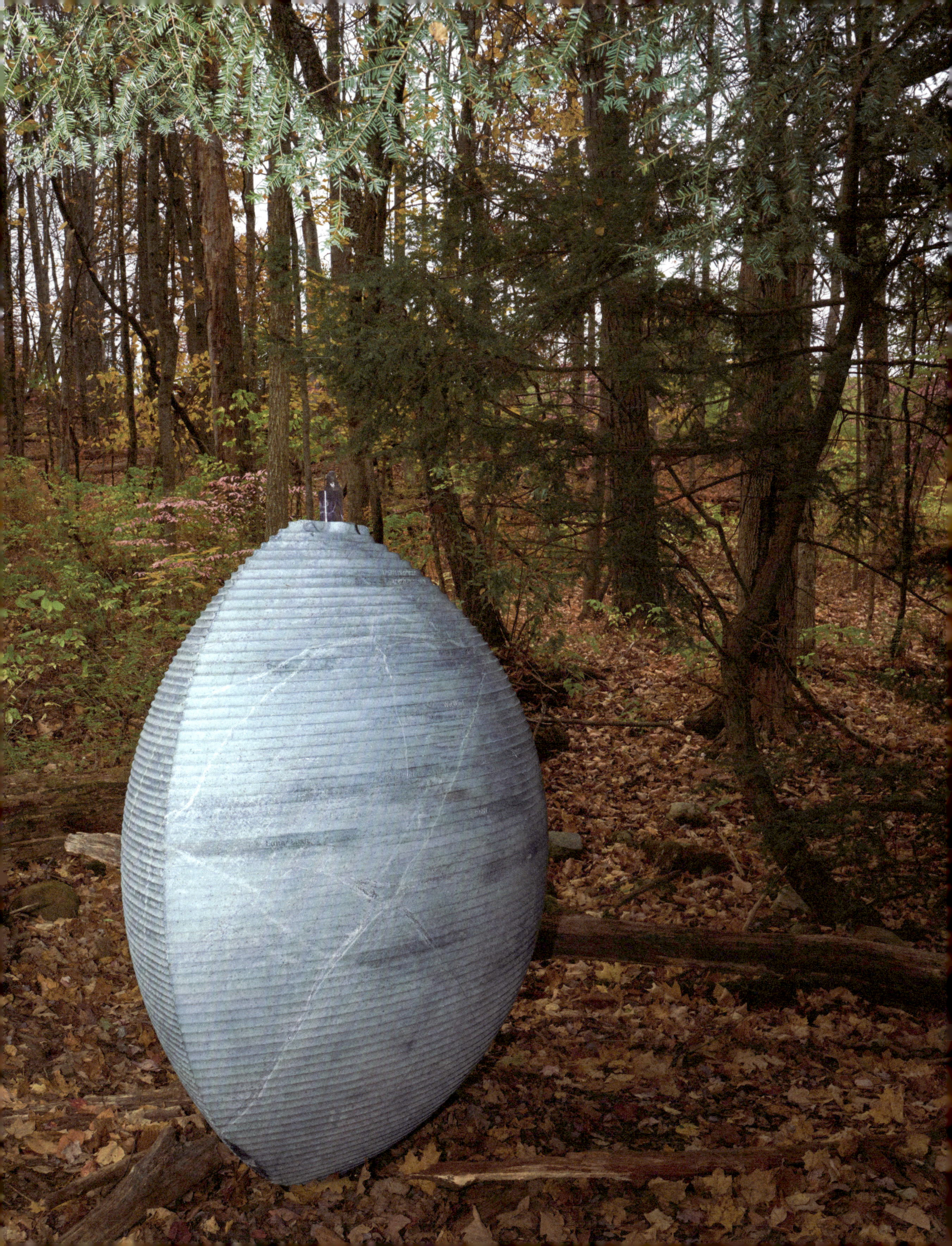

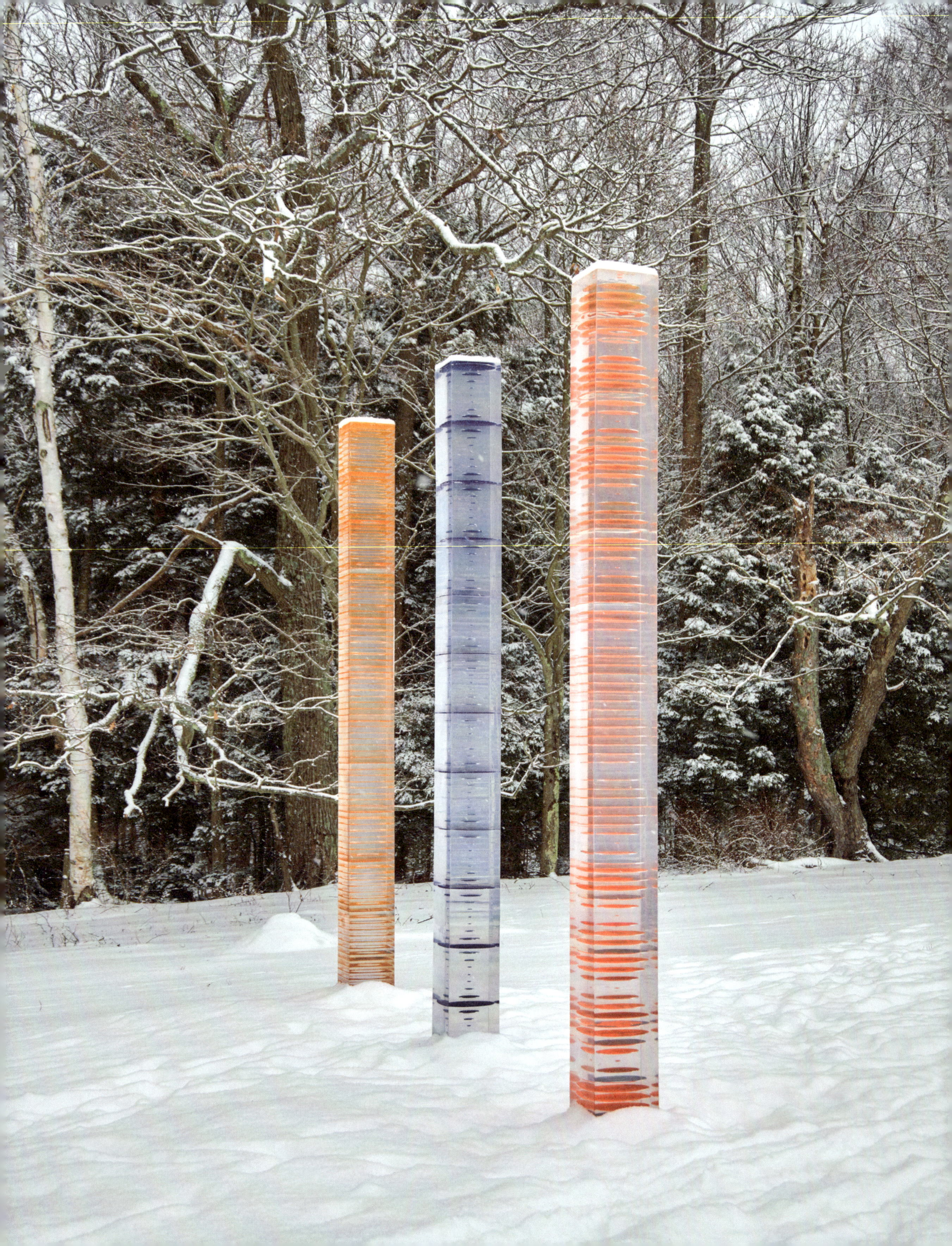

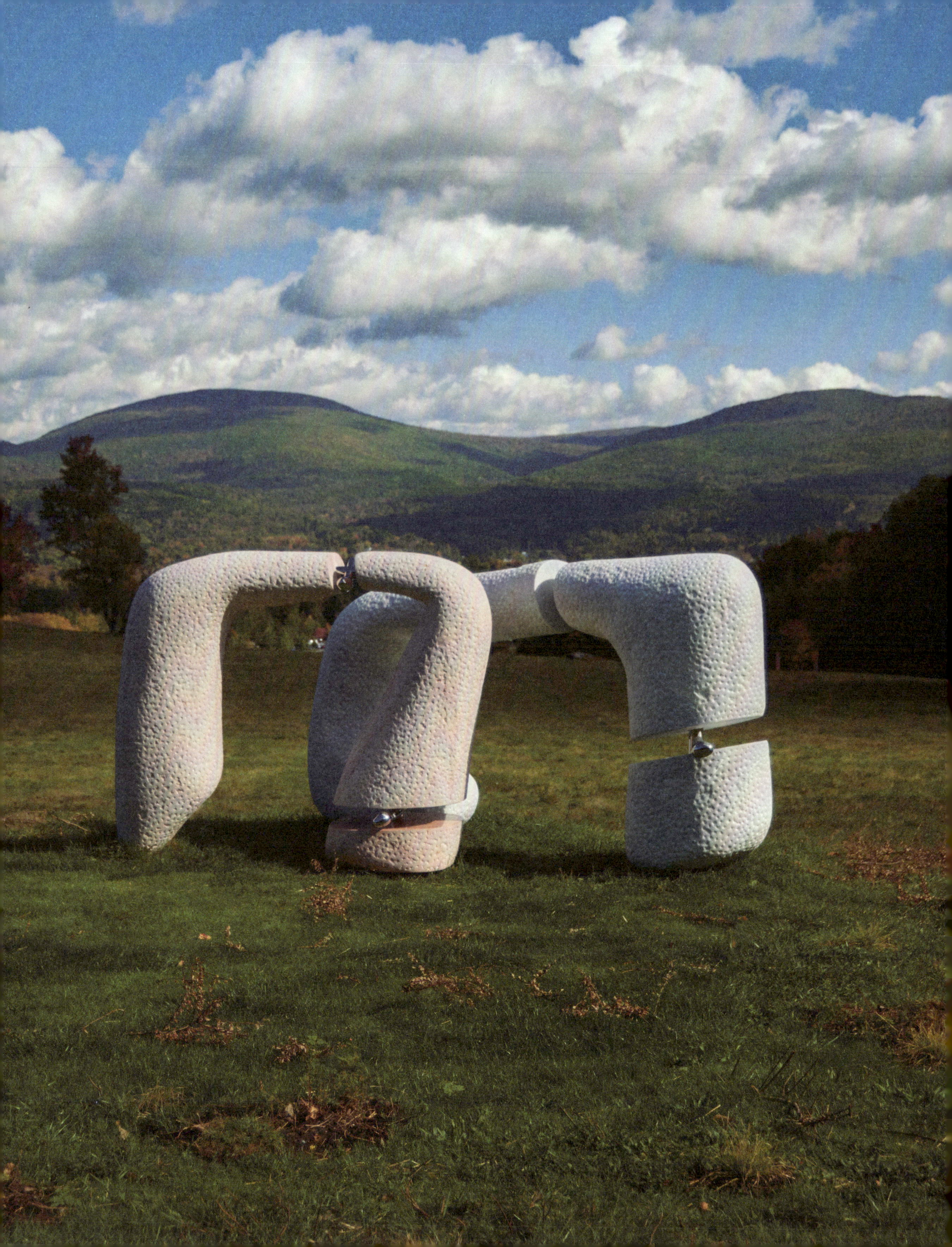

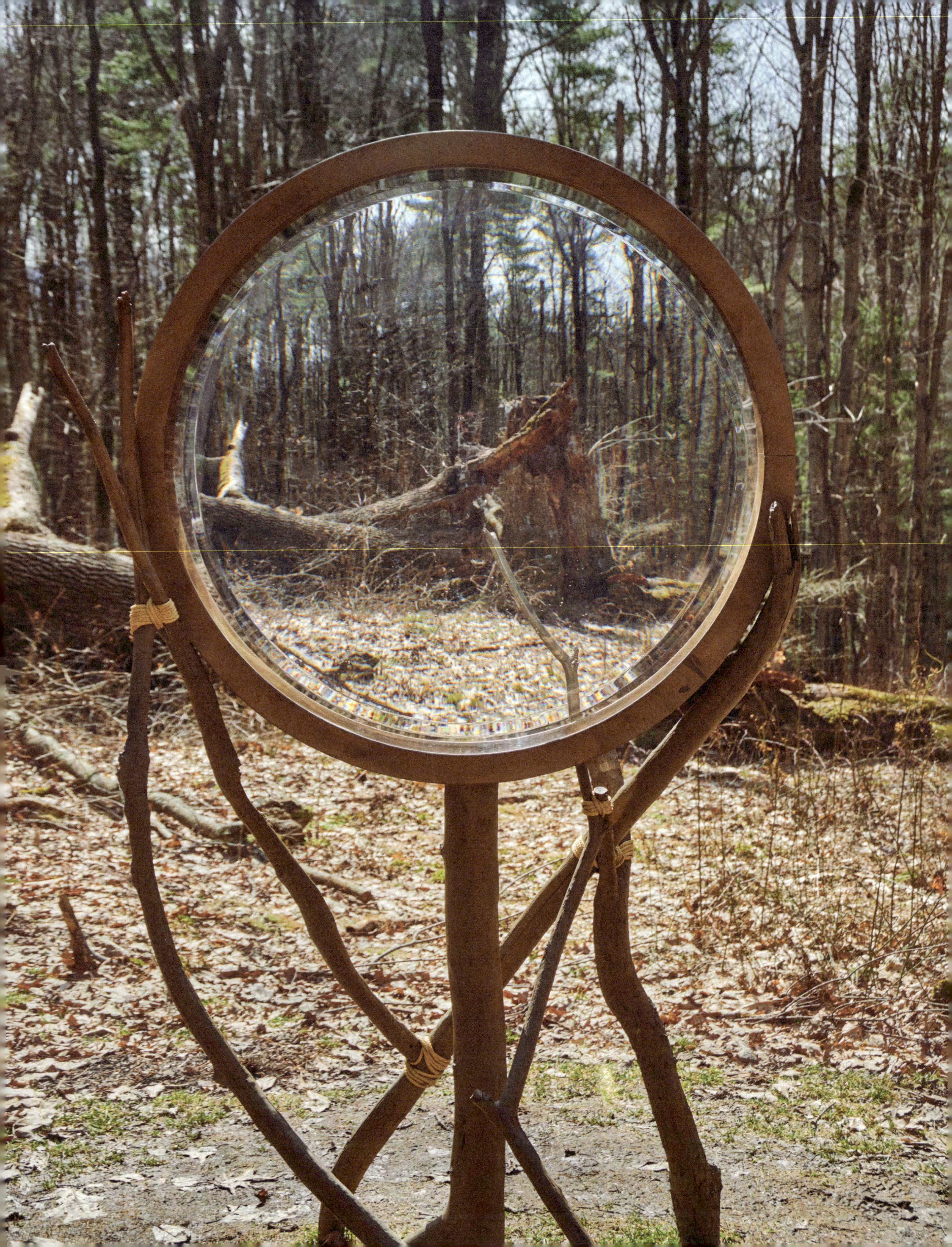

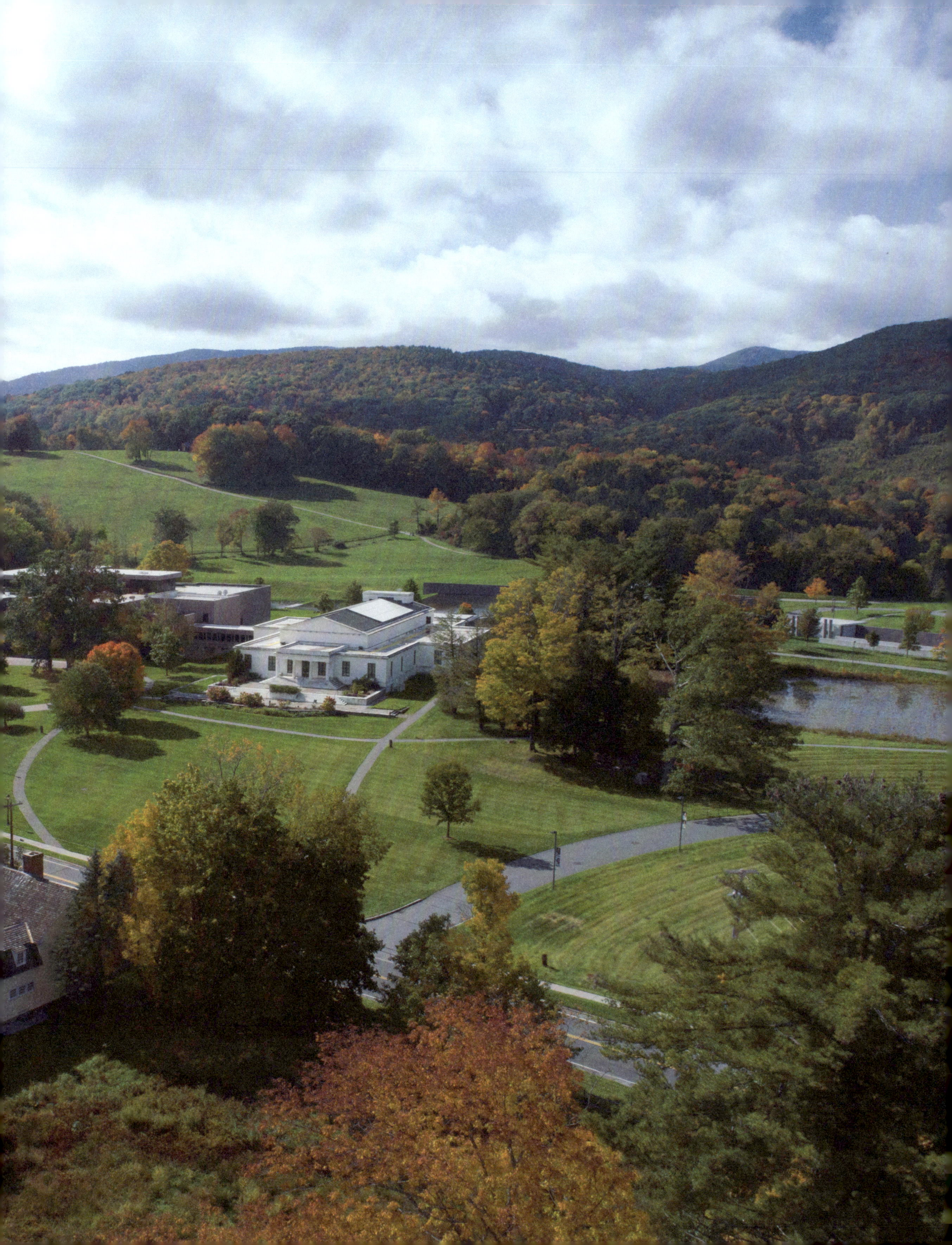

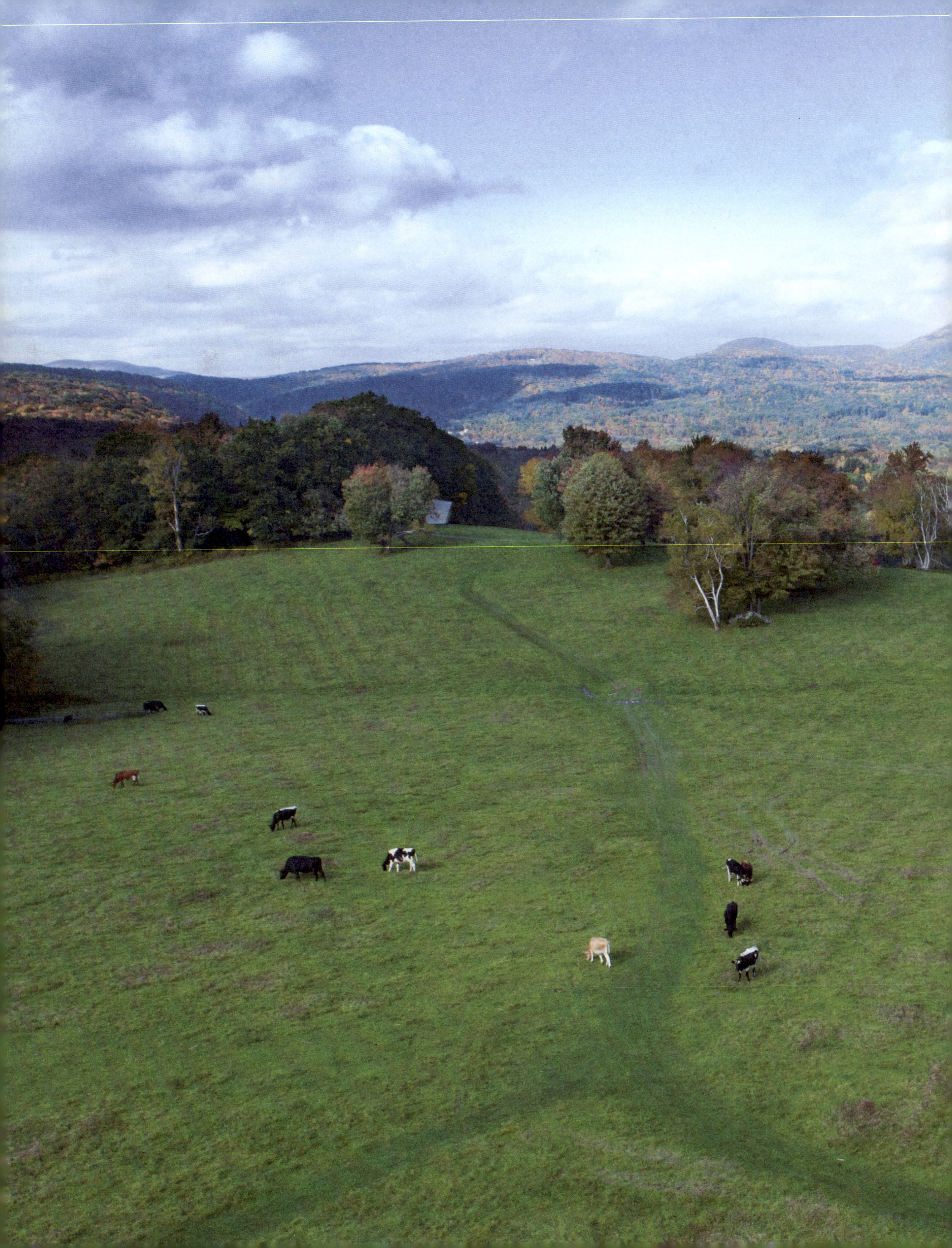